LONELY PLANET'S

1000

ULTIMATE

SIGHTS

FROM THE WORLD'S LEADING TRAVEL AUTHORITY

CONTENTS

FOREWORD

I want to see that.

There are so many places in the world where I've ended up as a result of one tantalising glimpse in a movie, one photographic poster taster, one intriguing museum display, one seductive line in a novel. That one tiny temptation is all it took; actually getting there has, on occasion, taken decades, but eventually I'm standing there thinking: 'well there it is, I'm finally seeing it'.

Of course, some sights are so well known, so overexposed in so many movies, that the reality can never match up to the expectation. We've 'seen' it so many times before we actually see it for real that the world's Eiffel Towers, Sydney Opera Houses, Grand Canyons or Taj Mahals all inevitably disappoint. Although my wife and I did, quite accidentally, contrive to arrive for the first time at the Taj on our first wedding anniversary, a perfect intersection of romantic location and romantic date.

The big sights are always worth a big effort, but it's the small ones, the unusual ones which often live in the memory. Encountering a sight without preconceptions and anticipation can make all the difference. It was a pleasant surprise encountering the bust of Frank Zappa in Lithuania, and Graceland is so overwhelmingly the rock-excess focus of Memphis that it was a thrill to discover some down-to-earth rock history at Sun Studios. Sometimes actually getting there brings home

just how interesting or important the sight is: it wasn't until I stood at Vindolanda on Hadrian's Wall and gazed across to darkest Scotland that it came home to me that this was the ultimate frontier for the Roman Empire. This was where civilisation ended – one more step and you were in among the wild men.

Wildlife sightings are always a special thrill because they simply are not a sure thing – they might turn up or you might just be unlucky. But when it works ... well, seeing an Alaskan brown bear snatch a salmon out of a raging stream and guzzle it down in a couple of teeth-gnashing gulps is a sight you never forget.

Big egos are just as intriguing as big bears. Hearst Castle is a reminder of the US media magnate William Randolph Hearst (said to have inspired the movie *Citizen Kane*), but it's hard to imagine a bigger ego than North Korean despot Kim Il Sung, immortalised by his gigantic Mansudae Monument statue in Pyongyang. Other sights need no reminders to stay with you; the story of sheer injustice brought home by the Anne Frank House in Amsterdam brings a lump to my throat every time I encounter another connection to that young Nazi victim.

I may have already seen a wide selection of these 1000 sights, but there are plenty more I'm determined to get to one day. The Nazca Lines in Peru, Skellig Michael in Ireland, the market at Kashgar in China, even Chornobyl in the Ukraine. They're all on my list.

Tony Wheeler
Lonely Planet founder

The amazing eroded 'fairy chimneys' of Cappadocia, Turkey, seen from the air (see p217)

ULTIMATE ITINERARIES

▶ BEST OF BRITISH

'Stately home' is an understatement for the expansive Castle Howard, which leaves visitors agog at its theatrical grandeur. **p83**

Beautiful Oxford is a haven for literature enthusiasts, not least as it's the home of the original Alice in Wonderland. **p134**

Fairy folklore abounds at the enchanted Llyn y Fan Fach in the enchanting Black Mountains of Wales. **p276**

The fascinating Bletchley Park Museum houses the Enigma machines and other technology that helped Britain win the war. **p166**

Sporting enthusiasts come to worship at the birthplace of golf amongst ruins and great views at St Andrews, Scotland. **p294**

▶ ONLY IN AMERICA

If you suspect the Truth is Out There, then Roswell will confirm it for you with extraterrestrials making their presence felt all over town. **p68**

Mix with Frank Sinatra and the Mob at the memorabilia-crammed Mulberry Street Bar in New York. **p348**

Book well in advance if you want to get a seat at the pinnacle of American sport, the Super Bowl. **p294**

The rainbow hues of the Grand Prismatic Spring in Yellowstone National Park make it one of the world's most stunning geothermal springs. **p181**

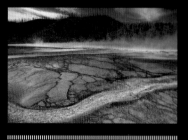

The Washington National Cathedral is a tribute to America's inclusiveness, open to all faiths and incorporating local motifs in its European design. **p87**

Pack your raygun: riding on Prague's metro trains into Flora Station feels like a bizarre trip into 1970s Soviet sci-fi. **p162**

In Brussels' annual Waiters' Race contestants must carry a bottle and three glasses 2.5km without spilling a drop. **p249**

A series of 16th-century decorative fountains, Bern's Kindlifresserbrunnen depict folkloric and historical characters, including a baby-eating ogre! **p89**

The Jomsvikings, the world's largest viking re-enactment society, makes rampaging warriors out of humble citizens across Europe. **p311**

In typical Dalí style, the Teatre-Museu Dalí, in the artist's home town of Figueres, Spain, is a museum that's full of surreal surprises. **p60**

The glittering gold- and gemstone-swathed stupa of Shwedagon Paya, in Burma, houses eight of the Buddha's hairs. **p201**

Divers flock to investigate the mystery of the 'Japanese Atlantis' in Yonaguni-jima: ancient underwater ruins or just nature waxing geometric? **p67**

As well as its fearsome reptilian namesake, the Komodo National Park in Indonesia boasts an extraordinary network of iridescent coral reefs. **p159**

The classic Chinese landscaping of the gardens at Beijing's Summer Palace offer a tranquil retreat from the modern metropolis. **p250**

It may not be the prettiest or the sweetest smelling, but the Rafflesia plant of Indonesia and Malaysia is the world's biggest flower. **p125**

Montana was a great stomping ground for dinosaurs, and young enthusiasts now follow in their footsteps with the Montana Dinosaur Trail. **p196**

Harry was not the only beloved Potter: familiar, storybook-perfect details still abound in Beatrix Potter's Lake District. **p134**

The monsters come out for New York's Halloween Parade, the biggest game of dress-ups you've ever seen. **p142**

Everyone loves a fireworks display, and on Bonfire Night (Guy Fawkes Night) they happen all over England. **p263**

An ice-cream from the Gelateria di Piazza in the picturesque Tuscan village of San Gimignano is a memorable treat for kids and adults alike. **p175**

The Romans left their enduring mark at Libya's Leptis Magna, where well-preserved temples, forums and baths evoke ancient times. **p23**

From its origins around 100BC, through a thriving Mayan civilisation and its collapse, Palanque, Mexico, has many stories to tell. **p57**

Hidden in a forest in India are the 12,000-year-old Bhimbetka cave paintings, depicting an array of animals and humans engaged in diverse activities. **p178**

Unlikely as it seems, there are thousands of marine creatures in Canada's Rocky Mountains – or at least there were 515 million years ago, at Burgess Shale. **p195**

A once-lost monument to greatness, Egypt's Abu Simbel temple ensures Ramses II will always loom large in history. **p74**

Set among forests and caves, Croatia's Plitvice Lakes – a network of 16 lakes linked by waterfalls – are as stunning as they sound. **p277**

The reward at the end of Iceland's greatest hike is the Landmannalaugar pools: a warm bath for tired feet in spectacular surrounds. **p183**

Bird-watchers flock to South Africa's Kruger National Park for the thrill of spotting the large and impressive Big Six bird species. **p115**

The Great Blue Hole in Belize is an ocean sinkhole 145m deep; its star attractions are huge marine stalactites. **p145**

Standing next to the venerable General Sherman sequoia in California's Sequoia National Park – the world's largest living thing – is an awesome and humbling experience. **p193**

Eeriness is a once-thriving town that is now completely abandoned: Prypyat in Ukraine is in Chornobyl's 'Alienation Zone'. **p278**

The Apartheid Museum in Johannesburg is a place of sober reflection on 52 years of government-sanctioned racial oppression. **p232**

Visitors walk among ancient ghosts in Rome's seemingly endless underground catacombs, which originally held the remains of early Christians. **p307**

One of history's most famous natural disasters – the eruption of Mt Vesuvius that buried Pompeii – left shockingly precise traces of the lives it extinguished. **p151**

Shameful memories linger in Cape Coast Castle in Ghana, where captured people waited to be shipped to the New World as slaves. **p37**

n the Château de Versailles, a palace that drips extravagance from every gold-leaf-coated surface, one can see why the revolutionaries revolted. **p74**

n perfect harmony with the harbour it sits on, the Sydney Opera House is as iconic as they come. **p171**

The world's greatest monument to ove, India's Taj Mahal is also one of ts most graceful buildings. **p307**

The Chrysler Building is not only he literal pinnacle of the art deco aesthetic, it's also classic New York. **p313**

Barcelona wouldn't quite be Barcelona without Antoni Gaudí and his fabulous, inspired, still-unfinished Sagrada Família church. **p335**

The spectacular, wind-buffeted cliffs of Vestmanna, in the Faroe Islands, are home to a surprising array of bird species. **p255**

Lonely, isolated and nearly devoid of human life, the former asbestos-mining town of Wittenoom in Western Australia is an almost-forgotten outpost. **p59**

Paradise Harbour on the Antarctic Peninsula doesn't have much going on, unless you count waddling penguins, huffing whales and icebergs calving from glaciers. **p136**

Secreted away in remote Kamchatka, the Valley of Geysers – the second biggest geyser field in the world – vents the earth's ire in near-obscurity. **p148**

A treasure such as Caroline Atoll, an extraordinary lagoon reef in the Republic of Kiribati, is lucky to be so remote – it remains largely unspoiled. **p158**

9

ULTIMATE
ITINERARIES

GREATEST WILDLIFE SPECTACLES

It's animal magic: witness dazzling visions as creatures of all colours, shapes and sizes feed, court, fight and migrate.

001 LÁTRABJARG BIRD CLIFFS, ICELAND

The famed white cliffs of Dover get their hue from the chalk stratum. At Látrabjarg, the very far western extremity of Iceland (and Europe), the rock faces – some over 400m high, and about 12km along – aren't naturally white. When you hear that these cliffs host the summer roosts of millions of seabirds, you'll guess what those stains are: an unbelievable quantity of guano. The swirling, squawking cacophony of puffins, razorbills, guillemots, fulmars, cormorants and kittiwakes is extraordinary; even if you're not into birdwatching, the comic antics of the puffins and the sheer scale of the mob are mesmerising.

Access is easiest with a car, though a bus (www.sterna.is) runs three times weekly from June to August from Isafjordur, the Westfjords region's main town.

002 MONARCH BUTTERFLY ROOSTS, MEXICO

Instinct is a curious thing. How does a creature that lives only for brief weeks or months know how to find its way to a spot thousands of kilometres away, without ever having been there before? It's not as if insects are great map-readers. Yet, somehow, countless millions of monarch butterflies make the annual migration south from summer territory in the USA and Canada to spend winter in Mexico's oyamel fir forests. Seeing clouds of these pretty orange, black and white insects would be impressive enough, but they also roost on trees in numbers huge enough to bend branches.

The picturesque town of Angangueo, about 130km west of Mexico City, is a handy base for visits to El Rosario Butterfly Biosphere Reserve.

003 KING PENGUIN ROOKERY, ST ANDREWS BAY, SOUTH GEORGIA

March of the Penguins is one of those great art-house films: strong, silent characters, for much of the movie not a lot happens, then it's over – but somehow it's incredibly powerful. Which is something you'd also say about penguin odour; you'll certainly smell them before you see them. But you'll forget the stink when you see the rookery: over a quarter of a million birds – big ones, too, reaching almost a metre tall – mingle and trumpet, resplendent in their black tuxedos and orange collars. It's a scene that's simultaneously hilarious, noble, cute and magnificent.

South Georgia is commonly visited on voyages to the Antarctic Peninsula from Ushuaia in Argentine Tierra del Fuego, via the Falkland Islands.

ARIADNE VAN ZANDBERGEN / LONELY PLANET IMAGES

A crowd of wildebeest and zebras takes a drink stop during the Great Migration across the Serengeti

005 BROWN BEARS FEASTING, ALASKA, USA

There's nothing like the flavour of flapping-fresh fish, straight from the river. Especially if you're a brown bear with a taste for dog salmon. From early summer, shimmering masses of salmon return from their oceanic feeding grounds and head upriver to spawn; when they hit rapids and small cataracts, they make easy prey for bears – it's a conveyor-belt sushi joint. At the falls on the McNeil River, 1.5km upstream from its mouth in southwestern Alaska, huge browns, bulky from years of salmon feasts, gather to flip fish from the stream. Dozens of bears can be spotted at any one time.

Only 10 viewing permits are issued for each day between June and August, allocated through a lottery; for details, visit www.wildlife.alaska.gov.

004 GREAT MIGRATION, SERENGETI NATIONAL PARK, TANZANIA

One wildebeest is amusing: a shaggy, skinny cow with a head seemingly too narrow for a brain. But 1.3 million wildebeest – that's unimaginably impressive. In a breathtaking spectacle, particularly from above, vast herds of gnu sweep across the East African savannah in an annual circuit, accompanied by hundreds of thousands of zebras, gazelles and elands – and the predators that feed on the rumbling masses. The wildebeest spend the December to May rainy season in the southern Serengeti, nosing northwest before crossing into Kenya's Masai Mara National Reserve. Most dramatic is the mass crossing of the Grumeti River, where crocodiles wait to snap up unlucky wildebeest.

The exact timing of the migration varies each year, but the Grumeti crossing usually occurs between May and July.

006 ELEPHANT GATHERING, SRI LANKA

When King Mahasen built the Minneriya Tank, a vast reservoir, in the 3rd century AD, he probably wasn't thinking of animal welfare. Now the focal point of a national park, the lake comes into its own as the dry season bites, with elephants trundling in from reserves around the region. Forming enormous herds, they head to the tank for the world's biggest pool party, known simply as the Gathering, where 300 or more thirsty pachyderms graze the lush grass, drink and play in the water. It's a unique opportunity to watch how elephants interact (noisily and boisterously, as it turns out).

Elephant numbers at Minneriya usually peak around August or September; jeep safaris organised through local hotels get you close to the lakeshore action.

11

007 BATS OF DEER CAVE, SARAWAK, MALAYSIA

Head to Borneo's Gunung Mulu National Park to get two superlatives for the price of one: the world's most impressive bat gathering, and the planet's most gag-inducing stink. Sadly for those of a delicate olfactory sensibility, it's tricky to experience one without the other, and three million wrinkle-lipped bats create a lot of poop. Rest assured though, the spectacle is worth the stench. Settle into a viewing spot by the mouth of this colossal cavern and wait for dusk: on some telepathic signal the bats come flooding out as one snaking, coiling stream, heading off to hunt for airborne bugs.

Deer Cave is visited by daily guided tours from park headquarters, where there's accommodation ranging from hostel beds to garden rooms; see www.mulupark.com.

008 ORCA FEEDING, VALDÉS PENINSULA, ARGENTINA

The orca, you might think, is just a big, chubby dolphin. And dolphins are so cute and friendly. So why are orca also called 'killer whales'? Head to Punta Norte, on Argentina's Valdés Peninsula, and it becomes abundantly clear. The beach here is home to sea lions nursing pups – favourite orca snacks. One group of orca has developed a unique strategy: when they get peckish, they launch themselves from the surf right onto the beach, grabbing a tasty pup before the next wave breaks and allows it to wriggle back into the sea. It's risky – stranding would be disastrous – but breathtakingly dramatic to watch.

Sea lions pup in January, so orca attacks mostly occur between February and April, three hours either side of high tide.

009 STARLINGS ROOSTING, SOMERSET LEVELS, ENGLAND

Late afternoon on a misty winter's day, head to the wetlands of Westhay Moor National Nature Reserve. As dusk falls, a patch of sky darkens; a cloud is gathering. But it's behaving strangely – ebbing and flowing, clumping and twisting – and it's vast, an expanse of black, shifting sinuously. It's starlings, millions of them in a swirling mass, gathered in a huge flock for safety, dipping to escape the attentions of raptors. Finally, in one smooth flow, like a genie returning to its lamp, the swarm gathers and swoops down to roost. And then you remember to breathe.

Westhay is 5km northwest of Glastonbury, off the B3151; aim to arrive an hour before sunset to watch the starlings roost.

010 SARDINE RUN, SOUTH AFRICA

You might think watching fish is none too exciting – something for a computer screensaver, not an unforgettable, once-in-a-lifetime spectacle. Well, it depends – if the fish are part of a swirling, silvery mass stretching over 7km long, it gets a lot more interesting. As millions upon millions of sardines dart and bunch their way around the Eastern Cape and along the KwaZulu-Natal Coast, the waters boil with diving gannets and cormorants, along with thousands of hunting seals, dolphins and sharks. Whether you're watching from the safety of a boat or snorkelling near the embattled shoals, it's a phenomenal sight.

The 'sardine run' doesn't happen every year, and its location can't be predicted, but it generally takes place between May and July.

GREATEST WILDLIFE SPECTACLES

MOST FAIRYTALE-LIKE EUROPEAN CASTLES

All you Cinderellas and Prince Charmings: you will go to the ball, at one of Europe's grandly fortified fantasies.

The most famous German castle will inspire you to build your own Magic Kingdom, or sing Wagnerian opera

011 PRAGUE CASTLE, CZECH REPUBLIC

Calling Pražský hrad a castle is a masterful understatement – it's really a compact walled city, with cathedral, palaces, streets and houses. A succession of ambitious rulers enhanced the original 9th-century fortifications, somehow blending complementary Romanesque, Gothic, baroque and Renaissance delights. But in truth there's one better place to be than in the castle – that's outside it, looking up. As the sun's glow fades on a summer evening, or the snowflakes drift in and out of the street lights on a chill winter's night, few sights are more stirring than the view from among the statues on Charles Bridge across to the hilltop redoubt.

Explore the thousand-year history in the Story of Prague Castle exhibition, in the Old Royal Palace's Gothic vaults. For more, see www.hrad.cz.

012 EILEAN DONAN, SCOTLAND

Brooding, solitary, rugged...and that's just the gatekeeper. Eilean Donan, perched atop an island on Loch Duich, is the castle that launched a thousand Scottish tourist brochures. And why not? Just the approach will have your mental bagpipes wheezing, clopping across the arched stone bridge towards the grey battlements, mist drifting across the rippling water... at least, that's how it was in the many movies filmed here, and to be fair, it's often like that in reality. Inside, it's a fair re-creation of former glories – the medieval castle was pulverised in 1719 by English troops, then rebuilt in the early 20th century.

Buses from Inverness and Fort William stop in the village of Dornie, near the castle (www.eileandonancastle.com), which opens March to October only.

013 SCHLOSS NEUSCHWANSTEIN, BAVARIA, GERMANY

It's hard to credit that Bavaria's 'mad' King Ludwig II never clapped eyes on Disneyland. The Wagner-loving royal, obsessed with romantic epics of knightly lore, created castles of stereotypical fairytale grandeur. His apotheosis came with Neuschwanstein, started in 1869 atop a wooded outcrop: witch-hatted turrets, Minstrels' Hall, grand throne room – all that's missing is a wicked sorcerer and perhaps a distressed damsel incarcerated in a tower. You don't need to join the hordes inside to appreciate Ludwig's vision: stop at the Marienbrücke (Mary's Bridge), itself picturesquely spanning a waterfall in the Pöllat Gorge, for unforgettable views of the castle.

15

To arrive at the castle like a pampered prince or princess, take a horse-drawn carriage up from nearby Hohenschwangau village.

GLENN VAN DER KNIJFF / LONELY PLANET IMAGES

014 CASTELL DE PÚBOL, CATALUNYA, SPAIN

If you believe fairytales are real, perhaps you're ready for the surreal. This medieval monument at La Pera, a compact Gothic-Renaissance affair, was fascinating enough before it was bought by Salvador Dalí in 1968. But after he installed his wife Gala here, and refurbished it to his own, er, unique tastes, it became something else. His trademark left-field flourishes lurk to wrong-foot unwary visitors: as an example, Gala's tomb in the subterranean crypt is guarded by a stuffed giraffe. Of course. Even ignoring the oddities, it's a charming place perched above a very strollable, traditional village.

Regular buses between Palafrugell and . Girona stop at La Pera, about 2km from the Castell. See www.salvador-dali.org for more.

015 TINTAGEL, CORNWALL, ENGLAND

Let me tell you a story about a boy who pulled a sword from a stone to become king, aided by a wizard called Merlin… The legend of King Arthur has been so long entwined with Tintagel Island that it was probably already in the mind of the Earl of Cornwall when he ordered his castle built here in 1233. Today, his stronghold is all the better for lying in ruins; crossing the fragile-looking bridge from the mainland builds the atmosphere for wanders among the clifftop site, where waves crash against the rocks below. Even the screeching seagulls sound mystical here.

Stop in at Tintagel Old Post Office (www .nationaltrust.org.uk), an absurdly lovable jumble of a 14th-century house, on your way to the castle.

016 PALÁCIO NACIONAL DA PENA, SINTRA, PORTUGAL

Palaces, you say? How many? In Sintra, you can't move for tripping over them. There's the ruined Castelo dos Mouros overlooking the town, where another white palace dominates the main plaza. The fantastical Quinta da Regaleira sits amid its lush gardens; then there's Monserrate, an exotically faux-Moorish affair. But the crown goes to pastel-turreted Palácio Nacional da Pena. Somewhere, buried under the castellated walls of the current 19th-century edifice, lurk the relics of a medieval convent. But you'd never know it: instead this kitsch confection of Gothic, Manueline and Islamic styles dominates, housing an Aladdin's cave of treasures.

Suburban line trains depart Lisbon every 15 minutes for the 45-minute run to Sintra, making it an easy day trip from the capital.

017 CHÂTEAU DE PEYREPERTUSE, LANGUEDOC-ROUSSILLON, FRANCE

As you meander along mountain roads in France's far southwest, hilltop fortresses loom above, some standing proud, others only snaggle-tooth ruins. Did noble knights set forth from these castles on fine steeds to battle evil? Actually, there's no way to break this gently: the knights were the bad guys here. The 13th-century Albigensian Crusade saw tens of thousands of Cathar 'heretics' slaughtered – and these bastions saw the Cathars' last stands. The castle at Peyrepertuse, largest and most vertiginously sited, now hosts displays of falconry and medieval combat, but wander to the battlements, gaze over the rugged landscape, and imagine the lives (and deaths) of its erstwhile inhabitants.

A 195km, full-day backroads drive between Carcassonne and Perpignan visits the four most impressive Cathar castles.

018 CORVIN CASTLE, HUNEDOARA, ROMANIA

Because sometimes fairytales are actually nightmares… Europe's spookiest castle is, appropriately, located on Dracula's patch in Transylvania; some say Vlad was imprisoned here. If you don't feel a shiver down your spine on approaching over the bridge, with the river cascading far below, you don't have a fear gland: the only reason there aren't vampires here today is because the werewolves ate 'em all. It was the stronghold of the powerful Hungarian Corvin family in the 15th century; more recently, Ceaușescu spitefully built hideous steelworks alongside the castle. Even so, the ugly neighbourhood can't diminish the grim gravitas of the massive stone walls, turrets and Gothic bulk.

The nearest transport hub is Deva, 18km north, from where buses make the run of 30 to 40 minutes to Corvin Castle.

019 TITANIA'S CASTLE, EGESKOV SLOT, DENMARK

In a land where beloved queens and princesses still live in enchanting – if not enchanted – castles, it's apt that such palaces are everywhere. And Egeskov is a paragon of castledom: set in beautifully landscaped, peacock-prowled gardens, the 16th-century towered bastion sits inside its moat, accessed via a drawbridge. Within its walls nestles the real

At sunset, you can imagine you're back in 14th-century Poland, riding up to your own castle

020 MALBORK CASTLE, POLAND

Bigger isn't always better – but try telling that to boys. The Teutonic Knights were clearly out to impress when they built this vast edifice, reputedly Europe's largest Gothic castle. Declaring Malbork (then called Marienburg) their capital in 1309, the knights kicked off a rush of property development, expanding the original convent into an enormous fortification with towers, deep moats, strong walls, an armoury and a palace for the Grand Masters. All that didn't prevent capture, first by Poles and then by Prussians, and the castle was virtually razed during WWII. Now restored, it houses an extensive museum – but it's the monumental building that wows.

Malbork (www.zamek.malbork.pl) is a 45-minute train ride from Gdańsk, itself worth exploring for its wonderfully restored medieval centre.

treasure: head to the 1st floor to see possibly the planet's most magical doll's house, Titania's Castle. Elaborately furnished and decorated with tiny treasures, it was built at the request of an English army officer's daughter to house the fairies that lived in the garden.

Egeskov has several museums and no fewer than four mazes – spend half a day exploring the grounds and castle; see www.egeskov.com.

MOST FAIRYTALE-LIKE EUROPEAN CASTLES

MOST IMPRESSIVE WATERFALLS

The bigger they are, the harder they fall – feel the power of the planet's mightiest and most beautiful cataracts.

021 VICTORIA FALLS, ZAMBIA/ZIMBABWE

Explorer David Livingstone could be accused of dampening expectations by naming these falls after England's doughty queen: dour and staid they're not. The locals, though, got it spot on, calling the falls Mosi-oa-Tunya – 'the smoke that thunders'. They're monstrously loud, and the mist rising as the Zambezi River plunges 108m into the gorge below – over 12,000 cubic metres per second at its heaviest flow – rises in vast clouds. See them from above, from below, from Knife Edge Point, from the Devil's Pool and from Cataract View, at sunrise and by moonlight – just make sure you see them.

Although flow is greatest between April and June, the best time for sunset photography is arguably October to December, when spray is not too heavy.

Satisfy your waterfall-lust with the 275 cataracts at Iguazú Falls

022 NIAGARA FALLS, USA/CANADA

Let me hear you shout it: Waterfalls are fun! Louder! And again! It's fortunate that Niagara is so truly awesome (up to 2800 cubic metres per second awesome, since you ask) or the various and extremely numerous shots of commercialised hokum might overwhelm the sight. But it is, and they don't – in fact, you'll probably visit, climb or ride several of the attractions to drink in many facets of the falls. Top of the list has to be a voyage on the *Maid of the Mist*, the 11th incarnation of the venerable boat that first sailed into the spray in 1846.

Tickets for the *Maid of the Mist* (www .maidofthemist.com), which sails from April to October, cost US$13.50/7.85 for adults/under-13s.

023 REICHENBACH FALLS, SWITZERLAND

Elemental, my dear Watson! Set among the deep gorges and rugged peaks of Switzerland's Bernese Oberland, the Reichenbachfälle seem appropriately dramatic as the backdrop for the final stand of Sherlock Holmes. It was at the roaring 250m-high cascades near Meiringen that the famous detective tussled with his arch-enemy, Professor Moriarty, before both tumbled into the cataract in the 1891 tale 'The Final Problem'. Today, Holmes fans flock to the falls, hiking over the top and down to the plaque marking the ledge where the fictional fight is believed to have been set.

For an atmospheric approach, catch the historic cable railway alongside the falls, running from Willingen mid-May to early October. See www.reichenbachfall.ch.

024 KAIETEUR FALLS, GUYANA

These remote falls may not be the highest, the heaviest or the most famous – but they're probably the wildest. Secreted away in the lush interior of Guyana – hardly an over-touristed neighbourhood – the Potaro River plummets 250m from a sandstone plateau. On the trail to the falls you might spot vivid blue butterflies, scarlet birds and the golden dart-poison frog; listen for screeching howler monkeys. Then crawl to the edge of the precipitous overhang, and look down at the roaring curtain, with white-collared swifts darting out from behind the cascade. Now, that's adrenalin.

The falls can be reached on charter flights from Guyana's capital, Georgetown, or an epic multi-day overland journey involving minibuses, boats and trekking.

KERRY LORIMER / LONELY PLANET IMAGES

025 IGUAZÚ FALLS, ARGENTINA/BRAZIL

Historically, Argentina and Brazil haven't always been the best at sharing; in fact, they're usually up for a scrap, whether it's over land (Uruguay, say) or soccer honours. But at Iguazú – Iguaçu to the Brazilians – the falls to end all falls are apportioned between them. OK, so the biggest drop is a 'mere' 82m – but with a staggering 275 cataracts extending for 2.7km along the Iguazú River, the combined might is jaw-dropping. And deafening: don your waterproofs and stroll to the lookout beneath the Garganta do Diabo (Devil's Throat) to feel the raw power of the cascades.

Brazil's Parque Nacional do Iguaçu (www.cataratasdoiguacu.com .br) is open 9am to 5pm, later in summer; Argentina's Parque Nacional Iguazú (www.iguazuargentina.com) is open 8am to 6pm.

19

026 DÉTIĀN FALLS, CHINA

What is it about waterfalls that encourages pride that verges on ludicrous? Hence Détiān is proclaimed 'the world's second-largest waterfall along a national border' – the gushing 200m-long stretch of cascades straddles China's Guǎngxī province and northern Vietnam (though China gets most of the flow). But you don't come here for the stats, or the tremendous roar of the rushing water, or for the fun of snapping a photo of yourself at the border marker. You come because it's gasp-inducingly beautiful: a verdant vision framed by looming karst outcrops and serene rice paddies.

Midsummer is the best time to appreciate the power of the flow; avoid winter, when the falls are relatively thin streams and fog dominates.

027 GULLFOSS, ICELAND

Iceland is where good geography teachers go when they die: a geological wonderland, its unique otherworldly landscapes go some way to explaining why most Icelanders believe in elves and goblins. Huge glaciers cover over a tenth of the country, hot water spurts at the eponymous Geysir, technicolour mountains loom in the interior, geothermal springs steam – and waterfalls cascade. Gullfoss is a multistepped affair that surges down into a mighty gash carved into the land; magical when the sun sparks rainbows into life, it's arguably even more enchanting in winter, when snow glistens and rime coats the rocks all around with a sparkling shell.

Gullfoss is easily reached from Reykjavik on a Golden Circle tour, or by bus with Reykjavík Excursions (www.re.is).

028 SUTHERLAND FALLS, NEW ZEALAND

Unsurprisingly, in the 'Land of the Long White Cloud' it rains a fair bit, especially on the wet west coast of the South Island. After the frequent downpours, New Zealand's many cataracts gush even more wildly. Milford Sound, that most photogenic fjord, is renowned for the falls streaming down its sides. The best is on the approach, accessible only by hiking the four-day, 53.5km Milford Track: Sutherland Falls, a 580m-high torrent tumbling from a lake perched on the valley walls. If the sun shines, wonderful; if the rain pours – and it probably will – better still.

Walkers on the Milford Track must book places in huts along the route – see www.doc.govt.nz. From October to April you must hike south to north.

029 JIM JIM FALLS, AUSTRALIA

What's more of a thrill: floating in a remote plunge pool while gazing up at a 215m-high cascade dashing over rust-red rock cliffs? Or wondering whether a 5m-long prehistoric reptile is about to sink its jagged fangs into your leg? At Jim Jim Falls, deep in Kakadu National Park in Australia's Northern Territory, you get both: a rufty-tufty 4WD track, then a 1km scramble along a rugged trail, leads to this spectacular outpouring. But before you dive into the swimming hole, so tantalisingly cool in the heat of the outback, ask local advice: saltwater crocodiles have been known to lurk here.

Visitors to Kakadu (www.environment.gov.au/parks/kakadu/) must pay a A$25 park fee; passes can be bought at centres in Darwin, Katherine and the park itself.

030 ANGEL FALLS, VENEZUELA

Spoiler alert: romantics, look away right now. The world's highest single-drop falls (979m high in total, with an 807m plunge) are not named for some celestial being – though the sight of this white ribbon plummeting down the side of the mist-cloaked, flat-topped tepui is almost heavenly. No, the moniker honours aviator Jimmie Angel, who in 1933 became the first to overfly the falls. The local Pemón people are more poetic, recognising the falls' breathtaking height – so tall that in the dry season much of the water evaporates before reaching the bottom – with the name Kerepakupai merú: 'falls of the deepest place'.

Several operators in nearby Canaima offer overflights (from around US$60) and two- or three-day tours in motorised dugout canoes, usually running from May or June to November.

MOST IMPRESSIVE WATERFALLS

If you thought you never wanted to see a falling angel, this Venezualan drop will change your mind.

GREATEST ROMAN SIGHTS

What did the Romans ever do for us? Take note, Monty Python: over two millennia on, the ancient empire's relics still set jaws dropping.

around the site of the modern-day city of Nîmes, got thirsty, 2nd-century Roman administrators built a vast canal system to deliver water. The zenith of the effort was the Pont du Gard, its 35 arches soaring 50m above the valley floor, and all constructed without mortar – no mean feat when you consider some of the stone blocks weigh over 5 tonnes each. Incredibly, the canal descends only 12m along its 50km length.

The Pont du Gard is 21km northeast of Nîmes; buses run the 45-minute journey from Nîmes up to five times daily.

031 JERASH, JORDAN

Yes, the well-preserved site of Jerash has the expected tick list of monuments and relics: triumphal arches, broad colonnaded streets and plazas, theatres, baths and temples. But although you can take in opera in Verona's Roman arena, and music in Orange's vast theatre, there's a truly authentic sight that's pretty much unique to Jerash: gladiators in battle! Each day the huge hippodrome – which in its heyday seated some 15,000 roaring Romans – rings to the sounds of horses' hoofs dashing around in a chariot race, legionaries performing army drill, and gladiators fighting to the 'death'.

The Roman Army and Chariot Experience takes place twice daily Saturday to Thursday, and once only on Friday; for details see www.jerashchariots.com.

032 DIOCLETIAN'S PALACE, SPLIT, CROATIA

If you're a Roman emperor, you don't just settle into a cosy country cottage when you retire. Over the 10 years preceding the abdication of Diocletian in AD 305, he built this deluxe coastal palace, a heavily fortified but grandiose retirement villa. Today Diocletian's Palace is a compact walled community, bustling and romantic at the same time, its charms only enhanced by centuries of additions within the walls of the Roman fortress. Admire the grand columns and capitals of the Peristil (entrance court) and Diocletian's domed mausoleum, now the Cathedral of St Domnius, before delving into the palace's basement halls.

The Split Card (€5; www.visitsplit.com) gives free admission to several museums, as well as discounts on galleries, restaurants and hotels.

033 PONT DU GARD, FRANCE

When the Romans decided to do something, they generally got it done – conquering 'barbarians', subduing swaths of the known world, creating monuments of dizzying grandeur. When Colonia Nemausensis, the settlement based

034 LEPTIS MAGNA, LIBYA

Olives: you love them or you hate them. The Romans adored them, and Leptis Magna, on Libya's Mediterranean coast, grew to be a mighty power through trade in olives, as well as exotic animals heading to the imperial capital, Rome. This is a site that lives up to its billing: it's still magnificent, with well-preserved temples, forums, theatres, circus and the fascinating Hadrianic Baths. Wandering beneath monumental arches and along colonnaded streets it's easy to imagine yourself a citizen of the 2nd century AD, toga draped over arm, en route to watching a few lions snacking on their favourite Christian titbits in the circus.

Learn about the city's pre-Roman history and admire mosaics, reliefs and statues from the site in the impressive Leptis Magna Archaeological Museum.

Marvel at the durability of Roman craft at the Leptis Magna Archaeological Museum, Libya

23

Between the Forum and the Colosseum, two of Rome's highlights, you'll wonder where the day went…and the soles of your shoes

035 VINDOLANDA, HADRIAN'S WALL, ENGLAND

Life as a Roman wasn't all orgies and days out at the Colosseum. Rome's legions were posted to far-flung, dangerous reaches of the empire. Built AD 122–128, the emperor Hadrian's eponymous wall – 80 Roman miles (about 117km) fortified with milecastles and turrets – did a decent job of keeping out vengeful Picts, but life was still tough for the garrisons. Vindolanda Roman Fort, an impressively excavated site just south of the wall, and its museum offer insights into the soldiers' existence; as well as the well-preserved ruins, finds include leather footwear, jewellery, weapons and a party invitation.

Combine a visit to Vindolanda (www .vindolanda.com) with a circular walk touching the wall and nearby Housesteads (www.english-heritage.org .uk), the UK's best-preserved Roman fort.

036 BAALBEK, LEBANON

Talk about building works going over schedule; Baalbek's Temple of Jupiter was started in 60 BC and wasn't completed for some 120 years. But when you see the scale of the thing, that timeline starts to seem more reasonable – it's monstrously large, with columns almost 23m high and 2.2m across, its foundation stones weighing over 1000 tonnes. Baalbek's temples are diverse: some are delicate, notably the Temple of Venus, while the Temple of Bacchus is graced with wonderfully decorated ceilings and friezes. In all, some 10,000 slaves are believed to have worked on Heliopolis, the city's Roman name.

For a touch of more recent history, stay at the colonial-era Palmyra Hotel (961 8 370230), opposite the ruins.

GLENN BEANLAND / LONELY PLANET IMAGES

038 FORUM, ROME, ITALY

This is where it all began. On the Palatine Hill in the 8th century BC, Romulus offed twin brother Remus and founded his great city, naming it after himself. Wouldn't you? Below lies the Forum, heart of Roman life – and death: by tradition, Romulus's tomb lay beneath the black-marble Lapis Niger. Here, devotees worshipped, the Senate governed, and ordinary citizens gathered and shopped in the markets of the Mercati di Traiano and Piazza del Foro. Then it was down the road to the Colosseum for a spot of gladiatorial slaughter before rustling up a bite for the evening's orgy…

Daily guided tours and audio guides (€4 each), both available in English, breathe life into the ruins.

037 POMPEII, ITALY

Pompeii's catastrophe became its legacy. On 24 August AD 79, the volcano Vesuvius blew its top and clouds of ash smothered the city, which was rapidly buried (along with 2000 of its citizens) under a dense layer of hot pumice fragments. Lost for a millennium and a half, it wasn't rediscovered until 1594; today its streets and houses comprise one of the most poignant places on the planet. Particularly interesting for the liberal-minded (or prurient) are the decidedly naughty frescos preserved under the pumice – look for the erotic artwork in the Terme Suburbane and Casa dei Vettii.

Pompeii is a sprawling site – invest in a guidebook or audio guide, and try to avoid the midday heat in summer.

039 VOLUBILIS, MOROCCO

Possibly the best aspect of Morocco's prime Roman site is the juxtaposition of cultures: just a skip from the narrow alleys of Meknès' medieval medina and the Islamic pilgrimage centre of Moulay Idriss, the well-preserved ruins of Volubilis are striking. The attraction isn't so much the monuments – though the 1300-sq-metre Forum is particularly impressive – but wandering the streets, peering into skeletal houses to gawp at intricate mosaics, or just perch on the hillside, imagining bustling life here as it was 1800 years ago.

The most convenient way to reach Volubilis is to hire a *grand taxi* for the return journey from Meknès, 33km away.

040 BUTRINT, ALBANIA

One word sums up the Roman strategy for success: adaptation. Butrint is a spectacular example of how Roman settlement was built upon, then subsumed by, other cultures. The result is a mesmerising melange of historical influences, where Roman houses and temples were built among or on top of Hellenistic remains; blended into the Roman monuments are relics of Byzantine, Venetian and Ottoman rule. The location is dreamlike, a wooded peninsula on a marshy coastline; the sun setting over the acropolis, orange glow reflected in the seas, is a transcendent sight.

Ferries run from Corfu (Greece) to Saranda, from where buses and taxis make the 19km run south to Butrint.

GREATEST ROMAN SIGHTS

TOP BATTLE SITES

Time moves on and generations come and go, yet war persists. Over and over, battle lines have been drawn – take aim and shoot for these key sites.

043 BATTLE OF LITTLE BIGHORN, USA

Remembered as the most significant conflict of the Great Sioux War, fought between Native Americans and the US army, the Battle of Little Bighorn (also known as Custer's Last Stand) raged over two days in June 1876. Three thousand men engaged in a battle that was crucial in the natives' attempts to preserve their way of life. The combined power of the Sioux and Cheyenne people prevailed and gave rise to the legend of Crazy Horse and Sitting Bull. The grassy plains of the battlefield are now a National Monument.

Little Bighorn National Monument lies off Interstate 90 near Crow Agency.

041 BATTLE OF RORKE'S DRIFT, SOUTH AFRICA

In the days when Britain's empire spanned the globe, South Africa was the hub of an immense tussle for power and exploitation of resources known as the 'Scramble for Africa'. The continent was pillaged in much the same way as the East Indies had been in the centuries before. And guess what? The locals didn't like colonialism! Cue the 1879 Anglo–Zulu War and a series of increasingly bloody battles. At Rorke's Drift, a 4000-strong gang of rampaging natives besieged a missionary and trading post occupied by a tiny reserve of 140 British troops. Bedlam ensued, the natives were defeated and colonial rule continued until 1910.

Get to Rorke's Drift by following route R68 on the final leg of a 428km drive from Johannesburg. Bed down at the plush Rorke's Drift Lodge (www.rorkes driftlodge.com).

042 BATTLE OF THERMOPYLAE, GREECE

Ancient Greece was more than academia, mythology and the birth of the Olympic Games; they also knew how to fight a good ruck. Persia, undaunted by defeat in its 492 BC attempt to conquer Greece, came back for a second bite at the cherry in 480 BC, and so began the Second Persian Invasion of Greece. This time, things would be different. A Persian force estimated at 300,000 men marched in along the Malian Gulf pass at Thermopylae, vastly outnumbering the 8000-strong Greek defenders. Swords clashed, warriors were slain and the inevitable Persian victory saw the conquering invaders overrun the country as they marched on to Athens.

Geographical changes at Thermopylae mean the battlefield is now beneath 20m of soil. Drive the ancient pass on the road from Lokris to Thessaly, 135km northwest of Athens.

044 BATTLE OF ALÉSIA, FRANCE

Life was certainly cheap back in Roman times, made for living and reduced to the basest elements. Food, drink, sex… and war. And when the Romans went to war, they did it in impressive style. In 52 BC, as Julius Caesar's troops moved steadfastly through Gaul – present-day France, Luxembourg and Belgium – the stakes got higher and the battles more orgiastic. At Alésia, opposing forces fought for control of the strategic town; some 350,000 men traded blows as swords, javelins and crossbows wreaked their havoc. Caesar triumphed, Gaul fell to the Romans and the seeds of modern French culture were sown.

The village of Alise-Ste-Reine – 55km west of Dijon – lays claim to being the site of the battle; archaeological remains include the primitive forum, temple and forges.

045 BATTLE OF OLLANTAYTAMBO, PERU

If you're going to pick a fight, there are better places than the high Andes of Peru. But that's exactly what Spanish conquistadores did during their 40-year campaign against the Incas, when they launched an attack on Emperor Manco Inca's town of Ollantaytambo in 1537. Whether or not fighting at 2800m above sea level had any bearing on events is unknown, but suffice to say the Spanish (all 100 of them and their 30,000 native allies) were given the runaround before they eventually fled to Cusco under cover of darkness. The battle site is notable for its archaeological remains and huge Inca terraces overlooking the town.

Ollantaytambo, a popular town for hikers on the Inca Trail, is 65km from Cusco; hop on a frequent train or bus service for a day trip to see the ruins.

046 BATTLE OF SEKIGAHARA, JAPAN

For those who know Japanese history, and perhaps fans of the '80s novel and TV series *Shogun*, the Battle of Sekigahara in 1600 marked the end of the Shogunate in Japan. The Tokugawa clan were the victors, but the victory planted the seeds for a long-brewing revenge. It led to the eventual fall of the clan and the rise of Japan as an empire, launching the country into the modern world and paving the way for its military supremacy in Asia. Visiting the town of Sekigahara now, it's difficult to imagine 150,000 men in a pitched battle that lasted only six hours.

Sekigahara is a rural town in central Japan, 375km west of Tokyo and served by the mainline train service from Nagoya to Osaka.

047 BATTLE OF AGINCOURT, FRANCE

Medieval battles must have been a sight to behold. Legions of armour-suited warriors called to arms, wielding a blood-curdling array of daggers, swords, spears, axes and clubs. And that's before we even get to battering rams and catapults, not to mention mind-boggling torture devices. All these and more were employed in 1415 at the Battle of Agincourt, the decisive battle in the Hundred Years' War fought between Henry V's English troops and French battalions under the command of Charles d'Albret. Today you can visit the battlefield museum and get up close and personal with some of the gruesome weapons used.

The Centre Historique Médiéval d'Azincourt (www.azincourt-medieval.fr) allows you to relive all the glory and gore. Visit in October to see a re-enactment.

048 BATTLE OF GETTYSBURG, USA

The now tranquil town of Gettysburg, 235km west of Philadelphia, saw one of the American Civil War's most decisive and bloody battles. It's also where Lincoln delivered his famous Gettysburg Address. At the Gettysburg National Military Park you can pick up a map that details a self-guided tour, with sombre sights including the Wheatfield, which was strewn with more than 4000 dead and wounded. The Civil War Heritage Days festival takes place from the last weekend of June to the first weekend of July and features elaborate battle re-enactments - the closest thing you can get to time travel.

You can see other re-enactments throughout the year. See www .gettysburg.com/livinghistory.

049 BATTLE OF THE SOMME, FRANCE

Few conflicts in recent history resonate like that of the Battle of the Somme, six months of hellish fighting at the peak of WWI. From July to November 1916, wave after wave of British and French soldiers toiled to force back German troops who had occupied northern France for over two years. The Allies would eventually prevail, but not before more than one million men had fallen victim to the terrible carnage. Where innumerable shells once ripped these tranquil fields apart, shattering the landscape as well as those manning the front line, today the fields resound with a poignant serenity.

The 46m-high Thiepval Memorial to the Missing, 32km northeast of Amiens, remembers 72,000 Commonwealth soldiers whose graves are unknown.

050 CỦ CHI TUNNELS, VIETNAM

You don't have to be on the front line to be in the thick of the battle – countless wartime leaders commanded operations from secret bunkers and covert spy bases worked at cracking secret codes. In Vietnam, this effort reached extraordinary levels. Underlying much of the countryside near the town of Cu Chi, a huge network of tunnels formed the major infrastructure of the 1955–75 war with the US. As well as an operational base, the tunnels contained hospitals, weapons caches and quartermasters' stores, allowing guerilla fighters to stay ahead of the enemy.

Tours leave Ho Chi Minh City for the 40km drive to the tunnels; ask around to find the best operators.

MIGHTIEST MONOLITHS

They're big, bold lumps of rock, yes – but they're also sacred sites, colonial outposts and even home to lost worlds.

051 ULURU, AUSTRALIA

An iceberg in the outback, Uluru is 378m high above ground – but there's twice that bulk beneath it. Still, the surface portion of this monster in Australia's Northern Territory is impressive enough: it's a 10km walk around the rock, and a two-hour climb up – though the local Anangu people ask you not to; Uluru is sacred, and key to their Dreamtime stories. One legend asserts it is the outcome of warring tribes: as the leaders fought, Earth herself, racked with grief, created Uluru as bloodshed made stone. It's a plausible story when you watch the rock turn from eye-scalding orange to mellowing red as the setting sun moves across its sides.

Uluru-Kata Tjuta National Park, 445km from Alice Springs, is open daily from just before sunrise to sunset; see www .environment.gov.au/parks/uluru.

052 SIGIRIYA, SRI LANKA

Sigiriya – Lion Rock – is an impressive volcanic nub rearing 200m above precisely landscaped gardens in the heart of Sri Lanka's Cultural Triangle. As a geological feature it's nice enough; but since AD 477, when coup-fearing Prince Kasyapa decided to hide out here and make it his stronghold, it's been so much more than a lump of stone. Atop this strategic boulder you'll see remnants of Kasyapa's lofty fortress, a masterpiece of construction accessed through the Lion Gate, the huge stone paws of which can still be seen. The lower reaches are decorated with frescos depicting his 500 comely concubines, looking fine despite their 1500 years.

Sigiriya is 10km east of the main road between Dambulla and Habarana. Frequent buses run from Dambulla from about 7am.

053 TORRES DEL PAINE, CHILE

Like the sharpened prongs of a devil's trident, the three spiky namesake towers of Torres del Paine comprise the iconic image of Chilean Patagonia. They are as magnificent as they are hostile – when you look at these great granite shards, glacially eroded over tens of thousands of years, you feel that you might have entered a land where people have no business, and only llama-like guanacos should roam – the peaks are hard-edged, and the wilderness truly wild. In fact, with comfy refuges and well-marked trails, the park is well set up for visitors – though this doesn't detract from the landscape's fearsome air.

December to February is the best time to trek in Torres del Paine, when the weather is more clement and daylight hours are longer.

Climb these blue towers of Patagonia, Chile, and discover the true meaning of awesome

054 BEN AMERA, MAURITANIA

It's almost as massive as Uluru, but have you ever heard of it? Ben Amera sits squat, solitary and largely ignored in the barren desert of North Africa, a long, long way from the eyes of, well, pretty much anyone. It's plonked 5km from the small village of Tmeimichat, and the best way to catch a glimpse of this little-known, 400m-high mass is by riding the desert train between Nouadhibou and Zouerate. That's an experience in itself: the longest train in the world, a 3km-long, 220-car monster of rolling stock that grinds slowly through the sandscape, delivering iron ore across Mauritania's empty interior.

Ben Amera is about 400km west of Nouadhibou; some local tour operators arrange camping by the rock for a night.

055 SAVANDURGA, KARNATAKA, INDIA

Bald and bold as an elephant's rump, Savandurga – two separate hills, one black, one white – bulges up amid the forest of the Deccan Plateau. Pilgrims are drawn to the temples in its foothills, but hardy climbers ascend the mass itself to investigate its crevices and explore the fort upon its flanks. It's not an easy hike up – though some arrows mark the way, a local shepherd guide is a safer option – but it's worth it to marvel at the how-did-they-build-it-here architectural remains, to scramble between boulders and to stand by the shrine on the lofty summit and gaze out across the green valleys below.

Savandurga is 60km from Bangalore; the climb (two to three hours) should not be attempted during rains, when it becomes very slippery.

29

Aliens may not choose Wyoming for their earthly visit, but that means more nature walks and local wildlife for the rest of us

056 ROCK OF GIBRALTAR, UNITED KINGDOM

No other monolith can claim such a curious mix: Spanish sunshine, mischievous monkeys, Mediterranean guardianship and good ol' British boozers round the corner. The 426m-high slab of stone watching over the Straits of Gibraltar at the mouth of the Med is the centrepoint of this small British enclave off southern Spain. A troupe of Barbary macaques runs amok in the rock-top nature reserve, while caves Swiss-cheese the limestone beneath: explore this underbelly to see where Neolithic man sheltered 30,000 years ago, and where centuries of army generals have hacked strategic defensive tunnels to ensure the Iberian rock keeps the Union Jack flying.

The Spain–Gibraltar border is open 24 hours and is free – ignore touts trying to sell entry 'tickets'; see www.gibraltar.gi.

057 RORAIMA, VENEZUELA

Mist-shrouded, flat-topped, mysterious: tepuis are the venerable old men of the South American rainforest, imposing mesas dating back two billion years – they're some of the oldest geological formations on the planet. And Roraima is king of them all, its near-vertical, waterfall-dripped sides rising to 2810m and, seemingly, to another world. On top a hidden ecosystem awaits,

CAROL POLICH / LONELY PLANET IMAGES

058 DEVILS TOWER, WYOMING, USA

Impressive 386m-high protrusion of igneous rock, or alien landing pad? Since Steven Spielberg gave Devils Tower a starring role in *Close Encounters of the Third Kind*, many have pondered whether the monolith is indeed calling to extraterrestrial beings. There's certainly plenty of life here: it sits in a park of ponderosa pine, deer, prairie dogs and bears (the tower's native name translates as 'Bear Lodge'). While ET has yet to appear, the place is still special – it's been worshipped by Northern Plains tribes throughout the ages, and in 1906 was declared the USA's first National Monument.

There's no public transport to Devils Tower. Drivers should take the scenic route via the town of Hulett; see www.nps.gov/deto.

059 EL CAPITAN, CALIFORNIA, USA

The great grey granite of Yosemite National Park was first formed 500 million years ago, but it's the successive millennia of artful erosion and gradual glaciation that have sculpted today's national park into its current beauty: a U-shaped valley of breathtaking splendour. Standing sentinel in this show-off section of Californian hinterland is 910m-high El Capitan, one of the largest lumps of granite in the world. Known to the local Ahwahneechee as Tu-tok-a-nu-la (after the chant of the inchworm, allegedly the only creature able to scale the mountain), El Capitan is now the Holy Grail of rock-climbing, though thankfully you don't need to dangle off it to marvel at its magnitude.

Yosemite is around 320km from San Francisco – a four-hour drive, or six hours by a combination of train and bus; see www.nps.gov/yose.

060 PEÑA DE BERNAL, MEXICO

Bernal's Boulder is a chunky customer. Looming 350m above tiny San Sebastian Bernal, it makes its incongruously craggy presence clearly known. Yet travellers don't know about it, tucked as it is in little-visited Querétaro state – a short ride from Mexico City but apparently off the beaten track. It's a fun hike to the small chapel halfway up for views across the valleys. Better still, look for the booty – legend has it that when the sun shines right, an arrow-shaped shadow points to a cave on the peña's side where a giant snake guards a precious treasure.

San Sebastian Bernal is 60km from Querétaro City; a sound-and-light show illuminates the monolith every Saturday.

developed in utter isolation: unique frogs, flowers and carnivorous plants have evolved unusual habits in their Venezuelan eyrie, which was first climbed by European explorers in 1884 and subsequently inspired Arthur Conan Doyle to pen the tale of a dinosaur-tramped Lost World.

Roraima is 22km northeast of Paraitepui; tours can be arranged in Santa Elena, the nearest major town.

MIGHTIEST MONOLITHS

MOST ROMANTIC SPOTS

Come over weak-kneed and misty-eyed at the planet's best places to fall in love.

063 'EIFFEL TOWER', LAS VEGAS, NEVADA, USA

If you like love declared with actual, rather than metaphorical, fireworks, it's got to be Vegas, baby. King of kitsch, incapable of understatement, brash and larger than life, Las Vegas puts the razzmatazz into romance. It's all fake – a city of 1.8 million in the desert? – so embrace it. Ascend the 140m replica Eiffel Tower for a dash of Parisian passion, and discover the city's most amorous aspect: a view of 'Venetian canals', Chapel O' Loves and the illuminated spumes of the Bellagio's fountains, performing a dreamy dance at regular intervals below.

The Eiffel Tower Ride costs US$10/15 day/night; the Bellagio fountain show happens every 15 minutes, from 8pm to midnight. Check out www.parislasvegas.com and www.bellagio.com.

061 TOMB OF ABÉLARD & HÉLOÏSE, PARIS, FRANCE

Naming the most romantic spot in the most romantic city is a tall order. But the tomb of medieval lovers Abélard and Héloïse – ill-fated heroes of Paris' oldest love story – has at least a historic claim on the title. Theirs is a tale of an affair discovered: Abélard was castrated, Héloïse sent to a nunnery. But now they lie side by side in Père Lachaise Cemetery – along with Proust, Oscar Wilde, Jim Morrison and other famous dear-departeds. Grab a map of the graveyard, pay your respects to the illustrious dead and leave a letter by the lovers' crypt – a tradition said to ensure you find your own soulmate.

Père Lachaise is located in the 20th arrondissement; the nearest Metro stops are Philippe Auguste, Père-Lachaise and Gambetta. See www.pere-lachaise.com.

062 HEART REEF, GREAT BARRIER REEF, AUSTRALIA

Why say it with flowers when you can say it with coral instead? Discovered in 1974 by a sharp-eyed pilot, Heart Reef, in the middle of Queensland's idyllic Whitsunday Islands, is Mother Nature gone all gooey. A 17m-wide run-of-the-mill outcrop when viewed from boat level, from above this particular isolated ring of reef appears distinctly, undeniably, romantically heart-shaped. To coo at it yourself, board a floatplane, though it's just one of the attractions here: also look out for the luscious greens of the 74 islands, the sandy swirl of Whitehaven Beach, and a seemingly never-ending ocean of paradisiacal blue.

Scenic flights over the Whitsundays (www.whitsundaytourism.com) depart from Airlie Beach; a 65-minute flight will take in Heart Reef and Whitehaven.

064 PLAZA DE LOS COCHES, CARTAGENA, COLOMBIA

Cartagena oozes romance. Its walled old town is a pastel-hued warren of colonial mansions, blooming balconies and elegant towers – which is why it was used as a film set, for the 2008 adaptation of Gabriel García Márquez's novel *Love in the Time of Cholera*. It's the perfect backdrop for Márquez's amorous allegory; indeed, though it's not named in the book, Cartagena is clearly the town he had in mind. The Plaza de los Coches became the 'arcade of scribes', where the protagonist pens love poetry; as you pass the houses and horse carriages of the colonnaded square you may feel similarly inspired.

Cartagena, on Colombia's Caribbean coast, is hot year-round, though blessed by sea breezes; December to April is the dry season.

The beauty of the Taj Mahal's architecture is enhanced with 28 types of precious stones from all over India and other parts of Asia

065 APHRODITE'S BEACH, CYPRUS

Commune with the goddess of love herself: according to legend, it was from the foam at Petra tou Romiou – Aphrodite's Beach – that the Greek deity emerged on a zephyr-blown scallop shell, having formed in the sea from Uranus' amputated privates. That the sand here was the stomping ground of a goddess is not hard to believe – the beach is a beauty, with Mediterranean turquoise-blue waves lapping a tumble of outlying rocks and an undeveloped stretch of shore. Bring a picnic, go for a paddle and make a sunset toast to Aphrodite, in her spiritual home.

Petra tou Romiou is on the B6 road between Lemesos and Pafos; the beach is accessible via steps near the cafe.

066 TAJ MAHAL, AGRA, INDIA

The world's greatest monument to love, or its most outlandish romantic gesture at least, is India's Taj Mahal, the marble materialisation of one man's passion for his beloved wife. When Mumtaz Mahal died in childbirth, husband Shah vowed to build her the most beautiful tomb ever seen. It took him 22 years, but by 1653 he'd made good on his promise – and the Taj is no less magnificent today. Visit at dawn, when a pink glow warms the smooth white walls, to best appreciate the master craftsmanship of the inlaid mosaics and the graceful symmetry of the domes and minarets. Mumtaz would have been proud.

The Taj Mahal is open from 6am to 7.30pm daily except Friday. Agra is around 200km from Delhi.

33

067 HUÁNGSHĀN (YELLOW MOUNTAIN), CHINA

The views from the country's 'loveliest mountain' are exactly what you want from your Oriental landscape: this is postcard China, a vista of karst mountains and pines enveloped in wispy mist, best enjoyed at sunrise. There are countless other tourists, but the (many) stone steps to Huángshān's summits – including 1873m Lotus Peak and 1683m Beginning to Believe – are still worth the crowds and effort for those views (cheats can take the cable car). Plus there's extra romance in these hills: keen couples buy padlocks and secure them to the handrails, tossing the key into the abyss below – thus securing their love forever.

Huángshān, in Ānhuī province, can be reached by bus (70 minutes) from Túnxī, which is on the train line to Shanghai.

First seduce them with the views, then lock your loved one to you at China's Huángshān

DIANA MAYFIELD / LONELY PLANET IMAGES

068 ALLEY OF THE KISS, GUANAJUATO, MEXICO

Somewhere amid the colonial charm and mummy-filled catacombs of Unesco-listed Guanajuato, a tragic tale unfolds… Above the narrow Callejón del Beso – the Alley of the Kiss – two facing balconies almost touch. It was here that the daughter of a Spanish aristocrat, forced by her father to marry a noble, carried on hand-holding trysts with her impoverished true love living opposite. Predictably, this did not end well: Dad caught them at it, and plunged a dagger into her heart. Now couples exchange a kiss below those ill-fated overhangs to ensure 15 years of personal happiness; those who don't pucker up get seven years of suffering instead.

Guanajuato, in Guanajuato state, is virtually the geographic centre of Mexico and is 370km northwest of Mexico City (four hours by bus).

069 THE MEETING PLACE, ST PANCRAS INTERNATIONAL, LONDON, ENGLAND

The 9m-high couple canoodling beneath the station clock (a replica of the 19th-century original) makes an unambiguous statement: *The Meeting Place*, artist James Day's lovebirds-made-bronze, aims to sum up the romance of rail travel – and of this terminus in particular. St Pancras was almost demolished in the 1960s, despite its Grade-I listed Gothic facade and vast-spanned train shed. Today it has been restored and embellished to become home to the cross-Channel Eurostar fleet. As you stand by the statue's huge embrace you feel not only the thrill of the pair's reuniting, but also the tantalising prospect of a whole continent beckoning beyond.

The Eurostar journey takes two hours and 15 minutes from St Pancras to Paris, and one hour and 51 minutes to Brussels. See www.eurostar.com.

070 JULIET'S HOUSE, VERONA, ITALY

Romantic by association if not in atmosphere, the Casa de Giulietta throngs with tourists eager to have their 'Romeo, Romeo' moment on its fabled balcony. The heaving terrace – which may or may not have been linked to a Juliet, who may or may not have existed – is attached to a humble 13th-century home, rumoured to have once been a brothel, now scrawled with amorous graffiti. For a more peaceful impression of the town that gave birth to Shakespeare's star-crossed lovers, head up the Torre dei Lamberti: looking down on the alleys, ancient amphitheatre and the Adige River's bridges and bends, you can't deny the city's romance.

Entrance to the courtyard of Juliet's House is free; there is a fee to enter and stand on the balcony.

MOST ROMANTIC SPOTS

MOST NOTORIOUS PRISONS & DUNGEONS

Unlock the secrets of some of the world's most chilling, historic and poignant penitentiaries.

071 PORT ARTHUR, TASMANIA, AUSTRALIA

Backed by untouched forest on the shores of a tranquil bay, Port Arthur should be prime real estate. Instead, this remote outpost on the Tasman Peninsula is plain spooky, cloaked in an air of Gothic gloom. Though originally built as a flour mill, in 1857 the site was converted into a notorious, reputedly escape-proof penitentiary, which held some of the so-called 'villains' deported Down Under by the Brits. Tours following the fortunes of individual inmates bring home the reality of prison life in the 19th century; stories of the 1996 massacre, when a crazed gunman indiscriminately killed 35 tourists, add more up-to-date pathos.

Port Arthur (www.portarthur.org.au) is 60km east of Hobart via a scenic drive (part of the Convict Trail Touring Route); allow 90 minutes.

072 TUOL SLENG/S-21, PHNOM PENH, CAMBODIA

Brace yourself for a brush with man at his most monstrous. In 1975 this former high school in the Cambodian capital was converted into a prison by the Khmer Rouge to inflict unspeakable suffering on the regime's alleged enemies. Classrooms became torture chambers; chalk and textbooks were replaced with gruesome implements designed to extract information with maximum pain. Tuol Sleng closed in 1979 when Pol Pot was toppled, but not before 17,000 inmates were murdered. Today you can walk among the classrooms and corridors lined with blank-faced photos of the victims to ensure the atrocities perpetrated here are never forgotten.

Tuol Sleng Museum is open daily; the Killing Fields of Choeung Ek, where many of the inmates were executed, is 12km southwest.

073 CAPE COAST CASTLE, GHANA

It looks like a luxury villa from up top; a little crumbly, perhaps, but the high white walls and terraces of this Unesco-listed castle overlooking Ghana's Atlantic coast are still as imposing as its 17th-century architects intended. It's what lies beneath that is so chilling: featureless dungeons that, during the height of the slave trade, would have been packed with more than

1000 captive souls. They'd be held here for months before being shipped to the New World; descend there now and you can begin to imagine the hellish wait for those trapped there, a taunting sea breeze through the few barred windows their only contact with the world beyond.

Cape Coast is a three-hour bus journey from capital Accra; the admission fee includes a guided tour.

DAVID WALL / LONELY PLANET IMAGES

Port Arthur, Tasmania, serves as an important reminder of Australia's convict past

074 ALCATRAZ, SAN FRANCISCO, USA

Perhaps the planet's most famed prison, this wild isle in the middle of San Francisco Bay only served as a jail for 29 years. But what years they were – Alcatraz was a super-prison, a penal experiment to counter the rising crime in 1930s USA. It incarcerated some of the most notorious ne'er-do-wells of the time, including Al Capone and Robert 'Birdman' Stroud. But there's more to this isolated outcrop; an audio guide will point out the prison cells, but also the bird colonies and reminders of the 1969–71 Native American occupation, which ultimately secured the future of the USA's persecuted tribes.

Ferries leave for Alcatraz from San Francisco's Pier 33 every 30 minutes from 9am. Advance booking is essential; see www.nps.gov/alcatraz.

075 TOWER OF LONDON, ENGLAND

If only the walls could talk… First built as a stronghold for William the Conqueror in 1070, the Tower of London has, over the centuries, protected kings, safeguarded the crown jewels and incarcerated some of Britain's biggest-hitting prisoners. Guy 'Gunpowder Plot' Fawkes, the 'Little Princes' (allegedly illegitimate sons of Edward IV), Sir Walter Raleigh, all were locked within the Thames-side fortress. Many more were executed in its grounds – Henry VIII used its chopping block for dispatching two unwanted wives. Today the Tower is more genteel (unless you believe the ghost stories…), but take a tour with a Yeoman Warder to hear them recreate this bastion's grisly past.

The Tower of London (www.hrp.org.uk/ Toweroflondon) is open daily and costs from £16/9 per adult/child; once inside, Yeoman tours are free.

076 CONCIERGERIE, PARIS, FRANCE

From grandeur to the guillotine, this former palace in the middle of Seine Île de la Cité has a chequered past. A one-time palace of the medieval kings of France, and home to Sainte-Chapelle (an exquisite example of Gothic Rayonnant architecture and a must for those with a penchant for stained glass), the Conciergerie became the main detention centre for pesky reactionaries during the French Revolution. Dark and pestilent cells, which you can tour today, held those opposed to the new regime; during the 1793–94 Reign of Terror, more than 2700 souls lost their heads after being sentenced here – a grim tally for a grand site.

Entrance to the Conciergerie, open daily, costs €7 (€11 including entry to Sainte-Chapelle); see http://conciergerie .monuments-nationaux.fr.

077 KAROSTA, LIEPAJA, LATVIA

Law-abiding citizens can feel the full force of KGB interrogation at this former jail on the Baltic coast. Still operating as a deeply unpleasant prison as recently as 1997, this interactive museum puts you in the shoes of the anti-Stalinists and military deserters who populated its dingy confines. Visitors, now temporary inmates, are photographed, frogmarched, yelled at and examined as they tour the miserable digs and (reputedly haunted) guardhouse. Those who want a fuller taste of criminal incarceration can opt for ghoulish night tours, complete with prison rations and a stay in a cell: you get a mattress, a metal mug and not a lot else.

Karosta, 5km from Liepaja on the west coast, is open 10am to 6pm daily, May to September; night tours by arrangement. See www.karostascietums.lv.

Watch the resident birds of Alcatraz at play, safe in the knowledge that you'll head back to San Francisco at the end of the day

078 CHÂTEAU DE CHILLON, LAKE GENEVA, SWITZERLAND

'And mine has been the fate of those / To whom the goodly earth and air / Are bann'd, and barr'd – forbidden fare.' So penned Lord Byron about imprisoned monk Bonivard after a visit to this practically perfect medieval castle. (It's got turrets! A moat! And lake-view battlements!) The poet, who scratched his name onto a pillar here, was moved by the rather beautiful dungeons – more cathedral nave than dingy basement – in which the monk and other renegades had been chained over the centuries. Now that non-criminals are allowed into the stronghold, you can be similarly inspired by its watchtowers, ancient toilets and literary graffiti.

Château de Chillon (www.chillon.ch), 3km from Montreux, at the eastern end of Lake Geneva, it's open daily from at least 10am to 4pm (longer in summer).

079 ROBBEN ISLAND, CAPE TOWN, SOUTH AFRICA

When the 1984 pop song implored the world to 'Free Nelson Mandela', the leader of the African National Congress had already spent 18 years behind bars here. Robben Island, an isolated outcrop 7km off Cape Town, had been utilised as a jail by the colonising Dutch since the 1650s. Decreed the lowliest category of prisoner, Mandela received few privileges and had a tough life, but his will was unshakable. It's now a World Heritage site, and tours of the island – from Mandela's cell to the limestone quarry in which he was forced to work – give a feel for the hardships endured, while an ex-inmate provides you with a harrowing eyewitness account.

Ferries to Robben Island (www.robben-island.org.za) depart at 9am, 11am, 1pm and 3pm (weather permitting) from Cape Town's V&A Waterfront.

080 DEVIL'S ISLAND, FRENCH GUIANA

It should be a tropical paradise – a lush isle floating 15km off the north coast of South America. But Île du Diable was hell. It was a dumping ground for 80,000 French felons from 1852 to 1946, and few ever left: conditions were squalid, the heat unbearable, and the mosquitoes were malarial and voracious. Even if inmates did find a way through the jungle and rough seas, a run-in with crocs awaited. Henry Charrière was one who did escape; though some doubt its veracity, his book *Papillon* tells a believably macabre tale.

Ferries and (more comfortable) catamarans leave for Devil's Island from Kourou; the crossing takes 1½ hours.

MOST NOTORIOUS PRISONS & DUNGEONS

FLASHIEST LIGHTHOUSES

These top light-spotting spots are guaranteed to dazzle.

MARJANIEMI, FINLAND

To get a good feel for the romance of lighthouse-keeping – the storms, the constant wind, the tumult of crashing oceans – spend a night in one. Getting to Hailuoto island by ferry adds to the nautical adventure. Hurry, though; continental rebound (the earth rising back up after being compressed from the glacier-weights of an ice age) will eventually see the island join the mainland. If you can't get out there soon, a webcam is in operation (www.luotokeskus.fi/webcam) and will give you some immediate vicarious adventure.

EDDYSTONE, ENGLAND

The lighthouse on the Eddystone Rocks is the fourth such structure to bear the Eddystone name. The Great Storm of 1703 (a hurricane that blew for a week) destroyed the first incarnation, which had begun operating in 1698. The second structure, ready in 1709, was a wooden wonder, but was destroyed by fire in 1755. The third attempt was made from stone and lit in 1759, but the rock it was built on was unstable, so the structure was dismantled 120 years later – today you can visit the reassembled lighthouse at Plymouth. In 1882 the current structure was lit, a sleek, modern-looking tower built near the stumpy remains of Eddystone III.

CAPE HATTERAS, USA

You'll know it by the barbershop spirals coiling around the tower. And possibly the height – Hatteras is the tallest lighthouse in the USA at 63m. An earlier incarnation was completed in 1803 but was damaged during the Civil War. The current building was first lit in 1871. Due to erosion of the shore, the Cape Hatteras lighthouse was moved, in 2000, from its original location at the edge of the ocean to safer ground approximately 800m inland. There's a visitor centre and museum at the site. It remains an active lighthouse, guiding vessels past the treacherous Diamond Shoals off the North Carolina coast, cause of some 2000 wrecks over 400 years.

GREEN CAPE, AUSTRALIA

What better place to find a lighthouse than the tip of a bay bearing the rather unfortunate name Disaster? Green Cape lighthouse, in New South Wales, has seen a few wrecks in its time, most significantly the SS *Ly-ee-Moon*, which ran aground in 1886, just three years after the lighthouse was lit; 71 sailors died and 15 were rescued by the keeper. Disaster Bay is at the border of two national parks (Croajingolong and Ben Boyd), and the lighthouse is perched above the epitome of an Australian bush beach: chalky, fine sand, rugged cliffs festooned with tea trees, wild blue waters and the lingering scent of eucalyptus.

HOOK HEAD, IRELAND

The great granddaddy of lighthouses, Hook Head is arguably the oldest working light in the world. The site had humble beginnings, reportedly as far back as the 5th century, with monks lighting a beacon there. The structure as it stands today has existed for 800 years. It's an automated light, squat and a little…plump (they say horizontal stripes emphasise a thick waist, so it might just be an illusion). Access to the light is by tour, organised through the visitor centre. A historical teaser – have you ever wondered where the phrase 'by hook or by crook' comes from?

SLANGKOP, SOUTH AFRICA

Looking out from the infamous Cape of Good Hope, Slangkop was built in 1914 but first lit in 1919. A few years prior to its construction, the SS *Maori* was wrecked, highlighting the need for a beacon. The brilliant white of the structure will have you pondering the repainting cycle, which must be constant – you can ask the keeper on a guided tour. This cast-iron lighthouse overlooks Kommetjie, a village about 30km from Cape Town, where you can combine your light-spotting with some crayfishing – crayfish is a local speciality.

CAPE PALLISER, NEW ZEALAND

The Cape Palliser lighthouse, built in 1897 and resplendent in its wide red bands, is a cynosure to ships navigating the Cook Strait, located off the southern tip of New Zealand's North Island. Inland it looks over fine food-and-wine country, so it's a gourmet light-spotter's paradise and, as you'd expect in New Zealand, the adventure activities in the region are many. The light is still in service – but you can still climb up the 250 steps to get a light's-eye view of ocean and land.

CREAC'H, FRANCE

The black-banded Creac'h, standing tall (seriously tall, at 54.85m) on Île d'Ouessant (Ushant), is one of the most powerful lighthouses in the world. The French Atlantic coast is famous for its churning, storm-swept oceans, made treacherous by the numerous granite outcrops that lie off the Brittany shore. The Creac'h cuts across these waters with a beam that reaches 60km away. A lighthouse museum provides an insight into its workings. As a bonus, a visit to the Creac'h is an opportunity to visit the nearby Stiff Lighthouse, one of the older lighthouses still in use, built in the late 17th century.

PONDICHERRY, INDIA

In a country most would associate with English colonialism, Pondicherry (Puducherry) is a strongly French-influenced town in the south of India. It grew from sleepy village to significant trade centre for the French East India Company, which eventually replaced a log fire on a hill with a lighthouse to give ships fair warning. The lighthouse shot out its first beam in 1836 and remained in use for 150 years. It stands now as a monument, but is being restored as a museum to the French architecture of the town.

GIBBS HILL, BERMUDA

The Gibbs Hill lighthouse stands high on a hill in Southampton, and climbing to the platform gives you a view of the entire island, with Caribbean splendour all around. Early in the year you might catch a glimpse of migrating whales. At such a height, the beacon can be seen up to 60km away. Back on the ground there's more standard tourist fare, with a cafe and gift shop; the owner's grandfather was the last keeper before the lighthouse was automated, so the romance is not all gone.

BIGGEST STATUES

Size really is everything! See the world's super-statues – celebrations of religious devotion, political persuasion and the downright kitsch.

091 MOTHERLAND, VOLGOGRAD, RUSSIA

Decreed on its unveiling in 1967 to be a symbol of 'the people's infinite love of the Motherland and its unshakable solidarity with the Communist party', today this mammoth matriarch in Russia's southwest is looking decidedly less than unshakeable: her 85m of sword-waving, cape-flailing concrete is now listing 20cm off-kilter, and is in danger of imminent collapse. Which would be a shame – she's quite a sight, a typically Soviet neoclassical/kitsch behemoth, built to commemorate victory over the Nazis at Stalingrad (Volgograd's former name). To gaze up from her base is to feel the force of Stalinist patriotism – just don't stand under her teetering frame for too long…

Trains leave from Moscow's Paveletsky Station for Volgograd and take around 19 hours; see www.poezda.net.

092 STATUE OF LIBERTY, NEW YORK, USA

Probably the world's most famous super-sized statue, Lady Liberty has symbolised freedom to all those passing through New York's harbour since 1886. A gift from the French to a USA freshly emerged from civil war, she remains just as potent a presence today. Her own liberty was compromised following the 9/11 attacks: security concerns saw her pedestal (home to a museum) closed until 2004, while access to the uppermost observation deck – a 354-step climb up into her spiky crown – only resumed in 2009. But now she is open for business once more, standing guard over an altered NYC perhaps, but one that's no less impressive.

Liberty Island can be reached by ferry from Battery Park, Manhattan; for information on visiting, including crown access, see www.nps.gov/stli.

093 MOAI, EASTER ISLAND

Big, yes; statues, almost not. The mysterious moai of Easter Island, huge heads carved from the volcanic tuff up to 750 years ago by the ill-fated Rapa Nui, were almost all toppled – the result of tribal rivalry. Today, a few of the 600-odd moai have been re-erected to restore full upright grandeur; reaching almost 10m, these monoliths dot the remote Pacific outpost. A few look out to sea, many lay unmoved from the quarry at Rano Raraku, but all provoke questions: what exactly were they for? And why did their creators disappear before they'd provided an explanation?

Easter Island is 3790km and a five-hour flight from Santiago de Chile; most flights continue on to Tahiti, six hours away.

094 CHRIST THE REDEEMER, RIO DE JANEIRO, BRAZIL

This incredible lump of soapstone could tempt even the most stalwart of atheists to convert. It isn't so much the size of Rio's 38m Christ that's so affecting, or even its aspect – though his open-armed embrace is strangely soothing for such a giant. It's his position: perched atop the 710m-high Corcovado mountain, this art deco effigy lords it benignly over Rio's bay and bustle below. On a clear day, ride the cog railway or trek up the 220 steps through Parque Nacional da Tijuca to join the main man way up on his pedestal – and feel that little bit closer to heaven.

The cog train takes 20 minutes from Cosme Velho station to the foot of the statue; see www.corcovado.com.br.

JUDY BELLAH / LONELY PLANET IMAGES

43

Feel the arms of Christ reaching for you as you climb to view Rio de Janeiro from above

095 MEMENTO PARK, BUDAPEST, HUNGARY

Lenin, Marx, Engels – a conflab of communist bigwigs and bombast has gathered on the outskirts of the Hungarian capital. Following the fall of the Communist Party in 1989, the icons of the regime, which dotted Budapest in order to remind its citizens just how good communism was, were shipped wholesale into this unique open-air museum. Now 42 artworks – muscle-bound workers, flag-waving comrades and political machinators – stand in a field. The star exhibit is a bit of Stalin – during the city's 1956 revolution his effigy was destroyed, and all that remains are his impressive pair of big bronze boots.

The park is in the 22nd district, Southern Buda; a direct bus leaves at 11am from downtown. See www.szoborpark.hu.

096 GIANT NED KELLY, GLENROWAN, AUSTRALIA

Glenrowan was the site of infamous outlaw Ned Kelly's last stand – and it appears he's still standing. Just off the Hume Highway, 240km north of Melbourne, a Big Ned greets Australian road trippers. Big Things have sprouted all over the country – from bananas to crustaceans, they've become kitsch icons – but this 7m-high, metal-hatted man has greater significance than oversized fruit. It was here, in 1880, that the nation's beloved bandit was finally captured after a siege at the Glenrowan Inn. The original inn is no more, but a walking tour and museum point out key Kelly spots.

The Ned Kelly Memorial Museum and Glenrowan Tourist Centre are both on the town's main street; see www .glenrowantouristcentre.com.au.

44

Experience the calm that emanates from this mighty Buddha in Sichuān province, China

097 ANGEL OF THE NORTH, ENGLAND

A rusty eyesore? Or the most important piece of modern public art in Britain? It seems sculptor Antony Gormley's hilltop-poised Angel, looming 20m above the outskirts of Gateshead, has fast converted sceptics who'd branded spending £800,000 on a lump of steel preposterous. Now this weighty statue welcomes droves of travellers with its wide-winged embrace – a gesture of famed northern hospitality that stretches as wide as a jumbo jet. But the Angel isn't just a sight to be snapped: it's a dramatic declaration – through the combination of engineering skill and artistic audacity – of the regeneration of a resurgent region.

The statue is located just outside Gateshead and can be visited by the Angel bus service; see www.simplygo .com for timetables.

098 SPHINX, GIZA, EGYPT

If age defines importance then the Great Sphinx of Giza is undoubtedly the world's statue supremo. Hewn from the underlying rock around 2500 BC by Pharaoh Khafre – whose pyramid the reclining half-man, half-lion seems to guard – the Sphinx is also massive: its feline torso is 74m long,

its human head 20m high. Time is taking its toll – its nose is long gone (possibly lopped off by a disgruntled Sufi Muslim in the 14th century), its beard is in the British Museum, and pollution and rising groundwater are eating away at its insides. But for now, both the Sphinx's air of mystery and its massive proportions remain resolutely intact.

The Sphinx and Pyramids are illuminated by a sound-and-light show up to four times daily; for details see www .soundandlight.com.eg.

100 MAITREYA BUDDHA, EMEI LAKE, TAIWAN

If laughter is contagious, this chuckling bronze colossus will have passers by in stitches. The statue overseeing Emei Lake in northern Taiwan's Hsinchu County is 72m of broad-bellied, cheeky-grinned Laughing Buddha, an enormous incarnation of the bodhisattva of the future, who will – so the prophecy goes – descend from heaven and bestow an 'abundance of joy and happiness' to all his followers. For now, visitors should be happy just to admire his plump proportions, stroll the leafy lakeside and surrounding mountains he smiles over, and drink a reviving cuppa – the Emei region is known for its special 'beauty tea'.

High-speed trains run to Hsinchu Station (www.thsrc.com.tw/en), from where you can board a bus to Fuxing Station for Emei Lake.

099 GRAND BUDDHA, LÈSHĀN, CHINA

At 71m tall, with shoulders broader than buildings, toenails bigger than people and 5m-long eyebrows, the Buddha of Lèshān is a mountain of a man – quite literally, as he sits hewn from the cliffs of Sìchuān province, overlooking the confluence of the Dàdù and Mín rivers. Conceived by a monk in AD 713 to cast a calming influence on the turbulent waters, he's a bit moss-covered but otherwise doing well for his 1300 years. Pay your respects from the terrace by his ear before descending the twisty staircase to be dwarfed by his monstrous feet.

Boat tours (which pause for photos) or cheaper ferries (which don't) offer river views of the Buddha; board from the docks along Binjiang Lu.

BIGGEST STATUES

BEST UNDERGROUND SIGHTS

Delve below the surface to see the awesome art, communist caves and top-notch train lines that lie beneath...

101 PATHET LAO CAVES, LAOS

Caves make brilliant wartime hideouts. In 1964, the communist movement Pathet Lao moved its headquarters to a series of caves near Vieng Xai; secreted away along a narrow and precipitous valley, it was virtually unassailable. Six of these caves can now be visited: inside are former meeting rooms, government offices, markets, temples, printing presses, hospitals, army barracks and more. Wooden walls, as well as natural formations, divide the caverns into various rooms, still decorated with images of Lenin and Che Guevara, and incongruous facades and gardens are built onto the front of the caves.

Pick-up trucks run from Sam Neua, the main town of Houaphanh Province, to Vieng Xai; journey time is about 50 minutes.

102 PARIS CATACOMBS, FRANCE

In 1785, to solve the problem of Paris' overflowing cemeteries, bones of the buried were exhumed and relocated to the tunnels of disused quarries, 20m beneath the city streets. This continued for around 100 years, and 300km of tunnels are lined with skulls, tibias and femurs, almost artistically arranged. In the 2km open to the curious (or the ghoulish), it's estimated that six million individuals are represented. During WWII the tunnels were used as a headquarters by the French Resistance. Today they make a macabre attraction; urban spelunkers are often caught illegally roaming the unstable closed-off section.

The catacombs are accessed from avenue Colonel Henri Rol-Tanguy, near Denfert-Rochereau station; only 200 people are allowed in at one time. See www.catacombes-de-paris.fr.

103 CARLSBAD CAVERNS NATIONAL PARK, NEW MEXICO, USA

From above, it's a land of cacti and shrub. But beneath lies a geological Swiss cheese. There are more than 117 caves lurking under the badlands of New Mexico, and they put on quite a subterranean show: sulphuric acid has gnawed the limestone into theatrical auditoria, shimmering stalactites, delicate draperies and soda straws. There are cave sights for all: big ones for claustrophobes, tunnel crawls for the brave. Slaughter Canyon Cave has the most festive feel – a desert hike from the main labyrinth, it's home to the 'Christmas Tree Room', where the rock is bedecked in crystals that look like a glitter of fairylights.

Greyhound buses serve the caverns. Self-guided and ranger-guided tours are available; the latter must be booked ahead. See www.nps.gov/cave.

Deep in these 117 caves in New Mexico, your explorations might uncover a troll or two

104 SAGADA BURIAL CAVES, PHILIPPINES

Sumaging Cave is an exhilarating adventure guaranteed to bring out your inner Indiana Jones or Allan Quatermain. The route takes you crawling through narrow crevices, wading through water and scaling the sides of deep ravines, and in some sections the smooth limestone is so slippery that you have to go barefoot (watch where you step!). Guides light the way (and the stunning calcium formations) with gas lanterns. The connected Lumiang Burial Cave is fascinating for its eerie collection of centuries-old wooden coffins. Other, slowly decomposing, caskets can be seen hanging from the cliff face.

Sagada is in the Mountain Province of Luzon island; local *jeepneys* (minibuses) can take you to the caves from nearby Bontoc.

CROWN MINES SHAFT 14, SOUTH AFRICA

South Africa proudly lays claim to the world's deepest pub, 226m down a Johannesburg gold mine known as Shaft 14. This is one of the deepest mine tours you can take, and despite being located in a kitsch theme park, it gives an authentic glimpse of gruelling mining life. When the mine opened in 1897 there was only candlelight to work by, up to 40°C heat, ear-shattering drills and dangerous gases – along with miserable wages. Migrant miners of many languages learned to send messages by slapping their boots in rhythms, the origin of the *isicathulo* or gumboot dance.

Shaft 14 is just one attraction at Gold Reef City theme park (www.goldreefcity.co.za), in the southern suburbs of Johannesburg.

47

106 HOTEL SIDI DRISS, TUNISIA

If you've ever wished to set foot on the planet of Tatooine, of *Star Wars* fame, the village of Matmata in the Tunisian Sahara might be as close as you can get. The Berber underground dwellings here are built around a deep sunken courtyard, with cave-like rooms coming off the sides, which means they remain at a comfortable temperature year-round. But Hotel Sidi Driss has an added attraction for movie buffs: the hotel was used as the set for Uncle Owen and Aunt Beru's house in the original *Star Wars* movie, making it a rather surreal place to stay.

The hotel is a 40km share-taxi or bus ride from Gabes; specify 'Matmata Ancienne', as some services terminate in 'Matmata Nouvelle', 15km away.

107 CAVE OF SWIMMERS, GILF KEBIR, EGYPT

Figures doing front-crawl in the middle of the desert? The sea of sand that ripples around the remote Gilf Kebir in Egypt's far southwest was not always dry, it seems. In 1933 explorer László Almásy discovered a cavern where prehistoric paintings seemed to show people swimming. His conclusion? When these 10,000-year-old scribbles were made, there was water here for them to swim in. It's a mission to reach; the crew of *The English Patient* didn't bother – the cave, a key location, was re-created in Tunisia. But if you do make the trip you'll find one of the greatest ancient galleries in the world.

The Gilf Kebir is on the Egypt-Libya border, and is difficult to access. Only visit with an experienced tour operator.

48

Stop and admire Moscow's art deco Mayakovskaya station, just don't miss your train

JONATHAN SMITH • LONELY PLANET IMAGES

108 MAYAKOVSKAYA, MOSCOW METRO, RUSSIA

Flair and function combine to glorious effect in the bowels of the Russian capital. The Moscow metro, inaugurated in 1935, boasts 182 stations, used by nine million Muscovites daily. Impressive stats, but not as impressive as the stations themselves: marble columns, rousing mosaics and mighty chandeliers festoon these platforms. There are many beauties, but Mayakovskaya, on the Zamoskvoretskaya line, is pick of the stops: its vaulted, art deco hall is a flourish of pink and chrome, with frescos depicting happy Soviets toiling in fields as today's commuters toil less cheerfully below.

The 12 lines of the Moscow metro (http://engl.mosmetro.ru/) are open 6am to 1am daily; a single ride costs RUB26.

ACTUN TUNICHIL MUKNAL, MAYA MOUNTAINS, BELIZE

Hike through snake-infested jungle. Ford three rivers. Plunge into a dark and secret cave. Clamber amid jaguar-shaped stalactites and ancient artefacts. Wade, chest-deep, through subterranean streams. And then you will find her: the Crystal Maiden, a 1100-year-old skeleton who shimmers like diamonds within her cathedral-like confines. This is Maya mystery of the highest order – few delve into this cavern in central Belize; even fewer know anything about the unfortunate young lady within. It's believed she was sacrificed over a millennium ago, and only rediscovered in 1989, when her calcite-dusted bones became the source of her sparkly moniker.

Only two tour operators are permitted the guide trips into this cave, which lies 12km southof Beal of the Village.

GROTTE DE FONT-DE-GAUME, FRANCE

Vézère Valley is full of prehistoric rock art, but this cave is arguably the best, containing one of the most astounding collections open to the public. You can get close to about 25 of its 230 figures of mammoths, bison, reindeer and bears, and wonder at the meaning they held for their Cro-Magnon creators 14,000 years ago. Many of the animals, carved into rock or delicately shaded with pigments, are caught in remarkably lifelike movement.

The Grotte is in the Dordogne, 1.5km from Les Eyzies. Book ahead as there is a daily limit on visitors. See www.monuments-nationaux.fr

BEST UNDERGROUND SIGHTS

BEST LITERARY SIGHTS

You've read about them, now visit the places that figured in or inspired some of the finest words in history.

113 CUEVA DEL MILODÓN, CHILE

In a cave in Patagonia in the 1890s, German pioneer Hermann Eberhard discovered the partial remains of an enormous ground sloth. The sloth would become the inspiration for Bruce Chatwin's book *In Patagonia*. Growing up coveting a scrap of the *milodón's* skin kept in a cabinet in his grandmother's house in England, Chatwin headed off for Patagonia in search of its origin. Taking advantage of the book's phenomenal popularity, the 30m-high cave today pays homage to its former inhabitant with a life-size plastic replica of the animal.

The cave is 25km from Puerto Natales; Torres del Paine buses from the city pass the entrance.

111 STRATFORD-UPON-AVON, ENGLAND

The author of some of the most quoted lines ever written, William Shakespeare was born in Stratford-upon-Avon in 1564 and died in the same town in 1616. Today he's a tourist attraction that verges on a cult of personality. Experiences in the unmistakably Tudor town range from the touristy (medieval re-creations and bard-themed tearooms) to the humbling (Shakespeare's modest grave in Holy Trinity Church) and the sublime (taking in a play by the world-famous Royal Shakespeare Company). Five houses linked to the Bard's life – from his birthplace to the childhood homes of his wife and mother – form the centrepiece of the action.

You can buy individual or combination tickets for the two homes, which are run by the Shakespeare Birthplace Trust (www.shakespeare.org.uk).

112 BRONTË PARSONAGE MUSEUM, ENGLAND

Wend your way across the bleak moors to pay a visit to the Brontë Parsonage Museum situated in the hilltop town of Haworth. The family house preserves rooms as they would have appeared in the writers' day. Here you can see the small table Charlotte and Emily circled as they read *Jane Eyre* to each other. Sadly, all four highly creative siblings died before age 40. Charlotte, prevented from finding love until her late 30s by their exacting father, only knew brief romantic happiness. You may well go away from the Parsonage subdued, an appropriate mood in which to approach the (all the more remarkable) bruising passions of *Wuthering Heights*.

The museum is in the centre of Haworth, near the Yorkshire city of Bradford. For further information and tour details, see www.bronte.org.uk.

114 BAKER STREET, ENGLAND

Literature's most famous detective is celebrated in the Sherlock Holmes Museum in – where else? – Baker Street in London's West End. Though the museum gives its address as 221b Baker Street, the actual fictional abode of Sherlock Holmes is the former Abbey National building (look for the clock tower) a bit further south. Fans of the books will enjoy examining the three floors of reconstructed Victoriana, deerstalkers, burning candles and flickering grates, but may baulk at the dodgy waxworks of Professor Moriarty and 'the Man with the Twisted Lip'. The only disappointment is the lack of material and information on Holmes' creator, Arthur Conan Doyle.

The museum (www.sherlock-holmes .co.uk) is just a couple of minutes' walk from Baker Street tube station.

115 GREEN GABLES, CANADA

On Canada's Prince Edward Island (PEI) the soil is red and the lobsters are red, but the most famous 'red' is the little redhead called Anne of Green Gables. On the north coast, in the seaside-silly town of Cavendish, stands the Green Gables farmhouse that inspired the book's setting. Today it's a National Historic Site, filled with period furnishings and literary memories of Anne and Gilbert and co. And if you've got a bit more Anne in you, there's always Avonlea, the Cavendish theme park based on the Green Gables story.

PEI's Beach Shuttle bus runs between the island capital, Charlottetown, and Cavendish. In town, the Cavendish Red Trolley cruises along Highway 13, stopping at the Green Gables farmhouse.

117 PAZIN, CROATIA

The central Istrian town of Pazin is pretty much famous for one thing only: the chasm that so inspired Jules Verne he used it as a setting in his novel *Mathias Sandorf*. The Pazin Cave is a deep abyss of about 100m, through which the Pazincica River sinks into subterranean passages forming three underground lakes. Visitors can walk a 1200m path into the abyss. If you really want to make it a Verne vigil, come in the last week of June for the town's Days of Jules Verne festival featuring, among other events, re-enactments from the novel.

Pazin has train connections to Pula, Zagreb and Ljubljana. Check out the chasm online at www.pazinska-jama.com.

119 WHITE HORSE TAVERN, NEW YORK, USA

Brendan Behan summed up many a writer when he described himself as 'a drinker with a writing problem'. So many writers have turned to grog, it's almost a cliché, but the watering hole that may top all others in the literary annals is the White Horse Tavern in Manhattan's West Village. In the 1950s this pub became the haunt of the likes of Norman Mailer, James Baldwin, Anaïs Nin, Jack Kerouac and, most notoriously, Dylan Thomas, who famously had his last drinking session here – 18 whiskies at his own count – before falling ill and dying a few days later. His portrait now hangs in the bar.

The tavern is at 567 Hudson Street, on the corner of 11th Street.

MT SINAI, EGYPT

They're probably the most quoted bits of literature in history: the Ten Commandments, supposedly delivered to Moses atop the summit of Mt Sinai. It's a place of nightly pilgrimage for travellers. The climb begins at St Catherine's Monastery – built beside the reputed location of the Burning Bush – and can be made on one of two trails: the easier camel trail or the taxing 3750 Steps of Repentance, laid out by one monk as a form of penance. The two trails meet about 300m below the summit, from where all walkers must take a steep series of 750 rocky and uneven steps to the top.

St Catherine's Monastery is about 2.5km from the railhead. At Mokpe, which is served by buses from Dahab. Vehicles or St Catherine's are generally used by the monastery for returning walkers off the mountain.

ERNEST HEMINGWAY HOUSE, FLORIDA, USA

From 1931 to 1940 Ernest Hemingway lived in this gorgeous Spanish colonial house in Florida's Key West. *The Short Happy Life of Francis Macomber* and *Green Hills of Africa* were produced here, but Papa didn't just work; like all writers he wasted a lot of time, specifically by installing Key West's first saltwater swimming pool. The construction project set him back so badly he pressed his 'last penny' into the cement on the pool's deck. It's still there today, along with the descendants of his famous six-toed (polydactyl) cat, who basically rule the house and grounds. The author's old studio is preserved as he left it.

The house is at 907 Whitehead Street and is open daily to visitors. Information at www.hemingwayhome.com.

JAMES JOYCE TOWER, IRELAND

Dublin is one of literature's pin-up cities. It is the only city of its size to have spawned four Nobel laureates for literature (George Bernard Shaw, William Yeats, Samuel Beckett and Seamus Heaney), and it was the star of James Joyce's epic *Ulysses*. The historic Mortello tower in Sandycove is a James Joyce museum that keeps a number of treasures, including a precious edition of *Ulysses* illustrated by Henri Matisse. Below the tower is a seawater pool mentioned at the close of *Ulysses'* first chapter. In the tradition of Joyce celebrating 'heroic commonplace', many locals become everyday heroes by braving the skin-shrinking temperature of the sea sans swimming costume.

The tower is about 12km from Dublin. Check how to get there.

MOST OVERSIZED ANIMALS

Mass matters – at least, in the natural world, where bigger can mean better fed. These giant critters deserve your respect – and, maybe, fear.

121 KOMODO DRAGON, KOMODO NATIONAL PARK, INDONESIA

Here be dragons! OK, so there are no wings, no fiery breath (though you wouldn't want to get too close when it hasn't flossed for a while), but the planet's heftiest lizard truly is a monster – up to 3m long and 160kg. And it likes the taste of flesh: though tales of attacks on humans are exaggerated, bites usually become infected with bacteria from the dragon's saliva – nasty. The *ora*, as it's called locally, is confined to just five islands in Indonesia; of those, Komodo and Rinca comprise Komodo National Park, where you'll have a good chance of spotting at least one.

Rinca island is just two hours by boat from Labuanbajo on neighbouring Flores; it's a popular day trip, and boats are easily chartered.

122 GREEN ANACONDA, PANTANAL, BRAZIL

In the interests of fairness it should be observed that the anaconda is not the longest snake: that honour (shiver) goes to the reticulated python. But never mind the length, feel the width: this bus-long beast – some extend over 8m – has an enormous girth that contributes to a mass often well over 200kg. That's more than two Mike Tysons, and you'd have a better chance against twin Mikes in a fight, too. Brazil's Pantanal, prime anaconda-spotting territory, is big on superlatives: the world's largest freshwater wetland, it's home to plenty more monsters – giant anteater, capybara, jaguar and giant river otter.

Anacondas are tricky to spot; try driving the Estrada Parque, a dirt road through the south-centre of the Pantanal – snakes often cross during the day.

123 GIANT WETA, NEW ZEALAND

Imagine if a grasshopper and a cockroach got married. And their kid started weightlifting and taking a lot of steroids. Then got into medieval battle re-enactments. That's the giant weta: this colossus of an insect, the world's biggest, has a 20cm span across its spiky legs, and plate armour to cover its 10cm-long body. Its manners are as ugly as its appearance: it's prone to hissing when disturbed. Sadly, your chances of being hissed at are slim – populations are now mostly on New Zealand's small offshore islands – but you could spy cave weta at Zealandia, part of Karori Sanctuary in Wellington.

Weta are nocturnal, so up your chances of a sighting by joining the daily Zealandia by Night tour; visit www.visit zealandia.com.

The thrill of seeing a real live pachyderm in its South African habitat can positively pack a punch

124 AFRICAN ELEPHANT, ADDO ELEPHANT NATIONAL PARK, SOUTH AFRICA

Lions are fearsome. Giraffes warm the cockles. Spotting a leopard is a major safari thrill. But there's nothing like seeing an elephant close up to really inspire awe: they're just so, well, *big*. When he looms almost 4m tall and weighs over 6 tonnes, an encounter with a bull in his prime – tusks 2m long and more – is unforgettable, and more than slightly frightening. Addo Elephant National Park in South Africa's Eastern Cape is, unsurprisingly, a pachyderm hot spot, with 450 grey giants roaming its diverse biomes. It's a far cry from the park's early days – when it was gazetted in 1931, only 11 elephants survived within its boundaries.

Citrus fruits are not allowed – fed oranges and grapefruits in the past, elephants have been known to mob cars containing fruit.

Canadian polar bears may look sleepy, but don't let them get close enough for a goodnight kiss

125 POLAR BEAR, CHURCHILL, CANADA

Cuddling not encouraged – like many of your favourite big beasts, the polar bear is nowhere near as friendly as it looks. This goes double if you're a seal: steer clear of that lumpy-looking ice floe, or you're dinner. The planet's largest bear (along with Alaska's Kodiak subspecies) is also the world's mightiest land carnivore: over 2.5m long and up to 680kg. For a near-guaranteed meeting with this predator, brave the October chill in Churchill, Manitoba: that's when hundreds of bears arrive en masse, hungrily awaiting the feast to come when Hudson Bay freezes over.

The safest way to approach bears is aboard a Tundra Buggy, a closed-cabin truck with huge wheels; try www.tundrabuggy.com.

126 GIANT SALAMANDER, JAPAN

As the cliché claims, small may be beautiful – but big? Not so often. Take the giant salamander: it grows up to 1.8m long and can weigh as much as 64kg, making it the planet's largest amphibian. Also, the ugliest. Though you can choose between the Chinese variety and the slightly smaller Japanese species, they share one characteristic: only their mothers could love them. They've got bandy legs, broad snouts, weird little eyes and a mottled, lumpy complexion to make a hormonal teenager shudder – amphibian acne ain't pretty. They're understandably shy; scout the streams around Maniwa

LEE FOSTER / LONELY PLANET IMAGES

isn't the easiest), everything about it is massive. Even its heart is the size of a car. Long hunted and still endangered, perhaps 10,000 blue whales survive, but they're relatively easy to spot; head to Dondra Head, near Mirissa on Sri Lanka's southern coast, for a good chance of a sighting.

Calm seas from December to April make this period the best for spotting blue and sperm whales off the Sri Lankan coast.

128 SALTWATER CROCODILE, KAKADU NATIONAL PARK, AUSTRALIA

In horror films, as in life, the scariest things aren't the ones you can see – they're the ones you can't. And that's almost the most frightening thing about the saltwater crocodile. Because at least if you can see its armoured bulk – 6m-plus and well over a tonne of scales, fangs, claws and blankly malevolent eyes – you know which way not to head. Trouble is, one could be lurking just beneath the river's surface and you wouldn't know till you're dragged under. So keep a very close eye on any particularly large log in Kakadu National Park: if it blinks, run.

Spot salties safely on a wildlife-watching cruise on the East Alligator River at Cahill's Crossing or Kakadu's billabongs; try http://kakaduculturecamp.com.

in western Honshu and you might catch a glimpse if you're lucky.

Visit Asa Zoo, in the Asakita-ku suburb of Hiroshima, to see the salamander breeding program – if the idea of breeding salamanders isn't too repulsive. See www.asazoo.jp.

127 BLUE WHALE, DONDRA HEAD, SRI LANKA

Let's not mess around: the blue whale is the biggest. Of anything, at any time. This colossal cetacean is believed to be the largest creature that's ever existed on earth, bar none. Measuring upwards of 30m long and weighing up to 90 tonnes (or maybe more – weighing whales

129 OSTRICH, NAIROBI NATIONAL PARK, KENYA

Seeing a bird that's taller than you are is a weird sensation, and the ostrich is a weird-looking critter in any case: big eyes with beautiful eyelashes (to protect against sun and sandstorms), fluffy feather-duster cape, a neck that changes colour in

breeding season, legs like bamboo poles and a brain smaller than its eyeball. On the plus side, this 2m-tall flightless bird can spring 70km/h and lays eggs weighing 1.5kg – quite an omelette. A suitably surreal place to spot ostrich is Nairobi National Park, where you can meet those enormous eyes with the high-rises of Kenya's capital as a backdrop.

Entry to Nairobi National Park requires a rechargeable SafariCard, which can be bought and loaded at the main gate; see www.kws.org/about/safaricard.html.

130 GIANT TORTOISE, GALÁPAGOS ISLANDS

Poor Lonesome George. What use is living for a century if you're the last of your kind? George, the only known giant tortoise of the Pinta Island subspecies, is certainly unlucky, but then so were most of his cousins: it's unfortunate that as well as being slow-moving, Galápagos tortoises are so tasty – a tragically bad combination that made them living larders for hungry sailors. Now protected, the 11 subspecies of this enormous reptile – many weighing over 350kg – lumber lethargically around the islands, notably the highland areas of central isle Santa Cruz, where you'll see them at El Chato Tortoise Reserve.

Meet Lonesome George, along with a number of tortoises from other islands, at the Charles Darwin Research Station; www.darwinfoundation.org.

MOST OVERSIZED ANIMALS

MOST INTRIGUING LOST CITIES

War, weather, cosmic intervention or simply a case of purpose served…nothing lasts forever.

131 SKARA BRAE, SCOTLAND
More a village than a city, this prehistoric set of ruins in Orkney is of a small farming settlement over 5000 years old. It was discovered in 1850 after a wild storm revealed the stone remnants. Excavations (and more storms) showed the village had at least eight stone cottages, complete with beds, hearths and shelves. It seems erosion brought the village closer to the sea, until it was abandoned and left to the enshrouding sands for four millennia. Today, erosion continues to threaten the site, and visits in winter depend on weather conditions.

The best way to Shetland is by air, but flights vary due to weather and season. Check with Flybe (www.flybe.com) for schedules.

132 BABYLON, IRAQ
Babylon, settled around 2500 BC, became a great centre of the Mesopotamian world 500 years later, when Hammurabi, the first king of the Babylonian empire, made it his capital. It was destroyed in the 6th century BC by the Assyrians, and then left to fall into ruin in the 2nd century BC, following the death of Alexander the Great. The ruins of Babylon conjure images of a biblical past: the great Tower of Babel; the beautiful hanging gardens…and there's that certain disco song that just won't leave your head…

Only the most hardened of travellers are currently visiting Babylon, 85km south of Baghdad. Babel Tours (www.babel-tours .com) runs escorted itineraries.

133 TAXILA, PAKISTAN
Founded by an ancient Indian king sometime around the 7th century BC, Taxila (or Takshashila) is a tale of three lost cities. The first was built on a hill, later known as Bhir Mound. In an Old Testament–style confusion of begats and political intrigue, the city was lost to a new Taxila, known as Sirkap, built by Greek invaders. It enjoyed a period of significance in the world of philosophy and the arts, which continued under the Kushans, who took over and refounded Taxila as Sirsukh. Eventually, the city was lost to the Huns in the 6th century, who destroyed it and left it in ruins. Visit the site today, about 30km northwest of Islamabad. The Taxila Museum houses all manner of artefacts, which help you get a feel for the complex history of this once-great city.

Aim for a March or November visit, avoiding the winter cold and the heat and rain of the summer and autumn months.

134 DUNWICH, ENGLAND
Here was a town basking in glory, a major seaport and one of the largest cities in medieval Britain, said to have been the capital of East

Ancient Palenque's rich and remarkable history is recorded in hieroglyphs adorning the interior walls of the Temple of the Inscriptions

Anglia – but all built on sand. In the late 13th century a storm blew in, demolishing a good part of the town. Coastal erosion chipped in and before you could say 'cursed city', only a few cottages remained (actually, a few hundred years passed as the town slipped into the ocean). Tales of haunted beaches abound, and at low tide you might well hear the muted tolling of church bells beneath the waves.

Dunwich Museum has a scale replica of the city in its heyday – without the coastal erosion (www.dunwichmuseum.org.uk).

135 PALENQUE, MEXICO

At the foot of the Chiapas mountains in southwestern Mexico, Palenque is an archaeologist's treasure trove. The city appears to have existed at least since 100 years BC. Five hundred years later it became a major population centre of Classic Mayan civilisation, complete with myth and legend: child kings, invasions, decapitations, court intrigue and finally the abandonment of the city.

Palenque has a jungle climate, so prepare accordingly – take sunscreen, insect repellent and plenty of water.

57

Angkor Thom's houses and public buildings decayed long ago, leaving us with just a skeleton of extravagantly beautiful religious structures

136 ANGKOR, CAMBODIA

Crumbling stone temples in the python grip of jungle vines, a flash of turmeric-coloured robes disappearing into the alcoves of ancient temples. Angkor has its fair share of tourists, but its size means you'll easily find a place to get lost in the distant past. The greater city was enormous, new research suggesting it covered 3000 sq km. Built by a succession of Khmer god-kings from AD 900 to 1200, it had a population close to one million, and was the capital of the Khmer empire. It's been suggested that climate change (affecting water supply) caused the city to be abandoned some 500 years ago.

Angkor is 20 minutes north of Siem Reap. Guided tours abound, from helicopters to tuk-tuks and elephants.

139 HERCULANEUM, ITALY

Like nearby Pompeii, Herculaneum was lost to a river of Vesuvian lava and ash in AD 79. An upper-class town, home to members of the imperial family, it was uncovered about 250 years ago and remains a treasure trove for archaeologists. The pyroclastic flow that enveloped the city carbonised organic matter, preserving structures and human bodies. Most enticing, though, are the hundreds of scrolls found in the Villa of the Papyri, texts from the only ancient library to have survived into modern times.

Take the 25-minute *Circumvesuviana* train from Naples. Allow a day to tour the site.

137 WITTENOOM, AUSTRALIA

Way out west, in the desert-dominated state of Western Australia, you'll find a town if not fully lost, so close to being a ghost as makes no difference. Officially no longer a town, and not receiving government services, this place supported an asbestos-mining industry until the mid-1960s, when health concerns over the lung-clogging stuff spelt its demise. A handful of residents remain but it's tough going. Some may know of it in theory (it was made famous by Australian band Midnight Oil's hit 'Blue Sky Mine'); to experience it, take a long (1100km!) drive north from the state's capital, Perth. A lonely drive to a very lonely place.

Karijini National Park, with red rock formations, deep gorges and enticing swimming holes, might just make this epic drive worthwhile (www .westernaustralia.com).

138 DARWIN, CALIFORNIA, USA

Darwin, like many thousands of towns in late-19th-century USA, sprung up on the back of a lucky strike, in this case, of silver. But these are flash-in-the-pan places – the town became derelict just four years from its settlement in 1878, as prospectors leapt on to the next lucky strike. It was revived in the early 20th century as copper became a commodity. You might bump into a resident today, though chances are it'll be tumbleweed caught on a desert wind. The edge of Death Valley seems an appropriate place to visit the remnants of a Wild West town, so grab a bottle of whisky for the picnic as you head out.

There's only one lonely road to this ghost town, spurring from State Highway 190, 75km southwest of Stovepipe Wells.

140 CARTHAGE, TUNISIA

It's never enough for a great city to be destroyed only once. After 900 years exerting power in North Africa and southern Europe, Carthage succumbed to the wrath of the Roman Empire (needled for so long by the elephant-led armies of Hannibal). Later rebuilt by the Romans and raised to new glory, it once again found itself at the nexus of conflict and was destroyed by Arab Muslims expanding their own sphere of control. Today, on the outskirts of Tunis, you can visit the crumbling remains of Roman baths, temples and villas being absorbed by the sprawl of the capital city.

Transport links to the capital, Tunis, are excellent. Carthage is just 15km north of Tunis; numerous day trips are on offer.

MOST INTRIGUING LOST CITIES

CRAZIEST BUILDINGS

When architecture becomes archi-texture, strange things arise, such as these weird and wonderful constructions.

143 ATOMIUM, BRUSSELS, BELGIUM

Atomium was originially built as the main pavilion for the 1958 Brussels World Fair, and its design replicates the structure of an iron-crystal molecule at a magnification of 165 billion times. The aluminium-clad steel structure features nine spheres at a diameter of 18m each, joined by tubes with a diameter of 3m each; the entire kit is 102m high and weighs more than 2400 tonnes. The structure includes a restaurant in the top sphere and art and scientific exhibitions, chiefly about 'peaceful uses of atomic energy', in the other spheres. There's also a permanent exhibition about the 1958 World Fair.

The Atomium is open daily from 10am to 6pm; the nearest train station is Heysel (Brussels). Details are at www.atomium.be.

141 PALAIS IDEAL, HAUTERIVES, FRANCE

The story of Hauterives' Palais Ideal is as intricate as the building's many turrets and towers. It was constructed over 33 years (from 1879) by the local postman, Ferdinand Cheval, after he supposedly tripped over a rock and took inspiration from its shape. Resembling the sort of structure you might expect to stumble upon deep in a jungle, not 90km from Lyon, the stone, cement and mortar construction is about the size of two suburban homes. Cheval began building it at night after work, before becoming more obsessed as the years ticked past.

From Lyon, take the A7 south to Chanas, turning east here and following the D131 and D121 to Hauterives. For a preview, visit www.facteurcheval.com.

142 TEATRE-MUSEU DALÍ, FIGUERES, SPAIN

A purple-pink building topped by boiled eggs and Oscar statues? Smack in the middle of a dowdy Spanish town? This can only mean one thing: Salvador Dalí! In the town of his birth, Figueres, Dalí created this incredible museum, full of surprises (and that's not just the artworks). The building itself aims to surprise, from the collection of sculptures outside the entrance, to the pink wall along Pujada del Castell, topped by a row of Dalí's trademark egg shapes and what appear to be sculptures of female gymnasts, and studded with what look like loaves of bread.

Figueres is on the train line between Barcelona, Girona and Portbou on the French border. For gallery details, see www.salvador-dali.org.

144 KUNSTHAUS GRAZ, AUSTRIA

Sitting splendidly on the bank of the Mur River, Graz's Kunsthaus, or art gallery, looks a little like a pillow and a little like a transplanted human organ. Designed by British architects Peter Cook and Colin Fournier, the gallery's shining facade is wrapped around a world-class contemporary art space, with exhibits changing every few months. It's a bold creation for a provincial city, perhaps reflecting Graz's relaxed attitude – how else to explain their ready acceptance of a building with a roof of 'stumps' that resembles a clear-felled patch of forest. The space-age look continues inside.

Gallery tours cover the exhibitions and the building itself. For gallery info, see www.kunsthausgraz.at.

145 MUSEU OSCAR NIEMEYER, CURITIBA, BRAZIL

Designed by Oscar Niemeyer, the celebrated architect behind the creation of the Brazilian capital, Brasília, the Museu Oscar Niemeyer will test your view of aesthetics. Like all great buildings – and probably more so – the art museum's appearance has an element of love-it-or-hate-it. Its main gallery is shaped like a reflective glass eye, balancing atop a yellow support, and is approached on curving ramps above a pool of water. Once inside the building commonly called the 'Eye Museum', you'll see that every aspect of the museum's design seems to marry beauty with whimsy.

The museum is open daily (except Sunday) from 10am to 6pm; last entry is at 5.30pm.

146 NATIONAL LIBRARY OF BELARUS, MINSK, BELARUS

You probably need to have a thing for libraries to really share the excitement about this library in Belarus' capital city, Minsk. North of the city centre, it was built in 2006 and is a fairly ghastly piece of hubris. The 22-storey building is a giant rhombicuboctahedron (look it up!) that is lit up at night and contains over two million records, as well as art galleries. More appealingly it also offers one of the few high views of Minsk, with the 22nd floor containing an observation platform, from where you can stare over the city from a height of 72m.

The observation platform is open from noon to 11pm daily. Check out the geometry ahead of time at www.nlb.by.

147 EXPERIENCE MUSIC PROJECT, SEATTLE, WASHINGTON, USA

The brainchild of Microsoft cofounder Paul Allen, Seattle's Experience Music Project bears a likeness to a smashed guitar. The curving, three-part shape has the stamp of architect Frank Gehry – you'll notice some correlation with his Guggenheim creation in Bilbao – but has come in for its share of criticism. *Forbes* named it among the 10 ugliest buildings in the world, while a *New York Times* writer described it as 'something that crawled out of the sea, rolled over and died'. It's almost secondary that inside there's a museum that trawls through music history.

The museum (www.empsfm.org) is directly beneath the landmark Space Needle, by the Seattle Center Monorail stop.

148 HANG NGA CRAZY HOUSE, DALAT, VIETNAM

Crazy by name, crazy by nature, this Dalat building is a free-wheeling architectural exploration of surrealism. Defying easy definition, it has echoes of Gaudí and has been a work-in-progress since 1990. It has nine strangely decorated rooms – some with ceiling mirrors, many with creepy animal statues with glowing red eyes – each named after an unlikely animal or plant, and all built into an organic-looking structure that resembles an enormous tree unfurling itself. It's filled with tunnels, walkways and ladders and you can wander around as you please: getting lost is part of the experience.

The Crazy House is about 2km from Dalat's Central Market. Buses travel to Dalat from most parts of the country.

149 CASA BATLLÓ, BARCELONA, SPAIN

A list of strange buildings would be incomplete without at least one entry from Antoni Gaudí. If La Sagrada Família is his master symphony and major stamp on Barcelona, then Casa Batlló is his whimsical waltz. The facade, sprinkled with bits of blue, mauve and green tiles, and studded with wave-shaped window frames and balconies, rises to an uneven blue-tiled roof with a solitary tower. Inside the main salon, everything swirls. The ceiling is twisted into a vortex around a sun-like lamp. The doors, windows and skylights are dreamy waves of wood and coloured glass. The roof, with its twisting chimney pots, is equally astonishing.

Casa Batlló is at Passeig de Gràcia 43, beside the Passeig de Gràcia metro stop.

150 SELFRIDGES, BIRMINGHAM, ENGLAND

Imagine, if you will, a peanut with acne. Perhaps that's a little unfair, but look closely at the skin of this Birmingham store and you'll start to see the resemblance. The department store, part of the busy Bullring shopping centre, is covered in around 15,000 aluminium discs. Designed by Future Systems, it was intended to represent a church, reflective of shopping's quasi-religious status in the modern world. It was constructed in 2003, bringing some shape and life to Birmingham; its contours are also said to reflect the billowing lines of fabric and waistlines. Or, as we suggested, a peanut with acne…

Selfridges and the Bullring shopping centre are on Park Street, in the heart of Birmingham.

BEST PUBLIC MURALS

Great art doesn't just exist behind velvet ropes in stuffy galleries. Hit the streets to see some of the hottest talent – and it's all for free!

151 DERRY, NORTHERN IRELAND

Nowhere did 20th-century politics explode more violently than Northern Ireland. Unrest between Protestants and Catholics raged from the late 1960s to '90s, commonly referred to as 'The Troubles' and defined by brutal terrorist acts. The northwestern city of Derry saw some defining confrontations. In the Bogside area, Tom Kelly, William Kelly and Kevin Hasson – 'the Bogside Artists' –

For nearly 30 years the fearful symbol of a city divided, the Berlin Wall now acts as a canvas for local artists happy to poke fun at the past

painted poignant murals offering staunch defiance and recording the plight of the fighters. Today their tributes to those injured and killed in the Battle of the Bogside and Bloody Sunday incidents are among the world's most poignant public artworks.

Known as 'The People's Gallery', the artworks span the length of Rossville Street, 500m from the city centre. Guided tours from the artists themselves cost £10 (www.bogsideartists.com).

152 COMIC STRIPS, BRUSSELS, BELGIUM

Brussels might be the seat of straight-laced European bureaucracy, but fortunately it's hiding a much brighter secret among its serpentine backstreets. The Belgian capital gave the world cartoon heroes such as Tintin and the Smurfs, and residents love comic-book culture so much that they have painted dozens of celebratory murals all across town. The project employs Belgian cartoon artists to paint original murals in certain districts, with the aim of linking the artwork to the chosen area. The result is a living gallery of giant superheroes, animated animals and baffling images of the absurd.

Why not time your visit with Brussels' annual comic-strip festival? Fête de la BD organises citywide events each September (www.fetedelabd.be).

153 BOGOTÁ, COLOMBIA

La Candelaria is Bogotá's old-town quarter, dotted with Spanish colonial and baroque architecture and imbibed with a bohemian spirit. Sandwiched between some of the city's toughest barrios, for many years the district was a nocturnal no-go zone, but heightened neighbourhood security has driven away some of the crooks who operated here. Instead, tourists are rediscovering the area's artistic vibe, vividly brought to life with first-rate graffiti murals. The low-rise buildings mean that everything's confined to single-storey elevations or roadside walls, but the mix of contemporary tagging and political comment gives a public voice to the local psyche.

January and February are good times to visit Bogotá – these are the driest months of the year with temperatures averaging 10°C to 20°C.

MARTIN MOOS / LONELY PLANET IMAGES

154 EAST SIDE GALLERY, BERLIN, GERMANY

Germany's Berlin Wall, torn down by the people in November 1989, was a target for Berliners' rage against the communist machine; the so-called East Side Gallery, the longest extant stretch of the Wall, has been covered with graffiti and more than 100 murals. Although vandalism and the elements have destroyed much of the gallery's impact, it's still a powerful reminder of the former regime of iron, with artworks ranging from Dalíesque freak shows to Pink Floydian bricks. Happily, a restoration project is under way.

The gallery is near the city centre; get the train to Ostbahnhof. For history and information about the conservation effort visit www .eastsidegallery.com.

63

This Pyongyang mural proclaims 'Long live the Great Victory of the Military Force Policy'. And who among North Koreans could disagree?

155 MISSION DISTRICT MURALS, SAN FRANCISCO, USA

The world-famous murals of the Latino Mission District adorn the walls of dozens of buildings. These poignant pieces of public art build upon the Mexican mural movement from the 1920s, as well as a good dollop of hungover-from-the-'60s hippie idealism. Common themes include Hispanic, Aztec and Mayan motifs, human rights, football, Carnival and Mexican cinema. The theme is 'community' and it's so thick in the air here you could carve it.

The District's centre is at 16th and Valencia and its cultural heartland is the area around 24th Street; see what's happening at www.sfmission.com.

156 TROMPE L'OEIL MURALS OF JOHN PUGH

In most lines of work, causing bodily harm would probably be frowned upon. For John Pugh, it's a sign of success. Specialising in trompe l'oeil murals, meaning 'trick the eye', his works have been commissioned across the USA and as far afield as Taiwan and New Zealand. Usually comprising near-photographic images on the sides of buildings, Pugh's art is so mesmerising that drivers have been known to run off roads and people have walked into non-existent doorways.

Pugh's best-known mural is at California State University in Chico, 280km north of San Francisco. Catch a Greyhound for the five-hour journey (www.greyhound.com).

157 BANKSY STENCILS

The works of enigmatic artist Banksy can be seen around the world, from the Israeli West Bank barrier to his (rumoured) home town of Bristol, England. Largely satirical takes on politics and culture, Banksy's pieces combine stencils with graffiti and have raised street art to the highest ranks (a fact he finds amusing). The prolific artist has said that he began creating stencils because graffiti took too long. To see his work in situ it's a case of hurry before it's painted over by the local council or before it goes up for auction at Sotheby's for more than £100,000.

Read Banksy's latest manifesto and see his work at www.banksy.co.uk.

TONY WHEELER • LONELY PLANET IMAGES

159 PYONGYANG, NORTH KOREA

What better way to spread propaganda messages than with large murals? It's a fact appreciated by North Korea's leader Kim Jong-il, who uses this trick to remind subjects that the socialist dream lives on in this most insular corner of Eastern Asia. From metro stations to hotel lobbies and even rural soy fields, North Koreans are never far from a jingoistic revolutionary painting. Usually depicting military might or anti-American rhetoric, the images are the height of communist-art chic. For the ultimate display, the annual Mass Games present vast human-formed murals in an orgiastic display of symbolic chest-puffing.

Visitors to North Korea are appointed an official chaperone. The simplest way in is with an established operator – try Koryo Tours (www.koryogroup.com).

160 ODE TO APHRODITE & HALA SULTAN, NICOSIA, CYPRUS

Seldom do Greek and Turkish ideologies mix favourably in Cyprus. But in the heart of Nicosia, the world's only divided capital city, artist Farhad Nargol-O'Neill has managed just that. In the northern half of town, known to the Turkish Cypriots as Lefkoşa, Nargol-O'Neill has illuminated a dreary-looking arts complex with a mural of vivid brilliance. Entitled *Ode to Aphrodite & Hala Sultan*, his cubist symbolism is not just a pretty picture, but also a sign of hope and reconciliation – the Hellenistic image of Aphrodite melds seamlessly with Hala Sultan, aunt of the prophet Mohammed.

Cross from South to North Nicosia at the Ledra Palace checkpoint, still pock marked with gunfire from the conflict.

158 LAKE CHELAN, WASHINGTON, USA

Creating the world and all the animals took the Great Chief Above a fair while, but eventually he got around to humans. Helpfully, he decided they needed an instruction manual, and proceeded to unleash his artistic tendencies with a series of red ochre pictographs depicting hunting and other activities. Though some are now underwater and many have been defaced, a few can still be seen on rocks at Lake Chelan in Washington state. Take a boat ride to check out the Creator's best Banksy impressions.

Lake Chelan (www.cometothelake.com) is an adventurer's paradise. Hire a bicycle (www.chelanbicycleadventures.com) to appreciate the Lake Chelan basin.

BEST PUBLIC MURALS

MOST MYSTERIOUS SIGHTS

The truth is out there, although sometimes it's a little hard to decipher, as the following mysteries testify.

161 YETI, THE HIMALAYA

In the Nessie mould comes the 'monster' of the Himalaya. Call it the Yeti or the Abominable Snowman – reports of a creature that resembles an ape-like human have been around for centuries, but began to enter the Western consciousness in the early 20th century. Interest was most furious in the 1950s, as mountaineers raced to the tops of the Himalayan mountains. Sparking most interest were Eric Shipton's 1951 photos of supposed Yeti footprints, while Edmund Hillary and Tenzing Norgay also reported encountering large footprints on their Everest climb in 1953. Debate rages about the Yeti's authenticity, but perhaps only it knows for certain. Or not.

The International Mountain Museum in the Nepali city of Pokhara has a display on the Yeti.

162 EASTER ISLAND, CHILE

For a tiny stone in a large ocean, Easter Island has made quite a big splash in the traveller psyche. The images of its stone *moai* (figures) are famous across the world, but what still isn't known is just how they came to be standing around the island's coast. From the Rano Raraku quarry, in the island's interior, where the *moai* were carved, the task of hauling 85 tonnes of large-headed stones – and repeating it hundreds of times – is an intimidating one even today, with technology at our fingertips, let alone in the 13th or 14th century. So, how did the residents of one of the most isolated settlements on earth manage it? In a word: dunno.

LAN Airlines (www.lan.com) flies to Easter Island from Santiago (Chile) and Papeete (Tahiti).

163 CROP CIRCLES, ENGLAND

Whether they've been created by local lads hooning through the fields, by isolated weather systems, or by geometrically minded aliens, crop circles have intrigued since they first began appearing in farmers' fields in the late 1970s. These patterns of flattened crops have a spiritual home of sorts around the Wiltshire town of Avebury, coincidentally also noted for its stone circles. For close encounters of the barley kind, several companies offer tours of crop-circle sites, while you can hang out with 'croppies' at their chosen watering hole, the Barge Inn, in the town of Honeystreet.

Avebury is 130km west of London; buses run to Avebury from nearby Salisbury, Swindon and Devizes. Honeystreet is 10km south of Avebury.

Alien landing strips or astronomical calendars? View Peru's giant Nazca Lines, including this magnificent condor, from above

164 YONAGUNI-JIMA, JAPAN

Japan's westernmost inhabited island – closer to Taiwan than Japan proper – was put on the 'what the?' map with an underwater find in the mid-1980s, when divers discovered what looked like underwater ruins. Rocks here had flat surfaces, right angles and straight lines. Manmade was the conclusion: Atlantis with a Japanese accent. More than two decades on, debate continues about whether the rocks are part of some ancient human structure or just nature in a Lego sort of mood. Either way, Yonaguni was firmly put on the map as one of Japan's best diving destinations.

Flights operate to Yonaguni-jima from Naha, while two ferries a week sail from the island of Ishigaki.

165 NAZCA LINES, PERU

It's the kind of archaeological site you simply couldn't invent if you tried. Giant hummingbirds, monkeys, spiders and other figures, all etched out into the Peruvian desert some 2000 years ago. And the killer is, they can't be seen from the ground. No one's quite sure how the ancient Nazca pulled off this artistic conjuring trick, but they mapped out an incredible 800 geoglyphs; shapes, straight lines and pictures on the plain. At ground level the area looks like an unimpressive stretch of red-brown earth. But when a light aircraft whisks you skywards, the huge figures of a whale, condor and pelican unfold before your eyes.

Flights over the Nazca Lines depart from the town of Nazca. There are buses to Nazca from Lima and Arequipa.

166 STONEHENGE, ENGLAND

Arguably one of the world's most important prehistoric sites, the ancient ring of monolithic stones at Stonehenge has been attracting a steady stream of pilgrims, poets and philosophers for the last 5000 years. Despite the crowds of visitors it's a mystical, ethereal place – a haunting echo from Britain's long-forgotten past and a reminder of a lost civilisation that once walked the many ceremonial avenues across Salisbury Plain. Although there are countless theories about what the site was used for – ranging from sacrificial centre to celestial timepiece – in truth no one really knows what drove prehistoric Britons to expend so much time and effort on its construction.

Stonehenge is 17km from the city of Salisbury; bus 3 runs from Salisbury bus station to the site.

167 NEWGRANGE, IRELAND

From the surface, Newgrange is just a flattened, grass-covered mound, about 80m in diameter and 13m high. Underneath, however, lies one of the most remarkable prehistoric sites in Europe, dating from around 3200 BC. The purpose for which it was constructed remains uncertain, although the alignment with the sun at the time of the winter solstice suggests it was designed to act as a calendar. At 8.20am during the winter solstice (19 to 23 December), the rising sun's rays shine through the slit above the entrance, creep slowly down the long passage and illuminate the tomb chamber for 17 minutes.

To visit Newgrange during the winter solstice, you must enter a lottery, which is drawn on 30 September each year. See www.newgrange.com/solstice-lottery .htm for details.

168 ROSWELL, NEW MEXICO, USA

Conspiracy theorists unite. In 1947, on a ranch near the New Mexico town of Roswell, a mysterious object crashed to earth. Nobody might have thought any more about it, except that the military made a big to-do of hushing it up, and for some folks that sealed it: the aliens were among us. International curiosity and local ingenuity have since transformed Roswell into a favourite haunt of aliens. Bulbous white heads glow atop the downtown street lights, and there's a UFO Festival (www.roswell ufofestival.com) held every July. Believers can check out the International UFO Museum and Research Center to confirm all their suspicions.

Beam Roswell onto your computer at www.roswellmysteries.com.

169 LOCH NESS, SCOTLAND

At a glance it's just a very large lake near the head of the Scottish Highlands, but if its tales and legends could add water it'd be the size of an ocean. In case you've been living in another solar system, Loch Ness is reputed to be home to a 'monster' – known more affectionately as Nessie – a dinosaur-like creature that occasionally makes guest appearances. Stories of a creature in the loch have been around for centuries, but it was a 1934 photo of a long neck and head that renewed

DAVID WALL / LONELY PLANET IMAGES

Join those who come to scratch their heads in wonder at Stonehenge, England's most iconic ancient site

interest in Nessie. And it's never faded, drawing generations of visitors to the shores of Loch Ness.

The town of Inverness, just north of the loch, is the best base for monster-spotters. Keep abreast of Nessie sightings at www.nessie.co.uk.

170 AREA 51, NEVADA, USA

Like Roswell on speed, Area 51 is a magnet for aliens and alien-spotters. This military base, part of Nellis Air Force Base, is a supposed holding area for captured UFOs, including those aliens scooped up in Roswell. It is reached along Highway 375, the official Extraterrestrial Highway, so named because of the huge number of UFO sightings along this stretch of concrete. While here, bunk down in Little A'Le'Inn, in the tiny town of Rachel, which accommodates earthlings and aliens alike, and sells extraterrestrial souvenirs.

Highway 375 begins around 180km north of Las Vegas, near Ash Springs.

MOST MYSTERIOUS SITES

VOLCANO!

Get up close (but not too close) to one of nature's greatest shows – the earth blowing its top.

173 STROMBOLI, ITALY

Known as the 'Lighthouse of the Mediterranean' for its permanent eruptive activity, Stromboli is part of the Aeolian Islands, an archipelago of seven volcanic peaks located off the north coast of Sicily. The most awesome of the islands, Stromboli belches regular explosions of dust and steam, spitting rocks and, at times, lava down the barren lava trail of the Sciara del Fuoco into the Mediterranean Sea. See Stromboli at its best by finding a fisherman to take you out on the water at dusk to watch the natural pyrotechnics. The Aeolians are accessible by ferry from Naples, and Milazzo on Sicily.

Watch the volcano do its thing as you eat seafood at L'Osservatorio (090 98 63 60), on the lower slopes of the peak.

171 SOUFRIÈRE HILLS, MONTSERRAT, LESSER ANTILLES

A volcano with true bang, the Soufrière Hills ended four centuries of dormancy in explosive fashion in 1995, blowing away one third of its own height and rendering the Caribbean holiday island of Montserrat almost uninhabitable. The geothermal belches calmed over the following decade, even prompting the re-opening of the airport, but in January 2007 the volcano erupted again, shooting out a cloud of ash that smothered both the island and its re-emerging tourism industry. If you make it to the island, the crater is off-limits but the Montserrat Volcano Observatory on its slopes is open to visitors.

The Observatory is open to visitors from Monday to Thursday. A documentary runs at quarter past every hour from 10.15am to 3.15pm.

172 RABAUL, PAPUA NEW GUINEA

The PNG island of New Britain is a constant bubble of geothermal activity, and in 1994 twin volcanoes erupted around Rabaul, a town many travellers considered to be the finest in the Pacific. Set inside a caldera, Rabaul had always flirted with danger, but in this two-pronged erosion the entire town collapsed beneath ash, leaving behind a strange, black wasteland. Today, the port continues to function, and there's a modicum of activity in the town, even as the Tuvurvur volcano still issues the occasional smoke signal. For a surreal volcanic experience you need do no more than wander the town, most of which is buried beneath your feet.

Rabaul Shipping has twice-weekly passenger boats sailing from Rabaul to Lae. The offices are open from 8am to 5pm Monday to Saturday.

174 HAWAI'I VOLCANOES NATIONAL PARK, USA

Hawai'i Volcanoes National Park is a huge preserve containing two active volcanoes and terrain ranging from tropical beaches to the subarctic Mauna Loa summit. The park's centrepiece is the steaming Kilauea Caldera, at the summit of the planet's most active volcano. Amid a landscape of craters and cinder cones, hills piled high with pumice, and hardened oceans of lava, you can pay rare witness to flowing lava. Here, the fluid lava mostly oozes and creeps along, and at the end of the Chain of Craters road you can follow a walking trail to see the active flow entering the sea.

Check in with the rangers at the Kilauea visitor centre for an introduction, information on guided walks and an update on volcanic activity.

175 WHITE ISLAND, NEW ZEALAND

White by name, but black by nature, White Island has been in almost constant eruption for the last three decades. Sitting in the Bay of Plenty, the island marks one end of the highly active Taupo Volcanic Zone, which also includes the volatile Mt Ruapehu and the geothermal fields of Rotorua. Although the latter is one of New Zealand's premier tourist attractions, the ever-changing colours and fury of White Island are arguably more impressive. The island can be visited by boat or helicopter from Whakatane, and once ashore at Crater Bay you'll witness an array of volcanic features.

Want to see the action from above? Book yourself a helicopter tour to White Island at www.vulcanheli.co.nz.

176 PARICUTÍN, MEXICO

Three hundred kilometres west of Mexico City, Paricutín is one of the youngest mountains on earth, and a volcano so unusual it quickly earned a place among the seven natural wonders of the world. During WWII an eruption suddenly began in the middle of a cornfield, a 410m-high cinder cone rose from the earth and lava flows covered an area of about 20 sq km (engulfing two villages). Today there's the surreal sight of a church spire poking above the solidified lava – all that remains of the two villages. It's a long trek on foot or by horse to the summit, but the view of the massive lava flow is mind-blowing, and you'll get to run, jump and slide down the deep volcanic sand on the descent.

Guides with horses (you'll also need a guide for walking) offer their services from the town of Angahuan.

177 MT PINATUBO, PHILIPPINES

In 1991, after around 600 years of dormancy, Mt Pinatubo, on the Philippine island of Luzon, produced one of the greatest volcanic jolts of the 20th century, shooting ash and rock 40km into the sky, decapitating almost 300m of its own summit and leaving a 2.5km-wide caldera in its place. The new summit is accessible to hikers – the climb begins from Santa Juliana, 40km from Angeles – and is also the scene of a virtual pilgrimage on 30 November each year, when the annual Pinatubo trek (the so-called March to Peace and Tranquillity) commemorates the eruption.

Power Up (02 631 4675) is a group of Manila climbers that can organise big and small climbs up Mt Pinatubo.

178 MT ST HELENS, WASHINGTON, USA

Once a classic symmetrical volcano, Mt St Helens showed a disdain for geometry on 18 May 1980 when an eruption blew around 400m off its peak and created a 1.5km-wide crater on its north side. Though much life has returned to the peak, the devastation is still clear, and the mountain continues to steam, with a new lava dome growing inside the crater. Around the mountain a number of hiking trails highlight the volcanic landscapes; climbers wanting to summit must obtain a permit. There's no technical climbing involved, but most of the ascent is through loose pumice fields and over chunks of lava.

Visit Seattle's fascinating Ye Olde Curiosity Shop (www.yeoldecuriosityshop.com) for a Mt St Helens ash globe (like a snow globe, but with ash).

179 HEKLA, ICELAND

Once believed to be the entrance to hell, Hekla was Iceland's most famous volcano until the plane-disrupting eruption of Eyjafjallajökull in 2010. Hekla – its name means Hooded One, referring to the mountain's perpetual cap of cloud – has shown watch-setting punctuality in recent times, boiling over pretty much every 10 years. The 1491m peak, around 70km east of Reykjavík, makes for a comfortable climb when it's inactive, and rewards walkers with a heated crater ringed by a snow-capped summit. If you venture here in winter, there are even snowmobile tours to the top.

Learn more about Hekla by taking in the multimedia exhibition at the visitor centre at Leirubakki (www.leirubakki.is).

180 GUNUNG BROMO, INDONESIA

In eastern Java sits a caldera 10km wide, covered by a sea of sand and punctured by a trio of volcanic cones. Steaming among them is Gunung Bromo (2392m), a volcano within a volcano, shadowed by Java's highest mountain, the highly active Gunung Semeru. As a grandstand to this remarkable scene, Bromo makes for one of the most remarkable outings in Southeast Asia. Most hikes to Bromo follow the Probolinggo approach, with the walk beginning atop the crater wall at Cemoro Lawang, crossing the Sand Sea for a sunrise spectacular atop Gunung Bromo.

Tours to Bromo are easily arranged in Malang, and you can also arrange jeep hire in hotels and at travel agents there.

MOST ASTOUNDING EGO TRIPS

Some people leave a bigger legacy than others. Explore the world's most arrogant architecture.

181 PALACE OF THE PARLIAMENT, BUCHAREST, ROMANIA

Was Nicolae Ceauşescu trying to compensate for something? The communist dictator's gargantuan Palace of the Parliament is the architectural equivalent of buying a Ferrari at 40; what autocrats do when they're having a mid-life crisis. It's a beast – the world's second-heaviest administrative building (after the Pentagon), weighed down by 1100 rooms, 12

Sombre North Koreans pay their respects (as is compulsory) to the Great Leader at the base of Mansudae in Pyongyang

storeys, oak panelling, gold leaf, much marble and an estimated €3.3 billion construction bill. Tours visit just 5% of this behemoth, including a step out onto the balcony from which Ceauşescu planned to address his people – had they not executed him before his palace was completed.

The Palace is open from 10am to 4pm; 45-minute guided tours run approximately every 30 minutes; English tours are available.

KEREN SU / LONELY PLANET IMAGES

182 ASTANA, KAZAKHSTAN

Is there an act more arrogant than shifting your nation's capital and rebuilding it after your fancy? In 1998 Kazakhstan's head honcho Nursultan Nazarbayev relocated the country's epicentre from Almaty to a town in the sub-Siberian north, renaming it Astana (imaginatively meaning 'capital'). More than 10 years on and, as well as declaring 6 July (his birthday) Astana Day, Nazarbayev has commissioned a raft of fantastical structures. These include Khan Shatyr, the world's biggest tent (containing heated gardens and mini-golf course) and Bayterek, a 105m tower where visitors are encouraged to place their hands in an imprint of Nazarbayev's own and make a wish.

Visit Astana between May and September; it's frosty from October to April, with temperatures hovering around -15°C from December to February.

183 ARCH OF CONSTANTINE, ROME, ITALY

Not only was Emperor Constantine (aka Constantine the Great) a vainglorious fellow, he was a pilferer too. His 'look how good I am' victory arch in the Roman Forum was not a fresh construction but rather cobbled together in 315 AD from other ancient monuments – a bit of Trajan statuary, a Marcus Aurelius frieze or two. If Constantine was arrogant enough to reuse what he fancied, he also ensured his feats were never forgotten – his arch spanned the Triumphant Road, along which new emperors processed en route to being crowned; as they passed underneath Constantine's monolith they were forced to acknowledge his eternal glory.

One entrance ticket (€12), valid for two days, includes admission to the Forum, Colosseum and Palatine Hill (www.pierreci.it).

184 MANSUDAE GRAND MONUMENT, PYONGYANG, NORTH KOREA

All bow to the cult of Kim! This bulky bronze of North Korea's Great Leader is the first stop on tours of the secretive nation. What's more, visitors are required to pay their respects to Kim Il-sung's 20m-high likeness: flowers must be placed at the big man's feet before the group lines neatly to genuflect in synchrony. North Koreans love Kim – at least in public. Kim loved Kim too – the Mansudae figure was built in 1972, a 60th birthday present-to-self. Though he died in 1994, through this mighty monument he watches his people still.

Travelling to North Korea independently is prohibited; you must visit on a tour. Wandering the streets alone is not allowed.

185 TRUMP TOWER, NEW YORK, USA

You're building a massive high-rise on New York's premier retail street. You're the country's most famous real-estate tycoon. You have a bit of an ego. So what do you call your 202m erection? You name it after yourself, of course! Trump Tower, just one of Donald Trump's army of eponymous edifices, is a shouty, shiny, soaring skyscraper, completed in 1983 and still turning heads on Fifth Avenue. Much of it is residential and office space, but the lower public retail areas hint at the glamour above: pink-white marble, massive mirrors and gleaming brass.

Trump Tower is at 721 Fifth Avenue. A one-bedroom apartment in the building costs around US$2.3 million (www .trumpsales.com).

186 TOM PRICE, WESTERN AUSTRALIA

In the good Aussie tradition of no-nonsense naming (Snowy Mountains, Great Sandy Desert etc), this outback outpost, established in 1962, was labelled after the chap who brought it prosperity. Thomas Moore Price was vice president of Kaiser Steel, and a key supporter of iron ore prospecting in the Pilbara region; in gratitude he now has a town, a mine and a mountain bearing his identity. He picked a fine spot: the wilds around Tom Price are Western Oz at its best – fiery red-gold outcrops, endless blue skies and, 50km east, the lush green gorges of Karijini National Park. Well done, Tom.

Mt Nameless, 4km west of Tom Price, offers good views, especially at sunset; access is by 4WD only. See www .tompricewa.com.au.

187 ABU SIMBEL, EGYPT

Gone but not forgotten – Ramses II made sure of that. Or at least he tried, with Abu Simbel. Dedicated to sun god Ra, god-king Amun and Ramses himself, this majestic temple is fronted by four 20m-high statutes (all of Ramses); inside, through the pillared hypostyle hall, lie wondrous paintings – most featuring our pharaoh, naturally. But despite Ramses' best efforts, Abu Simbel *was* forgotten, swallowed by sand. Not rediscovered until 1813, in 1964 it was moved, brick by brick – at a cost of US$80 million – to avoid being flooded by the Aswan Dam. Ramses would have expected no less.

Abu Simbel is a three-hour drive or 45-minute flight from Aswan; airfares include the short bus ride to the temple.

188 HACIENDA NÁPOLES, ANTIOQUIA, COLOMBIA

This is what a life of cocaine trafficking, violence and corruption can achieve – a bombed-out mansion and some sad plastic dinosaurs. That's disingenuous: Hacienda Nápoles may be worse for wear now, but before owner Pablo Escobar was gunned down in 1993, this was a flamboyant pleasure palace, built to show off just how rich and powerful the drug lord was. It had a bull-fighting ring, an airstrip, even a zoo. Most of the animals have now died or been rehoused, but a hippo herd remains, the only members of Escobar's gang still roaming his murky fantasy world.

Hacienda Nápoles (www.hacienda napoles.com, in Spanish) is 165km from Medellín; it has been converted into a theme park and is open from 8am to 5pm.

JOHN ELK III / LONELY PLANET IMAGES

189 CHÂTEAU DE VERSAILLES, FRANCE

Believing himself to be second only to God, in 1664 Louis XIV built a pad befitting his own sense of self-importance. And Versailles suggests he was self-important indeed. The gardens are immense, neatly regalised with statuary and fine fountains. But it's the palace – dripping with gold leaf, frescos, marble and mirrors – that reveals Louis's love for bling. As such a profligately OTT edifice, Versailles became a symbol of absolute monarchy – not popular with the revolutionaries, who pillaged the palace in 1789.

The Passport ticket (€18) allows entry to all of Versailles' sites, including the gardens, chateau and Marie Antoinette's rooms. See www.chateauversailles.fr.

But of course Hearst Castle has stunning pools and fountains, and statues from ancient Greece and Moorish Spain – doesn't everyone?

190 HEARST CASTLE, CALIFORNIA, USA

On commissioning his architect in 1919, newspaper magnate William Randolph Hearst wrote 'I would like to build a little something' – a masterful understatement for a creation that became the polar opposite: an opulent, ostentatious hyperbole in landscaping and stone. Hearst Castle boasted 165 rooms, multiple pools, even its own airport, and the main building was modelled on a Spanish cathedral. The entire estate received frequent additions; even as the jet set of the 1920s and '30s popped in for parties, souvenirs from Hearst's travels were being incorporated – a Roman mosaic, an Italianate terrace, another zebra for the zoo…

A range of tours is available (www.hearstcastle.org); on the evening tour costumed guides bring Hearst Castle history to life.

MOST ASTOUNDING EGO TRIPS

MOST INTERESTING BRIDGES

Get out and cross these super spans, from modern curves to ancient planks.

191 NISHISETO EXPRESSWAY, JAPAN

You can't let the small matter of an inland sea get in the way of a good bridge – when the fast-living Japanese wanted to speed up connections between the islands of Honshu and Shikoku, they certainly didn't. However, the Nishiseto Expressway isn't one bridge, it's a series of 10, hopping for 60km between islets in the Seto Sea to ultimately link the cities of Hiroshima and Imbari. There are two other bridge-clusters that span the same water but Nishiseto wins – for its sea views, village stops en route, and for being the only one you can cross on bicycle or foot, as well as by car.

For views of the Seto Sea bridges go to the Hanaguri Seto Observation Platform on Omi-shima Island and Mt Kiro-san on O-shima Island.

192 MILLENNIUM BRIDGE, GATESHEAD, ENGLAND

So much more than a way to cross a river, Tyne and Wear's Millennium Bridge (actually opened in 2002) is an architectural statement: its tilting span – the world's first tilting bridge – screams of Gateshead's reviving economic fortunes. It's useful too, providing pedestrians with a funky link to Newcastle, via the artily regenerated quayside area. And because the whole thing – footpath and 50m-high counterbalancing arch – works by seesawing on its struts, it's no bother to move it out of the way when big boats pass by: a low-energy manoeuvre that costs just £3.60 each time.

Gateshead Quays is home to the Sage music venue and the Baltic Centre for Contemporary Art. Bridge tilt times are at www.gateshead.gov.uk.

193 ÖRESUND BRIDGE, SWEDEN/DENMARK

Why link riverbanks when you can link countries? The Öresund Bridge disregards international boundaries to connect Danish capital Copenhagen with Malmö, Sweden's third-largest city. The journey along it – by road or by rail – is 16km, though technically just under half is bridge proper: a tunnel accounts for some of its length, the switch from underwater to over it occurring on a manmade island in the Öresund Strait. But when you do emerge from that tunnel it's like you're floating on water, the snaking, cable-stayed structure – with pylons soaring 200m up – delivering you seamlessly to a whole new nation.

Trains cross the Öresund Bridge every 20 minutes, connecting Copenhagen with Malmö; the journey time is around 35 minutes.

Carrying more than 4.5 million vehicles annually, France's Millau Viaduct is a work of industrial art

194 MILLAU VIADUCT, FRANCE

The 'missing link in the A75' seems the epitome of undersell as a description of this bridge behemoth. Yes, technically it does fill a gap in the much-needed motorway from Paris to Montpellier, fording (somewhat disproportionately) the Tarn River. But the Millau Viaduct is also the most astonishing, grand-scale construction ever to have graced such bucolic countryside. For over the quiet patchwork fields and villages of southern France sits the highest bridge in the world – the seven pylons are up to 343m tall – and simply the engineering pièce de résistance of the 21st century so far.

Millau Belfry (open June to September) offers good views of the viaduct, as does the visitor centre on the north side. See www.leviaducdemillau.com.

195 BROOKLYN BRIDGE, NEW YORK, USA

The movie star of the masonry world, Brooklyn's iconic suspension bridge has featured in many a movie, such is the cult status of its twin-arched towers and thick, geometric cables. It has a slightly murky past for something so attractive: constructed between 1869 and 1883, 27 men lost their lives in the process. Today, however, you can celebrate their efforts, and the foresight of architect John Roebling, who recognised the need to incorporate a grand promenade on a bridge in such a crowded city.

Brooklyn Bridge Park, Brooklyn, hosts outdoor cinema evenings in summer, with Manhattan and the bridge as a backdrop. Visit www.brooklynbridgepark.org.

Arguably the finest of Esfahan's bridges, the Khaju Bridge has always been as much a meeting place as a bearer of traffic

196 GALATA BRIDGE, İSTANBUL, TURKEY

There are no graceful arches or fancy curves; its lower tier is lined with cafes hawking kebabs. But this bridge carries much history on its modern shoulders, linking two culturally distinct parts of old Constantinople. Today's Galata Bridge was completed in 1994, but there was a causeway across the Golden Horn as far back as the 6th century AD. The link is still vital and swarms of İstanbulis use it daily, to transit, to gossip and to cast a line for silver fishes. Tourists come,

too, because the sunset view – the sky red-pink behind silhouetted minarets – is hard to beat.

Trams run across the Galata Bridge; the T1 line links the sights of Sultanahmet with the modern shops of Beyoglu.

197 MOSTAR BRIDGE, BOSNIA & HERCEGOVINA

A bridge that truly shaped a city, it was Mostar's bridge-keepers (*mostari*) that gave the city its name – such was the strategic importance of this arch over the Neretva River.

Originally constructed in the 16th century, the Old Bridge stood firm until 1993, when the Croat army bombed it to dust during the Balkan War. But there's no keeping a good span down. In 2004 a reconstruction was unveiled, the bridge gleaming, gorgeous and fit once more for boys to leap from: diving from the 21m apex into the shallow water below has been a local rite of passage for nearly 450 years.

The scenic rail route from Ploče to Sarajevo travels via Mostar; Mostar is 2½ hours from Sarajevo by train.

DIEGO LEZAMA · LONELY PLANET IMAGES

199 KHAJU BRIDGE, ESFAHAN, IRAN

If rain's been scarce, the Zayandeh River barely needs bridges at all – in some years it's been known to dry up as it tries to trickle through the Silk Road city of Esfahan. But the Khaju Bridge was worth building, river or not. An elegant thoroughfare-cum-pleasure-palace, it was constructed in around 1650 by Shah Abbas so his family could play in the water. Today its 110m-long, two-storey gantry of Islamic arches is still a popular hangout, with locals seeking shade in the niches. It also doubles as a dam, so if there *is* water flowing, it has the power to stop it anyway.

Esfahan is 7½ hours by train from Tehran. Khaju Bridge is southeast of the centre; haggle hard with taxi drivers.

sunset to see flocks of local villagers and orange-robed monks scurrying to and fro while the sky puts on a fine dawn/dusk show.

U Bein Bridge is south of Mandalay, near Amarapura; buses connect the two. The journey takes 45 minutes by bicycle.

train from nearby Kanchanaburi, to learn more of its grim creation at the little museum.

For more history, walk a 4.5km section of the Death Railway to Hellfire Pass, 80km north of Kanchanaburi.

198 U BEIN BRIDGE, MYANMAR (BURMA)

A fine advert for the practice of recycling, the U Bein Bridge across Taungthaman Lake was cobbled together in the 19th century from wood left behind when the Burmese capital was shifted from Inwa to Amarapura. These abandoned palace pieces have withstood the test of time: despite the structure's venerable years and rather rickety appearance, it's the longest teak bridge in the world. The 1.2km stilted span is well used too – visit just after sunrise or just before

200 BRIDGE ON THE RIVER KWAI, THAILAND

Plain, low-slung, nestled in jungle – this is not the most impressive bridge, perhaps, but it is one of the most poignant. The Bridge on the River Kwai, immortalised on film by David Lean's eponymous epic, was built by Allied prisoners during WWII to carry the so-called Death Railway. The bridge was subsequently bombed – the curved steel spans are original, the straight-sided ones are postwar replacements. Despite past damage, though, it's still possible to cross this eerie structure, on foot or by

MOST INTERESTING BRIDGES

MOST AMAZING NATURAL PHENOMENA

Nature is always amazing, but sometimes it pulls a really freakish rabbit out of a hat. Here's where to catch the strangest of the strange natural sights.

203 LAMBERT GLACIER, ANTARCTICA

In a world of shrinking glaciers it's nice to know there's always Lambert Glacier. The world's longest glacier drains about 8% of the Antarctic ice sheet and is up to 400km long and 200km wide at the point where it reaches the Amery Ice Shelf. The shelf itself is a seaward extension of the Lambert, and is a source for one of the rarest and most beautiful sights in the natural world: bottle-green icebergs, resulting from the high content of organic material inside the ice.

Getting to this extremely isolated part of Antarctica requires a long voyage and isn't cheap, so it is visited only rarely – just one or two tourist ships a year come here.

201 CATATUMBO LIGHTNING, VENEZUELA

Centred on the mouth of the Río Catatumbo at Lago de Maracaibo, this strange phenomenon consists of frequent flashes of lightning with no accompanying thunder. The eerie, silent electrical storm, referred to as Catatumbo Lightning, can be so strong and constant (150 to 200 flashes per minute) that it's possible to read by it at night, and it's said to be the world's largest single generator of ozone. Various hypotheses have been put forth to explain the lightning, but the theory that stands out is that cold winds descending from the Andes clash with hot, humid air evaporating from the lake, producing the ionisation of air particles.

On average, storms occur on 150 nights each year and are at their fiercest at times of high humidity.

202 PITCH LAKE, TRINIDAD & TOBAGO

Once thought of as a punishment from the gods, this bubbling lake of pitch is perhaps Trinidad's greatest oddity. Birdwatchers will find it of interest as well for the species it attracts. The 40-hectare expanse of asphalt is 90m deep at its centre, where hot bitumen is continuously replenished from a subterranean fault. The lake, one of only three asphalt lakes in the world, has the single largest supply of natural bitumen, and as much as 300 tonnes are extracted daily. The surface looks like a clay tennis court covered with wrinkled elephant-like skin, and during the rainy season you can sit in its warm sulphurous pools.

The lake is 22km southwest of San Fernando near the town of La Brea; guided tours are available – high heels are not recommended.

204 DON JUAN POND, ANTARCTICA

Antarctica's Dry Valleys are remarkable enough in what is already an impressive continent: huge, desolate spaces covering 3000 sq km without snow or ice. Here, algae, bacteria and fungi, some of it thought to be 200,000 years old, have been found growing *inside* rocks. The Onyx River flows inland from the coast and there's a lake, Lake Vanda, that is a balmy 25°C at its bottom. There's also Don Juan Pond, which is only 10cm deep but the most saline body of water on the planet, 14 times saltier than the ocean. It is so salty, in fact, that this shallow pond never freezes, even at temperatures of -55°C.

Vanda Station, 14km east of Don Juan Pond, is the closest settlement. Don't expect bright lights – it's only staffed temporarily by a small band of researchers.

205 RED LAND CRABS, AUSTRALIA

For most of the year you'll see little of the red land crabs of Australia's Christmas Island. They live in shady sites inside the forest that covers much of the island's plateau. Then, suddenly, at the beginning of the wet season, in around October or November, more than 100 million enormous red crabs suddenly emerge, breaking out of the forest like escapees, climbing down cliff faces and – more dangerously – crossing roads. All this so the female crabs can release their eggs into the Indian Ocean at precisely the turn of the high tide during the moon's last quarter.

Schedules are irregular, but you can fly to Christmas Island from Perth (www .virginblue.com.au) or Kuala Lumpur (www.malaysiaairlines.com).

206 SOLAR ECLIPSE, AUSTRALIA

For millennia, eclipses have fascinated those who witness them; Homer wrote about a total eclipse in the ancient Greek epic *The Odyssey*. Eclipses are some of nature's most awe-inspiring spectacles, and great excuse for a party. Solar eclipses occur a couple of times a year, but the total blocking of the sun is only visible from a small part of the earth's surface. A total solar eclipse will take place on 13/14 November 2012, and Cairns, in far north Queensland, will be one of the best places on earth to witness the incredible event.

Make your way to festival events being planned in Cairns and surrounding regions; details can be found at www .solareclipse2012.com.

207 RAIN OF FISH, HONDURAS

Virtually every year in June or July, dark storm clouds gather over the small town of Yoro and unleash a tremendous summer rainstorm. In the downpour appear thousands of silvery fish, flopping on the ground. Locals believe the phenomenon is nothing less than an act of god. They trace its origin to a 19th-century Spanish missionary who prayed for a miracle to feed the people. Biologists say it can be explained scientifically, but have yet to provide any conclusive evidence. Either way you look at it, it's an occasion for a party: the annual Festival de la Lluvia de Peces includes parades, music and lots of fried fish.

Base yourself in bustling San Pedro Sula, with its great entertainment and nightlife; from here it's a three-hour bus ride to Yoro.

208 MORNING GLORY CLOUDS, AUSTRALIA

Be up bright and early at dawn for the chance to watch a meteorological wonder roll into northern Australia's Gulf of Carpentaria. The Morning Glory is a tubular cloud (or series of clouds) up to 1000km in length, that rolls across the sky in the early morning, pushing great updrafts ahead of it. It's these updrafts that have made it one of the great places for gliding and hang-gliding adventures. First soared in 1989, Morning Glories have carried gliders for more than 700km and up to six hours.

The Morning Glories usually occur from September to late October. Burketown in northern Queensland makes a good base for viewing.

209 POROROCA TIDAL BORE, AMAZON RIVER, BRAZIL

At the mouth of the Amazon, the Atlantic's tide occasionally – when the moon is right – gets the better of the outpouring river. The result: the longest tidal wave on earth. In the predawn light you'll hear the monkeys screeching and a distant dull roar before you see the wave – all 4m of it charging upstream, taking all manner of shoreside debris, and some very intrepid surfers, along with it. The surfing record to date is a 12.5km ride lasting 37 minutes. You'll be able to enjoy the spectacle at the annual National Pororoca Surfing Championships in São Domingos do Capim in March.

The *pororoca* occurs twice a day, three days a month; waves are biggest in February and March.

210 RACETRACK, CALIFORNIA, USA

Who wouldn't expect a few oddities in a place like California's aptly named Death Valley? Prime among them is the mystery of the 'racing' stones in the valley's remote north. These large, flat stones, some of which weigh as much as 180kg, have 'raced' across the earth, leaving grooves in the dry, cracked lake bed behind them. Nobody has actually ever seen any of the rocks move, and science's best guess is they've been blown across at times when the lake bed is slippery from rain or frost.

You can camp in Death Valley, but with furnace-like temperatures you might prefer an air-conditioned lodge (www .nps.gov/deva).

GREATEST MANSIONS & GRAND HOUSES

Who wants to be a squillionaire?
Well, if you get to live in houses like these…

KARL BLACKWELL / LONELY PLANET IMAGES

211 | MARBLE PALACE MANSION, KOLKATA, INDIA

The extraordinarily grand 1853 Marble Palace Mansion is indulgently overstuffed with statues and lavishly floored with marble inlay. The house is a blend of neoclassical and traditional Bengali architecture, and filled with chandeliers, mirrors and clocks. Amid the eclectic jumble of objects you'll find a mahogany bust of Queen Victoria and paintings by Rubens and Titian. There's also a lake and an aviary with peacocks and cranes. Yet the mansion's fine paintings droop in their dusty frames and the antique furniture is haphazardly draped in torn old dust sheets. It would make a great horror-movie set.

The Mansion is still a private residence and you can only see it by tour. You'll also need a permit from West Bengal Tourism.

212 | CHEONG FATT TZE MANSION, MALAYSIA

Built in the 1880s, the magnificent 38-room, 220-window Cheong Fatt Tze Mansion was commissioned by Cheong Fatt Tze, a local merchant-trader who left China as a penniless teenager and ended up as 'the Rockefeller of the East'. The mansion blends Eastern and Western designs, with louvred windows, art nouveau stained glass and beautiful floor tiles, and is a rare surviving example of the eclectic architectural style preferred by wealthy Straits Chinese of the time. The house sits on the 'dragon's throne', meaning that there is a mountain (Penang Hill) behind and water (the channel) in front – the site was chosen for its excellent feng shui.

The building was rescued from ruin in the 1990s. You can visit it and also stay in the exclusive hotel (www.cheongfatttze mansion.com).

213 | WERRIBEE MANSION, AUSTRALIA

The 19th century was boom time for this corner of Australia; at one stage during the gold rush, Melbourne was the richest city in the world. The good times are reflected in the city's lavish Victorian architecture. Werribee Mansion was built in the Italianate style by the Chirnside family, wealthy pastoralists, in 1877, and is a solid testament to colonial ambition. It sits in charming formal gardens with a lake, glasshouses, a grotto and a sculpture walk.

The Werribee Park Shuttle runs return services from central Melbourne. Check www.werribeeparkshuttle.com.au for schedules and fares.

In a nation filled with stately homes, Castle Howard is among the grandest of all

214 VILLA D'ESTE, ITALY

In Tivoli, near Rome, the High Renaissance Villa d'Este was a Benedictine monastery before Cardinal Ippolite d'Este (Lucrezia Borgia's son) transformed it into a pleasure palace in 1550, and withdrew here to recover from his disappointment after a failed bid to be pope. It's set around a courtyard, and has frescoed ceilings and a central room looking out onto the fantasyland of the gardens, with their hundreds of whimsical water features: fountains, pools, grottoes, nymphs, dragons, winged horses and a water organ.

The villa is open from Tuesday to Sunday from 8am to one hour before sunset.

215 CASTLE HOWARD, ENGLAND

Stately homes may be two a penny in England, but you'll have to try pretty hard to find one as breathtakingly stately as Castle Howard, a work of theatrical grandeur and audacity set in the rolling Howardian Hills. This is one of the world's most beautiful buildings, instantly recognisable from its starring role in the '80s TV adaptation of *Brideshead Revisited*. It took three earls' lifetimes to build; it's still inhabited by the Howard family, but you can take tours of the house and grounds (18th-century walled garden, roses, delphiniums, temples, fountains and all).

Castle Howard is 15 miles northeast of York, off the A64. There are several organised tours from York.

Gaze upon the Catherine Palace, so baroque it will surely make your eyes water

216 FALLINGWATER, PENNSYLVANIA, USA

A Frank Lloyd Wright masterpiece from the 1930s, Fallingwater is a typically clean-lined, cantilevered structure that appears to float over a waterfall. It was built for the Kaufmann family, wealthy department-store owners, in the woods of southern Pennsylvania. The house is made of locally quarried stone, bringing it into harmony with the landscape –

it's almost like rocks have risen up out of Bear Run creek and shaped themselves into the house. Inside it has an almost Japanese minimalism, with the sound of the waterfall burbling in every room. It's set in forested gardens that also blend seamlessly with the natural environment.

To see inside the house you must take one of the hourly guided tours; reservations are recommended.

217 CHÂTEAU DE CHAMBORD, FRANCE

Chateaux don't get any grander than Chambord, built in the 16th century by François I so he could hunt deer and hang out with his mistress. Its most famous feature is its ingenious double-helix staircase. Attributed by some to Leonardo de Vinci, the two helixes ascend three storeys without ever meeting. Then there's the Italianate rooftop terrace, where you're surrounded

ARNO BURGI / CORBIS

218 CATHERINE PALACE, RUSSIA

The baroque Catherine Palace was initially built by Peter the Great's wife, Catherine I, as a summer pleasure palace. Elizabeth, her daughter, spent her life remodelling and extending the palace with the help of her architect Bartolomeo Rastrelli, who later designed the Winter Palace. In her day the entire exterior was picked out in gilt. Catherine II made slightly less flashy additions such as the Agate Room and a Chinese drawing room. The Catherine Palace was raided and gutted by German forces during WWII, but has since been largely restored. Don't miss the stunning (replica) Amber Room with its solid amber panels and amber parquetry floor.

The Catherine Palace is in the village of Tsarkoye Selo, an easy day trip from St Petersburg.

219 SLEEPER-MCCANN HOUSE, MASSACHUSETTS, USA

The lavish 'summer cottage' of interior designer Henry Davis Sleeper has over 40 rooms and is also known as the Beauport House. Sleeper toured New England in search of houses about to be demolished and bought up selected elements from each: wood panelling, furniture, wallpaper, coloured glass and china. In place of unity, Sleeper created a wildly eclectic but artistically surprising – and satisfying – place to live. The mansion sits on rocks overlooking Gloucester Harbor and has Arts-and-Crafts-style terraces leading down into a series of garden 'rooms'. The house is in Gloucester, Massachusetts.

You can visit the house between June and October, Tuesday to Sunday from 10am to 5pm. The last hourly tour begins at 4pm.

220 POWERSCOURT, IRELAND

Powerscourt is a phoenix house, gutted by fire in the '70s but now restored to its full Palladian glory. It started out as a 13th-century castle but was remodelled in the 18th century – additions included a stunning double-height Georgian ballroom. The house is set in the Wicklow Mountains amid 47 acres of Italianate gardens with fountains, grottoes, terraces, cascades, fish ponds, a walled garden and a mile-long beech avenue with 2000 trees.

Visit the nearby village of Enniskerry, built in 1760 by the Earl of Powerscourt so his labourers would have somewhere to live.

by so many towers, cupolas, domes, chimneys, mosaic slate roofs and lightning rods that it's like being in a small city. It was here that the royal court assembled to watch military exercises, tournaments and the hounds and hunters returning from deer-stalks.

Chambord is in the Loire Valley. Get a train from Paris Austerlitz to Blois; there's a Blois–Chambord shuttle from May to September.

GREATEST MANSIONS & GRAND HOUSES

MOST BIZARRE MONUMENTS

If it's lived and breathed – or even if it hasn't – it's probably been immortalised somewhere, as the following list testifies.

At Memento Park, the heroes of communism – and Stalin's boots – live on, and on, and on...

221 PETER THE GREAT STATUE, MOSCOW, RUSSIA

Peter the Great wasn't particularly kind on Moscow. Though he built the city's tallest structure, the 90m-high Sukharev Tower, he also relocated Russia's capital to swampland in the northwest (St Petersburg), leaving the spurned ex-capital to fall into decline. So it's odd to find this truly gargantuan statue now standing in front of Moscow's Krasny Oktyabr (Red October) chocolate factory. At 94.5m, or twice the size of the Statue of Liberty without her pedestal, Peter towers over the city. Not all Muscovites are impressed; some radicals even attempted – unsuccessfully – to blow the thing up.

The statue is on Bolotny Island, on the Moscow River, immediately opposite the Cathedral of Christ the Saviour.

222 WASHINGTON NATIONAL CATHEDRAL, WASHINGTON, DC, USA

This enormous cathedral is an iconic feature of Washington, DC's skyline, and wouldn't look out of place in Europe, except for a few uniquely American accents: the column capitals on the north side of the building include igloo motifs, while one of the interior stained-glass windows is studded with a moon rock. Most bizarrely, among the gargoyles arranged around the parapets is the carved head of… Darth Vader. Yes, Luke's asthmatic papa. His presence resulted from a 1980s competition in which children were invited to design decorative sculpture for the cathedral – Darth was submitted as a futuristic representation of evil.

The Darth Vader gargoyle is near the top of the northwest tower, on the north side.

223 MEMENTO PARK, BUDAPEST, HUNGARY

In most former Soviet states, the heroic statues of Lenin and Marx etc were consigned to the scrapheap, but in Budapest they're a wee bit proud of their communist debris. So much so, they created Memento Park, which is home to almost 50 statues, busts and plaques of Lenin, Marx, Béla Kun and 'heroic' workers. Ogle at the socialist realism and try to remember that at least four of these monstrous relics were erected as recently as the late 1980s. Among the collection are the replicated remains of Stalin's boots, all that was left after a crowd pulled the enormous statue down during the 1956 Uprising.

The park is 10km southwest of the city centre; a direct bus leaves from in front of the Le Méridien Budapest Hotel on Deák Ferenc tér at 11am.

87

224 ENEMA MONUMENT, ZHELEZNOVODSK, RUSSIA

The world is full of monuments to obscure items, but whoever thought the humble enema would be worthy of celebration? In 2008, the Russian town of Zheleznovodsk unveiled a bronze sculpture of three angels carrying a 360kg syringe bulb, honouring one of the popular spa resort's signature treatments: enemas from the mineral waters that rise from springs around the town. At the unveiling, a banner was strung across the walls of the adjoining spa, proclaiming the message, 'Let's beat constipation and sloppiness with enemas.' Very moving…literally.

Nearby Pyatigorsk is the main mineral resort in the region; from here *marshrutka* (share taxi) 113 leaves from Upper Market for Zheleznovodsk, taking around 20 minutes.

225 MANNEKEN PIS, BRUSSELS, BELGIUM

Known throughout the world, Manneken Pis – a little boy cheerfully taking a leak into a pool – has somehow become a national symbol for the Belgians, who've adopted him as an emblem of their indomitable and irreverent spirit. The statue's origins are lost in legend: some say he's modelled on a boy who extinguished a fire, others say he was a nobleman's son. On occasion the city dresses him up in one of his 700-odd costumes. And there's more – his little 'sister', Jeanneke Pis, squats in an alley on the north side of Grand Place, and Zinneke, a mongrel dog with a cocked leg, stands in St Géry.

Manneken Pis is three blocks from the Grand Place.

At Kindlifresserbrunnen, ogres are as famished as the next man

226 ROCKY BALBOA STATUE, ŽITIŠTE, SERBIA

Even if you've watched all six of the *Rocky* movies very closely, you've probably still failed to note whether Rocky Balboa ever fought in Serbia. But that hasn't stopped the small Serbian town of Žitište erecting a 3m-high bronze statue of the rags-to-riches boxer. Unveiled in 2007, it was an effort to show the town's fighting spirit and boost morale after years of bad luck (such as floods) and publicity (such as murders). The local resident who dreamed up the idea – a staunch *Rocky* fan (no surprises there) – claimed that since Rocky Balboa had to fight for all he achieved, it felt as though he might have come from Žitište.

Žitište is around 90km north of Belgrade, near the Romania border.

227 KINDLIFRESSERBRUNNEN, BERN, SWITZERLAND

One of the famous features of the picture-postcard Swiss capital of Bern is its 11 decorative fountains dating from the 16th century, all of which depict fantastical folkloric characters or historic figures. Most are along Marktgasse as it becomes Kramgasse and Gerechtigkeitsgasse, but the most famous lies in Kornhausplatz: the Kindlifresserbrunnen (Ogre Fountain). Begin from the toes up and it's kind of warm and embracing. The ogre has one child snuggly in a basket and another tucked under his arm. Look higher and the mood changes, with the ogre stuffing the head of a child into his mouth. Just the spot, really, to take your kids if you want to scare the living ogres out of them.

The fountain is in the centre of the old town, near the landmark Zytglogge (clock tower).

230 FRANK ZAPPA BUST, VILNIUS, LITHUANIA

Frank Zappa's links to Vilnius, Lithuania's capital, are tenuous to say the least (OK, nonexistent), but when the city looked a bit empty after all the Lenin busts were packed away in the early 1990s, the local Frank Zappa fan club seized the moment. Following the rocker's death in 1993 the city became the first to erect a monument in his honour, with a stone bust standing atop a very tall column. Behind it, a wall was airbrushed with Zappa images, making for a monument that, remarkably, has become one of the most popular in the city.

The bust is at Kalinausko gatvė 1, west of Vilniaus gatvė.

228 MOLINIÈRE BAY UNDERWATER GALLERY, GRENADA

Art galleries are all the same, right – white walls, wood floors, pretentious patrons? Well not this one. Sitting beneath the surface of the sea in Molinière Bay, 3km north of St George's on Grenada's west coast, is where you'll find this gallery. Life-size sculptures depicting a circle of women clasping hands, a man at a desk and a solitary mountain biker are among the collection. Artist Jason Taylor has created a garden of art that is a platform for sea life. As the pieces age, coral will grow on them, creatures will make their homes around them and they'll become a part of the sea.

To see the art you'll have to get in the water with one of the local scuba-diving companies.

229 DUKE OF WELLINGTON STATUE, GLASGOW, SCOTLAND

There's nothing even slightly out of the ordinary about the Duke of Wellington statue outside of Glasgow's Gallery of Modern Art, except for the traffic cone on his head. As a matter of course, this very heroic-looking duke, placed here in 1844, wears an orange traffic cone, jauntily tilted on his head (as, quite often, does his horse). It's a tradition that dates back more than two decades – revellers climbing the statue to place a traffic cone on the duke – and one that authorities have tried at times to stamp out with threats of prosecution. Unsuccessfully. We're not condoning anything illegal, but gosh he looks fetching in orange.

The gallery is at 111 Queen Street.

MOST BIZARRE MONUMENTS

ART NOUVEAU ICONS

The most enduring examples of one of history's most alluring styles.

233 MÉTRO ENTRANCES, PARIS, FRANCE

The art nouveau entrances to Paris' Métro are emblematic of the style, but also of the city, and so beloved it's hard to believe they were reviled when they first appeared. The entrances, made from glass and wrought iron and as light as insect wings, were designed by the architect Hector Guimard, who is history's most overlooked art nouveau genius. Although his Métro signs are recognisable, who would recognise his name? He died unregarded in New York. Sadly, many of the entrances have been demolished (and one given to Montréal).

The last remaining fully original and fully intact entrance is at Porte Dauphine, on Line 2.

231 MUCHA'S 'PRINCEZNA HYACINTA', PRAGUE, CZECH REPUBLIC

When it comes to art nouveau graphic design and commercial art, the Moravian artist Alphonse Mucha wears the (star-wreathed) crown. Some of the most recognisable images of the art nouveau period come from his posters for liqueurs, cigarettes and the theatre, featuring piercing-eyed Slavic maidens in flowing poses. *Princezna Hyacinta* was from a poster advertising a ballet based on a fairytale. The actress who played the title role, with her vivid blue eyes, poses against a midnight sky holding a strange device worked with silver hyacinths and wearing a starry diadem.

The Mucha Museum (http://mucha .tyden.cz) holds an impressive collection of Mucha's paintings, lithographs, decorative panels and drawings.

232 KLIMT'S 'JUDITH I', VIENNA, AUSTRIA

Gustav Klimt is arguably the definitive art nouveau painter, with his languid, sensuous women and rich use of gold and tarnished shadow. Judith was a biblical heroine of a sort, a Hebrew widow who saved her people by bedding and beheading the general of the opposing army. Lavishly gilded and collared, robed in an underwater blue, with stylised golden trees seeming to grow out of her shoulders, Klimt's Judith holds the decapitated head in her spidery hand. She bares a breast and wears an expression of triumphant sexual ecstasy. Perhaps it's no wonder Klimt raised staid hackles throughout his career.

You can visit *Judith I* – if you dare – in Vienna's Upper Belvedere (www .belvedere.at). The gentler but similarly iconic *The Kiss* is also in the collection.

234 LALIQUE DRAGONFLY ORNAMENT, LISBON, PORTUGAL

The dragonfly was especially beloved by the artists of the art nouveau movement. They were used outright in many designs and the arabesque designs in their wings were imitated in the architecture. Peacocks and scarab beetles were also nouveau faves – not to mention enigmatic, sensual women. This astounding corsage pin (the wings are hinged to move) by radical jewellery and glass designer René Lalique puts it all together in one scintillating hybrid goddess. She took the Paris World Fair of 1900, where she was displayed, by storm. She now lives in the Gulbenkian museum in Lisbon.

The ornament appears on the front cover of AS Byatt's *The Children's Book*, a wonderfully erudite, soapy account of the Arts and Craft Movement.

235 BEARDSLEY'S 'THE TOILETTE OF SALOME', LONDON, ENGLAND

The writhing ink lines of a Beardsley femme fatale are synonymous with the decadence of the Aesthetic Movement, which was a huge influence on art nouveau. Aubrey Beardsley was an illustrator devoted to depicting the sensual and the grotesque. *The Toilette of Salome* is a typical work. It shows Salome getting all dolled up to wreak a bit of erotic and murderous vengeance on John the Baptist. She's depicted smirking under the powder puff of a malignant clown attendant, a de Sade book on the shelf next to her. The work was an illustration for Wilde's scandalous play, *Salome*.

A version of the *Toilette* is held by the British Museum (www.britishmuseum .org). Take the tube to Russell Square.

236 TIFFANY WISTERIA LIBRARY LAMP, ORLANDO, FLORIDA, USA

The wonderfully named Louis Comfort Tiffany was an art nouveau innovator whose combination of technical skill and design genius has earned him an enduring place in the canon. His invention of the opalescent glass process allowed effects in glass production never before seen, and he used the technique in the service of a marvellous aesthetic that wed sumptuous, saturated colour to the ethereal effects of light. The Wisteria Library Lamp, with its drippy form suggesting heavy flowers on a tree-inspired iron foot, is Louis Comfort at his best.

The Library Lamp is in the comprehensive Tiffany collection of Orlando's Morse Museum (www.morsemuseum.org).

237 WILLOW TEA ROOMS, GLASGOW, SCOTLAND

Charles Rennie Mackintosh, he of the famous straight-backed chair and stylised rose, reached the apotheosis of his art in the Willow Tea Rooms on Glasgow's Sauchiehall Street. (Sauchiehall means Alley of Willows, and willows are a decorative motif throughout.) Mackintosh was the architect for the building and worked on every aspect of the design, including the teaspoons and aprons. The cream – as it were – of the tearooms is the Room de Luxe, with its white and silver freshness highlighted with dove pinks and deep purples and featuring Mackintosh's trademark chairs and botanical leadlights.

Drop into the charming Room de Luxe for scones, but take a book (on design, of course) – there are usually long queues.

238 GELLÉRT BATHS, BUDAPEST, HUNGARY

Having a soak in this pillared, elaborately tiled thermal pool has been likened to taking a bath in a cathedral. Floating around here, it's easy to feel like the surreal empress in out-there artist Matthew Barney's film *The Cremaster Cycle*, the final chapter of which was filmed here. The baths are attached to the similarly sumptuous nouveau palace of the Gellért Hotel, and are fed by springs from Gellért Hill, which are supposed to have healing properties. The light is dim, the details ornate and the whole environment designed to put you in the kind of languorous trance depicted in so many art nouveau paintings.

Help that trance along by having a massage at the Gellért Spa (see www .gellertbath.com).

239 CASA MILÀ (LA PEDRERA), BARCELONA, SPAIN

This undulating beast is a madcap masterpiece by the one-off Catalan architect Antoni Gaudí, built from 1905 to 1910 as a combined apartment and office block. Formally called Casa Milà, it is better known as La Pedrera (the Quarry) because of its uneven grey stone facade, which ripples around the street corner. This is art nouveau at its wildest and most exuberant, channelled through Gaudí's unique vision and expressed in sweeping curves, swelling organic forms and unexpected twists. The wave effect is emphasised by elaborate wrought-iron balconies.

The building is at 261-265 Carrer de Provença and entry costs €10.

240 TASSEL HOUSE, BRUSSELS, BELGIUM

The Tassel House is often talked of as the first house to be completely art nouveau in its design. Built by Victor Horta for the Belgian scientist Émile Tassel, it has a sinuous line and a delicate airiness that is pure nouveau. The exterior curves out in a graceful bay window and the interior makes much use of glass to bring light into the house. There are murals, stained glass, iron pillars resembling slender trees, and mosaic features. Horta designed the entire house, right down to the door handles.

The Tassel House is at 6 rue Paul-Emile Jansonstraat. It opens its doors only occasionally, but the exterior is well worth a look.

MOST AWESOME CANYONS & GORGES

Carved by water over millennia, these gashes in the Earth are deep, dark and delightful.

241 GEECH ABYSS, ETHIOPIA

When you hike along the escarpment of the Simien Mountains there's no end to the heady views, but still the first sight of the Geech Abyss is confronting. As you creep out across a narrow rock band, a shadowed pit opens out below, as deep and dark as the supposed heart of Africa. From one niche pours a thin stripe of a waterfall, leaping more than 500m to the unseen bottom below. Wrapped around it are rock walls that fall so sheer they seem never to end. And it's a view you'll share with some very ancient cousins, as endemic gelada baboons inevitably graze just metres from where you stand.

Treks through the Simien Mountains usually reach the Geech Abyss on the second day; treks can be arranged in Debark, about three hours' drive from Gonder.

242 FISH RIVER CANYON, NAMIBIA

Nowhere else in Africa will you find anything quite like Fish River Canyon. Despite the seeming enormity of this statement, the numbers don't lie: the canyon measures 160km in length and up to 27km in width, and the dramatic inner canyon reaches a depth of 550m. Although these figures by themselves are impressive, it's difficult to get a sense of perspective without actually witnessing the enormous scope of the canyon. In order to do this, embark on a monumental five-day, 85km hike that traverses half the length of the canyon.

The hiking route is only open from May to mid-September and advance bookings need to be made through Namibia Wildlife Resorts (www.nwr .com.na).

TIM HUGHES / LONELY PLANET IMAGES

243 KALI GANDAKI, NEPAL

Stand somewhere such as Kopra Ridge, draping from the slopes of Annapurna South, looking into the deep shadow that is the Kali Gandaki gorge, and you quickly understand what a looming chasm it is. From the gorge floor to the summit of Dhaulagiri – the seventh highest mountain in the world – there's an elevation difference of around 5500m, making this the deepest gorge in the world. Long a trading route between Nepal and Tibet – the river funnels up through Mustang towards the China–Tibet border – it's more recently been one half of Nepal's most popular trekking route, the Annapurna Circuit.

To walk the Circuit, or simply up into the Kali Gandaki, sherpas, guides and porters can be arranged in Pokhara or through a host of international tour companies.

Nepalese magic at the Kali Gandaki gorge

Tiger Leaping Gorge, China: not even the Panthera tigris could jump those raging waters

244 CAÑÓN DEL COLCA, PERU

The 100km-long Cañón del Colca is set among 6000m-high volcanoes, and ranges from 1000m to more than 3000m in depth – more than twice as deep as the Grand Canyon. For years there was raging debate over whether this was the world's deepest canyon, but recently it ranked a close second to neighbouring Cañón del Cotahuasi, which is just over 150m deeper. A two-day hike into the canyon is popular, while it's also possible to hike for five days, crossing the 5100m Paso Cerani. Keep a watch for condors.

The city of Arequipa is the access point for the canyon. Buses travel to Chivay and then continue to Cabanaconde, at the end of the canyon's main road.

245 SAMARIA GORGE, CRETE, GREECE

At 16km, Crete's Samaria Gorge is touted as the longest in Europe. It begins just below the Omalos Plateau, carved out by the river that flows between the peaks of Avlimanakou (1858m) and Volakias (2115m). Its width varies from 150m to 3km and its vertical walls reach 500m at their highest points. Hiking through the gorge is one of Crete's most popular activities, and though around 170,000 people wander through it each year, time spent in this stupendous gorge is still an experience to remember.

You can get to the gorge easily from Hania by bus, then catch a ferry from Agia Roumeli back to Hora Sfakion or other south-coast towns.

246 GRAND CANYON, ARIZONA, USA

Grand by name, grand by nature – this is the world's most famous ditch, and with good reason. Stand on its rim and it's as though the earth abandons you, plunging 1600m down to the Colorado River. Apart from the sheer volume of the crack before you, what stuns about this natural icon are the colours – black, red, brown – which seem to change with the moving sun. The Grand Canyon is generous to visitors, yielding its beauty in a variety of manners: stand on the rim, hike to the canyon floor, or raft through its belly.

Learn all you need to know about a Grand Canyon visit at the official park website (www.nps.gov/grca).

DANNY CARLO / ALAMY

248 TIGER LEAPING GORGE, CHINA

This whimsically named gorge in Yúnnán is one of the deepest in the world, measuring 16km in length and a giddy 3900m from the waters of the Jīnshā River to the snowcapped mountaintops of Hābā Shān to the west and Yùlóng Xuěshān to the east. Hiking through the gorge was once an obscure adventure, though in recent years it has become the 'can't miss' experience of northern Yúnnán. Plan on three to four days to do the hike, though it can be done in two. The best time to come is May and the start of June, when the hills are afire with plant and flower life.

Lijiāng is the leaping-off point for Tiger Leaping Gorge. Check with cafes here before setting out for the latest weather news.

247 KINGS CANYON, AUSTRALIA

The image of the Australian outback is built on natural wonders such as Kings Canyon, with its sheer, 100m-high walls sliced into the red desert landscape. The 1km gorge is carved from a dominating sandstone plateau, crowned in many places by bizarre, weathered sandstone domes. At the head of the gorge is the spring-fed Garden of Eden, where a moist microclimate shelters a variety of plants. The best way to experience the canyon is by setting out on the Kings Canyon Rim walk, a 6km loop that offers an awesome view into the canyon from several angles.

The canyon is around 330km from Alice Springs along the unsealed Mereenie Loop Road; a 4WD is recommended.

249 TARA RIVER CANYON, MONTENEGRO

Slicing through the mountains at the northern edge of Durmitor National Park, the Tara River forms a canyon that drops to 1300m at its deepest point. Stretching for more than 80km, it is the deepest canyon in Europe, just a few hundred metres shy of the depths of the Grand Canyon. Rafting through the canyon is one of Montenegro's premier tourist attractions. It has a few rapids but it's no cauldron, so don't expect an adrenalin-fuelled white-water rodeo. You'll get the most excitement in May when the last of the melting snow revs up the flow. The classic two-day trip heads through the deepest part of the canyon.

Various operators run rafting trips daily from May to October.

250 YUSUFELI GORGE, TURKEY

With its 1500m-high walls compressing the Çoruh River, this gorge in eastern Anatolia offers some of the world's best white-water rafting. It has a succession of Grade 4 and 5 rapids with welcoming names such as King Kong and High Tension, though the gorge's great joy is its scenery: the tall, craggy rock walls and snapshots of traditional village life. Rafting outings vary from day trips to multi-day epics – to run the river's 300km length will take around a week, building up to its finale: the paddle through Yusufeli Gorge.

Various local operators run trips out of the town of Yusufeli; May and June offer the best water levels.

MOST AWESOME CANYONS & GORGES

MOST AMAZING MARINE ANIMALS

From the world's largest animal to gruesome creatures of the dark and tiny bioluminescent microplankton, our oceans are full of staggering creatures.

251 MOLA MOLA, NAMIBIA

One look at the mola mola, or ocean sunfish, and you'd swear it was swimming on its side. There's no sensible reason why, it has dorsal and ventral fins just like all fish, but it just looks weird. Maybe the mola mola's construction – all squashed as if it's been through a mangle – just plays tricks with the eyes. Whatever the case, this odd-looking chap is unique. It's also immense, being the ocean's heaviest known bony fish (tipping the scales at an average weight of 1000kg). Truly, this is one fish about which fishermen can justifiably hold their arms out and say, 'It was this big!'

Mola molas can be seen off the coast of Namibia's Walvis Bay – the appropriately named Mola Mola Safaris organises tours (www.mola-namibia.com).

252 BLUE WHALE, CALIFORNIA, USA

The majestic blue whale is the largest animal ever known to have lived on the planet, growing up to 30m in length and weighing up to 180 tonnes. To give those figures some context, we're talking a quarter of a football pitch and the equivalent of 24 double-decker London buses. You need an awful lot of krill to fuel an engine like that – about six million per day to be exact. Conservative estimates say that as few as 10,000 blue whales remain, split between the northern and southern hemispheres, so good sightings are rare. Most tourists prefer to see the photogenic orca, but the thrill of seeing a wild blue is the ultimate big beast buzz.

The best place to see a blue whale is on their late-summer migratory passage through the Monterey Canyon, off California. Try Monterey Bay Whale Watch (www.montereybaywhalewatch.com) for itineraries.

253 SEA HORSES, SULAWESI, INDONESIA

Everyone loves sea horses, the diminutive little fellows whose cute looks mean they are both endeared and endangered. And what's not to love? For starters, they don't look like any other ocean dwellers. Their long snouts, curved bodies and upright swimming style are unique, while sea horses are famous for the role that dad plays in giving birth to the babies. Their small size and cunning camouflage make them hard to spot in the wild, even more so because they are usually found hidden away in corals. Alas, they are also much prized for ornamental and medicinal purposes – some 25 million are traded each year.

At the Wakatobi Resort in Sulawesi you can dive to search for pygmy sea horses and learn about marine conservation (www.wakatobi.com).

Not only does dad give birth, but he wears polka-dot pyjamas too; a Sulawesi sea horse struts its stuff

Nothing quite matches the electric beauty of Indonesia's emperor angelfish

254 DUGONG, PHILIPPINES

Something about the dugong makes you want to exclaim 'You're supposed to be in a field somewhere! Go eat some grass!' And the unassuming dugong may just oblige. For this humorous beastie is known as the 'sea cow' and it's often found munching along the seabed, languidly scoffing through favourite fields of marine grasses. The devil-may-care attitude might seem a bit blasé considering some of the beasts roaming the oceans, but the dugong's size means it's only targeted by serious hunters like sharks, orcas and crocs. Be grateful dugongs don't move any faster – it makes spotting them a whole lot easier.

Palawan Island in the Philippines is a desert-island destination that offers a good chance of seeing the dugong – Pioneer Expeditions take guided tours (www.pioneerexpeditions.com).

255 DOLPHINS, AZORES, PORTUGAL

Who in the world hasn't dreamt about swimming with dolphins? Of all the creatures inhabiting our oceans, few tug the heartstrings more than these little critters. Maybe it's their high intelligence or their permanent smiley demeanour, but we've adopted them as paragons of animal virtue and it's officially super-cool to be 'dolphin friendly'. Which is a good thing, of course, so long as our attempts to conserve don't lead to intrusion or exploitation. Dolphins live in captivity around the world for our entertainment, but if you can get to their habitat the experience will be all the more rewarding.

Travel to the Azores, 1500km west of Portugal, and experience ethical dolphin swimming with the Dolphin Connection Experience (www .dolphinconnectionexperience.com).

256 GALÁPAGOS TORTOISE, GALÁPAGOS ISLANDS, ECUADOR

Tortoises have become an icon of ecological conservation. Graceful, platonic and born of ancient stock, all species are endangered due to human encroachment and black-market trading. Size isn't everything, but jumbo tortoises are a splendid sight and none are bigger than those of the Galápagos. True to the islands' reputation for harbouring unique species, the endemic Galápagos tortoise is a monster – up to 2m in length, 400kg in weight and with a reported lifespan of 150 years. So rare are some subspecies that one old chap, Lonesome George, has become a media star because he has no females with which to mate.

The best way to Galápagos is to fly via Quito with TAME (www.tame.com.ec). Always book island tours with a reputable operator.

257 EMPEROR ANGELFISH, RAJA AMPAT ISLANDS, WEST PAPUA, INDONESIA

Coral reefs are the richest ocean environments, known as 'underwater gardens' and landscapes of enthralling beauty. The fish found here are aquatic poster boys – *Finding Nemo*, anyone? – and Indonesia's Raja Ampat Islands have one of the most diverse reefs of all. If you think clownfish are clichéd, there are 1300 other species from which you can pick a favourite. Of all the shapes, sizes and colours on offer, the emperor angelfish is mesmerising. Juveniles are deep blue with vivid rings of electric blue and white, while adult patterns morph into stripes of blue and yellow. A more beautiful creature is hard to imagine.

The Raja Ampat Islands are in West Papua – fly to Sorong via Jakarta. Operators such as Papua Diving (www.papua-diving.com) provide a range of resort and boat dives.

258 GREAT WHITE SHARK, GANSBAAI, SOUTH AFRICA

Of all the world's mighty predators, few instil fear like the great white shark. Stories abound of swimmers snatched from the sea and the *Jaws* films of the 1970s and '80s fuelled their fearsome reputation. Real attacks are uncommon but it pays to exercise caution, for the great white is a super-efficient ambush hunter. Growing up to 6m in length and packing a bone-crushing array of razor-sharp teeth (a shark re-grows worn out teeth and can get through 35 million in its lifetime), the great white targets large fish species, dolphins, porpoises, seals and even some whales.

At Gansbaai in South Africa, shark diving is the pièce de résistance. Several outfits will pop you in a cage and scare your pants off for around ZAR1200 – see www.sharkbookings.com.

259 NOMURA'S JELLYFISH, JAPAN

No bones, no brain and no blood. That's a funny recipe for any creature but a combination that serves the jellyfish well. Like all great designs the jellyfish exudes simplicity – employing basic propulsion to move around and using the ocean's buoyancy to support their mass – in a manner unchanged by evolution. Some species are phosphorescent, others flash brightly to lure prey and many have deadly stings. Nomura's jellyfish are none of these things, but they are huge. Growing up to 2m across and weighing in excess of 200kg, they're confined to the waters of the East China Sea around the coastlines of China, Korea and Japan.

Nomura's jellyfish is considered a menace so you won't find many sightseeing tours – your best bet could be a ferry from Osaka or Kobe to Shanghai (www.chinajapanferry.com).

260 CROWN-OF-THORNS STARFISH, EGYPT

The world's oceans contain more than 2000 known species of starfish and probably a fair few that haven't been found yet. And what a creature this is! We're talking about an animal that has eyes on the ends of its arms, breathes through its feet and can remove one of its two stomachs to aid in digesting prey. And that's not all. If an arm should fall off it can grow a new one, and some species wear poisonous sheaths comprising thousands of spines. The crown-of-thorns starfish is king of the genre – vivid in colour and packing a serious venomous whack.

Crown-of-thorns starfish can be found in the Red Sea – search inside the hull of the wrecked *Giannis D*, in the Straits of Gubal (www.emperordivers.com).

MOST AMAZING MARINE ANIMALS

SALTIEST SITES

The plains, caves, lakes and tunnels that add flavour to your travels.

263 GREAT SALINAS, ARGENTINA

The Great Salinas in Cordoba is a collection of large salt dunes in the central northwest of mainland Argentina. It is said that the origin of these mountains lies in a large gap in the Mar, a tectonic fault which exposed the saline seafloor from which the great dunes were formed. The area is also known to be in a constant hurricane; in times of flooding, a surface of saline creates a pristine mirror to the sky. This is the place to show off your extra-dark sunglasses with UV protection – even if your only audience is the sky.

Take Highways 9 and 60 north out of Cordoba for the 200km drive to Las Salinas Grandes.

261 SALT-CRYSTAL FORMATIONS OF DEVIL'S GOLF COURSE, NEVADA, USA

In the centre of the Southern Californian desert, Nevada, sit elements of nearly every major geological era. Death Valley National Park is one of the lowest points in the western hemisphere, one of the hottest places in the world, and it also plays host to an incredible salt phenomenon. The bizarre, moonlike field of salt crystals at Devil's Golf Course, in the centre of the park, will take you back to the world of dinosaurs and prehistoric wonders. The crystals are fragile to touch and should be handled with care; it's not an actual golf course – park rangers advise that you leave the golf balls at home.

Most people visit Death Valley from the west (Las Vegas) or east (Los Angeles) on Interstate 15. Baker, California, is a good gateway town.

262 NAMAKDAN CAVES, PERSIAN GULF, IRAN

In January 2006 a group of Czech geology students discovered an area touted to become the largest salt-cave system in the world. The students stumbled upon the hidden treasure in the Namakdan Mountain on Qeshm Island, and could hardly believe their eyes – underground salt lakes, glistening dripstones and sparkling domes of pure salt stood majestically before them. Unlike limestone, which takes thousands of years to grow, the jewels of the salt caves grow just days or weeks after rain, forming beautiful dripstone crystals. The student discoverers named the cave the Three Naked Men (coined while bathing in its salty glory?).

Qeshm's Hara Protected Area is a mangrove forest restricted to fishing and ecotourism use, and migratory home for 25% of Iran's native bird population.

264 SALT CATHEDRAL OF ZIPAQUIRA, COLOMBIA

If you need a reason to go to church, the small town of Zipaquira will give you one. Several kilometres from the town, in Cundinamarca, sits one of the world's only salt cathedrals, built in a tunnel of mines from 200-million-year-old salt deposits. As you wind your way underground, take note of the 14 small chapels on the descent, each of which illustrates the events of Jesus' last journey. Each station has a cross and kneeling platforms, several of which are carved into the salt structure. You won't be alone; more than 3000 churchgoers worship in this shimmering cathedral every Sunday.

Zipaquira is a city of 100,000 residents, with an attractive Spanish colonial old town. It's 50km north of Bogotá, easily reached by train or bus.

265 QĪNGHǍI LAKE, CHINA

Ever wondered whether salt lakes exist inland? Set between the snowy mountains of Tibet and the grasslands of the Qīnghǎi region lies China's largest interior salt lake, situated some 3200m above sea level and covering nearly 4400 sq metres. Located on the Qīnghǎi–Tibetan plateau, this area is often looked on simply as a passage to Tibet or northwest China – indeed, the lake attracts lots of migratory birds, which stop here on their way across Asia. The main attraction is Bird Island: huge numbers of birds congregate in the breeding season, between March and early June.

Tour buses to Bird Island depart from the bus station in Xining – allow two hours for a visit.

267 SALT PLAINS OF SALAR DE UYUNI, BOLIVIA

Dreaming of a white Christmas? Pack your Santa hat and make the trek to the world's most enduring salt plains, spanning nearly 12,000 sq km in the Potosí region of Bolivia. In some places the salt is over 10m thick; in the wet season the plains are covered with a thin sheet of water. Take a photo of your shadow on the sparkling plains or visit the salt-mining area, where tonnes of the stuff are piled into giant mounds. When it's time for bed don't go past a salt hotel, where you'll be handed a candy bar when entering your shimmering white bedroom.

4WD trips start in Uyuni, but with so many on offer it pays to shop around and seek the advice of fellow travellers.

269 CARDONA SALT MOUNTAIN, SPAIN

In the hilltop town of Cardona, some 90km northwest of Barcelona, sits a group of majestic mountain masses made entirely from salt. The mountains, partner to the town's historic castles, form a solid backdrop to this picturesque city; reddish-brown and clay in parts, and translucent in others. When you've had your mountaintop moment, make a trip to the portico of St Vincenç in Cardona, where the fragments of painted vaults will give you a strong sense of the sacred.

Want to see the murals but can't get to Cardona? Fragments are displayed at Barcelona's Museu Nacional d'Art de Catalunya (www.mnac.cat).

266 GREAT SALT LAKE, UTAH, USA

Size does matter. The Great Salt Lake, located in northern Utah, lays claim to being the largest salt lake in the western hemisphere, no mean feat. The lake used to be part of prehistoric Lake Bonneville, and is also known as America's Dead Sea. It's home to millions of creatures able to survive the high saline levels, such as waterfowl and other birds, including the largest staging population of Wilson's phalarope in the world – a boon for birdwatchers. If you're looking to get lost for a while, why not take a salty cruise to one of the lake's 11 recognised tidal islands.

Antelope Island has superb beaches that offer great swimming opportunities. Take Interstate 15, heading north from Salt Lake City (www.utah.com/stateparks/great_salt_lake.htm).

268 WHITE-SALT MOUNTAINS OF TRAPANI, ITALY

Next time you have an urge to reach for the moon, why not get a leg-up from one of the glistening white-salt mountains and shallow *saline* (salty pools) in Trapani, western Sicily? These saltpans were formed by the evaporation of seawater, and are situated majestically along the coast road between Trapani and Marsala. Here, life still centres around the ocean, as it has for generations, with industries such as tuna fishing, coral harvesting and salt production. Be sure to take in the sight of the 100-year-old windmills that sit alongside the *saline*, slowly fanning the winds of salt harvesting.

If you want to unearth the history of this local industry, there are dedicated museums in converted salt-mills at Nubia and Trapani.

270 SALT TUNNELS OF SOLOTVYNO, UKRAINE

Solotvyno is not the most stunning destination, but it certainly attracts thousands of visitors each year. The Soviet-looking Ukrainian mining town runs one of the most successful tourist businesses in Eastern Europe, albeit a long way underground. The town's working salt mine, situated near the Romanian border, offers speleotherapy – an unusual form of treatment for people with respiratory conditions. The mine has a unique microclimate because of the salt particles in the air. Patients descend more than 300m underground, where they breathe in the salty atmosphere while sitting or lying in rock-walled grottoes that glisten and sparkle.

Treatment costs about US$22 a day and usually takes place over 18 to 20 daily or overnight visits.

BEST BATHS

No longer just a means to be clean, luxury baths are fast becoming hot destinations and must-see sights.

271 CHAMPAGNE-GLASS WHIRLPOOL BATH, NEW YORK, USA

If you've ever dreamt of soaking your troubles away in a mammoth glass of champagne, this could be your lucky day. That's right, at the Pocono Palace Resort, only a couple of hours' drive from New York City, you too could be relaxing in a 2m-tall champagne-glass whirlpool bath for two. If that's not cheesy enough, look around your suite and savour the faux Roman columns, the circular bed, the mirrored walls and the private heart-shaped swimming pool.

It's not just rakish decadence – you can also cool things down with pursuits such as miniature golf and billiards (www .covepoconoresorts.com).

273 HOT WATER BEACH, NEW ZEALAND

Thermal waters brew just below the sand at Hot Water Beach on New Zealand's North Island. During the peak tourist season it looks like it's been set upon by giant rabbits – for two hours, at either side of low tide, you can dig your own hole in the sand with a spade rented from the local cafe, then sit back, relax and warm your behind in your own natural spa. Luckily your rapidly roasting limbs will be regularly refreshed by cool waves from the incoming seawater.

Hot Water Beach lies on the east coast of the beautiful Coromandel Peninsula, 12km southeast from the town of Whitianga.

272 LES BAINS DE MARRAKECH, MOROCCO

For a bathing experience that indulges all your *One Thousand and One Nights* fantasies – think glorious sunlit courtyards, tinkling fountains, carved alcoves and scattered rose petals – Les Bains de Marrakech is just the ticket. As well as the traditional *hammam* (bathhouse) experience, involving an unceremonious scrub-down with black soap and a wire mitten, you can choose from gentler options such as chocolate body massages or candlelit baths for two. In between treatments you're encouraged to sprawl out on an indecently comfortable pile of cushions and drink your own body weight in mint tea.

Rock the Kasbah – Les Bains (www .lesbainsdemarrakech.com) is snuggled away in the ancient medina, the historic heart of Marrakesh.

Dig your own personal spa pool at New Zealand's Hot Water Beach – DIY never felt so good

Soak and swim through steam clouds at the Blue Lagoon for the the quintessential Iceland experience

274 BEPPU, JAPAN

This town on the coast of Kyushu is associated in Japanese minds with one thing: hot springs. Millions of litres of steaming hot water spill daily out of around 3000 springs, providing a dazzling array of bath-time treats. On offer for your bathing pleasure are mammoth modern indoor spa complexes, small outdoor springs, simmering mud baths and even 'sand baths' where you can be buried up to your neck in hot sand by a lady with a shovel. When you're done getting wet, it's time to discover why Beppu is nicknamed the 'Las Vegas of Japan'.

Beppu is on the southwestern island of Kyushu, a six-hour train ride or 90-minute flight from Tokyo.

275 CHODOVAR BREWERY BEER BATHS, CZECH REPUBLIC

For the ultimate beer-on-skin experience, you can relax in the Czech Republic's first underground beer spa. Large stainless steel tubs (including tubs for two) are filled with a specially brewed bathing beer and crushed herbs and are topped off with a creamy foam 'head'. As you bubble away in all that malty goodness you can partake in a glass or two of the local brew from the bathside bar. Apparently it's all excellent for the pores.

The wonderfully named Beer Wellness Land (www.chodovar.cz) charges CZK600 for a 40-minute beer bath session.

276 SZECHENYI BATHS, HUNGARY

Budapest is a city famed for its thermal baths. Sample the city's bathing habits at the Szechenyi Baths – a meandering neo-baroque complex of pools, ranging from icy cold to steaming hot – in the middle of the city park. Originally a medical treatment centre, this is the place to come for a massage, a sauna and a dip in the huge open-air thermal pool filled with local families, tourists and gentlemen playing chess on floating boards.

Szechenyi (www.szechenyibath.com) comprises a full wellness centre with a range of holistic treatments, from fat-burning to physiotherapy and gymnastic programs.

FRANS LEMMENS / LONELY PLANET IMAGES

278 BLUE LAGOON, ICELAND

Iceland's answer to Disneyland and the country's number-one tourist attraction, the Blue Lagoon is sometimes dismissed as overcrowded and overpriced. But what's not to like about floating in a steaming pool of milky blue (at a spot-on 38°C), surrounded by a landscape of dark and twisted lava fields, with a futuristic geothermal plant puffing away in the background? When you're fed up of the main pools, you can have a steam bath in a lava cave, a waterfall massage or a sauna. You'll no doubt leave with your spirits renewed and baby-soft skin.

Conveniently located near Reykjavík and Keflavík International Airport, Blue Lagoon is one of Iceland's most accessible attractions (www .bluelagoon.com).

277 DOGO ONSEN, JAPAN

Japan's oldest hot springs facility at a rumoured 3000 years old, Dogo Onsen is at the centre of many a folk tale. Its centrepiece, the Honkan bathhouse, is the oldest public bathhouse in Japan. An intricate three-storey timber structure, it looks like a fairytale castle and is said to be the inspiration behind the enchanted bathhouse in Miyazaki's animated film *Spirited Away*. Splash out on a first-class ticket and you'll get a hot soak, your own relaxation room, a *yukata* (kimono) and a post-bath snack of green tea and crackers.

The onsen is in Matsuyama, Shikoku, and can be reached by the regular tram service, which terminates at the start of the spa's shopping arcade.

279 VINOTHERAPY, FRANCE

Being rubbed with grape seeds, slathered in honey, oil and wine yeast and submerged up to the neck in a wine-casket bath might sound like a hedonistic Roman orgy but it is, in fact, vinotherapy – a spa treatment to be had at Les Sources de Caudalie in Bordeaux using grape extracts. It seems that bathing in the stuff rather than drinking it is one of the best beauty treatments, with the power (apparently) to reduce wrinkles, stress and even cellulite. Les Sources is set in a vineyard, so you can also ingest your grapes the traditional way with a glass or two.

A half-day treatment including a red wine soak costs a cool €210 – strictly no sipping the bathwater (www.sources -caudalie.com).

280 DEAD SEA, ISRAEL/ JORDAN

King Solomon, Cleopatra and the Queen of Sheba were among the early believers in the benefits of a Dead Sea spa, one of the world's first health resorts owing to the medicinal properties of the area's waters and minerals. Since then, the climate has inspired a huge array of therapies such as thalassotherapy (bathing in Dead Sea water) and balneotherapy (a treatment using the black mineral mud of the Dead Sea). There are resorts on both the Israeli and Jordanian sides, offering health packages to cure everything from psoriasis to arthritis.

If you don't want to pay big-ticket resort prices, then hit one of the beaches. Israel's Ein Gedi is among the best.

BEST BATHS

MOST INTRIGUING CLOCKS & CALENDARS

The humble wristwatch ain't the only way to keep an eye on the time. Check out these chronological contraptions.

As complex and as beautiful as the planets themselves: Prague's astronomical clock

281 HORNSBY WATER CLOCK, AUSTRALIA

Is it a fountain? Is it art? It is a water wheel? Is it a public abomination? Not everyone agrees on this one-man-band of a timepiece, but one thing's for certain – you can set your watch by it. Officially titled *Man, Time and the Environment*, the clock, unveiled in 1930, is a kinetic sculpture made by Victor Cusack. Figures representing Aboriginal history and local fauna cluster over it; the edges of the fountain are marked with Roman numerals, which are swept past by a water-operated hand. For good measure there's also three water-powered clocks in the Greek, Chinese and Swiss styles, not to mention a carillon that sings the hour.

The water clock is in the Hornsby Mall in Florence Street. Hornsby is about 25km north of Sydney.

283 CLOCK TOWER, SIGHIŞOARA, ROMANIA

The medieval citadel town of Sighişoara is famous for being the birthplace of Vlad Ţepeş, the historical Dracula, and tracking down some gory lore is the main game for most of its visitors. But some travellers allow themselves to be distracted by the clock tower and its pageant of automated characters. The tower in itself is quite impressive: it used to be the main entrance to the fortified city, and from its 64m height you'll get the best views in town. The clock dates from 1648 and its cavalcade of figures (Peace with an olive branch, Justice with scales, Law with a sword) are carved from linden wood. The executioner is also present and the drum-player strikes the hour.

Want to call it a night? Try the restored Casa cu Cerb (www.casacucerb.ro). Hey, it was good enough for Prince Charles.

284 'GILT COPPER CLOCK WITH A ROBOT WRITING CHINESE CHARACTERS WITH A BRUSH', BEIJING, CHINA

The name sounds like sci-fi, huh? But the reality is altogether more courtly – this is a robot of the old school, with plenty of old-world charm. The clock dates from the 18th century and lives in the Clock Exhibition Hall of the Forbidden City, along with a host of other elaborate and ingenious timepieces, mostly gifts to the Qing emperors from foreign parts. The robot, bewigged and dressed in 18th-century fashion, sits at a gilt chair and writes the eight characters that form the auspicious phrase 'boundless longevity'. Two more automatons display the scroll. Take a bow, ye olde robot!

Try to get to the Exhibition Hall at 11am or 2pm, when the clocks are set in motion.

282 ASTRONOMICAL CLOCK, PRAGUE, CZECH REPUBLIC

Why are all those tourists gathering at the foot of the Old Town Hall? They're waiting for the city's most famous clock to do its thing, that's why. The clock is a centuries-old, intricate system of interlocking time devices, showing the movement of the planets, the seasons, the moon and the zodiac. But what makes it popular are the animated figures that move on the hour. Its four external figures are Vanity (looking in his mirror), Death (a skeleton tolling a bell), a Jewish miser holding a bag of gold, and an Infidel (a turbaned Turk). You'll also see a parade of the Twelve Apostles.

The clock puts on its hourly show between 9am and 9pm daily; it's found in Prague's Old Town Square.

285 CARILLON, LA CHAUX-DE-FONDS, SWITZERLAND

The carillon stands outside the International Watchmaking Museum in the watchmaking city of La Chaux-de-Fonds, near the French border. Just in case you lose track of the time, the carillon is here to help. Every quarter-hour it comes up with a different musical chime, accompanying it with a hypnotic rippling of coloured metal. Its songs and colours change with the season. And because this is Switzerland, it also has a solidly housed digital clock that's accurate to within a 100th of a second, of course.

To get to La Chaux-de-Fonds, take a train to Neuchâtel; trains run from all major Swiss cities and there's a regional train.

286 JANTAR MANTAR, DELHI, INDIA

Wandering around this astronomical observatory is a little like being in an abstract sculpture exhibition. The function of these monumental instruments may be obscure to most of today's visitors, but they make an impressive display, especially the Samrat Yantra, a giant triangular sundial that points toward the North Pole. The observatory is one of five constructed in the early 18th century by Jai Singh, a maharaja of Jaipur. The stone and marble instruments still work; their functions range from measuring time to predicting the coming of the monsoon. They also make a splendid backdrop for photographs.

Jantar Mantar is located in New Delhi and is open daily from 9am until sunset.

287 CHICHÉN ITZÁ, YUCATAN, MEXICO

At Chichén Itzá you'll find the world's most famous Maya ruins, a ceremonial hub featuring the characteristic step pyramids, altars, a steam bath, ball courts and 'time temples'. The Maya had a complex understanding of celestial bodies and the seasons, and some of the buildings at Chichén Itzá have a calendar function. The most famous and spectacular of these is the towering 'El Castillo', or Kukulkan Pyramid. At the vernal and autumnal equinoxes the sun hits the pyramid in such a way as to cause a shadowy illusion of a serpent crawling down to join the carved stone snake's head at the bottom.

If you can't get to Chichén Itzá for the equinox, don't despair – a sound-and-light show recreates the effect throughout the year.

288 SUNDIAL BRIDGE, CALIFORNIA, USA

This futuristic structure was conceived by Spanish architect Santiago Calatrava, who also came up with the design for the Athens Olympic Stadium. The bridge spans the Sacramento River and leads into the Turtle Bay Exploration Park. It's quite the engineering marvel, a freestanding structure of pylons and cables that has no supports in the water (and thus manages to avoid the salmon spawning habitat). The 66m-high support tower, a radiant white blade that looks like it's leaning back against the weight of the bridge, also functions as a giant sundial. But don't leave your watch at home: the sundial is only accurate once a year, at the summer solstice.

The Turtle Bay Exploration Park is in Redding, California. Take Interstate 5 and turn off at the Central Redding Exit 678.

289 JENS OLSEN CLOCK, COPENHAGEN, DENMARK

This can-do clock has so many functions you almost expect it to make you a cup of tea. And it's quite a looker, to boot. Up a 105m clock tower at the top of city hall, it's a series of delicate gold cogs housed in a vitrine. It was the brainchild of Jens Olsen, a locksmith-turned-watchmaker and astronomical enthusiast. The clock, which is mechanical and has to be wound once a week, was 50 years in the making and displays solar, local and sidereal time, sunrises and sunsets, firmament and celestial

It's stunning, sure, but how do you tell the time? Incredible instruments on display at Delhi's Jantar Mantar observatory

pole migration, planet revolutions, the Gregorian calendar and even changing holidays such as Easter.

The Rathaus City Hall is open from 8.30am to 4.30pm Monday through Friday, and from 10am to 1pm on Saturday.

GREENWICH MERIDIAN, LONDON, ENGLAND

Greenwich Mean Time just doesn't get any meaner than this. Although it's all very arbitrary, there's something about being at the spot where two hemispheres meet – it's the ultimate east-meets-west. The meridian is the line that divides the eastern from the western hemisphere, and in the Meridian Courtyard of the Royal Observatory you can put a foot on either side of it for that king-of-the-world, globe-straddling feeling. Or maybe you're a quieter type and just want to see the red time ball drop from the top of the Observatory at 1pm, as it has since 1833.

The ultimate way to experience the Observatory is on the Meridian Line. For the lowdown on meridian events, visit www.rmg.co.uk/royal-observatory.

MOST INTRIGUING CLOCKS & CALENDARS

TOP WWI SIGHTS

The Great War: 28 July 1914 to 11 November 1918. Sixteen million dead, 22 million injured and a continent destroyed by the most appalling fighting. Here are some of the most poignant reminders.

291 WILFRED OWEN'S GRAVE, ORS COMMUNAL CEMETERY, ORS, FRANCE

Wilfred Owen was a British poet and one of WWI's most celebrated voices. Owen enlisted in October 1915, and his work was heavily influenced both by battlefield trauma and the writing of his friend, Siegfried Sassoon. His pathos-laden poems are synonymous with the horror of war and regarded as the finest records of first-hand experience – 'Anthem for Doomed Youth' is among the most famous. Owen was tragically killed one week before Armistice Day – the telegram informing his mother was delivered amid victory celebrations – and his grave can be found in the cemetery at Ors, where the simple white headstone stands among those of fallen comrades.

The village of Ors is on the road between Le Cateau and Landrecies, 85km southeast of Lille and most easily reached by car.

292 TRENCH OF DEATH, DIKSMUIDE, BELGIUM

The Western Front comprised a trench network covering thousands of kilometres, extending southeast from Nieuwpoort on the Belgian coast to the French border with Switzerland. Bitterly cold, waterlogged and thick with mud, the trenches offered soldiers precious little protection, yet formed a vital link with the reserve cantonments behind the front line. Few trenches remain today but in the Belgian countryside, near the town of Diksmuide, one small section known as the 'Trench of Death' has been preserved. The conservation work and tidy maintenance make it hard to appreciate the grim conditions, but this remains a unique example of life in the battlefield.

The Trench of Death is 1.5km from the centre of Diksmuide, 45km southwest of Bruges, which makes a good base for exploring other battlefields and cemeteries in the area.

293 ARMISTICE GLADE, RETHONDES, FRANCE

11 November 1918; the end of the Great War. After four long years, and with Europe on its knees, Germany accepted the armistice conditions proposed by the Allies. Under the command of Marshal Ferdinand Foch of the French army, the selected congressmen assembled to sign the treaty. The location Foch chose was the carriage of his own personal train, secluded in the tranquil forest of Compiègne. Today the forest hides a glade with a war memorial, under the gaze of a statue of Foch. Alongside lies a reconstruction of the Armistice Carriage – the original was seized by Nazi troops during WWII and destroyed in 1945.

The Armistice Glade is situated on route D546, between Rethondes and Compiègne, just 80km northwest of the centre of Paris. SNCF (www.sncf.com) run trains from Paris' Gare du Nord to Compiègne.

In 1914, a world-altering shot was fired on this historic Ottoman-era bridge in Sarajevo

294 GALLIPOLI, TURKEY

Away from the front lines of northern Europe, some of the fiercest fighting occurred at Gallipoli. This bloody eight-month campaign proved disastrous for Allied forces – some 34,000 Brits, Aussies and Kiwis perished here. The Gallipoli peninsula is 240km southwest of İstanbul, flanked by the Aegean Sea on one side and the Dardanelles channel to the other. The Allied plan was simple – send a flotilla up the Dardanelles to seize control of İstanbul and open a naval passage to Russia. The reality was very different, as Ottoman troops provided unflinching resistance.

İstanbul-based Trooper Tours (www .troopertours.com) will take you around the key sites in Gallipoli; tours run from one day up to nine days.

295 LATIN BRIDGE, SARAJEVO, BOSNIA & HERCEGOVINA

When Archduke Franz Ferdinand of Austria was assassinated in Sarajevo on 28 June 1914, few would have imagined the carnage that would follow. Targeted by a revolutionary movement known as Young Bosnia, Ferdinand's death was the catalyst that led Austria-Hungary to declare war on Serbia. Germany, allied to Austria-Hungary, would soon join the fold. The spot of Ferdinand's death was close to the Latin Bridge in the heart of the city and a small plaque commemorates the event. There's no fuss and precious little pomp, but for budding historians a visit here forms part of the ultimate WWI pilgrimage.

Sarajevo is one of Europe's up-and-coming cities, so combine your history fix with top shopping and entertainment; the summer months of June to August offer pleasant temperatures.

111

296 TYNE COT CEMETERY, ZONNEBEKE, BELGIUM

Of all the Commonwealth cemeteries marking the fallen heroes of WWI, Tyne Cot is the largest, containing 11,954 graves of soldiers from the UK, Canada, Australia, New Zealand, South Africa and the West Indies; 8367 of the plots are unnamed. The cemetery also carries the names of a further 35,000 soldiers who were never found. At the centre of the graves, the traditional Commonwealth Cross of Sacrifice stands atop a German pillbox, overlooking row upon row of uniform white headstones. There's no more evocative or powerful introduction to the sorrow of war.

Zonnebeke is 75km south of Bruges. Combine a visit to Tyne Cot with a trip to the Memorial Museum Passchendaele 1917 (www .passchendaele.be), located in a converted mansion in Zonnebeke.

297 POPPY FIELDS, FLANDERS, BELGIUM

'In Flanders fields the poppies blow; between the crosses, row on row…' From probably the most celebrated of the WWI poems, these beautifully evocative opening lines were penned by a Canadian Lieutenant Colonel, John McCrae, in homage to a lost friend. As war ravaged the countryside and churned the earth, the disturbance stimulated the growth of poppies; they illuminated the countryside and have since become the defining image of remembrance to the dead. The poppies still bloom each year, providing nature's own homage to the bravery of those who made the greatest sacrifice.

Poppies are in bloom on most of the Western Front battlefields from April to early July, but unseasonal weather can affect their growth.

298 LOCHNAGAR CRATER, LA BOISSELLE, FRANCE

The Battle of the Somme was one of WWI's defining battles; five months long and more than one million dead. Yet few know that its roots lay deep beneath the battlefield. British forces explored all avenues in their attempt to outfox the Germans and started the offensive by blowing them up from below. Tunnelling teams rabbited under enemy positions, laying 10 monumental mines that were detonated simultaneously. Stuffed with 28.8 tonnes of explosives, the assault gave Allied forces an early advantage in the battle for strategic territory. Lochnagar's huge crater – 90m across and 30m deep – can still be seen today.

The Lochnagar Crater is south of the village of La Boisselle, 155km north of Paris. From the village, follow the signs for the aptly named 'La Grande Mine'.

299 MENIN GATE MEMORIAL, IEPER, BELGIUM

The battlefields around Ypres saw appalling conflict and many men were lost here, never to be found. At the eastern end of town stands Menin Gate, a soaring memorial to more than 54,000 of the soldiers whose final resting place remains unknown. Every evening, the road beneath the arch is closed to traffic and buglers from the local fire brigade sound the Last Post, the haunting commemoration to soldiers lost in war. On summer evenings the event draws large crowds who stand silent in

DENNIS JOHNSON / LONELY PLANET IMAGES

Pay your respects to the fallen among the ordered headstones of Belgium's Tyne Cot cemetery.

remembrance; in winter, cold, bleak and windswept, the bugle notes drift away unheard.

Ypres is now known by its Flemish name of Ieper. Menin Gate is at the edge of the city centre, close to the marketplace; the Last Post is sounded at 8pm.

300 CHRISTMAS TRUCE MEMORIAL, FRELINGHIEN, FRANCE

Amid the horror of front-line fighting, stories of simple humanity have become legend; none more so than the Christmas Truce of 1914.

With the war still in its infancy, hundreds of Allied and German soldiers fighting near the French town of Frelinghien downed their guns on Christmas Day and engaged in a remarkable truce. Official records are sketchy but the most famous story recollects a football match on the battlefield – nobody has been able to corroborate this, but sufficient evidence of the truce exists for the event to be marked with a memorial plaque in the village.

Frelinghien is 90km southwest of Calais; combine it with a visit to Ieper, 15km to the north. The memorial is in the public park at the edge of the village.

TOP WWI SITES

TOP ORNITHOLOGICAL SIGHTS

Modern-day shooting parties armed with cameras and binoculars flock to these birdwatching hot spots.

301 PARROTS & FRIENDS, QUEENSLAND, AUSTRALIA

Australia's isolation has seen some unusual birds evolve, along with the continent's peculiar animals. The laughing kookaburra really does sound like it's laughing, while the spectacular-tailed lyrebird sounds like any bird or other sound it chooses to mimic – in touristed areas it can often make a camera shutter sound. Then there are bowerbirds, which compete for female attention by creating towering nests from pretty shiny things; the flightless emu – the world's second-largest bird after the ostrich; and a seemingly endless array of brilliantly coloured parrots. These birds can be seen all over the country, but one place you're sure to encounter them all is Currumbin Wildlife Sanctuary in Queensland, where flocks of friendly lorikeets are a hallmark attraction.

Currumbin Wildlife Sanctuary (www.cws .org.au) is on the Gold Coast.

302 PENGUINS, ANTARCTICA

Vast icy landscapes of haunting beauty are one drawcard for travellers; penguins, the symbol of Antarctica, are definitely another. With their comical waddle, social nature and will to live in the most inhospitable terrain on earth, penguins capture the imagination. Because of the scarcity of people, quiet observers may find themselves approached by curious birds. The four main species are the Adélie, chinstrap, gentoo and emperor, and they number literally in the millions. Emperor penguins are known for their valiant breeding cycle, marching miles from the ocean to their ancestral breeding grounds, enduring bitter winters huddled together there to incubate their eggs, then making the arduous journey back again to finally feed.

Penguins will be a feature of all tours. The International Association of Antarctica Tour Operators website (www.iaato.org) provides lots of contact information.

303 ALBATROSS, OTAGO PENINSULA, NEW ZEALAND

Here at one of NZ's hottest attractions the drawcard is the birdlife. Taiaroa Head is the site of the world's only mainland royal albatross breeding ground, where you can observe the spectacle of albatrosses with wingspans of up to 3m coming in to land like a succession of 747s. Stewart Island is the best place to see the much-loved but very shy national icon, the kiwi, a flightless fluffy brown ball. The island is also home to rare penguins, the endangered yellow-eyed penguins, named for their yellow feathered eye masks.

The Royal Albatross Centre at Taiaroa Head is open daily and offers various tours as well as colony viewing. Bookings are essential: 03 478 0499.

304 HUMMINGBIRDS, THE PANTANAL, BRAZIL

A major destination for birdwatching trips, the Pantanal is home to more bird species than all of North America. In this wetland region birds fly in flocks of thousands and six different species may nest on a single branch. The biggest Brazilian bird is also found here – the flightless rhea, which resembles a small ostrich. The smallest birds are the numerous types of hummingbird. These little birds, with their dazzling iridescent colours, may be seen all over the country. They flit rapidly from one spot to the next, and can even fly backwards. The Brazilian name for them is *beija-flor* (flower-kisser).

You can arrange guided tours (or head off on your own) from the gateway towns of Cuiabá, Corumbá and Campo Grande. Reservations are needed for all accommodation in July.

305 TOUCANS, ECUADOR

Like Brazil, Ecuador has a huge diversity of birdlife – over 1500 species. Among the best known and most colourful groups are toucans, which have huge rainbow-coloured beaks, sometimes as long as their bodies, enabling them to reach berries at the end of branches. Toucans live at forest treetop level and are often best seen from boats. Also at home in the rainforest canopy are macaws, particularly the blue-and-yellow variety. These large parrots' clumsy antics and raucous music provide plenty of entertainment while exploring the jungle around the headwaters of the Amazon River.

The riverside town of Tena is a natural jumping-off spot for rafting; many tour operators can be found on Avenida 15 de Noviembre.

306 WATERBIRDS, DANUBE DELTA, ROMANIA

If you want to go birdwatching in Europe, word is that the Danube delta is the place to go. This network of channels, lagoons, reed islands, woods and pastures on the Black Sea coast, though sadly depleted by the activities of humans, remains a natural wonderland. Ornithological highlights include thousands of pelicans, herons, ibis, ducks, warblers and white-tailed eagles, but the real appeal of the region is the proximity you can get to them. Areas of the wetlands are only accessible by kayak or rowboat, from where you can watch the wildlife a mere arm's length away.

The visitor permit required to enter the Danube Delta Biosphere Reserve can be purchased from travel agencies and hotels in the gateway town of Tulcea (for around US$4).

307 BALD EAGLE, ALASKA, USA

Much like great cats, birds of prey command respect and are always an object of fascination. One of the most sought-after birds to sight is America's emblematic bald eagle. Living atop lofty mountains and soaring to heights of 3000m, they represent freedom, the nation's highest value. These magnificent raptors with their white heads and tails can be found in every state except Hawaii, but are most prevalent on the northwest coast. The best place to see them in large numbers is on the Chilkat River in Alaska from October to December, when they gather for the annual salmon run.

Chilkat Bald Eagle Preserve has excellent eagle-viewing areas about 30km from Haines along the Haines Highway.

308 BIG SIX, KRUGER NATIONAL PARK, SOUTH AFRICA

Kruger is the place to spot South Africa's 'big six' birds. They are the southern ground hornbill, Pel's fishing owl, lappet-faced vulture, saddle-billed stork, martial eagle and the kori bustard. Although not the most beautiful of creatures (particularly the vulture), they are mostly easy to spot, and all are large and impressive. Just as thrilling for the traveller are the ostriches, often seen streaking across the savannah, and the common-as-muck but oh-so-beautiful glossy starling, a shimmering jewel-like iridescent blue.

There are safaris and accommodation options for all budgets at Kruger; the northern section, particularly around the Luvuvhu River, is the best area to spot the birds.

309 BIRDS OF PARADISE, PAPUA NEW GUINEA

This archipelago has much wonderful natural habitat still intact. The stars of the show are the fantastical birds of paradise, of which there are more than 40 species, all individually bizarre. With brilliant colours and showy, sweeping plumes, they engage in dazzling courtship displays, jumping, carolling and opening their feathers like Chinese fans. Another well-known character is the cassowary, a large flightless bird that has a horny casque on its head to help it crash through the thick rainforest, as well as a fiercely sharp middle toe that gives it a (probably exaggerated) reputation as the world's most dangerous bird.

Varirata National Park is one of the top birdwatching sites. It's an easy drive along the Sogeri road from Port Moresby.

310 FLAMINGOS, RIFT VALLEY, KENYA

You're sure to have seen this image before (it's part of the lovely flight scene from *Out of Africa*, for example): a flock of flamingos like a swirling drift of pink petals covering a lake. But seeing it in the flesh is one of those spine-tingling moments that stay with you forever. The noise is raucous. Up close, the elegant birds are almost comical, performing their elaborate, synchronised courtship dance. The lake in question is Kenya's Lake Nakuru, but sadly, for reasons that aren't quite certain, the numbers of flamingos returning to the lake is dropping each year. It's worth catching while you can.

Lake Nakuru National Park is 2km south of the centre of Nakuru. There is a large public campsite just inside the main gate (adult/child US$10/5).

BEST MUSIC PILGRIMAGE SIGHTS

Choose the perfect soundtrack to accompany these toe-tapping musical pilgrimages, and pay homage to iconic voices, venues and seriously rockin' tunes.

313 ABBEY ROAD, LONDON, ENGLAND

As well as a recording studio of note (at number 3), Abbey Road houses quite possibly the most famous zebra crossing in the world. It was at this studio in leafy north London that the Beatles recorded their 1969 album, *Abbey Road* – acclaimed by many as their best. The cover shot of the band crossing the road out the front of the studios is instantly recognisable, and was taken by a photographer friend in a shoot lasting 15 minutes (while a policeman held up traffic). These days, fans snatch at any gaps in the passing traffic to recreate the shoot.

Abbey Road is in St John's Wood, London NW8. The studio is a five- to 10-minute walk from the St John's Wood tube station on the Jubilee line.

311 GRACELAND, MEMPHIS, TENNESSEE, USA

In a city packed with musical sights, Graceland is the king. In the spring of 1957, at age 22, Elvis Presley spent US$100,000 on this house, and he lived here until his death in 1977 – he's buried next to the swimming pool along with his closest relatives. Elvis had the place redecorated in 1974, and it's a virtual textbook of '70s style, baby. Behind the white-columned facade you'll find a retro-cool, yellow-and-blue media room, avocado-green kitchen appliances, and the fake waterfall and green shag-carpet ceiling in the awesomely kitsch Jungle Room. But wait, there's more: jumpsuits, memorabilia, cars, even Elvis' planes. Thankyouverymuch.

While in Memphis, Sun Studios (www.sunstudio.com) is another music legend must-see. If too much Elvis is never enough, stay at (where else?) the Heartbreak Hotel (www.heartbreak hotel.net).

312 PÈRE LACHAISE CEMETERY, PARIS, FRANCE

The world's most opulent (and visited) cemetery, this enormous necropolis contains the mortal remains of some 800,000 people. Their names read like a Who's Who of French history and the arts – Balzac, Proust, Delacroix, Pissarro, Piaf – but the most venerated tomb belongs to Doors rock-god, Jim Morrison, who died in Paris in 1971. Prior to complaints from Morrison's family, pilgrim traditions included fans drinking, taking drugs and having sex atop Jim's grave. There's now a permanent security guard and code-of-conduct leaflet, making you wonder whether Jim is looking on and finding the new arrangements rather lame.

Morrison's grave is in Division 6; maps locating noteworthy graves are posted around the cemetery, but it's worth purchasing a detailed map from one of the nearby newsstands.

314 MOTOWN HISTORICAL MUSEUM, DETROIT, MICHIGAN, USA

The Motown Museum is a string of unassuming houses that became known as 'Hitsville USA' after Berry Gordy launched Motown Records here in 1959 with a US$800 loan. The 'Motown Sound' was soul music with a distinct pop influence, and stars that rose from the label include Stevie Wonder, Diana Ross, Marvin Gaye, Gladys Knight and Michael Jackson. Gordy and Motown split for the glitz of Los Angeles in 1972, but you can still step into humble Studio A and see where the Four Tops and Smokey Robinson recorded their first hits.

In recent years, it's been rap, techno and hard-edged rock that have pushed Detroit to the forefront of the music scene, with homegrown artists including the White Stripes and Eminem.

315 COUNTRY MUSIC HALL OF FAME & MUSEUM, NASHVILLE, TENNESSEE, USA

For country-music fans all over the world, a trip to Nashville is the ultimate homage, a nod to the musicians that taught us how to bleed through our hearts and see the beauty in the simple, while creating a song out of an empty bottle of booze. The Hall of Fame and Museum is a monumental and worthwhile hats-off to the city and its country-music history. It's chock-full of artefacts like Elvis' gold Cadillac, Gene Autry's string tie and the handwritten lyrics to 'Mammas Don't Let Your Babies Grow Up to Be Cowboys'. Everything's state-of-the-art, and touchscreens allow access to recordings and photos from the Country Music Foundation's enormous archives.

No music-lover's trip to Nashville is complete without a night at the Grand Ole Opry (www.opry.com), a country-music stage concert held every Friday and Saturday night year-round.

117

Gold records at Nashville's Country Music Hall of Fame & Museum

The Beatles – bow legged stances, silly jackets and all – preserved for the ages at Hamburg's very own shrine to Beatlemania

316 PRESERVATION HALL, NEW ORLEANS, LOUISIANA, USA

The 'Big Easy' is front-runner for the title of most musical city in the USA. It birthed blues, jazz and brass bands, and every pop movement that's been built on them. A veritable museum of traditional and Dixieland jazz, Preservation Hall is a New Orleans pilgrimage – but like many religious obligations, it ain't necessarily easy, with no air-con, limited seating and no refreshments. Still, with white-haired grandpas on tubas, trombones and cornets raising the roof every night, it's worth the discomfort of sitting on the floor for an entire set. 'When the Saints Go Marching In' is a guaranteed goose-bump moment.

Preservation Hall has affordable shows nightly from 8pm – get in line early to snag a good seat, or book one of the *very* limited VIP seats at www.preservationhall .com/tickets.

317 BEATLEMANIA, HAMBURG, GERMANY

Beatlemaniacs will have surely ticked off the sights of Liverpool, but how about Hamburg? In the swinging '60s, the Beatles cut their musical teeth in the German city – John Lennon once said 'I might have been born in Liverpool, but I grew up in Hamburg.' You can take a slightly surreal journey through the band's career at the five-floor Beatlemania museum, full of entertaining interactive exhibits (including recreated Abbey Road Studios) and rare memorabilia (such as the Beatles' first recording contract, which was signed in Hamburg). It also stages concerts and fashion shows; look for the giant yellow submarine bulging from the building's facade.

While in Hamburg, check out the Beatles-Platz (square), designed like a vinyl record. It's at the intersection of the famous Reeperbahn and Grosse Freiheit.

318 APOLLO THEATER, NEW YORK, USA

The Apollo Theater has been Harlem's leading space for concerts and political rallies since 1914. Virtually every black artist of note in the 1930s and '40s performed here, including Duke Ellington and Charlie Parker. After a recent renovation, the Apollo's interior is more beautiful than ever: gold sconces and balconies and plush red seats. Its famous weekly Amateur Night, 'where stars are born and legends are made', still takes place on Wednesdays, with a wild and ruthless crowd that's as fun to watch as the performers. Previous Amateur Night winners include luminaries such as Ella Fitzgerald, Billie Holiday, James Brown and even Jimi Hendrix.

From the Apollo, you're not far away from the famed soul-food fixins of Sylvia's at 328 Lenox Avenue.

319 CLARENCE HOTEL, DUBLIN, IRELAND

When in Dublin, U2 fans make a beeline for this boutique hotel, owned by Bono and The Edge. They were regulars in the bar here back in the day, so when the hotel was up for sale in the 1990s, they decided to invest in its restoration, turning it into the sort of place they'd like to stay in now they've become rich and more discerning. Fans looking for band memorabilia (and/or a celeb sighting) may be disappointed, but there are other reasons to linger, not least the Tea Room (actually an upmarket restaurant) and the cocktails in the cosy Octagon Bar.

The Clarence is in Temple Bar, the city's party district, so you'll have no problem finding drinking dens in which to whet your whistle and enjoy some local *craic* (good times).

320 THE CROCODILE, SEATTLE, WASHINGTON, USA

For many, Seattle equals grunge (aka the 'Seattle sound'). A guitar-and angst-driven derivative of punk, grunge grew out of garage rock, where slacker dudes with nothing else to do jammed in their garages. And then in the early 1990s, grunge exploded onto the international scene, and live-music venue Crocodile Café was at its epicentre. The club's stage showcased virtually every important Seattle band during the grunge years (and there were many, including Soundgarden, Pearl Jam, Mudhoney and the big kahunas, Nirvana). After its shock closure and reopening in 2009, it continues to rank as one of the best rock clubs in the country.

Check out forthcoming gigs at the venue's website, www.thecrocodile.com. Stop by the Back Bar for a slice of wood-fired pizza.

BEST MUSIC PILGRIMAGE SIGHTS

MOST BREATHTAKING VIEWING PLATFORMS

Not for those prone to vertigo – these lofty lookouts give epic views of falls, forests and fjords.

321 PULPIT ROCK, NORWAY

Sometimes it's best to leave it to nature. While glass floors and skyscrapers can be impressive, in Norway it's a mighty lump of stone that offers the best outlook. Preikestolen – Pulpit Rock – looms 604m above Lysefjord, one of myriad incisions along Norway's west coast. There are mountains aplenty hereabouts, but this summit seems built for purpose: its almost perfectly flat top juts out over the water (no safety barriers here), commanding uninterrupted if vertiginous views. Scarier still, peer down the cracks in Preikestolen's surface – caused by 10,000 years of glacial action – and hope no new ones form just then…

It's a two-hour hike (one way) from the road to Pulpit Rock, best done from April to September. For info, see www.ryfylke.com.

322 SKY TOWER, AUCKLAND, NEW ZEALAND

In a land renowned for natural wonders, it's a humanmade site that provides the best – or, at least, most terrifying – views. At 328m, Auckland's Sky Tower is the country's tallest building. And this being New Zealand (where there has to be a way to jump off, into or under everything for 'fun') they can't just leave it at that. A handful of high-adrenalin options are available, 192m up: gaze out from the enclosed glass rotunda; don a harness to walk a dizzying lap outside; or plunge (with safety wire) at 85km/h to the plaza below – less lookout than leap-off.

The Sky Tower (www.skycityauckland.co.nz) is open from 8.30am to 10.30pm Sunday to Thursday, until 11.30pm Friday and Saturday. Basic admission is NZ$25; the SkyJump and SkyWalk cost extra.

323 ILLAWARRA FLY TREETOP WALK, AUSTRALIA

There's no better way to commune with the kookaburras, cockatoos and crimson rosellas – the Illawarra Fly Treetop Walk puts you in the canopy of Australia's temperate and tree-cloaked Southern Highlands.

Hovering 25m above the ground, between stands of eucalyptus, sassafras, blackwood and mulberry, this 500m-long platform gives the wingless a glimpse of the avian lifestyle. And the bird's-eye views are spectacular, from close-ups of tree-dwelling flora to sweeping panoramas of the surrounding escarpment, part of the country's grand Great Dividing Range. Climb up Knights Tower, 20m higher than the walkway itself, for an even loftier lookout.

On the second Saturday of every month the Illawarra Fly Treetop Walk (www .illawarrafly.com) opens from 6am to 9am for a sunrise experience; booking is essential.

There's not a great deal separating you from that stupendous view beyond Norway's Pulpit Rock

GRAEME CORNWALLIS / LONELY PLANET IMAGES

324 GRAND CANYON SKYWALK, ARIZONA, USA

Striking architectural achievement or environment-defacing monstrosity? Opened in 2007, the Grand Canyon Skywalk – a 20m-wide, glass-and-concrete horseshoe projecting out over a side canyon of Arizona's gorgeous gorge – doesn't sit well with purists who like their natural wonders just as that. The majority of the land-owning Hualapai Indian tribe are pleased, as their coffers are filled. And so are many visitors: the views from this cantilevered platform are undeniably breathtaking – not least due to the see-through floor, putting seemingly nothing but air between you and the red-rock depths hundreds of metres below.

The Skywalk (www.grandcanyonskywalk .com) is part of the Grand Canyon West development; entrance costs US$43.05 plus US$29.95 for the Skywalk.

325 KNIFE-EDGE POINT, VICTORIA FALLS, ZAMBIA

Noise – a relentless, violent roar. The pale arc of a rainbow. Spray like smoke, billowing into the air as if the river were actually on fire. Victoria Falls – known locally as Mosi-oa-Tunya – is the Zambezi's death plunge, the point at which the mighty river flings itself off a 100m-high basalt precipice to snake into gorges. Its scale is alarming, especially when witnessed from Knife-Edge Point. Walk over the footbridge to this sturdy buttress where – if the mist is being blown in the opposite direction – you can gaze at the falls and the churning abyss below.

March to April is peak flood season – the falls are in full flow, but spray can obstruct views; water levels are lowest in November and December.

326 WATERFALL TRAIL, IGUAÇU FALLS, BRAZIL

Bring a poncho: you *will* get wet. For this raised walkway, suspended above the river, delivers falls-fans right into the mighty rumble of Iguaçu – or so it feels when you're being sprayed and serenaded by around 1500 cubic metres of water a second. This South American cascade – a 3km-wide, 80m-high tumble of 275 separate falls, dripping in tiers through the jungle – is shared between Brazil and Argentina. And it's on the Brazilian side that the Waterfall Trail leads out to the viewpoint below the Garganta do Diabo (Devil's Throat) – Iguaçu at its most thunderous and spectacular.

Arrive early – photography on the Brazilian side is best in the morning; the park opens at 9am (www.cataratasdoiguacu.com.br).

327 IL BINOCOLO, MERANO, ITALY

Viewing platforms go self-referential in the Italian South Tyrol. Conceived by architect Matteo Thun as an addition to the already lovely gardens at Trauttmansdorff Castle, this lookout suspended over the trees resembles a pair of opera binoculars. And as binoculars should, it gives a fine focus to those who dare step out onto its transparent gantry: over the vineyards, orchards, rooftops and mountainsides around the sophisticated town of Merano. It's a grand garden to gaze over, too. Arranged around the neo-Gothic palace are swaths of rhododendrons, terraced water gardens, exotic palms, a house of bees and the world's oldest vine.

On selected evenings in June, July and August, Trauttmansdorff (www .trauttmansdorff.it) opens for Garden Nights, alfresco concerts in the grounds.

328 DACHSTEIN SKY WALK, AUSTRIA

Hang out over a heap of mountains – the glass-bottomed gantry jutting out from this 2700m massif in Austria offers 360-degree views across state lines *and* international borders: Slovenia's Triglav summits and the Czech Republic's Bohemian forests can be seen. If you can bear to look, that is – it's a dizzying prospect. And the wind and snow frequently flurry, making this an exposed, if exhilarating promontory. The journey up is even more hair-raising: the cablecar from the Türlwandhütte rises nearly 1000m to the Hunerkogel station, skimming the limestone cliff face (you can see every crack and crevice) by what feels like mere inches.

The Dachstein glacier enables year-round downhill and cross-country skiing; check weather and slope conditions at www .derdachstein.at.

Expect to be dazzled – and doused – by the Garganta do Diabo on the Brazilian side of the Iguaçu Falls

329 AIGUILLE DU MIDI, CHAMONIX, FRANCE

So close you could touch it: that's the sensation aroused when you're standing on the viewing platform of the Aiguille du Midi, with (on a clear day) the snow-smothered monster of Mont Blanc visible dead ahead. The Aiguille is no minnow itself – this spiky mountain rears up 3842m into the air. But it's a democratic peak: a two-part cablecar ride from the town of Chamonix below zips from valley bottom to the top – a 2800m altitude gain – in just 20 breathtaking minutes. This enables anyone with a head for heights to get intimate with the legendary massif – a perspective usually reserved for expert mountaineers.

The Aiguille is the starting point for some routes up Mont Blanc; paragliding is also possible, though not in July or August. See www.chamonix.com for more.

330 PETRONAS TOWERS SKYBRIDGE, KUALA LUMPUR, MALAYSIA

This viewing platform is perhaps better looked at, rather than from. The two-storey Skybridge linking the 41st and 42nd floors of the two Petronas Towers is an engineering marvel; with its huge supporting 'legs' it looks like the bolt holding the twin 452m-high skyscrapers together. At night it's even more impressive, when the entire complex glitters brighter than a Christmas tree. The view from the bridge, 170m up, is pretty good, too: the super-quick lift whizzes you up to see the green spaces of the Malaysian capital mingling with the other high-rises.

The Skybridge is closed Monday; the best place for a view of the Petronas Towers is the Menara KL tower.

MOST BREATHTAKING VIEWING PLATFORMS

WEIRDEST PLANTS

As you travel through life, don't forget to stop and smell the roses…or not. Some of these flora are, quite literally, breathtaking.

331 GIANT SEQUOIA (SEQUOIADENDRON GIGANTEUM), CALIFORNIA, USA

Giant sequoias are the planet's largest living things (by volume). You can pay your respects to the record holder, nicknamed General Sherman, in the Giant Forest of Sequoia National Park, California. Estimated to be more than 2000 years old, the General measures 83.8m tall and 31.3m in circumference at the base, which makes it neither the tallest (the accolade belongs to another species of sequoia, the coast redwood) or the thickest (many African baobabs have greater girths) – but it's probably one of the most impressive living things you'll ever see. Wandering through the grandeur of the Giant Forest and observing its scale is quite a humbling experience.

There is a choice of long or short hiking trails throughout the Giant Forest that take in the General as well as other notable trees, including the see-through Telescope Tree.

332 ROSE OF JERICHO (ANASTATICA HIEROCHUNTICA), MIDDLE EAST

The rose of Jericho (actually nothing like a rose) survives in the desert by curling up into a tight, dry ball and waiting for the next rainy season, when it revives and unfurls with the first raindrops. This curling up and drying out can occur repeatedly over many years, leading to its alternative name: the resurrection plant. This miraculous ability, together with its origins in the Holy Land, have given the rose of Jericho religious significance, and individual long-lived plants have been passed down through generations of families, stored in their dry state and brought out at special occasions for a brief comeback appearance. A bit like the Rolling Stones, really.

Good places to hunt for this plant are the barren plains around the Dead Sea and the canyons and wadis of the Negev Desert in Israel.

333 SQUIRTING CUCUMBER (ECBALLIUM AGRESTE), GREECE

The fun thing about this plant is that its fruit, which look like small bristly cucumbers, explode violently when ripe and squirt their juicy content and seeds a considerable distance. In the plant world this just about qualifies as fastest gun in the west. The liquid can cause skin irritation, but also has anti-inflammatory properties and is traditionally used to aid sinusitis. Squirting cucumbers grow in sandy and stony areas throughout Greece, Malta and Turkey – a good place to watch one go off is on the slopes of Mt Pelion in Thessaly, Greece.

Time your visit to Mt Pelion for August, when the plants are most active, and wander the ancient cobbled mule pathways connecting mountain and seaside villages.

334 WELWITSCHIA MIRABILIS, NAMIBIA

Resembling nothing so much as an alien life form in the Namibian desert, this plant is thought to be a living relic of the Jurassic era. Along with a short stem and roots, it consists of two leaves, which are the only leaves it ever grows – and never sheds – making it unique among plants. Long and leathery, the leaves continue to grow, spilling out onto the ground and getting torn and split over the years. And it can be many years – a *Welwitschia* plant is thought to live for between four and 15 centuries.

These are best spotted along the aptly named Welwitschia Drive in the Namib-Naukluft National Park. The other-worldly landscape makes a worthwhile day trip from Swakopmund.

335 RAFFLESIA (RAFFLESIA ARNOLDII), INDONESIA/MALAYSIA

This parasitic plant wins the title of world's biggest flower. In fact it's all flower, having no leaves, stem or roots. The huge, fleshy bloom, with its acne-like white spots, grows to over a metre across – and smells of putrefying roadkill. Seeing one in its natural habitat can be a challenge as they usually grow in steep, leech-infested jungle. Your best bet is the Batang Palupuh Nature Reserve, West Sumatra. In Malaysia, the Orang Asli people, who traditionally used the plant for healing after childbirth, now take tourists to see the blooms.

Flowers bloom from August to November. Batang Palupuh Nature Reserve is 16km north of Bukittinggi; local buses go to the nearby village of Palupuh, where guides can be hired.

337 TITAN ARUM (AMORPHOPHALLUS TITANUM), INDONESIA

Its Latin name means 'gigantic misshapen penis'. This more or less describes its appearance. Its local name is 'corpse flower', which more or less describes its smell. This delightful specimen has a central shaft that grows taller than a man and emits the scent of rotting meat to attract pollinating insects. It's native to the rainforests of Sumatra, but it only flowers in the wild once every couple of years so you may have to get yourself to the botanic gardens of Sydney, Bonn or Washington, DC, to see one in its full glory. Just don't forget your gas mask.

Flowerings of cultivated plants are usually big media events. Check the What's On page of the Sydney Royal Botanic Gardens website (www.rbgsyd.nsw.gov.au) for notices.

339 LIVING STONES (LITHOPS), SOUTH AFRICA/NAMIBIA

In southern Africa, especially in the Karoo desert, you might stumble over a strange-looking brown or grey stone with a split across the surface. On closer inspection this will turn out to be a succulent plant, which has evolved so well that it can be hard to distinguish from the sand and rocks of its surroundings. *Lithops* survive the harsh conditions by growing partly underground and devoting most of their size to water storage. In autumn and winter they suddenly shrug off their disguise and show their true nature by sprouting daisy-like flowers.

Scout for living stones at the Goegap Nature Reserve in South Africa's Namakwa region, which is famous for having 200 species of succulents and an extraordinary display of spring flowers.

336 MIRACLE FRUIT (SYNSEPALUM DULCIFICUM), WEST AFRICA

The red berries of this shrub, known in its native tropical West Africa as *taami*, *asaa*, or *ledidi*, are tasteless. However, they have the seemingly miraculous power of changing the taste of other foods eaten after them. Any acidic food, like lemon, lime or vinegar, suddenly tastes sweet. The berries contain a glycoprotein called miraculin, which in the presence of acid activates the tastebuds responsible for sweetness. A word of warning though: if you try miracle fruit, go easy on the acid, or you'll end up with a sore mouth and stomach.

This and other medicinal plants of Africa can be found at the Aburi Botanic Gardens in Ghana, an hour's minibus ride from the capital, Accra.

338 PITCHER PLANT (NEPENTHES RAJAH), SABAH, MALAYSIA

A plant that consumes frogs and small mammals sounds like something you don't want to stumble over in a dark Borneo jungle. In fact, the pitcher plant prefers to eat insects, and is generous enough to share its bounty. Monkeys drink rainwater from the plant's tube-like funnel, whose slippery sides are designed to catch small critters; and diving spiders attach a line to the lip of the cup, abseil down into the liquid and use a bubble of air as a scuba tank while they fish for prey.

This endangered species only grows wild in the highlands of Mt Kinabalu and neighbouring Mt Tambuyukon, both located in Kinabalu National Park in Sabah, Malaysia.

340 WOLFFIA GLOBOSA, THAILAND

Unlike a camel, a single one of these tiny round green blobs could easily pass through the eye of a needle. Hundreds of them will fit on your fingertip. This is the world's smallest plant. It can be found floating in slow-moving streams and ponds throughout the tropics. In Thailand it's known as *khai-nam* (water eggs) and has been harvested as a vegetable for generations. *Khai-nam* looks like a dark green dip, and is a good source of protein.

Look for *khai-nam* among the tropical bounty in the fresh-food markets of Chiang Mai, such as Talat Thanin (off Thanon Chang Pheuak).

MOST MARVELLOUS MONASTERIES & CONVENTS

Find your spiritual side in cities and on mountains at these global retreats.

Climb the stairway to heaven – or, in this case, to Bhutan's most famous monastery, the breathtaking Tiger's Nest

341 SANTA CATALINA, AREQUIPA, PERU

The nuns once had it good in Santa Catalina. This elegant Mudéjar-style convent was founded in 1580 by a wealthy widow who accepted only upper-class nuns – with servants. A strict sister put a stop to all that in the 1870s, and in 1970 the Peruvian government declared tourists could nose inside. Now there are far more visitors than holy ladies scurrying about this walled citadel; the remaining 30-or-so nuns reside in one corner, while the pastel-painted alleys, flower-filled courtyards, secret staircases, even the Silence Yard where sisters would sit and pray the rosary, are open to all.

Santa Catalina (www.santacatalina.org .pe) is open daily from 9am to 5pm; it has a small cafe serving snacks and pastries.

342 SELIME, CAPPADOCIA, TURKEY

The lush Ihlara Valley harbours around 60 Byzantine chapels, churches and monasteries – you just can't see most of them. Because here in Cappadocia the volcanic tuff is so soft it was once easier to build dwellings into it than on it. The locals became troglodytes – including the monks of Selime, who lived in its underground network of dorms, kitchens, stables and a cathedral. When it was first hollowed out in the 13th century, bright frescos adorned the walls; today, little decoration remains. But it's still an atmospheric experience to enter this cave complex, before emerging, blinking, to admire the weird rock-valley views outside.

The Ihlara Valley is 16km long; the walk from Ihlara village (southern end) to Selime (northern end) takes seven to eight hours.

343 MONTSERRAT, SPAIN

Ascend a mountain, meet an icon – that's why people come to Montserrat, an 1230m outcrop 40km from Barcelona. Up here lives La Moreneta, a small black Virgin statue that, it's claimed, cannot be moved: a past bishop tried, but she wouldn't be budged. So instead they built a chapel to house her here, which has grown over the years into the Montserrat Monastery – a complex incorporating a museum, a hotel, even a post office. But it's the Basilica everyone beelines for, to kiss the icon's feet and ask for her blessing.

Plan to visit Montserrat's Basilica at 1pm (noon on Sunday) to hear the famous Escolania boys' choir singing hymns.

SALLY DILLON / LONELY PLANET IMAGES

344 TIGER'S NEST, BHUTAN

Nothing's prosaic in Bhutan. The lotus-born Buddha didn't walk to this auspicious spot, 3000m up in the Himalaya: he flew on the back of a tigress. And when the original builders later constructed the monastery, they used not bolts to anchor it, but the hairs of female spirits. Such is the mysticism that surrounds Bhutan in general, and Tiger's Nest Monastery in particular. The imposing fortress, a cascade of flared roofs and white walls, clings to a cliff face 900m above the Paro Valley. Without a flying feline you'll have to get there by foot.

The steep walk to Tiger's Nest starts from a trailhead at 2600m and takes around 1¾ hours.

127

All that glitters is quite possibly gold in Luang Prabang's best-known and most-visited monastery

345 WAT XIENG THONG, LUANG PRABANG, LAOS

Monks don't permanently confine themselves to monasteries in sleepy Luang Prabang – get up early and you'll see processions of tangerine-robed devotees strolling the streets for alms. But that doesn't mean the monasteries aren't worth a look, especially 16th-century Wat Xieng Thong, practically the only one of Luang Prabang's many such buildings not to have been sacked over the centuries, and perhaps the country's most resplendent. Called the 'Golden City Monastery', its interior is dripping in the stuff: the main temple is embellished with shimmering motifs from the Laotian Ramayana, while a golden Buddha surveys the scene.

November to January is the best time to visit; from February to May the air over Luang Prabang becomes smoky due to slash-and-burn agriculture.

346 ST CATHERINE'S, MT SINAI, EGYPT

Thou shalt not make a list of 10 without including this place – St Catherine's is one of the world's oldest Christian monasteries, built at the foot of the mountain on which Moses allegedly received the Ten Commandments. Its religious significance cannot be underestimated: priceless icons are kept within its 11m-high walls, such as a shrub growing on the grounds, purportedly a direct descendent of the Burning Bush. It's a great staging post for a short pilgrimage, too – strike out early from St Catherine's to summit 2285m Mt Sinai at sunrise and watch the day break over this biblical land.

Leave St Catherine's at 2am or 3am to summit for sunrise; it gets very cold at night in winter, so bring layers.

347 HANGING MONASTERY, DÀTÓNG, CHINA

Looking a lot like it might not be standing by the time you've finished reading this sentence, this precarious place of worship in Shǎnxī province teeters on stilts on the side of a mountain. Not just any old mountain, mind: this is Héng Shān, one of Taoism's most sacred. And the peak's holy influence is doing the trick, as the Hanging Monastery's fluted roofs, rickety walkways and rare combination of Confucian, Taoist and Buddhist elements have survived for 1500 years. Its architectural mechanics are astonishing given its age – but that doesn't stop it looking like it's all about to fall down…

Hanging Monastery is 65km from Dàtóng; while here, visit Yúngǎng Caves (16km from Dàtóng), home to China's earliest Buddhist carvings.

348 RILA, BULGARIA

Heaven forbid you've sinned before visiting Rila Monastery. The building is imposing, but it's the frescos you should fear, for on the walls are daubed myriad interpretations of the Last Judgment – winged devils scratching out people's eyes, transgressors boiling alive and a naked man being sawn in half. Apocalyptic art aside, it's a marvellous monastery. Originally founded in the 10th century, today's structures are 19th-century Renaissance replacements (due to fire): black-white-red candy-striped colonnades and thick brick domes. Nestled into the foot of the Rila Mountains, it's pretty as a picture – even if its pictures aren't pretty.

Rila Monastery is an easy day trip from capital Sofia; local buses make the journey in 2½ hours.

349 SKELLIG MICHAEL, COUNTY KERRY, IRELAND

If being a monk is about paying penance and removing yourself from society, then budding brothers should look no further. Skellig Michael is a tiny, sheer-sided pinnacle of rock, exposed to the Atlantic elements. For the community that lived here from around the 6th century, life would have been tough indeed. They'd had enough by the 1100s and abandoned the place – leaving it to the flocks of puffins. But the monks' legacy remains, remarkably well preserved due to the inaccessible location: spartan beehive huts, vertiginous stone steps and a chapel perched at the island's craggy summit.

The shortest boat trips to Skellig Michael leave from Portmagee on the Iveragh Peninsula; the crossing takes 45 minutes.

350 NOVODEVICHY CONVENT, MOSCOW, RUSSIA

Come commune with the big names of Russia's past: composer Prokofiev, writer Chekhov, former First Lady Raisa Gorbachev – just three of the glitterati buried within the walls of Moscow's baroque convent. Built in the 16th century as a nunnery-cum-fortress, its defensive aspect didn't stop the Bolsheviks booting out the sisters and reclaiming the place – five-domed cathedral, striking red churches, gilded belfry – as a museum. Thankfully this secular rebirth saved its treasures from a revolutionary razing. Restored to religious purpose in 1945, Novodevichy is one of the few spots in which to celebrate both the ecclesiastical glories and great names of Mother Russia.

Sportivnaya is the nearest metro station; visit in winter to sledge and skate on nearby Novodevichy Pond.

MOST MARVELLOUS MONASTERIES & CONVENTS

MOST UNUSUAL STADIUMS

You might not be a sports fan, but that doesn't mean you can't marvel at some of the world's most weird and wonderful stadiums – grab a ticket and join the crowd.

351 ESTÁDIO MUNICIPAL DE BRAGA, BRAGA, PORTUGAL

For years soccer stadiums were desolate places of run-down grandstands and tired terraces. But a new wave of architecture is changing the landscape. In the northern Portuguese city of Braga, engineers eschewed traditional design and transformed the former Monte Castro quarry into an internationally acclaimed arena. With spectator stands running down only two sides, the ends have been left open to reveal the site's former industrial use – a soaring wall of granite backs one goal, while the other offers panoramic views of the rambling city below. The result is a truly unique venue that appears to be part of the mountain from which it is hewn.

SC Braga play in the top division of Portuguese soccer and frequently compete for the big prizes. If you can't see a game, take a stadium tour for €5 (www.scbraga.pt).

352 ESTADIO CHIVAS, GUADALAJARA, MEXICO

Sports fans around the world love bragging about their fanaticism, arguing over who are the most loyal, loudest and most passionate supporters. Followers of Mexican soccer team Club Deportivo Guadalajara, known as Chivas, could lay claim to these titles but they also have a brand-new stadium with a name worthy of the crown – the Volcano. But this moniker has nothing to do with the crackling atmosphere; rather, it's in tribute to the amazing design. Blended into the undulating landscape, the 45,000-capacity stadium rises from a grass-covered cone, with a white roof that floats above like a ring of smoke. It's a sight that blows the opposition away.

Guadalajara is Mexico's second-largest city, home to four million people and blessed with a rich cultural heritage. The soccer season runs in two halves: August to December and January to May.

353 BEIJING NATIONAL STADIUM, BEIJING, CHINA

When birds build a nest, it's usually with twigs. Lightweight and malleable, they're the perfect material for tiny beaks. But when the Chinese built *the* Bird's Nest, they used 110,000 tonnes of reinforced steel, spent US$431 million and employed a workforce of thousands. And it shows. From the outside, the intermeshed girders have been woven into one immense structure, giving the stadium vast strength and earning its famous nickname. Built for the 2008 Summer Olympic Games, the stadium was an instant hit with the Chinese public, with up to 30,000 visiting each day simply to gawp at the spectacular 80,000-seat arena.

You can join the locals on a tour of the stadium (www.n-s.cn) for CNY50 per person.

SEAN CAFFREY · LONELY PLANET IMAGES

Stylish *and* practical: the interlocking mesh aesthetics of the Beijing National Stadium

Singapore's Float@Marina Bay, a new location for a new era in stadium design

354 THE FLOAT@MARINA BAY, SINGAPORE

Singaporeans are past masters at expanding their tiny island through a program of land reclamation, so finding space for a new multipurpose stadium was no big deal – they just built it on the sea. The Float@Marina Bay is a soccer-pitch-sized steel platform, located slap-bang in the glitziest area of town. Overlooked by swish five-star hotels and the iconic Singapore Flyer Ferris wheel, the platform is moored in the trendy Esplanade district. The single grandstand seats 30,000 spectators and is jam-packed for events such as the F1 Grand Prix, National Day celebrations and, in 2010, the Summer Youth Olympics.

You can get to the Esplanade and Float@Marina Bay using the MRT subway service – hop off at Raffles Place, City Hall, Promenade or Esplanade.

355 HIPPODROME D'AUTEUIL, PARIS, FRANCE

There's nothing as romantic as a Paris cityscape, and the view from Hippodrome d'Auteuil is as good as it gets. Perched in the grandstand of this old stadium, your eyes will be drawn away from the galloping horses below and towards the distant spectacle of the Eiffel Tower. Sit back, crack a can of 1664 lager and tuck in to a *sandwich mixte* as you check the form in the *Paris-Turf* newspaper. Backing the winner is the aim of the game, but it's not essential. Whichever way it goes, there's no mistaking that this is a quintessentially Parisian experience.

Dating from 1874, the annual Grand Steeple-Chase de Paris is held in late May and is one of France's most important races; admission costs €3 to €8.

356 GOSPIN DOLAC, IMOTSKI, CROATIA

Kids dreaming of soccer stardom often start out as ball-boys. But pity those of Croatian team NK Imotski, for they have some serious retrieving to do. Imotski is a diminutive Dalmatian town in the lofty Biokovo Mountains – it's a hilly place with nary a flat patch to lay a soccer pitch. At the tiny 4000-seat Gospin Dolac stadium, perched atop a rocky bluff and overlooked by a medieval fortress, the ball-boys dread being posted to the far touchline; any stray balls hurtle directly over a 500m cliff to the distant Blue Lake below.

The Biokovo Mountains are close to the Bosnian border and Imotski is 280km south of Zagreb; the soccer team competes in the Croatian second division (www.nk-imotski.hr).

357 VELTINS-ARENA, GELSENKIRCHEN, GERMANY

In today's corporate age of megabucks sponsorship, modern super-stadiums have to work hard to earn their keep. And Gelsenkirchen's Veltins-Arena works harder than most. Not content with playing host to the Schalke 04 soccer team and 62,000 avid spectators, this arena is a chameleon that plays host to any number of events. Apart from big-ticket soccer fixtures like the Champions League final and World Cup clashes, the stadium has also hosted boxing, ice hockey, a winter biathlon and even opera. With a slide-out pitch and space-age fibreglass roof, this is a true 21st-century stadium wonder.

German soccer is among the cheapest in Europe; tickets for FC Schalke 04 (www .schalke04.com) games start at €15.

358 ESTADIO ALBERTO J ARMANDO, BUENOS AIRES, ARGENTINA

If Guadalajara's Volcano is the perfect soccer stadium name, then the colloquial handle for Boca Juniors' ground must be the worst. In Spanish, it sounds flamboyant – La Bombonera – but the English translation is 'the Chocolate Box'. So-called for its unusual design – three towering grandstands and one flat wall – the stadium is the beating heart of La Boca barrio. Even by South American standards, this place rocks, so much so that the wall is said to sway in the cacophonous atmosphere.

The big game against rivals River Plate is one of world soccer's essential fixtures – US operator World Football Travel (www .worldfootballtravel.com) can fix you up with match tickets and travel packages.

359 KAOHSIUNG NATIONAL STADIUM, KAOHSIUNG CITY, TAIWAN

If you could harness the energy of a top-draw sports event, the electricity grid would go into meltdown. Nobody's worked out how to do that yet, but Taiwanese boffins have done the next best thing; they've made the world's first stadium that exploits the sun. Covered in 8844 solar panels and designed in the vision of a coiled dragon's tail – one end peeled open and back on itself to reveal the 55,000 colourful seats within – this arena produces all of its own power and even feeds the surrounding neighbourhood when it's not in use.

Kaohsiung City is in southern Taiwan, connected to Taipei by the 345km-long high-speed rail service (www.thsrc .com.tw), which travels at 300km/h and completes the journey in 90 minutes.

360 HPCA STADIUM, DHARAMSALA, INDIA

In a country boasting the second-largest cricket venue in the world – Kolkata's 82,000-capacity Eden Gardens – there's stiff competition for the title of best wicket. But size isn't everything and top prize goes to the tongue-twisting Himachal Pradesh Cricket Association Stadium in the northern city of Dharamsala. Thankfully known as HPCA Stadium, this little gem is surrounded by wonderful scenery. At more than 1450m above sea level, the backdrop of the snowcapped Dhauladhar mountains and picturesque Kangra Valley is enough to hit anyone for six.

In 2010 HPCA Stadium gained international acclaim as a venue in the Indian Premier League cricket tournament (www.iplt20.com) – numerous overnight buses make the 13-hour journey from Delhi.

MOST UNUSUAL STADIUMS

SIGHTS FROM BRITISH CHILDHOOD LITERATURE

Lit-lovers, prepare for an onslaught of childhood nostalgia. What better way to pair Britain's picture-book scenery than with its well-loved children's classics?

361 ALICE IN WONDERLAND & OXFORD, ENGLAND

The dreamy spires of genteel Oxford may call to mind pursuits more noble than chasing fairytales, but among the august institutions of higher learning one can pay homage to Lewis Carroll. Christ Church College, Oxford's grandest college, was Carroll's home, and the dean's daughter at that time was Alice Liddell, the inspiration for the heroine in Carroll's renowned tales, *Alice's Adventures in Wonderland* and its sequel, *Through the Looking-Glass*. Alice addicts can do an Alice-themed tour of the College, while the Museum of Oxford has Alice-related memorabilia. Alice's Shop on St Aldate's is a must – it's the original Old Sheep Shop from *Alice Through the Looking Glass*, today selling more Wonderland souvenirs than you ever dreamed possible.

Christ Church College has another literary connection – it was used as a location for the Harry Potter films. Information on touring the college is at www.chch.ox.ac .uk/visiting.

362 BEATRIX POTTER & THE LAKE DISTRICT, ENGLAND

Long before Pixar had us going gaga over talking animals, Beatrix Potter was busily drawing bonnets on Jemima Puddle-Duck, smart blue jackets on Peter Rabbit and aprons on Mrs Tiggy-Winkle (a washer-woman hedgehog), and giving these button-cute characters oh-so-English voices. Beatrix Potter fans will go potty at Hill Top farm, a few kilometres south of Hawkshead, a village in the glorious Lake District of England that's an enticing muddle of rickety streets, whitewashed houses and country pubs. Beatrix wrote and illustrated many of her heartwarming tales inside the picture-postcard farmhouse at Hill Top, and it's crammed with decorative details that fans will recognise from her illustrations.

In the village of Hawkshead, be sure to also check out the Beatrix Potter Gallery on Main Street, containing lots of original illustrations from Potter books.

363 THE WIND IN THE WILLOWS & THE RIVER THAMES, ENGLAND

Although born in Scotland, author Kenneth Grahame lived with his grandmother in Cookham Dean west of London, in a bucolic riverside area where old-world English charm is laid on thick. The Thames river scenes between Cookham and Henley inspired Grahame's writings – if you're after a bit of recreation, stroll the Thames Path for a spell, or take to the water (according to Ratty 'there is nothing – absolutely nothing – half so much worth doing as simply messing about in boats'). Pay a visit to Henley's River and Rowing Museum, where the Wind in the Willows exhibition brings the story of Ratty, Mole, Badger and Toad to life.

Looking to further indulge your inner child? Legoland (www.legoland.co.uk) is about 25km from Henley, in Windsor.

364 ROBIN HOOD & SHERWOOD FOREST, ENGLAND

Nottinghamshire is the heartland of Robin Hood and his merry men. Today, there are almost more tourists than trees in Sherwood Forest, although there are still peaceful spots to be found (but few outlaws). The visitor centre houses 'Robyn Hode's Sherwode', a cute but corny exhibition describing the lifestyles of bandits, kings, peasants and friars. One of the major attractions is the Major Oak, a hiding place for one R Hood, according to folklore – these days it's more likely he'd have to prop up the ancient tree, not hide in it.

To bed down, Sherwood Forest YHA Hostel (www.yha.org.uk) is a modern hostel, a mere bugle-horn cry away from the forest's visitor centre.

365 HARRY POTTER & KING'S CROSS STATION, LONDON, ENGLAND

This is the departure point for students of Hogwarts School of Witchcraft and Wizardry, made famous by its illustrious alumni, including one Harry Potter. In the books, the Hogwarts Express departs from Platform 9¾ – it's clearly marked between platforms 9 and 10, and there's even a luggage trolley disappearing into the brickwork (set up for countless photo opportunities). To visit, head for platform 8 from the main entrance or the tube exit. Then go to the end of the platform, turning left for platforms 9 to 11. No ticket is needed.

From King's Cross, pay a visit to the British Library (www.bl.uk). It receives a copy of every publication produced in the UK and Ireland.

366 PADDINGTON BEAR & PADDINGTON STATION, LONDON, ENGLAND

'Mr and Mrs Brown first met Paddington on a railway platform. In fact, that was how he came to have such an unusual name for a bear, for Paddington was the name of the station.' And so begins Michael Bond's 1958 story of a bear that travels all the way from darkest Peru with a note around his neck reading 'Please look after this bear, thank you'. The story of the polite but trouble-prone bear, with his love of marmalade sandwiches, became an English classic. There's a statue of Paddington Bear, on the concourse of Paddington Station.

Not far from Paddington Station is Kensington Gardens with another London literary landmark on the western side of the Serpentine – a statue of Peter Pan.

367 KING ARTHUR & TINTAGEL, ENGLAND

The legend of King Arthur and the Knights of the Round Table is a powerfully enduring one – the intricate plotlines conjure images of knights in shining armour, illicit romances in medieval castles and heroic quests for the Holy Grail, all set in a magical, mystical Britain. The spectre of King Arthur looms large over the Cornish village of Tintagel and its dramatic cliff-top castle. Though the present-day ruins mostly date from the 13th century, archaeological digs have revealed the foundations of a much earlier fortress, fuelling speculation that Arthur may indeed have been born at the castle, as local legend claims.

Enjoy the views – and a Cornish pasty – at the castle's Beach Café. More information is at www.english-heritage.org.uk.

368 THE WOMBLES & WIMBLEDON, ENGLAND

Wimbledon Common is a expanse of open space for walking, nature trails and picnics – or a spot of Womble-spotting. Wombles are pointy nosed, furry creatures that live in burrows where they help the environment by collecting and recycling rubbish in useful and ingenious ways (greenies ahead of their time). Wombles were created by author Elisabeth Beresford and originally appeared in a series of children's novels from 1968, but gained the following they rightfully deserved from a mid-'70s TV series. Though Wombles live all around the world, the story is based on the group living in Wimbledon Common.

You might also know Wimbledon for a certain tennis tournament, held annually in June and July. See www.wimbledon .org for info on attending.

369 POOH COUNTRY & HARTFIELD, ENGLAND

AA Milne captured the imagination of children with his books about a boy named Christopher Robin (after his son) and various characters – most notably the bear named Winnie-the-Pooh. The literary landscape was centred around the Milne family home at Cotchford Farm in Hartfield, East Sussex – visit and you can take an 'expotition' into the Ashdown Forest through Posingford Wood and across the Poohsticks Bridge to other Enchanted Places. Drop by Pooh Corner Shop (where the real life Christopher Robin used to buy sweets) to pick up Pooh-phernalia and Pooh-country maps.

Using public transport, Tunbridge Wells, southeast of London, is a good jump-off point for reaching Hartfield (there's an hourly bus). See www.pooh-country .co.uk for more.

370 FAMOUS FIVE & DORSET, ENGLAND

Seaside holidays with Julian, Dick, Anne, George and Timmy the Dog. Plus lashings of ginger beer. It can only mean one thing: Enid Blyton's Famous Five adventures. The prolific author wrote 21 tales of the Famous Five. She holidayed frequently at Dorset's Isle of Purbeck (actually a peninsula), and its glittering bays and crumbling cliffs are where many of the tall tales were set. Take the Swanage Steam Railway to Corfe Caste (the inspiration for Kirrin Castle) – in the village is the Ginger Pop Shop, run by a Blyton boffin and full of books and memorabilia.

While you're in the neighbourhood, visit the almost circular bay at Lulworth Cove, and the nearby 17th-century Lulworth Castle (www.lulworth.com).

GREATEST
HARBOURS

From cute coves to eminent estuaries, visit the world's best places to drop anchor.

371 NELSON'S DOCKYARD, ENGLISH HARBOUR, ANTIGUA, WEST INDIES

It's pleasing when places retain their sense of purpose: Nelson's Dockyard, the world's only Georgian naval harbour, may now be a fine museum, but it's also still a working port – albeit for yachts rather than Horatio's fleet. Nelson himself was stationed here from 1784 to 1787; this safe haven enabled the Brits to maintain a presence in the Caribbean. Today, you can maintain the dockyard's original spirit yourself: raise a rum in the former Galley, now the Galley Bar; shop in the bakery (which is still baking); and bed down in one of the old dormitories – now turned into more salubrious hotels. Interpretive plaques explain the history of the various buildings.

English Harbour is a 45-minute drive from the capital of St John's. The Dockyard is open from 8am to 6pm daily (see www. nationalparksantigua.com for more).

372 ALEXANDRIA, EGYPT

Venerable Alex is one of the world's oldest ports. Its Mediterranean vantage once sheltered the ships of namesake Alexander the Great, and warranted the construction of a bona fide World Wonder: the fabled Pharos lighthouse, one of the official Seven, stood 138m tall on outlaying Pharos Island. Sadly the city lost some of its luminance as its importance declined and a 14th-century earthquake tumbled the ancient beacon. But now Alex is on the up, its boats doing a fine trade in Egyptian cotton, its cultural significance bolstered by the new Bibliotheca Alexandrina, and underwater explorations unearthing relics suggesting this historic harbour harbours secrets still.

Alexandria is 225km north of Cairo. The Bibliotheca Alexandrina (www.bibalex .org) contains antiquities hauled up from the harbour.

373 PARADISE HARBOUR, ANTARCTICA

The clue's in the name – as long as you like your 'paradise' chilled, remote and populated by penguins. You won't see many other boats at this port-of-sorts on the Antarctic Peninsula. However, with luck you *will* see plenty: the mountains reflected mirror-clear in the floe-dotted water; icebergs calving with explosive ferocity off the faces of creaking glaciers; and comic gaggles of chinstrap and gentoo penguins waddling about their daily business. Spy a huffing whale or seal bobbing off the bow of your Zodiac inflatable (the best way to explore) and you've hit rush hour, Antarctic style.

Expedition cruise ships leave Ushuaia, southern Argentina, for the Antarctic Peninsula, from November to March; trips take between eight and 10 days.

374 KOCHI (COCHIN), KERALA, INDIA

Infused with the scent of cardamom, cloves and salt-air rippling off the Malabar Coast, Kochi is an exotic harbour with historic pinches of Dutch, Portuguese and English styling. The Chinese left the most iconic mark, however: billowing, 10m-high cantilevered fishing nets, an import from the court of Kublai Khan, dot the stretch of coast along Fort Kochi and Vypeen Island. It's not all such small-scale industry – this is Kerala's biggest port, after all – but with its meandering beaches, boat rides through the backwaters and shacks selling fresh fish suppers, this is a place to embrace the Arabian Sea's sleepier side.

Kochi has an international airport and three railway stations; trains to Mumbai take around 35 hours (see www.cochin.org).

375 HALIFAX, NOVA SCOTIA, CANADA

The native Mi'kmaq called this place Jiputug – Great Harbour. The visiting Brits ignored them, of course, naming it 'Halifax' after an irrelevant earl. But great it remained, the world's second-largest natural harbour, around which a lively city has grown. Halifax hasn't always prospered from its shore – in 1917 a ship carrying munitions detonated in the port, killing 2000 people. But this is ultimately a city of the sea, where immigrants arrived, where boats constantly come and go, and where waterfront cafes are the place to be.

The Maritime Museum of the Atlantic (http://museum.gov.ns.ca/mmanew), on Halifax's waterfront, is open daily (except Monday from November to April).

376 GUANABARA BAY, RIO DE JANEIRO, BRAZIL

Rio's bay is truly blessed. The wide waterway allows for ample shipping (and ample beaches, ideal for teeny-tiny bikini-flaunting). The higgledy-piggledy hills behind provide a deliciously wild backdrop for such a heaving conurbation. And high up above it all stands a statue of Christ, open-armed, granting his benediction to those below on a daily basis. The best way to take it in is to join him: ascend the cog railway up Corcovado Mountain late in the afternoon, when the light is shining back towards the harbour, then stay as late as you can to watch the sun dip into the sea. Heavenly.

The best months to visit Rio are September and October, when temperatures are pleasant but the humidity hasn't set in.

A spectacular harbour landscape is just one of Rio de Janeiro's shameless virtues

377 SYDNEY HARBOUR, AUSTRALIA

The bay that launched a thousand firework displays is no less impressive for being famous. It was obvious when Captain Cook first sailed by in 1770 that this was a special spot (though of course the Aborigines had known this for aeons); subsequent centuries have seen the harbour thrive, from first British settlement in Australia to modern-day Opera-House-Harbour-Bridge glory. But it's the nooks and crannies that make it so intriguing : from the prison (and campsite) on Cockatoo Island, to the fine sands at Manly, to the walking trails around historic North Head, the harbour is far more than one postcard view.

Ferries link sites across the harbour; an unlimited-travel daypass costs A$20 www.sydneyferries.info).

378 CLOVELLY, DEVON, ENGLAND

Clovelly is how you want your North Devon fishing village to be. An oh-so-cute cluster of wattle-and-daub houses spilling 120m down a steep cliff, it has cobbles and cats, a fisherman's cottage and a couple of pubs. The main street – Up Along/ Down Along, depending on your direction – is for foot traffic only; its bottom nuzzles the tiny harbour, a-bob with small boats. Time hasn't touched Clovelly – it's a privately owned village, so development is restricted. It does get crowded though, so stay overnight and, after the day trippers have gone, you'll be left with the cats, the charm and the gentle lap of the sea.

Entrance to the Clovelly visitor centre costs £5.95; walkers hiking the South West Coast Path can bypass this charge (www.clovelly.co.uk).

379 SKOPELOS, SPORADES ISLANDS, GREECE

Mamma Mia! What a harbour! At least, that's what the movie moguls thought when they chose rocky, forested Skopelos as the location for much of the ABBA musical. They had a point: the main town is as pretty as a film set, a tumble of whitewash walls, terracotta tiles and bougainvillea-festooned balconies, designated a Traditional Settlement of Outstanding Beauty to ensure development doesn't ruin the aspect. A harbourfront taverna is the place to watch the fishermen haul in their catch. Or negotiate the passageways up to the hilltop fortress for the best views and a singalong with the local musicians – ABBA or otherwise.

Skiathos airport is a 45-minute ferry ride from Skopelos; catamarans serve Skopelos from Thessaloniki in summer (three hours).

380 VICTORIA HARBOUR, HONG KONG

This is a harbour, Hollywood-style. The bay between Hong Kong Island and mainland Kowloon is a razzle-dazzle of lights and skyscrapers so big and brash you can barely see the strait they're hugging. It wasn't always this way: when Queen Victoria acquired it for the Empire in 1842, her consorts mocked her interest in such a backwater. But Hong Kong – or 'fragrant harbour' – came good, becoming the powerhouse of the South China Sea and a world-class sight.

The Star Ferry (www.starferry.com.hk) runs four routes across Victoria Harbour from 6.30am to 11pm daily.

GREATEST HARBOURS

MOST ENTERTAINING PARADES

There's no rain heavy enough to take the zip out of these humdingers.

381 NOTTING HILL CARNIVAL, LONDON, ENGLAND

The British capital's top summer knees-up, a celebration of the local Caribbean community, has enlivened this part of town since the 1950s. During the end-of-August bank holiday (the last Sunday and Monday in August) the neighbourhood explodes with reggae sound systems and Rasta styles. There's also calypso and soca, samba dancing, sassy outfits and animistic sculptures. It all climaxes on the Monday with a 5km parade of floats and revellers in feathered headdresses and Lycra suits. Ravers can fuel themselves at stalls selling Jamaican patties, jerk chicken and curries.

The parade attracts some two million partygoers – and a satellite population of pickpockets. Keep a good eye on your cash.

382 DURUTHU PERAHERA, COLOMBO, SRI LANKA

Duruthu Perahera celebrates the Buddha's first visit to Sri Lanka, during which he is said to have visited the Kelaniya temple in Colombo. The celebrations consist of three processions on the nights preceding the full moon. Whip-crackers lead each procession, followed by fire-ball performers, drummers, dancers and costumed performers. Decorated elephants parade between each of the groups, including, most spectacularly, an enormous tusker treading on a special white carpet. Hundreds of thousands of people attend the parades, which become more colourful and lavish as the nights go along. The one on the night before the full moon is the zenith.

The processions are held before the January full moon. Kelaniya temple is 7km northeast of Colombo's Fort zone.

DAN HERRICK / LONELY PLANET IMAGES

383 CONEY ISLAND MERMAID PARADE, NEW YORK, USA

The Mermaid Parade, a much-beloved marine-themed art parade, was kicked off in the 1980s to pay homage to the Mardi Gras that was held at Coney Island between 1903 and 1954. The festival is also about celebrating the start of summer. As well as mermaids you'll see costumes of fish, shells, Neptunes, octopuses, Coney Island amusement rides and the occasional lighthouse. Ever year cult celebrities are crowned as King Neptune and Queen Mermaid and preside over the parade. Past Neptunes and Mermaids have included David Johansen, Queen Latifah, David Byrne, Harvey Keitel, Lou Reed and Laurie Anderson.

The parade is held in mid-to-late June. To get to Coney Island, take the D, F, N or Q subway to Stillwell Avenue.

141

The Mermaid Parade is a sea of sequined and bejeweled revelers, with plenty of freakish aquatic-themed getups

The age-old struggle between good and evil provides the thematic backdrop for Bolivia's Oruru Carnival

384 JUNKANOO, NASSAU, BAHAMAS

More funk than junk, the Bahamas' national festival is at its wildest and best in the capital, Nassau. The parades start up at around 2am and generally go till 8am. Standing amid the crowd, you'll feel the music before you see its source – a frenzied barrage of whistles, horns, cowbells, drums and conch shells. Then the revellers whirl into view, wearing costumes that can weigh more than 90kg, adorned with glittering beads, foils and rhinestones. Many marchers spend all year planning their costumes, keeping the designs a closely guarded secret.

The parade takes place on 26 December and 1 January, and circuits around Bay and Shirley Streets.

385 UP-HELLY-AA, SHETLAND ISLANDS, SCOTLAND

The Shetland Islands were under Norse rule until 1469, and every year locals choose to honour their heritage by setting fire to a replica Viking longship (the Vikings were wont to burn ships to celebrate the rebirth of the sun). In the early evening hundreds of wannabe Vikings in full dress, complete with hats and swords, parade towards the galley with lit torches, pitching them aboard and burning the ship to ashes. The Vikings then go party-hopping, drinking a dram and dancing with one lady at each stop. Many heads are pounding like Thor's hammer the next day.

Up-Helly-Aa is held on the last Tuesday in January. Most parties are private, but a few are open to visitors.

386 HALLOWEEN PARADE, NEW YORK, USA

New York's Village neighbourhood is the place to be on 31 October, when the Halloween Parade arrives in a feast of dazzling fancy dress, with around 50,000 costumed revellers and another two million turning out to watch. The pageant was conceived in the mid-1970s by a local puppeteer who lamented the decline in the city's Halloween celebrations. The macabre holiday is certainly back with a vengeance. The parade is open to all in a costume who wish to march, so let your imagination run rampant and hit the Greenwich Village streets of Christopher, Bleeker and Houston.

Take the subway to West 4th Street to join the start of the parade. Get the lowdown at www.halloween-nyc.com.

387 ORURU CARNIVAL, BOLIVIA

Bolivia's largest annual celebration is a massive event that can draw around 400,000 people. Its centrepiece is La Diablada, the 'Dance of the Devils', an extraordinary parade that showcases demonic dancers in extravagant costumes. The 4km-long *entrada* (entrance procession) features 20,000 dancers and 10,000 musicians – so many people that the parade lasts up to 20 hours. It's led by a brightly costumed San Miguel character. Behind him, dancing and marching, come bears, condors, famous devils, Inca characters, conquistadores and Andean gods of evil. When the parade arrives at the soccer stadium, there's a series of dances telling the story of the ultimate battle between good and evil.

Oruru is 3700m above sea level, so you should arrive a few days early to allow your body to acclimatise.

390 KATTENFESTIVAL, IEPER, BELGIUM

Belgium's cat festival has a dark origin. It began as a 12th-century tradition that had the city jester throwing live cats from the belfry of the Lakenhalle (cloth hall). Cats, it was believed, personified evil spirits and this ritual, which continued until 1817, was a sure way to be rid of them. The modern version, in which toy cats are hurled from the belfry, started up in the 1930s. The festival is held every three years and on this day, the whole town purrs, with cat-shaped chocolates and marzipan for sale in all the shops. The big moment is Kattenstoet, a parade of giant cats.

The festival is held in the Grote Markt. Check with Ieper (Ypres) tourism (www.ieper.be) to see when it's coming up next.

388 LAJKONIK, KRAKÓW, POLAND

According to Polish legend, when the head of Kraków's defensive raftsmen defeated a Tatar marauder in the 13th century, he slipped into the Mongolian's robes and triumphantly rode into the city. The myth has been celebrated for more than 200 years with the procession of 'Lajkonik' through the Gothic city. Dressed in Mongol robes and accompanied by a musical troupe, the fairytale figure rides a hobby horse topped with feathers to the main square. En route the energetic larrikin dances, jumps, greets passers-by, pops into cafes, collects donations and strikes people with his mace (it's said to bring good luck).

Catch a tap from Lajkonik's mace on the Thursday after the Feast of Corpus Christi in the suburb of Zwierzyniec.

389 PROCESSION OF SNAKES, COCULLO, ITALY

One of Italy's strangest festivals, the Processione dei Serpenti is celebrated in the tiny Abruzzo hamlet of Cocullo by adorning a statue of St Domenic with jewels, bank notes and live snakes. The statue is then carried through the village, with the snakes coiling around both the statue and its bearers, before the squirming mass is released back into the forest, leaving the villagers supposedly immune from snake bites for another year. It's not as risky as it looks: the snakes are non-venomous and have had their fangs removed.

The festival takes place on the first Thursday in May. There's no accommodation in Cocullo, but it's only 40 minutes away by bus from Sulmona and 35 minutes from Celano.

MOST ENTERTAINING PARADES

UNDERWATER SIGHTS

The wildest blue yonder is the one beneath the waves.

393 MANTA RAY VILLAGE, HAWAII

No prizes for guessing the star attraction at this dive site off the Kona coast of Hawai'i (the Big Island), though half the fun is that dives here are conducted at night. Dive operators shine powerful lights into the water to attract plankton, which in turn attracts manta rays (which in turn attract divers). Manta-ray sightings are unreliable – you might see up to 10 rays and their magnificent 'wings', or you might see none. Dives during the new moon seem to be the best bet for manta encounters.

You can opt for the three-hour round-trip snorkel or do a certified one-tank manta-ray night dive. Book through www .hawaiiactivities.com.

391 UNDERWATER PYRAMIDS, JAPAN

Off the coast of the island of Yonaguni, there is a series of underwater structures that have thrown the New Age cat among the archaeologist pigeons ever since their discovery in 1985 by a local dive-tour operator looking for hammerhead sharks. The 'underwater pyramids' resemble Mayan ruins, with steps and terraces. Geologists still can't agree on whether the structure is an entirely natural one adapted by humans, or entirely manmade. Indications are that the site is 10,000 years old – from the Ice Age – which confounds received wisdom about the age of civilisations and drives Atlantis-seekers into a frenzy.

Go down and decide for yourself! Open Coast (www.opencoastravel.com) is a US company with bilingual guides that runs tours to Yonaguni.

392 NAVY PIER, WESTERN AUSTRALIA

As structures go, this 300m-long T-shape is not much of a sight. It's kind of a…pier (it was actually built by US troops in the 1960s). But underwater's where the action is. The proximity of Ningaloo Reef and the strong currents that sweep under the pier bring in a rainbow show of marine life, and the pylons are thickly coated with corals and anenomes. An unbelievable profusion of fish awaits your admiring gaze – lionfish, angelfish, squirrelfish, gropers, parrotfish and stargazers, to name just a handful, not to mention octopuses, nudibranchs and rays. Some rate it even higher than the Great Barrier Reef.

Because it's a military site, you'll have to dive Navy Pier with a tour operator. Day dives cost roughly A$170, night dives about $A190.

394 BATTLESHIPS IN CHUUK LAGOON, FEDERATED STATES OF MICRONESIA

The world of wreck diving owes a lot to the carnage of WWII – whole fleets of warships were sent down to Davy Jones' locker at Coron in the Philippines and Scapa Flow in Scotland. But nothing compares to the tiny state of Chuuk in Micronesia. The sandy seabed of this coral atoll forms an eerie graveyard for more than 300 Japanese battleships, freighters, submarines and aircraft, sunk in a single devastating American assault in February 1944. However, dive carefully – the wrecks still carry their original cargoes of tanks, ammunition, torpedoes, depth charges and mines!

Continental Micronesia (www .continental.com) flies into the tiny airstrip on Weno island from Guam four times a week.

395 CRISTÓBAL COLÓN, CUBA

The *Cristóbal Colón*, a Spanish ship, is the best-preserved wreck in a number downed off the coast of Cuba during the Spanish-American War. She was wrecked in 1898 during the Battle of Santiago de Cuba, one of several ships trapped in the bay by American craft. After a chase, which she lost after burning through all her high-grade coal, she was cornered by the Americans and her captain scuttled her in order to save the crew. She lies about 90km off the coast of Santiago. You can still see the cannon shells lying around her on the ocean floor.

The approach along the beach is made tricky by sharp rocks and big waves. If it's choppy weather, this is best done as a boat dive.

396 RAINBOW WARRIOR, NEW ZEALAND

Bombed by French government saboteurs in Auckland harbour in July 1985 to prevent her sailing off to protest French nuclear testing in the Pacific, the Greenpeace boat *Rainbow Warrior* was later refloated and scuttled off beautiful Matauri Bay in New Zealand's Northland to serve as a dive wreck and fish sanctuary. Coated in colourful corals and populated by goatfish, moray eels and other fish, it sits upright in 25m of water, wedged into the sandy ocean floor. Anemone, sponges and algae of all colours cling to the wreck; in its grave the ship is far more rainbow than warrior.

Book a day tour through www.divehqboi .co.nz, or visit www.divetours.co.nz to book a seven- or 15-day tour that includes a number of dive sites.

397 GREAT BLUE HOLE, BELIZE

When seen from above, the Great Blue Hole looks like the pupil of an eye. Seen from within, this Unesco World Heritage–listed ocean sinkhole is a visual treat for divers. Ringed by fringing reef, and approximately 400m in diameter, the Great Blue Hole drops away to around 145m. About 40m down are the formations that lure divers from around the world: marine stalactites up to 15m in length. Marine life is noticeable only by its absence – you might not see a single fish – but when you're swimming among stalactites, who gives a Nemo?

Day trips depart at 6am and return at 5.30pm, or you can overnight aboard a boat. The dive is only recommended for experienced divers.

398 TURTLE TOMB, MALAYSIA

Slow things down to turtle pace as you take to the seas off the Malaysian island that invariably figures in lists of the world's top dive sites: Pulau Sipadan. It's justifiably famous for the Drop Off, where, just a stroll from the shore, the ocean floor drops away 600m. It's also famous for its turtles. Green and hawksbill turtles abound, and 22m down you'll find the so-called turtle tomb, containing the skeletal remains of vast numbers of turtles who've been trapped in the deep underwater cavern and died there. You need to be a very experienced diver to stop the same thing from happening to you.

The diving season at Sipadan extends from April to December, but the conditions are best in July and August.

399 RED SEA STAR, EILAT, ISRAEL

The *Red Sea Star* is a bit like Stromberg's underwater lair in the James Bond flick *The Spy Who Loved Me* – unsurprising considering it's 5m below the Red Sea in Israel. The interior of this bar-restaurant resembles a mermaid's lounge room, with fishy fantasy motifs – including jellyfish-shaped stools and starfish lights – and huge windows through which curious (or vengeful) fish and other marine creatures eyeball the customers eyeballing their seafood platter. If you crane your neck, you might see a ship overhead from time to time.

Landlubbers will be relieved to find the rooftop Metro Bar is open from 7pm to 3am. The underwater bar opens from 10am; details at www.redseastar.com.

400 TAMAN PURA (TEMPLE GARDEN), INDONESIA

Taman Pura created quite a bit of ballyhoo in 2010 when rumours began to circulate in the Indonesian press about the discovery of a Hindu temple in Pemuteran Bay off the coast of Bali. Upon investigation, it was discovered that there is indeed a temple down there – but it's no submerged archaeological site. Rather, it was created as part of a reef conservation project funded by AusAID. Consisting of plinths, statues of Buddha and Ganesh and an ornate temple gate, all covered with marine flora and browsing fish, it's something of a wonder in its own right.

Go down there with the 'pirates' from the Sea Rovers Dive Centre (www.searovers .net), who also do dives to clean up the reef.

GREATEST GEYSERS

Bad day at the office? Feeling hot under the collar? You're not alone – even Mother Nature needs to let off steam from time to time.

401 EL TATIO GEYSERS, CHILE

Think of South America, and the Andes are never far from the top of the list, but how many know that this mammoth mountain range is home to the world's third-largest geyser field? Way up in the clouds, some 4300m above sea level, the El Tatio field comprises over 80 active geysers in one of the world's most challenging environments. Although no geyser erupts more than a few metres high, visitors come here for the extreme beauty and to witness the plumes of steam that condense in the frigid dawn air. A network of bather-friendly hot springs makes El Tatio all the more enticing.

Tours leave San Pedro at 4am for the rough 90-minute drive. Wrap up warm and take a towel to indulge in high-altitude hot-spring bathing.

403 SHIKABE GEYSER, JAPAN

Japan is awash with *onsen*, the traditional hot-spring bathing houses so deeply entwined in the nation's soul. This is a geothermal land – the same forces that bring rise to the hot springs also manifest themselves in volcanoes and earthquakes – but for such an active area the number of geysers is few. Japan has but four. In the fishing village of Shikabe, in the southeastern corner of Hokkaido Prefecture, this cute little blowhole is just metres from the seashore; it erupts every 10 minutes while you soak in the adjoining hot springs and take in the show.

Shikabe is 45km from the city of Hakodate, which has its own airport. Take a train for the one-hour journey.

402 ANDERNACH GEYSER, GERMANY

There are many things for which Germany is famous – lederhosen, beer festivals, winning on penalties – but gushing geysers are not among them. Granted, Aachen has the hottest springs in continental Europe, a toe-scorching 74°C no less, but most don't consider this a geothermal land. And they'd be right, because this is something entirely different. In the little town of Andernach, on the right bank of the Rhine in the western province of Rhineland-Palintate, you'll find the world's biggest cold-water geyser. Driven by CO_2, this spout fizzes some 60m with unflinching efficiency and is a source of much delight for the proud Andernachers.

Travel to Andernach by train from Frankfurt. The 132km-long ride follows the path of the Rhine and is one of Germany's finest.

The geyser at Shikabe, a rare sight in Japan

The scene at Lake Bogoria, a place of wondrous rapture

404 TRITON MOON, NEPTUNE

OK, so Neptune is 4.3 billion kilometres from earth and there's no easy way of getting there, but the planet's moon, Triton, sends off some major jet-like blasts. In 1989 the *Voyager 2* space mission captured images of gaseous nitrogen plumes shooting more than 8km from the moon's surface and dumping dusty residue more than 150km away – no mean feat considering that earth's largest recorded geyser, the extinct Waimangu in New Zealand, gushed to a height of around 300m. Somewhat closer to home, scientists believe that similar spurts occur on Mars, although nobody's ever seen them. With NASA recruiting for expedition volunteers, you could well be the first.

If you're stuck on earth, check out the guided tours available at huge observatories such as Paranal and La Silla in Chile (www.eso.org).

405 POHUTU GEYSER, WHAKAREWAREWA THERMAL VALLEY, NEW ZEALAND

Once upon a time, when geysers were geysers, New Zealand boasted the world's largest. Waimangu had a short-lived but dazzling life, active for just four years at the beginning of the 20th century but capable of shooting steaming jets to a height of 300m. New Zealand can still lay claim to almost 10% of all active spouts (not bad for a small country) and the richest pickings can be found in Whakarewarewa Thermal Valley. This geothermal area near Rotorua has over 60 vents, seven of which remain active. Pohutu is the pick of the bunch, unleashing a ferocious 30m-high blast pretty much every hour.

Access to Pohutu is via the somewhat-cheesy Te Puia New Zealand Maori Arts and Crafts Institute, on the outskirts of Rotorua (www.tepuia.com).

406 VALLEY OF GEYSERS, KAMCHATKA, RUSSIA

Few people know about Kamchatka. Isolated on Russia's easternmost boundary, north from Japan and much closer to Alaska than to Moscow, this wild peninsula straddles the Pacific Ring of Fire, resulting in some astonishing tectonic tantrums. So remote that you'll need a helicopter to get in, the Valley of Geysers was only discovered in 1941 but is now known to be the world's second-largest field, with more than 90 spouts along the 6km gorge. In a sign of just how unstable this area is, a 2007 landslide covered two-thirds of the valley – while many vents were blocked, the big one (Velikan – 'The Giant') remains active.

The Valley of Geysers is part of the Unesco-protected Volcanoes of Kamchatka. Get there via Petropavlovsk-Kamchatsky, the only city on this wild peninsula.

407 LAKE BOGORIA, KENYA

Lions, leopards, elephants, buffalo and rhinos – these are the Kenyan pin-ups that draw thousands of visitors each year. Safari expeditions are big business, but geyser tours as well? In the Kenyan Rift Valley, just a smidgen north from the equator, Lake Bogoria is a shallow, 35km-long saline lake in an area with strong volcanic origins. Wildlife still rules here – the lake is home to the world's largest population of lesser flamingos – but this protected reserve is also rich in geysers. At least 18 spouts have been identified and together with numerous hot springs they are renowned for their therapeutic values.

Lake Bogoria lies 260km north of Nairobi. Experience the rejuvenating powers of the spa waters at Lake Bogoria Hotel.

408 GEYSIR & STROKKUR, HAUKADALUR, ICELAND

Back in the days of primitive geyser tourism, visitors to Iceland's star attraction would stimulate eruptions by hurling foreign objects down the vent. Unsurprisingly, the spout that lends its name to all geysers – literally meaning 'to gush' – slowly got sick. Plumes reduced in frequency until, in 1916, Geysir coughed its last. Recent volcanic activity has rekindled it but, happily, Haukadalur has another pin-up performer. Once the smaller sibling, Strokkur is now a celebrity in its own right thanks to its reliable performance. Erupting once every eight minutes has, so far, been enough to prevent impatient tourists from clogging it with crap.

Tours to Geysir form part of the Golden Circle route, together with Gullfoss waterfall and the historic parliament at Thingvellir. Alternatively, it's an easy 125km drive from Reykjavík.

409 PANGALU GEOTHERMAL FIELD, NEW BRITAIN ISLAND, PAPUA NEW GUINEA

What's the capital of Papua New Guinea (PNG)? It's a good quiz question. Few countries prick the mass conscience less than PNG, a mostly undeveloped land and one of the world's last unexplored regions. This is another of the Pacific Ring of Fire countries, where volcanic eruptions, earthquakes and tsunamis are not uncommon. And guess what? Yep, there are geysers here as well. Halfway along the eastern side of the Willaumez Peninsula, on central New Britain Island, Pangalu Geothermal Field takes some getting to but intrepid visitors are rewarded with hot springs, boiling pools, fumaroles, mudpots and a flurry of small geysers.

If you want to visit PNG, you'll need to know that the capital is Port Moresby. The islands have a tropical climate but May to October is considered to be the dry season.

410 STEAMBOAT, YELLOWSTONE NATIONAL PARK, CALIFORNIA, USA

The fact that Yellowstone sits in the caldera of a supervolcano gives it a somewhat unfair advantage when it comes to geothermal grandeur. The park contains over 50% of the world's active geysers and some of the most famous, including trustworthy Old Faithful. It's also got the biggest, the somewhat gentle-sounding Steamboat, which sits in the Norris Geyser Basin and shoots to a maximum height of 90m. Don't count on it going off though – major eruptions can be up to 50 years apart – and even lesser blasts are unpredictable.

Yellowstone is open year-round. It's busy in high season; autumn can be a good time to visit. Crowds are smaller but watch out for sudden and significant snowfall.

GREATEST GEYSERS

MOST FASCINATING CORPSES

Gone but not forgotten – these lifeless leaders and mummified men are still very much with us...

413 ST BERNADETTE, NEVERS, FRANCE

Corpses don't come much comelier than St Bernadette, the pin-up of the passed away. The French nun, whose teenage Virgin Mary visions turned Lourdes into one of Christianity's key sites, is considered 'incorruptible'. Following her death in 1879, aged 35, she was exhumed three times – and declared intact on each occasion. Certainly her casket-enclosed body, on display in Nevers' Chapel of St Gildard, is pretty as ever – though if the angelic skin looks strangely waxy, that's because it is: it was felt her 'blackish colour' might put off pilgrims. Well, even the incorruptible need a touch up now and then.

Nevers is in the Burgundy region of central France; trains connect Nevers with Paris (two hours).

411 GRIP, PHILADELPHIA, USA

'And the raven, never flitting, still is sitting, still is sitting...' Still is sitting, in actual fact, in the Free Library of Philadelphia. The forbidding feathered creature, inspiration for 'The Raven', Edgar Allen Poe's famous poem, currently resides there, in a small glass case. He is Grip, and he has quite the literary past: beloved pet of Charles Dickens, he appeared in his master's novel *Barnaby Rudge* before Poe went on to immortalise him in verse. Dickens had the bird stuffed when it died in 1841; now it gazes over the library's rare books department, which includes works by Dickens and Poe themselves.

Grip is located on the 3rd floor of the Central Library, 1901 Vine Street; tours are available at 11am Monday to Friday (www.freelibrary.org).

412 JUANITA, AREQUIPA, PERU

Poor Juanita. Around 500 years ago, at the tender age of just 12 or 13, she was – so it's thought – taken up 6310m Nevado Ampato and sacrificed to appease the mountain. There she remained, cold and alone, until 1995, when a nearby volcanic eruption melted centuries of snow, uncovering her ceremonial resting place. Dubbed the Ice Maiden, Juanita was near-perfectly preserved by the high altitude and freezing temperatures. Now living at a lower altitude in Arequipa's Museo Santury, her muscles, stomach contents, even her once-fine clothes have provided a great, if ghoulish, insight into Inca life.

Arequipa's Museo Santury is open daily; Juanita is not on show from January to April, when another child sacrifice is displayed.

JON DAVISON / LONELY PLANET IMAGES

414 CAPUCHIN MONASTERY, BRNO, CZECH REPUBLIC

Not so much a fascinating corpse as fascinating *corpses* – lots of them, lying exposed in Brno's Capuchin Monastery Crypt. Most are monks: before the 18th century, these frugal souls reused the same coffin when a brother died; after the funerary rites were over, each dearly departed was removed from the recyclable casket and laid on the floor. Only it seems the well-aired catacomb – built by the appropriately named architect Moric Grimm – turned out to be ideal for body preservation. Wearing robes and clutching crucifixes, these tenacious holy men refuse to return to dust.

Brno is 210km east of Prague; frequent express trains connect Brno to the Czech capital (3½ hours).

415 POMPEII, ITALY

Nothing piques human curiosity like a mass catastrophe and few beat the ruins of Pompeii. While Pompeii's residents certainly weren't happy to be wiped out by the explosive belch of Mt Vesuvius, today's archaeologists are pretty pleased that they were. For the layer of *lapilli* (burning pumice) that coated the town in AD 79 preserved an unrivalled snapshot of Roman life, mummifying an entire city: its paved streets, amphitheatre, mosaics, villas, brothel – and its people. By pouring plaster into the cavities left by the disintegrated dead, their final poses have been captured for eerie eternity. Around a thousand souls have been found, several stored in Pompeii's Granai del Foro – a morgue from another millennia.

Pompeii (www.pompeiisites.org) is 40 minutes by bus or train from Naples; a one-day ticket for Pompeii costs €11.

Pompeii's excavated ruins are a profound mix of the monumental and the mundane

Tutankhamun's exquisite death mask on display in Cairo – and to think it was made to be buried in a hole in the ground...

416 TUTANKHAMUN, CAIRO, EGYPT

Ancient Egypt's most famous face hides over 3000 years of mystery. For behind that mask of glorious gold lies a crumbled body, unable to answer 'How did this 19-year-old pharaoh meet his early end? Was it murder? Malaria? A fall from chariot?' We may never know. But while scientists pick over his remains, visitors can follow the Tut trail. His Valley of the Kings tomb now sits empty; it was full of treasures when discovered in 1922, but these now reside in Cairo's Egyptian Museum. The museum is the place to come face to face with *that* mask and the more impressive Tut's inner coffin: 1.88m and 110kg of pure gold.

A Valley of the Kings entrance ticket permits access to three tombs only; visiting Tutankhamun's tomb costs extra.

419 LENIN, MOSCOW, RUSSIA

In good communist tradition, Lenin wasn't taken off to a subtle grave upon his death in 1924. A tomb was immediately erected in Moscow's Red Square so that the hero of the Revolution might continue to be worshipped. While the makeshift wooden structure has been replaced by one of stone, the man inside is remarkably little-changed, looking healthy (for his age) – the result of clever embalming and injections of mysterious 'balsam'. But he can't last forever.

Lenin's Mausoleum, at the northwestern corner of Red Square, is open from 10am to 1pm, Tuesday to Thursday, Saturday and Sunday; admission is free.

417 DAINICHIBO & CHURENJI TEMPLES, DEWA SANZAN, JAPAN

It takes extreme dedication to mummify yourself. But in the sacred mountains of northern Honshu, a group of monks gave it a go. The devotees of Dewa Sanzan followed a strict diet: nuts and seeds for a thousand days, pine and bark for a further thousand, plus tea made with poisonous sap – to purge the body of maggots. Then they'd meditate to death. Not all were successful – just a few *sokushinbutsu* mummies remain, one each in Dainichibo and Churenji Temples, near Mt Yudono. They don't look all that well, but pilgrims flock to see these men, who were on the ultimate quest for nirvana.

Visit from July to September, when all of Dewa Sanzan's temples are open; snowfall can make access difficult in winter.

418 HO CHI MINH, HANOI, VIETNAM

Apparently Ho Chi Minh, much-loved leader of Vietnam, wanted to be cremated following his death in 1969. Sadly for him, when you're this loved, your last wishes don't get granted. For the Vietnamese people like to still visit their liberator – his embalmed body remains on display in an austere, grey-granite mausoleum on Ba Dinh Square, the country's ceremonial heart. It was here that Ho Chi Minh declared independence on 2 September 1945; it's here that parades commemorate that day annually; and it's where smartly dressed devotees queue to enter the memorial, in order to shuffle past glass-enclosed 'Uncle Ho' himself.

The mausoleum is closed annually (usually October to November) for maintenance work to be carried out on Ho's body.

420 TOLLUND MAN, SILKEBORG, DENMARK

Forget Botox and anti-ageing creams – the secret to eternal youth, it seems, is to get buried in a pile of peat. It worked for Tollund Man. Extracted from Jutland's Bjældskovdal Bog about 2350 years after he was laid in it, this Iron Age 40-something looks good for his two-plus millennia. His head, tanned like leather by the peat's acidity, shows astonishing detail – lips, eyelids, wrinkles, even stubble are all visible on his blackened face.

Tollund Man and his contemporary, Elling Woman, are displayed in Silkeborg Museum, open daily from May to October (Saturday and Sunday only from November to April).

MOST FACINATING CORPSES

MOST BRILLIANT NIGHT SKIES

Stars were meant to knock you sideways. Here's where they still do.

423 PISAC, PERU

For the Incas, gazing at the heavens was about much more than horoscopes and romantic views. Instead the firmament featured a celestial roadway – the Milky Way. Priests possibly used this wide band of diffuse light as a route map for parallel terrestrial pilgrimages. You can tap into this mindset at Pisac, near Cuzco, with its sky-high complex of temples, citadels and terraces. While you're there have a close look at the Milky Way. The Incas saw negative patterns in it; dark cloud constellations are the gaps *between* the stars. See if you, like them, can spot a fox, a snake and a baby llama.

Pisac lies 33km northeast of Cuzco by paved road, and is a great starting point for a visit to the Sacred Valley.

421 HAWAI'I (BIG ISLAND), HAWAII, USA

You may plan to explore the smoking, steaming landscape around Crater Rim Drive, crawl through the lava tubes at Kaumana Caves or simply snorkel and sunbathe on the perfect white sand of Kauna'oa Bay. But it'd be a shame to leave the Big Island without at least one long look at the night sky – Hawai'i's altitude and isolation give it a distinct astronomical advantage. Twelve domed telescopes dot the 4.2km-high summit of Mauna Kea. But your best bet is the visitor centre 1.5km lower down, where they'll let you gaze through telescopes and gasp at constellations after dark.

The visitor centre is open from 9am to 10pm and will fix you up with hot chocolate as well as info (see www.ifa .hawaii.edu).

422 SLOVENIA

As Oscar Wilde put it: 'We are all in the gutter, but some of us are looking at the stars.' In theory you should be able to see a lot more stars in Slovenia – the country recently passed its first light-pollution law. As well as seeing Prague-like Ljubljana's charming architecture and skiing down Slovenia's alpine slopes, you might now notice carefully shaded street-lamps and low-glow public lighting during a trip here. The International Dark-Sky Association reckons the law will save Slovenia €10 million a year, and the planet some hefty greenhouse gas emissions.

Visit Portorož (the name means 'Port of Roses') for a good chance of clear skies – the coastal town has the country's highest annual sunshine levels.

424 SHERBROOKE, CANADA

Once the global hub of ice-hockey-stick manufacturing, Sherbrooke, Québec, didn't have many other claims to fame until recently. Visitors tend to use this French-speaking city as a springboard for the pristine rivers, mountains and lakes of the nearby Mont-Megantic National Park. But there is another reason to visit: both the park and the city have been designated the world's first International Dark-Sky Reserve. It's resulted in some 2500 light fittings being replaced – neatly cutting light pollution by a quarter. Look up and see much less of the city glow bleeding into the night sky.

Check out the work of the International Dark-Sky Association, which is dedicated to reducing light pollution, at www .darksky.org.

425 CALDERA DE TABURIENTE NATIONAL PARK, CANARY ISLANDS

Flung out into the sea off West Africa, the Canary Islands are the last chunk of land before a whole lot of ocean. La Palma is the island furthest west, and right at its tip is the Caldera de Taburiente National Park. It's such a good spot for star gazing that it's home to the Roque de los Muchachos Observatory, which has one of the most extensive fleets of telescopes in the world. When you're not staring at the night sky, hike the pine-clad, stream-scored slopes of the park's massive crater, then head to the beach to soothe those hamstrings.

If you can take the crowds, time your star-gazing pilgrimage to catch the riotous fun of the carnival season in February or March.

427 MCDONALD OBSERVATORY, TEXAS, USA

For a night-time event like no other, head more than 2000m above sea level to the top of Mt Locke. The McDonald Observatory, at Davis Mountains in Texas, enjoys some of the best dark skies in the continental US, ensuring jaw-dropping views of celestial splendour. It also holds regular star parties, allowing you to look through the kind of massive telescopes that make astronomers rub their hands together with glee. Marvel at the unrivalled views of planets, stars and galaxies – there's a whole universe out there waiting to be glimpsed.

The Observatory is open from 10am to 5.30pm. To book in for a star party, visit www.mcdonaldobservatory.org.

429 ATACAMA DESERT, CHILE

The Atacama is 1000 sq km of prime star-gazing country. What makes it so perfect for eyeballing the heavens? It's the driest desert in the world, and no rain means no clouds. It's lightly populated, which means no light spill. And the clear, dry, high-altitude air gives great visibility. In fact it's so perfect for star gazing that the European Southern Observatory operates two observatories here, one housing the Very Large Telescope (did Douglas Adams name that thing?). It's also where the Atacama Large Millimeter Array (ALMA), a huge new radio telescope, is being constructed.

The Atacama desert is on Chile's Pacific coast. It's a coastal inversion layer that keeps it so dry.

426 STONEHENGE, ENGLAND

Thought by some to be a giant, primitive observatory, Stonehenge suggests that going 'wow' at the heavens' twinkling bits is nothing new – building began on this monumental circle of standing stones around 5000 years ago. It's still a good place to star gaze today – out in Salisbury Plain in Wiltshire there aren't many lights around to interfere with nature's display. Wander the path around the site during the day, find a vantage point nearby, wait for the sun to go down, then think millennia-old mystic thoughts.

Cycling is a tranquil way to arrive at Stonehenge. Take National Cycling Network Route 45 from Amesbury.

428 SARK, CHANNEL ISLANDS

Get out of the cities to see more stars. Urban light pollution means you'll usually only see 100 with the naked eye; in a dark-sky zone you can pick out 1000. For a beautiful nightscape head to Sark, in the Channel Islands. This high plateau of granite is nearly 5km long and 2.5km wide, has few houses and no cars or street lights. Cycling its pock-marked, unpaved lanes by moonlight is magical – but bring a torch. Then gaze up from vertiginous cliffs above an inky expanse of sea and do some serious star counting.

See Sark in all its glory in Channel 4's adaptation of *Mr Pye*, the eccentric Sark-set novel by Mervyn Peake.

430 CARIBBEAN ISLANDS

Where better to gaze at a bejewelled blanket of stars than on islands where the breeze is warm, the night air is fragrant with frangipani and the rum is sweet. Find a romantic beachside, palm-fringed spot, lie back and stare into the velvety darkness. You and your beloved can even find and name a constellation of your very own.

On some islands the view is made all the more intense by the not-infrequent power cuts – proving a great dark-sky maxim: lights go off, stars come out.

MOST IMPRESSIVE CORAL REEFS

Coral reefs cover less than 1% of the world's oceans but support incredible biodiversity – pull on your snorkel, take a deep breath and check out these incredible underwater gardens.

431 GREAT BARRIER REEF, AUSTRALIA

Yes, it's an obvious choice, but the Great Barrier Reef is popular for good reason. The world's largest marine park stretches more than 2300km along the clear, shallow waters off the northeast coast of Australia. An extraordinary variety of species thrives in its tropical waters, including 400 types of coral, 1500 species of fish and 400 types of mollusc. An armada of tour boats shuttles snorkellers and divers to and from shore, providing myriad services and tours. Witness whales on their annual migration, car-sized cod fish and eerie shipwrecks at this Unesco World Heritage site.

Live-aboard boat *Spirit of Freedom* (www .spiritoffreedom.com.au) offers divers three-, four- and seven-day itineraries. In Cairns you'll find heaps more options for exploring the reef.

433 NEW CALEDONIA BARRIER REEF, NEW CALEDONIA

Coral reefs come in many shapes and sizes and the Pacific nation of New Caledonia boasts a sizeable double-barrier system; it's 1300km in length and surrounds the main island of Grand Terre. Lying up to 30km from the shore, the reef forms a huge lagoon containing a staggering array of marine life. Strap on your snorkel, take the plunge and you'll be confronted by species including triggerfish, tuna, sharks and tortoises, set against a backdrop of phosphorescent corals. Many species are endemic and Unesco considers this an area of outstanding natural importance – it placed the reef on the World Heritage list in 2008.

International flights arrive at Tontouta International Airport, 45km northwest of Noumea. The cooler months of July and August are a good time to visit.

432 ANDROS BARRIER REEF, BAHAMAS

The crystal waters surrounding Andros, the least populous of the Bahaman islands, form the world's third-largest reef system and offer truly unique dive experiences. The corals extend for 225km along the island's east coast and run to the edge of the dramatically named Tongue of the Ocean, an oceanic shelf that plunges from the 35m shallows to a pulse-quickening depth of 1800m. The experience is mesmerising, as is the opportunity to explore the wondrous coral caves of the Petrified Forest. Closer to shore, lagoon and mangrove areas offer less adrenaline-fuelled dives, rich in groupers, snappers and a variety of sponges.

Scuba divers heading to Andros have made Small Bay Hope Lodge their base since 1960. Dive trips, including night dives and shark spotting, are its speciality (www.smallhope.com).

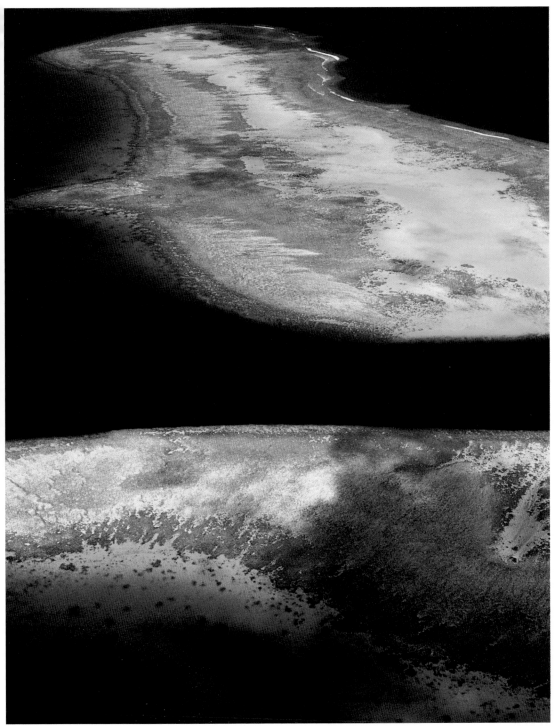

Indulge any and all *Blue Lagoon* fantasies in the blue heaven of New Caledonia

Off the radar until the last few years, Indonesia's Raja Ampat islands now see a steady traffic of live-aboard dive boats

434 RAJA AMPAT ISLANDS, WEST PAPUA, INDONESIA

Lying off the coast of Sorong in West Papua, Raja Ampat is at the heart of the so-called 'coral triangle', encompassing the reefs of Indonesia, the Philippines and northern Australia. The dazzling reefs that flourish here are considered some of the world's most spectacular, supporting a mind-boggling 1200 species of fish and 600 species of coral, some 75% of all known variants. So diverse is the ecosystem that one diver set a world record for the number of fish species seen in an hour – an astonishing 283. Add in multifarious sea fans, sponges and anthias fish of every possible colour and this is a destination without compare.

West Papua gets a serious amount of rain – 2000mm to 3000mm annually. The period from April to October offers the best chance of staying dry.

435 CAROLINE ATOLL, REPUBLIC OF KIRIBATI

The South Pacific is the ultimate desert-island destination. The Republic of Kiribati is a nation of 32 atolls and one solitary coral island, so isolated from civilisation that this is one of the world's most remote regions. It's also the location for an extraordinary lagoon reef. Caroline Atoll, 4200km east of the capital, Tarawa, is a tiny group of islets measuring just 13km long and 2.5km wide. The atoll's seclusion has allowed it to remain pristine and the reef blooms with lush corals and vivid species such as giant clams, coconut crabs and the Napoleon wrasse.

Caroline Atoll is part of the Line Islands. Air Kiribati (www.airkiribati.com.au) and Coral Sun Airways (www.coralsunairways.com) have domestic air connections.

MICHAEL GEBICKI / LONELY PLANET IMAGES

437 BELIZE BARRIER REEF, BELIZE

The Belize Barrier Reef is part of the greater Mesoamerican reef system that extends from Mexico's Yucatán Peninsula down to Honduras. The 300km length that follows Belize's Caribbean coastline shelters 100 types of coral and 500 species of fish. Scuba diving is the main draw and the reef has some of the best sites in the world including the Blue Hole, a 300m-wide, 124m-deep sinkhole. In 1996 Unesco bestowed World Heritage status on the reef, but global warming, pollution and uncontrolled tourism are threatening its health.

Ambergris Caye is the largest island in Belize and a prime spot from which to explore the reef. It's a 15-minute flight from the mainland (www.mayaislandair.com).

439 ABROLHOS BANK, BRAZIL

The oceans are earth's final unexplored frontier. Brazil's Abrolhos Bank, lying in shallow water near the southern coast of Bahia state, has long been of world importance due to the endemic species of mushroom-shaped corals. But in 2008 researchers discovered new reef structures that doubled the size of a system that was already the largest in the southern Atlantic. The reefs around the archipelago are now known to cover an area of 46,000 sq km and harbour previously unknown species of corals, molluscs and fish.

Access to the reef is best via the Bahian fishing town of Caravelas, which lies 920km from Rio de Janeiro.

436 ALDABRA ATOLL, SEYCHELLES

Aldabra is the world's second-largest atoll. Its location means there are no permanent residents and few tourists, but reef lovers might want to add it to their hit list. Surrounding the atoll are a series of shallow flats, slopes and deeper-lying reef systems, rich in pristine corals, fish and invertebrates. This bionetwork remains self-sufficient due to its protection from human interference, which has prevented stocks from depletion. In addition to the reef ecosystem, Aldabra supports species such as hammerhead sharks, barracuda, and over 150,000 endemic giant tortoises.

The nearest airstrip is on Assomption Island, 25km away. From here, take a dive cruise (www.ioexpl.com) or wait for one of the infrequent government supply ships.

438 KOMODO NATIONAL PARK, LESSER SUNDA ISLANDS, INDONESIA

Mention the name 'Komodo' and the mind races with images of the fearsome-looking dragon, the gigantic carnivore synonymous with Indonesia's islands. So it's no surprise to find that this chap is the star of the show in the aptly named Komodo National Park. But drag yourself away from the lizards and into the ocean and you'll find something equally extraordinary. The temperate waters support an iridescent network of reefs, abundant with the flamboyant life of sea horses, clown frogfish, blue-ringed octopuses and delicate tunicates. The contrast with the mean old Komodo dragon couldn't be greater.

To see the best of the park's reefs take a cruise with Komodo Liveaboard; it offers five- and six-day itineraries (www .komodo-liveaboard.com).

440 RØST REEF, NORWAY

High inside the Arctic Circle, Røst Reef was only discovered in 2002 and is the world's largest known cold-water coral system, covering an area of 120 sq km and lying at a depth of 400m. Røst is an island in the Lofoten archipelago, 200km southwest from Tromsø. Although the reef might be too far and too deep for the average diver, there are other options. Nutrient-rich currents flow around the islands, giving rise to a world rich in corals, wrecks and diverse marine life.

Harsh conditions mean you need to be competent to dive here. Amateurs should stick to snorkelling safaris run by operators such as Lofoten Opplevelser (www .lofoten-opplevelser.no).

MOST IMPRESSIVE CORAL REEFS

MOST INTERESTING SUBWAY STATIONS

These artful stops are reason enough to take your sightseeing underground.

Sculpting with light at Munich's Westfriedhof

441 BAKER STREET, LONDON, ENGLAND

Baker Street is where Sherlock Holmes lived in Arthur Conan Doyle's popular novels – hence the station's tiles, decorated with the detective's pipe-puffing silhouette. The station is a busy hub of the London Underground, serving five lines and carrying carriage-loads of tourists to Madame Tussauds and Regent's Park. Back in 1863, when the Underground was starting out life as the Metropolitan, the world's first underground railway, Baker Street was one of the stops. It's a survivor, unlike some of the other Underground stations, which have fallen into disuse and are glimpsed only as 'ghost stations' from the windows of trains moving between platforms.

Baker Street is on the Circle, Hammersmith & City, Metropolitan, Jubilee and Bakerloo lines. The Hammersmith & City platforms are the oldest.

443 T-CENTRALEN, STOCKHOLM, SWEDEN

There's so much to love about Stockholm's metro. First of all, it's called the *tunnelbana*. Second of all, it's often referred to as 'the world's longest art gallery' because almost every station in the system displays some kind of artwork. And thirdly, when it was dug out, the natural rock formation was left on Line B, giving cave-like arches to the concourses. T-Centralen, the system's hub, feels like you've entered into the Hall of the Mountain King, with rough arches painted up in traditional blue-and-white designs by Finnish artist Per Olaf Utvedt. There are also mosaic pillars and a mural depicting the *tunnelbana* workers on their scaffolding.

All local transport is run by Storstockholms Lokaltrafik (www.sl.se). There's an SL office in the basement of Centralstationen (not to be confused with T-Centralen).

444 KOMSOMOLSKAYA, MOSCOW, RUSSIA

Part baroque palace, part art gallery, part political exhortation, Komsomolskaya fights off some stiff competition from Moscow's marvellously elaborate subway stations to take the (highly decorated) cake. What makes it the greatest? The chandeliers, the hefty marble columns, the pale yellow arched ceilings picked out with snowy white decorative details… not to mention the mosaics. Inspired by Stalin's speech at the 1941 Moscow Parade, the mosaics depict Russian weaponry and glorious moments in the struggle for Russian freedom, and have been subject to some revisions over the years (including a retouch to remove Stalin himself).

Komsomolskaya is on the Koltsevaya line. It gets some major traffic, so visit outside peak hours to linger over the decor.

442 WESTFRIEDHOF, MUNICH, GERMANY

The architecture here is by Auer & Weber, but it's the work of Ingo Maurer that puts this place up with the big boys. In fact, the station is pretty bleak, all stark lines and concrete (the name means 'West Cemetery', so perhaps we should expect something a little sombre). But it's transformed by Maurer's light design. Huge lamps cast vivid colour over the walls and platforms, saturating the concrete with stained-glass blues, yellows and reds. And suddenly, wonderland! It's a place to ponder how easily the human desire for decoration can be satisfied. And maybe the place to shoot an '80s film clip.

Westfriedhof is a U-Bahn station on the U1 line. Rest up at the nearby neo-Renaissance mini-castle Hotel Laimer Hof (www.laimerhof.de).

445 HOLLYWOOD/VINE, LOS ANGELES, USA

OK, so perhaps it's tacky, but would you want the Hollywood/Vine station to be anything else? The LA subway gives it up for celluloid in this film-inspired station design including Yellow Brick Road paving, movie-theatre elevators, displays of 1930s projectors and even the notes to the 'Hooray for Hollywood' song in the handrails. The fake palm trees and vaulted ceilings recall the city's classic movie theatres. (If you look very closely, you'll see the ceilings are covered with film reels.)

161

Duck up to street level to pose with the stars on the Hollywood Walk of Fame, just outside the station.

446 BURJUMAN, DUBAI, UNITED ARAB EMIRATES

As you'd expect, Dubai's metro is a flashy affair. The stations are all modernist curves and whimsical decorations, with the themes being earth, air, fire and water. Despite its sci-fi sleekness, there are some carefully incorporated elements of traditional architecture, such as oriels and arches. The metro also tips a nod to the past by modelling its buildings on seashells, a reference to the city's pearl-diving heritage. Burjuman (also called Khalid Bin Al Waleed) is one of the most impressive stations, an underwater extravaganza of blue light and drippy, trippy jellyfish chandeliers.

Swim your way through your commute by visiting Burjuman as you pass between the Red and the Green lines.

447 FLORA STATION, PRAGUE, CZECH REPUBLIC

Prague may be a magic fairytale city above ground, but head down into its metro and it's pure 1970s – Soviet sci-fi style. The stations are decorated with geometric claddings that form long sleek perspectives and disappear into the tunnels. It's hard not to feel you should be donning your space gun and teleport bracelet and rushing down the platforms. Flora is one of the most stunning of the stations, with gold and burgundy spheres that whoosh past like light trails when you're coming in on a train. Ride Line A to get the effect. Don't miss the ticket halls with their murals of greenery.

Flora is just below the shopping mall Palác Flora, and close to the New Jewish Cemetery.

448 NAMUR, MONTRÉAL, CANADA

Montréal's subway system dates from the 1960s, and has housed the work of Québec's artists ever since its opening. The stations have varying levels of cultural excitement – some are notable more for their architectural features, like stained-glass windows that let in natural light to the concourses – but some are enlivened by sculptures and coloured tiles. Namur would be a fairly bleak station if it weren't for *Système*, a vast aluminium sculpture by Pierre Granche that hangs from the roof. Its interlocking structures recall molecules or geometric bubbles and give the station a magical, ethereal feel.

The station is on the Orange line – slightly ironic given its grey-and-steel colour scheme (well, it was opened in 1984…).

449 SYNTAGMA, ATHENS, GREECE

While the Athens metro is relatively new, several of its stations sport ancient artefacts dug up during the excavations. The process of tunnelling out the metro began in the early 1990s and was unprecedented in its cooperation between the engineers making the new lines, and archaeologists from the Ministry of Culture who worked alongside them to salvage and categorise the spoils under the city's surface. At Syntagma the finds included Roman baths, a sculpture foundry, an ancient road,

Burjuman metro station: as much a statement of intent as the rest of Dubai's singular architecture

an aqueduct and a river bed. Objects from the digs (or their replicas) are displayed at the station.

Want more ancient artefacts? Visit the National Archaeological Museum to see what was dug up in Athens in the 19th century.

450 UNIVERSIDAD DE CHILE, SANTIAGO, CHILE

There are many stations that have elements of art in them, but few compare with Universidad de Chile for the feeling you've stepped inside a gallery – or a Renaissance church.

The station walls are covered with a giant mural by Mario Toral that explores Chile's history in a grand heroic style that sometimes recalls Soviet art, sometimes an art deco cinema. But this is not bland public art. Toral pulls no punches, and all the pain of Chile's past – torture, fear, oppression – are there as well as its high points. It's a majestic achievement and well worth a detour.

There are other artistic highlights in them thar tunnels: try Santa Lucia station, with traditional Portuguese tiles donated by the Lisbon metro.

MOST INTERESTING SUBWAY STATIONS

ULTIMATE PREDATORS IN ACTION

They look fine and they look fierce, but watch out for those teeth. For a beast of a time, pay a visit to these happy hunting grounds.

453 JAGUARS, COCKSCOMB BASIN WILDLIFE SANCTUARY, BELIZE

Belize's most famous protected area is a huge swath of tropical forest that became the world's first jaguar sanctuary in 1984. Today it's home to an estimated 40 to 50 jaguars, as well as other wildlife: Belize's four other wild cats – the puma, ocelot, margay and jaguarundi – also roam here. Sightings are difficult, but they are possible, and often close to the park's headquarters. Night holds the best chance, with jaguars, ocelots and pumas often padding along the park entrance road late at night.

Visits are restricted to an eastern pocket where there's an information centre, accommodation and walking trails. Tours can be arranged at nearby Maya Center.

451 AFRICAN WILD DOGS, CHOBE NATIONAL PARK, BOTSWANA

Botswana's most famous national park is known largely for its enormous congregations of elephants and buffalo, but it also provides some of the best predator viewing on the continent. Chief among the hungry carnivores is the African wild dog – the so-called painted wolf – which is probably the most efficient hunter in Africa. Highly social and roaming in large packs, they are best seen on the open areas around Savuti Marshes in the west of the park. When the rains arrive in November and December, thousands of Burchell's zebras move into this area, attracting the wild dogs (and other predators).

To travel through the park, you'll need a high-clearance 4WD. Due to mud and flooding, Savuti may be inaccessible from January to March.

452 GREAT WHITE SHARKS, PORT LINCOLN, AUSTRALIA

The fact that some of the underwater scenes in *Jaws* were filmed around the South Australian fishing town of Port Lincoln is all you need to know about this shark-infested hot spot. The cool waters here are home to an impressive wealth of great white sharks, the fang-filled fish that can strike fear into even the fearless. Cage diving among the sharks is possible around the Neptune Islands, which are home to around half of Australia's total population of New Zealand fur seals, a favourite shark snack. Once here, you are dipped into the baited sea inside a mesh cage, with the great whites so near and yet hopefully still so far away.

Cage dives are offered by Calypso Star Charters (www.calypsostarcharter.com.au).

454 ORCAS, RESERVA FAUNÍSTICA PENÍNSULA VALDÉS, ARGENTINA

It may look like a pimple on the eastern face of South America, but Península Valdés is one of the continent's finest wildlife reserves, home to sea lions, elephant seals, guanacos, Magellanic penguins and a parade of passing southern right whales. Once a year (mid-February to mid-April), however, the action turns violent as orcas come to the peninsula's northern tip, Punta Norte, to feast on unsuspecting colonies of sea lions – the spectacular and famous footage from the *Trials of Life* documentary, in which orcas beached themselves to get at sea lions, was filmed here.

Puerto Pirámides, inside the reserve, is about 90km from the regional centre of Puerto Madryn and accessible by bus, but to travel around the peninsula a rental car is recommended.

455 BROWN BEARS, MCNEIL RIVER STATE GAME SANCTUARY, USA

Remember all those brown-bear-eats-leaping-salmon poster prints? Chances are they were photographed in this Alaskan reserve, which protects the world's largest concentration of brown bears. Here, each summer, bears gather at McNeil River Falls (up to 72 bears have been spotted at a time), snapping and chomping at spawning salmon as they leap through the falls on their journey upstream. The Alaska Department of Fish and Game has set up a viewing area and allows 10 visitors per day for a four-day period. The prime viewing season is July.

Visits are by permit only, and these are issued by lottery. Applications can be made through the Alaska Department of Fish and Game at www.wildlife.alaska.gov.

456 TIGERS, CORBETT NATIONAL PARK, INDIA

Few sights are as thrilling as spotting a Bengal tiger in the wild. India has 27 Project Tiger reserves, but Corbett, the original reserve and India's first national park, is still among the best for tiger tracking. Home to an estimated 10% of the country's estimated 1500 tigers, it offers safaris in jeeps and on the back of elephants, ranging out through the sal forest in search of the big cats. Sightings are down to chance, but if you visit towards the end of the dry season (late May or early June) waterholes will be scarce and grass cover minimal, optimising your chances.

To reach Corbett, take the overnight Ranikhet Express train from Delhi to Ramnagar, where permits and accommodation must be arranged at the Project Tiger office.

457 PITCHER PLANTS, MALIAU BASIN CONSERVATION AREA, MALAYSIA

Maliau Basin is known as Sabah's Lost World, and it's easy to see why. With no roads and no record of humans having entered the area until the early 1980s, it's a dense knot of genetic richness, winding rivers and lush rainforest. Among its 1800 plant species are six species of pitcher plant, a carnivorous plant with flip-top leaves that form a liquid-filled trap. Insects are drawn into the trap and devoured, and with a nascent tourism industry forming around the basin, visitors are now also being drawn towards these floral predators.

Independent visits to the basin are difficult, and there's no public transport, so arrange a guided tour from Tawau, about a five-hour drive away.

458 NILE CROCODILES, GRUMETI RIVER, TANZANIA

As wildlife spectacles go, the annual wildebeest migration through East Africa rates highly, especially when one million of the critters – a great seething mass of wildebeest – are forced to ford the Grumeti River in the Serengeti National Park's Western Corridor, with its hungry hordes of crocodiles. Occurring between May and July (usually in June), it's the most spectacular moment of the migration, with gigantic Nile crocs preying on the weakest of the wildebeest – you might never linger at the back of a group again!

Accommodation along the Serengeti's Western Corridor includes luxury tent camps at Kirawira and Grumeti River Camp. The river is also easily accessed from the park centre at Seronera.

459 POLAR BEARS, CHURCHILL, CANADA

The Manitoba town of Churchill makes a reasonable claim as the world's polar bear capital. It lies on the bears' migration route, between winters spent hunting on the frozen bay and summers on land. And though they might look like giant teddy bears, their bite is to be feared – polar bears are the largest of all bear species. The best (and safest) way to see them is aboard the purpose-built buggies that form the mainstay of the town's tourism each October. To avoid close encounters of the bear kind, local authorities maintain a 24-hour vigil from September to November, firing gunshots at night to shoo away any town-bound prowlers.

There are no roads into Churchill, but it can be reached by air or rail from Winnipeg.

460 LEOPARDS, YALA NATIONAL PARK, SRI LANKA

With trumpeting elephants, monkeys crashing through the trees, and peacocks in their finest frocks, Yala National Park is *The Jungle Book* brought to glorious life, complete with Bagheera the leopard. With more than 35 leopards, Yala West has one of the world's densest populations and is renowned as one of the best places in which to see these stunning cats. They're visible usually from around February to June or July, with the end of the dry season (March to April) providing the best viewing conditions as animals congregate around the park's shrinking waterholes.

The only way to visit the park is on a safari, which can be arranged in Tissamaharama.

TOP WWII SIGHTS

Barely 20 years on from the WWI armistice, Europe and the world were once again ravaged by war. Millions more lives were lost and poignant reminders can be found across the globe.

461 ANNE FRANK HOUSE, AMSTERDAM, THE NETHERLANDS

Auschwitz exemplifies what WWII meant for Jewish communities and, unsurprisingly, thousands tried to conceal themselves from the atrocities. The most famous exponent was Annelies Marie Franke, a young German girl forced into hiding with her family in the Netherlands. During her early teenage life Frank chronicled her secret existence in a series of powerful diaries, revered for the insight they offer into her astonishing way of life. Frank's family was eventually betrayed and she died in the Bergen-Belsen concentration camp, aged just 15, but the Frank home in Amsterdam was preserved and tells the moving story of one deeply personal battle against Nazi persecution.

Centrally located in the heart of Amsterdam, Anne Frank House is a 20-minute walk from Centraal Station. The museum is open daily (www .annefrank.org).

462 BLETCHLEY PARK MUSEUM, ENGLAND

With modern warfare relying on GPS, unmanned drones and bomb-defusing robots, it's sometimes difficult to imagine that WWII was predominantly a conflict played out in secret bunkers and reliant on intense human labour. But the formative computer technology employed in the rural English countryside was critical to Allied success. Hidden behind the facade of a traditional stately home, monolithic electromagnetic processors known as *bombes* whirred around the clock in an attempt to crack German Enigma codes. The museum at Bletchley Park houses replicas of these astonishing machines, together with wireless listening stations and archives detailing the history of the technology that gave rise to the modern-day computer.

Bletchley Park is located in the city of Milton Keynes; open daily, it's easily accessible from the city centre by train and bus (www.bletchleypark.org.uk).

ANN CECIL / LONELY PLANET IMAGES

463 USS ARIZONA MEMORIAL, PEARL HARBOR, HAWAII, USA

Big surf and volcanoes make Hawaii a dream-holiday destination, yet the visitors of 7 December 1941 came with more sinister intentions. Stationed nearby in the Pacific Ocean, six Japanese aircraft carriers launched a surprise attack that sank or disabled every US boat anchored at Pearl Harbor, taking almost 2500 lives in the process. The operation signalled the start of American involvement in the conflict – the US declared war on Japan the very next day – and today US veterans and bereaved relatives visit the memorial built on the submerged USS *Arizona* as part of their homage to those lost throughout WWII.

The USS *Arizona* Memorial Visitor Center (www.nps.gov/valr) is the gateway to this aquatic memorial in Honolulu – boat trips operate from 8am to 3pm daily.

167

The vessel itself may be submerged, but the memories aren't; visitors pay tribute at the USS *Arizona* Memorial

Hiroshima's Peace Memorial Park seeks to preserve the city's tragic legacy, and the lessons learnt

464 HIROSHIMA PEACE MEMORIAL, JAPAN

Hiroshima will forever be associated with the world's first deployment of the atomic bomb. On August 6 1945 at 8.15am, US bombers unleashed a weapon they mockingly called 'Little Boy'. It exploded 600m above the city and caused total carnage – 90,000 perished immediately and another 130,000 would die in the next five years as a result of their injuries or subsequent radiation sickness. Hiroshima was largely rebuilt, but one building, the Genbaku Dome, has been preserved in its bombed state. Fragile and skeletal, this poignant ruin was directly under the point of detonation and today forms part of the Unesco-protected Peace Memorial Park.

Hiroshima is 800km west of Tokyo. The Peace Memorial is centrally located on the Ota River and hosts the annual Peace Memorial Ceremony on 6 August.

465 KATYN WAR CEMETERY, RUSSIA

As war raged throughout Europe, human persecution on an unimaginable scale was occurring far from the front line. In the continent's furthest corners, mass murder was commonplace and many crimes only surfaced years later. One of the most hideous occurred in a remote forest near the Russian town of Katyn, where 22,000 Polish officers, doctors and high-ranking intelligentsia were massacred by the Soviet secret service – Soviet commanders would deny any involvement until the collapse of the USSR in 1990. Today the forest houses a moving cemetery, including memorial plaques that lend a dignified remembrance to those denied a dignified death.

Katyn is 22km from the Russian town of Smolensk, itself equidistant between Moscow and the capital of Belarus, Minsk.

466 KOKODA TRAIL, PAPUA NEW GUINEA

During WWII the Japanese hatched a daring plan to attack mainland Australia. The aim was to cross Papua New Guinea via the Kokoda Trail and launch a secret attack. However, the Aussies got wind of the idea and met them midway. The result was bloody combat where malaria, heat and sickness killed as many soldiers as the conflict itself. These days you can walk the same trail in a matter of days, but get ready for blisters, leeches and humidity – the least of the worries for those that fought here. The battle conditions are gone, but the rainforest and history remain.

Based in Australia, Kokoda Trekking (www.kokodatrail.com.au) runs six-day and nine-day guided tours along the trail.

467 CHUUK LAGOON, FEDERATED STATES OF MICRONESIA

Chuuk Lagoon abounds with rich, colourful coral and tropical fish, but divers heading here aren't interested in the ecosystem. What attracts them to this 70km-wide lagoon are the wrecks – Chuuk may hold the greatest proliferation of scuttled vessels anywhere in the world. It was used as a Japanese naval base in WWII, and US attacks in 1944 sank dozens of ships and downed numerous planes – there are even eerily encrusted tanks in the 35m-deep waters. Favourite dives include the *Fujikawa Maru,* complete with intact fighter planes in its holds, and the *Shinkoku Maru,* decorated by nature in soft corals and sponges.

Blue Lagoon Dive Shop (www.truk -lagoon-dive.com) can take you on guided snorkelling and deep-dive trips to some of the best wreck sites.

468 D-DAY BEACHES, NORMANDY, FRANCE

On 6 June 1944, Allied forces launched the largest amphibious invasion in history, landing 160,000 soldiers along an 80km stretch of the French coast, an astonishing mobilisation involving 5000 craft and an army of airborne reinforcements. Officially known as 'Operation Overlord', D-Day was the codename for a surge that lasted three weeks, changing the course of the war but with huge losses to the regiments fighting. Apart from some concrete bunkers, few signs of war remain but the major beaches are still marked with their operative codenames – Gold, Juno, Omaha, Pointe du Hoc, Sword and Utah – and cemeteries, museums and information centres commemorate one of the defining events of WWII.

Many beaches are reached easily from the town of Bayeux, 260km west of Paris and accessible by train or bus. Visit in early June for annual D-Day commemorations.

469 AUSCHWITZ CONCENTRATION CAMP, OŚWIĘCIM, POLAND

Few places are as chilling as Auschwitz. As the Nazi holocaust swept across Europe, six million Jews died in the most appalling genocide of the 20th century and more than one million perished in the Auschwitz network of concentration camps. So large was the facility that three main camps – base, labour and extermination – were supported by 45 satellite blocks in a compound designed to inflict horrific suffering. There's no easy way to approach the horror of gas chambers, crematoria and death camps, let alone the myriad individual possessions that personalise the atrocities, but Auschwitz speaks louder than any history book ever could.

Auschwitz is near the industrial city of Oświęcim, 35km from Katowice and 70km from Kraków. The museum is open daily – opening hours vary with the seasons (www.auschwitz.org.pl).

470 JEWISH GHETTO, WARSAW, POLAND

European Jewish communities not in the concentration camps faced grim conditions in overcrowded inner-city ghettos. Across the continent, Nazi commanders created closed communes that were sealed behind brick walls and patrolled by trigger-happy armed troops. Warsaw had the largest ghetto, where 450,000 Jews were annexed from the outside world. Conditions were dismal, yet, despite the suffering, a sense of resistance surfaced. Secret associations promoted cultural activities and forged trade links with the 'other side'. A full-blown revolt would eventually erupt, but was mercilessly crushed as Nazis razed the ghetto in 1943. Amid the carnage, a few buildings remained and are now commemorated with simple memorials.

You can find original ghetto buildings on Próżna Street – visit www.insightpoland .com for details of three- to four-hour guided tours.

TOP WWII SITES

OPERA HOUSES WITH IMPACT

Acoustic perfection is the resounding star in these temples of high art, but it wouldn't sound as sweet without the accompanying history and/or visual appeal.

471 TEATRO AMAZONAS, MANAUS, BRAZIL

Opera in the Amazon? Well, yes. Manaus is the Amazon's largest city, an incongruous pocket of urbanity in the middle of the jungle. Its famous opera house was opened in 1896, at the height of the region's rubber boom, and symbolises the opulence that was once Manaus. The artists and most of the materials (Italian marble and glass, Scottish cast iron) were imported from Europe; the wood is Brazilian but was sent to Europe to be carved. One truly homespun feature was the roadway outside the entrance – it's made of rubber, so late-arriving carriages wouldn't make too much noise.

The annual Amazonas Opera Festival is a three-week gala during April and May that brings high-quality opera deep into the rainforest.

The Sydney Opera House: turtles never had this much fun

472 PALAIS GARNIER, PARIS, FRANCE

The fabled 'phantom of the opera' lurked in this opulent opera house (aka the Paris Opéra), one of only two designed by Charles Garnier (the other is in Toulon). It was designed in 1860 to showcase the splendour of Napoleon III's France – unfortunately, by the time it was complete (15 years later) the second empire was but a distant memory and Napoleon III had been dead for two years. Still, this is one of the most impressive monuments erected in Paris in the 19th century – and in a city full of architectural riches that's really saying something.

Take a guided tour, or visit the attached museum, full of costumes, backdrops, scores and other memorabilia; see www.operadeparis.fr.

473 OPERAHUSET, OSLO, NORWAY

Those Scandinavians sure know how to design modern opera houses. The new, white Oslo Opera House is a sheer delight – and is partially submerged in a fjord! The design was inspired by the image of two glaciers colliding – from afar, from some angles, it looks like a floating angular iceberg. Inside is a symphony of oak set in a translucent cube. The roof, though, might be the best treat. Essentially an urban promenade, its large, sloping planes extend down to the water. Follow the crowds up to scramble around, peer inside and look out over the fjord. It feels kind of like a playground for adults that happens to host opera.

Operahuset won the 2009 Mies van der Rohe Award, the EU Prize for Contemporary Architecture. See www.operaen.no for more.

474 STAATSOPER, VIENNA, AUSTRIA

In a city considered by many to be the world capital of opera and classical music, this is *the* premier opera venue. Built between 1861 and 1869, it initially revolted the Viennese public and Habsburg royalty and quickly earned the nickname 'stone turtle'. Both the architects took this poorly: one hanged himself and the other died of a heart attack two months later. Despite its frosty reception, its opening concert was Mozart's *Don Giovanni* and it went on to house some of the most iconic directors in history. Productions are lavish affairs – the Viennese take their opera *very* seriously and dress up accordingly.

Feeling peckish? Directly across from the Staatsoper is Café Sacher, of *Sacher Torte* (rich chocolate cake with apricot jam) fame.

ROSS BARNETT / LONELY PLANET IMAGES

475 SYDNEY OPERA HOUSE, AUSTRALIA

Full of admiration for the Sydney Opera House, famous architect Louis Kahn said: 'The sun did not know how beautiful its light was, until it was reflected off this building.' Danish architect Jørn Utzon's competition-winning 1956 design is Australia's most recognisable icon. Utzon is rumoured to have drawn inspiration from orange segments, palm fronds and Mayan temples, and the building has been poetically likened to a typewriter stuffed with scallop shells and the sexual congress of turtles. Construction commenced in 1959 and it was officially opened in 1973 after a soap-opera series of personality clashes, technical difficulties and delays.

One-hour tours of the Sydney Opera House depart half-hourly from 9am to 5pm; see www.sydneyoperahouse.com.

171

476 TEATRO ALLA SCALA, MILAN, ITALY

Like a true diva, Milan's legendary opera house normally only goes by one name: La Scala. Its austere facade seems at odds with its sumptuous interior: six storeys of *loggia* (boxes and galleries) are bedecked in gilt and lined in crimson, and, for evening performances at least, audiences are similarly turned out. Milanese money, old and new, is deliciously on display. Yes, there is a dress code and yes, tickets need to be booked well in advance. Otherwise, you can peak inside as part of a visit to the in-house Museo Teatrale alla Scala, provided there are no performances or rehearsals in progress.

Opera season begins on 7 December, also the feast day of Milan's patron saint (St Ambrose); see www.teatroallascala.org.

477 TEATRO COLÓN, BUENOS AIRES, ARGENTINA

Recently reopened to its adoring public after a three-year makeover, BA's major landmark and source of pride is the gorgeous and imposing seven-storey Teatro Colón, a world-class facility for opera, ballet and classical music. Opened in 1908, it was the southern hemisphere's largest theatre until the Sydney Opera House came along and stole its thunder. It occupies an entire city block, seats 2500 spectators and provides standing room for another thousand. Opening night was a presentation of Verdi's *Aida*, and visitors have been wowed ever since – the Colón was described by Mikhail Baryshnikov as 'the most beautiful of the theatres I know'. High praise.

Two blocks south of the theatre is El Obelisco, the striking, 68m-high symbol of modern Buenos Aires.

478 ARENA DI VERONA, ITALY

Verona is certainly a town worthy of romance and drama (do the names Romeo and Juliet ring any bells?). And this extends to its impressive open-air opera house. The pink marble Roman amphitheatre known as the Arena, situated in the corner of bustling Piazza Brà, was built in the 1st century AD and survived a 12th-century earthquake to become fair Verona's legendary open-air opera house, with seating for 30,000 people. This is where Plácido Domingo made his debut, and the annual opera season (from June to August) includes 50 performances by the world's top names. Not enough atmosphere for you? Just wait until the candles are lit around the stadium after sunset.

Tickets to sit on the stone steps are the cheapest option (cushion rental is available). See www.arena.it.

479 FESTSPIELHAUS, BAYREUTH, GERMANY

With the backing of 'Mad' King Ludwig II, Richard Wagner turned the town of Bayreuth into a mecca of opera and high-minded excess. Today, the annual Wagner Festival draws some 60,000 opera devotees; their pilgrimage ends at the festival's main venue, the fascinating Festspielhaus. Designed by Wagner himself expressly for his works, the theatre was built in 1872 and lacks much of the ostentation of other theatres from the era. Here, it's all about how best to cleverly showcase Wagner's works and grip the

A peek into the privileged inner circle: Milan's sumptuous La Scala

audience, from the hidden orchestra pit to the three storeys of mechanical works below the stage.

While in Bayreuth, also stop in to see the Markgräfliches Opernhaus (Margravial Opera House), a baroque bombshell built in 1750.

480 MAGYAR ÁLLAMI OPERAHÁZ, BUDAPEST, HUNGARY

The gorgeously opulent, neo-Renaissance Hungarian State Opera House is one of Budapest's most beautiful buildings. Near the banks of the Danube on the Pest side of the city, the opera house opened in 1884 and boasts one of the most elegant interiors in Europe. We might just like it best for its balls – the New Year's Eve gala, and the prestigious Opera Ball, held in February/March. The latter is a Hungarian society event in which the stage and auditorium of the opera house are transformed into a huge ballroom, and the ball is opened by more than 100 debutante dancers.

See if you can wrangle a ticket to the Opera Ball – go online to www.operabal .com. Dress code: white tie.

OPERA HOUSES WITH IMPACT

TASTIEST GOURMET SIGHTS

Pack an appetite and roomy trousers, and let your taste buds do some touring at these delicious destinations.

481 DONGHUAMEN NIGHT MARKET, BEIJING, CHINA

This bustling night market is a kaleidoscopic food zoo of all the Chinese food you could wish to try (with plenty of critters-on-a-stick you might not care for, into the bargain). For the squeamish, there are lamb kebabs, beef and chicken skewers, corn on the cob, noodles and candied fruit kebabs. For those harder-of-stomach, how about smelly tofu, or deep-fried and

Fittingly for the country that invented sushi, the Tokyo Fish Market is magnificent (and frenetic)

skewered creepy crawlies such as grasshoppers, scorpions, silkworms and centipedes? For many it might be a case of look but don't dare to buy, but the photo opportunities are outstanding. Dozens of stalls are set up here each evening (from about 5.30pm); vendors' signs are generally in Mandarin and English.

Want fancier fare? Head to nearby Courtyard for fusion cuisine and one of Beijing's best wine lists; see www .courtyardbeijing.com.

OLIVER STREWE / LONELY PLANET IMAGES

482 GELATERIA DI PIAZZA, SAN GIMIGNANO, ITALY

It's not only the incredible beauty of the walled Tuscan town of San Gimignano that will cause your heart to soar. Stop by the Gelateria di Piazza and your taste buds will applaud… As the pictures on the wall attest, many celebs have wrapped their lips around one of the gelateria's rich ice creams ('all the family thought the ice cream was delicious' attested one Tony Blair). Master Sergio uses only the choicest ingredients: pistachios from Sicily and cocoa from Venezuela. There are plenty of the traditional flavours, but you'll be tempted by unusual combinations such as rosemary-scented raspberry, or pink grapefruit and sparkling wine.

Give your appetite another thrill at the town's Museo del Vino (Wine Museum), where you can taste some of the choice local white wines.

483 LA GRANDE EPICERIE, PARIS, FRANCE

If grocery shopping normally bores you to tears, prepare to be stunned. The exquisitely presented chocolates, pastries, tins of biscuits, fruit and veg, seafood, cheeses, wines and other enticing edibles in this glorious food store within Le Bon Marché department store are a sight to behold (for our money, this beats the *Mona Lisa*). There are downsides to visiting this shrine to fine food, however. The first: no suitcase (or budget) will be big enough for all that you wish to buy and take home. The second: returning to your neighbourhood supermarket after visiting Le Grand Epicerie will likely reduce you to tears.

You're not too far from the Jardin du Luxembourg, so snaffle some supplies and dine alfresco in one of the city's most beloved parks.

484 TOKYO FISH MARKET, JAPAN

Come for the tuna auctions, stay for the sushi breakfast. After it's been fished from the sea and before it turns up on a sashimi platter, most of Tokyo's seafood transits through Tsukiji Market. This gigantic pulsating hub of Tokyo's gastronomic system pumps at a frenetic pace. Workers yell, slice blocks of ice, haul massive bluefin tuna, spit, stop for a smoke, laugh, bone an eel and yell some more. You'll have to trundle out here early to see the predawn arrival of fish and its wholesale auctioning (when visitors are permitted), but even at around 7am there's still some good market bustle and seafood-slinging going on.

175

Lines are unavoidable at Daiwa Sushi, Tsukiji's famed sushi bar (open from 5am). The sushi sets are a good bet if you're not comfortable ordering in Japanese.

These young boys have eaten so much Belgian chocolate, they have soldified into praline people

485 HOUSE OF MASTER BELGIAN CHOCOLATE-MAKERS, BRUSSELS, BELGIUM

Belgium produces a dreamy 220,000 tonnes of chocolate per year. Its unmatched reputation for sublime chocolate derives from the silky smooth texture created by extended conching (stirring) during the production process, and from the use of pure cocoa butter. A turning point for Belgian chocolate came in 1912, when pralines (filled chocolates) were born in Brussels. On that city's magnificent Grand Place, La Maison des Maîtres Chocolatiers Belges unites 10 of the country's choco-craftsmen in an upmarket boutique that also offers demonstrations in English (and the all-important taste-tests) at 4pm Saturday and Sunday.

Also stop by a Pierre Marcolini store – his innovative choc-creations are a top choice for Belgium's wealthy and fashion conscious.

486 DARJEELING, INDIA

It'll start on the train there (or indeed, any train in India) – the nasal call of the *chai wallahs* pacing the platforms, hawking their masala-spiced nectar. But that's nothing compared to Darjeeling itself. Once you switch to the narrow-gauge steam train that hauls you up to this 2000m hill station you're surrounded by the stuff: tea in the cafes, tea in the bazaars and a deep-green leafy profusion of tea cascading down the hillsides, with the might of the Himalaya behind. Between March and November (picking and processing season) take a plantation tour and marvel at what goes into a humble tea bag.

Of course, high tea is in order – take it at the Elgin or Windermere hotels. Shop for tea at Nathmull's Tea Room.

487 SPICE BAZAAR, İSTANBUL, TURKEY

Although somewhat tainted by tourist creep, this market can easily transport you back to its Ottoman-era heyday with the kaleidoscopic colours of its mounds of saffron, sumac, chilli and *salça* (tomato paste), its herbal teas and *lokum* (Turkish delight), and enough aphrodisiac remedies to make even a sultan blush. As well as *baharat* (spices), nuts and honey in the comb, there are truckloads of *incir* (figs) and *pestil* (fruit pressed into sheets and dried). This is a regular shopping spot for the city's best chefs. Don't be afraid to do as the locals do – try before you buy, and compare prices.

If you're in need of more sustenance than a market snack, Bab-i Hayat is a beautiful vaulted space over the eastern entrance to the bazaar.

488 MAISON MERCIER, ÉPERNAY, FRANCE

Épernay, the *capitale du champagne* and home to many of the world's most celebrated champagne houses, is the best place for touring cellars and sampling bubbly. The most popular champagne brand in France, Mercier, has thrived on unabashed self-promotion since it was founded in 1858 by Eugène Mercier, a trailblazer in the field of eye-catching publicity stunts and the virtual creator of the cellar tour. Everything here is flashy, including the 160,000L barrel that took two decades to build, the lift that transports you 30m underground, and the train taking you along part of the 18km of champagne cellars.

Stay in style at Le Clos Raymi (www .closraymi-hotel.com), once occupied by Monsieur Chandon (of champagne fame).

489 ROQUEFORT CAVES, FRANCE

In the heart of rural southern France, the village of Roquefort turns ewes' milk into France's most famous cheese. Its steep, narrow streets lead to natural caves, where seven producers ripen 22,000 tonnes of Roquefort each year – and some cheesemakers offer tours. La Société, established in 1842, has one-hour tours of its pungent caves (including tasters). It's now the largest Roquefort producer, churning out 70% of the world's supply. And did you know that the mouldy blue-green veins that run through Roquefort cheese are, in fact, the spores of microscopic mushrooms, cultivated on leavened bread? Er, yum.

Roquefort is a parking nightmare; it's better to leave your car beside the tourist office at the main, western entry to the village and walk in.

490 SAN MINIATO NATIONAL WHITE TRUFFLE MARKET, SAN MINIATO, ITALY

The *tuber magnatum pico* (white truffle) reigns supreme at the medieval hilltop town of San Miniato, roughly halfway between Pisa and Florence. The woods around here are famed throughout Italy as prime truffle-hunting grounds, and mid-September to December is when all the action takes place. The best way to enjoy it is via the town's white-truffle market, held on the last three weekends of November. During the festival, restaurateurs and truffle tragics come from every corner of the globe to purchase supplies, sample truffle-based delicacies in the town's shops and restaurants, and breathe in one of the world's most distinctive aromas.

From October to December, join a truffle hunt with Barbialla Nuovo Fattoria (www .barbiallanuova.it), an agritourism estate.

TASTIEST GOURMET SIGHTS

BEST PREHISTORIC CAVE PAINTINGS

Take a gallery trip back through time and darkness, heading underground to these timeless works of art.

493 CAVE HILL, AUSTRALIA

Less famous than Kakadu, but no less fascinating, is this small cave in central Australia. Part of the longest intact songline in the country, stretching from the Gulf of Carpentaria to the Great Australian Bight, it contains paintings dating back more than 20,000 years, telling the story of the Seven Sisters, or Pleiades, being pursued across the sky by a man called Wati Nyrhu. Climb to the summit of the hill and you will also be treated to a view that includes Uluru, more than 100km away, and its lesser-known companion, Mt Conner.

Located on Anangu Pitjantjatjara Yankunytjatjara lands, Cave Hill can only be visited on tours out of Uluru.

491 KAKADU NATIONAL PARK, AUSTRALIA

Australia's largest national park is also its ultimate treasury of Aboriginal cave art. Set among vast wetlands and high escarpments are around 5000 ancient art sites, most of which are unknown to, and unseen by, visitors. At Ubirr, the main gallery reveals a range of art, from as far back as 20,000 years right up to contact with white settlers (look for the hands-in-pocket figure smoking a pipe). Prominent features include the X-ray-style animals and paintings of the Rainbow Serpent and Namarrgarn Sisters. South of Ubirr is Nourlangie, an outlier of the Arnhem Land escarpment, famed for its paintings of Namarrgon (Lightning Man), which were repainted by an Aboriginal artist in the 1960s.

The Nourlangie galleries are open from 7am to sunset, with Ubirr open 8.30am to sunset in the dry season (April to November) and 2pm to sunset in the wet season (December to March).

492 BHIMBETKA, INDIA

Secreted in a forest of teak and sal trees 46km south of Bhopal are more than 700 rock shelters, with around 500 of them containing an array of prehistoric paintings – the oldest have been dated to around 12,000 years. A gamut of figures and scenes spill across the rocks: gaurs (Indian bison), rhinoceroses, bears and tigers, and scenes of hunting, initiation ceremonies, communal dancing and drinking, religious rites and burials. The latest paintings are crude geometric figures, probably dating from the medieval period, when much of the artistry was lost. Zoo Rock Shelter is famous for its variety of animal paintings, while Shelter 15 features a magnificent red bison attacking a helpless stick figure.

From Bhopal, ask a bus driver to drop you at the turning for Bhimbetka, about 6.5km past Obaidullaganj – it's a 45-minute walk from here to the caves.

494 JEBEL ACACUS, LIBYA

In Libya's far southwest corner rise dark basalt mountains with Saharan sand dunes piled high into many of the cliffs. It is a natural work of art to match the paintings adorning so much of the rock. The paintings cover a period stretching from about 12,000 BC through to AD 100 and capture changes in flora, fauna and lifestyles. Some of the most beautiful of the Jebel Acacus' paintings are around the small mountain of Awanini, especially a hunting scene in ochre and white, in which the hunter and his prey appear to dance across the rock. Nearby is one of the Acacus' famed wedding scenes, a 6000-year-old painting that shows the women washing hair and trying on dresses.

Permits are required to visit the Jebel Acacus, but your tour company will probably arrange this without you even knowing.

495 CUEVA DE LAS MANOS, ARGENTINA

Translated from the Spanish, it means Cave of the Hands. Simple but appropriate nomenclature, with this site near the Patagonian town of Perito Moreno, along the Rio Pinturas, appearing like one giant Mexican wave from prehistory. Inscribed onto the Unesco World Heritage list in 1999, its walls were stencilled with human hands almost 10,000 years ago. Of around 800 images, more than 90% are of left hands, including one with six fingers. For variety, there are also images of guanacos, rheas and more recent abstract designs.

Guides in Perito Moreno organise day trips to the caves. Free guided walks are given every hour by knowledgeable staff.

496 CAVE OF SWIMMERS, EGYPT

In Egypt, you've just about stepped off the map if you make it as far as the mountainous Gilf Kebir on the Libyan border. And you might believe you've stepped out of reality when, here in the parched Western Desert, you stumble onto cave paintings showing people swimming. Yes, swimming, in water, not in the dry, sandy, rocky wadi that surrounds the cave. Brought to fame in the movie *The English Patient* (which actually used a re-created set in Tunisia), the cave art reflects the fact that 10,000 years ago this parched spot was a far wetter place.

Access to the remote cave is difficult – few tours even head here. Your best chance of securing a guide is in Al-Kharga, the largest and most developed of the Western Desert's oases.

497 CAVE OF ALTAMIRA, SPAIN

When an artist as revered as Pablo Picasso is reputed to have declared that 'after Altamira, all is decadence', you know that the art in this Cantabrian cave is something special. Most notable are the 21 bison painted across the cave ceiling, the figures remarkably preserved over millennia by the depth of the cave. Altamira's modern significance is that it was the first cave discovered with prehistoric art, stumbled upon in 1879 but not authenticated until 1902. The World Heritage–listed cave closed to the public in 2002 (a replica opened in its place) but plans have been announced to reopen it in 2011.

The cave is near Santillana del Mar, about 30km west of Santander.

498 GROTTE DE LASCAUX, FRANCE

France's Vézère Valley is prehistoric central, with its cliffs and earth pitted with caves that served as ancient, and now enduring, canvases. Prime among them, on a hillside 2km from the town of Montignac, is Grotte de Lascaux, often called the 'prehistoric Sistine Chapel'. Visitors enter a brilliant replica of the original cave (which was closed to the public in 1963 because of fears about damage to the art), which is covered in more than 2000 figures of beautifully textured animals – horses, stags, bison, even a rhinoceros. Highlights include a 5.5m-long bison – the largest animal ever found in prehistoric art – and a single human figure at the bottom of a 5m-deep pit.

For a virtual tour through Lascaux, visit www.lascaux.culture.fr.

499 CHURCH HOLE CAVE, ENGLAND

Throughout most of history, it was believed that there was no rock art in Britain. Then, in 2003, among the limestone cliffs of Cresswell Gorge, on the Derbyshire–Nottinghamshire border, archaeologists discovered engravings of animals, including deer and birds, inside Church Hole Cave. Bang went the theory. The art has been dated to around 13,000 years of age, and in 2009 a swish new visitor centre opened at the site. Visitors can now venture inside Church Hole Cave to view the art.

Rock-art tours run only from March to September; the cave is closed at other times to protect roosting bats.

500 CHAUVET CAVE, FRANCE

In December 1994, three cavers squirmed into a cave in a limestone cliff in France's Ardéche region and discovered animal bones and a painting of a mammoth in red ochre. Looking further, they found a host of paintings and engravings, now believed to be the oldest known examples of cave art in the world, dating back around 33,000 years. Due to its relatively recent discovery, research work continues inside the cave, which is not open to the public.

You can make a virtual visit to Chauvet Cave at www.culture.gouv.fr/culture/arcnat/chauvet/en/index.html.

BEST NATURAL SPRINGS

Steaming fumaroles, boiling pools and hissing vents – feast your eyes and soak your limbs at these spectacular geothermal springs.

501 RIFT VALLEY, ETHIOPIA

Africa's Great Rift Valley is a whopping 6500km-long geographical fault system that cleaves the continent from top to bottom. The Ethiopian section bubbles with seismic energy and contains some of the world's most inhospitable terrain. In the country's northwest is the Danakil Depression, a low-lying bowl pitted with saline lakes, where temperatures can soar to 50°C. You want it hotter? Well, there's a volcano here as well. Mt Dallol hasn't erupted significantly since 1926 but hot brine springs burst forth vigorously. As the water evaporates the salt crystallises, forming distinctive white, red and yellow structures coloured by sulphur and potassium.

There's no preferred time to visit Danakil – it's roasting all year round! Book with a reputable tour operator to ensure safety and comfort.

502 OYMYAKON, SIBERIA, RUSSIA

If a town ever needed a hot spring, this is it. Redefining the meaning of cold, Oymyakon holds the record as the world's chilliest permanently inhabited place. So how cold is cold? Well, a record low of -67.7°C was recorded here in 1933 and the average winter temperature is a ridiculous -45°C. So muffle up well before you explore this wondrous land of snow-capped peaks, panoramic vistas and far horizons. And if you ever thought Mother Nature was heartless, think again. Oymyakon means 'non-freezing water', which means that, depending whether you're in the freezing tundra or searching out the steaming-hot spring, the mercury can easily trouble both ends of the thermometer.

Oymyakon is a three-day drive from the nearest population centre, Yakutsk, which you can reach by plane from cities such as Moscow and Seoul.

503 DECEPTION ISLAND, ANTARCTICA

There's something very cool about a hot spring in a cold place, and they don't come much colder than this. Deception Island is an Antarctic wonder, a ring-shaped volcanic isle with a flooded interior, typified by barren mountain bluffs, huddles of chinstrap penguins and the continent's only geothermal lagoon. The beach at Whalers Bay is a popular landing point for visitors – even more popular when guides pull out spades to dig impromptu soak-holes in the sand. Hot water from below fills the pools to provide a spa experience like no other.

Unless you're a budding Captain Scott, a chartered cruise package is the only way in. Don't even think about visiting at any time other than the Antarctic summer.

JOHN ELK III / LONELY PLANET IMAGES

Prismatic by name, prismatic by nature: only at Yellowstone National Park

504 WAIMANGU VOLCANIC VALLEY, ROTORUA, NEW ZEALAND

In NZ, thermal beaches, hot rivers and conical volcanoes are par for the course, so where should you head for the ultimate hot spring? Rotorua makes a good base for exploring the Waimangu Volcanic Valley. Formed after an 1886 eruption, this is the world's youngest geothermal system and contains splendours such as Warbrick Silica Terrace and some intriguing crypto-geysers. More importantly, this is where you'll find Frying Pan Lake, the world's largest hot spring and thus an essential must-see for any aficionado.

Rotorua is one of the main towns on the North Island, a 230km drive from Auckland, and well served with campgrounds and hostels.

505 GRAND PRISMATIC SPRING, YELLOWSTONE NATIONAL PARK, USA

Yellowstone is one of the world's premier geothermal areas and Grand Prismatic is its largest spring. Few on earth are as visually stunning. For starters, it's huge – 90m across and 50m deep – but the clue to the beauty lies in the name. Prismatic means 'resembling a prism' and the water's rainbow hues run the spectrum from earthen reds to the deepest violets. It's at the heart of the magically named Midway Geyser Basin, and you'd be advised not to take a dip – Grand Prismatic pumps out more than 2000L per minute at a temperature topping 70°C.

Try visiting the spring in winter, when the crowds fall away and the steam effects get truly eerie. Rug up against the freezing temperatures.

Monkey see, monkey do: primate action at Yamanouchi, Japan

506 JIGOKUDANI MONKEY PARK, YAMANOUCHI, JAPAN

There are some springs where you're just not meant to bathe. Boiling temperatures, noxious gases or inaccessible locations can stump the most ardent adventurer. And then there are the ones where someone else got there first. Welcome to Jigokudani Monkey Park. Remote and accessible only on foot, this little-visited corner of Joshinetsu Kogen National Park is famous for the troops of wild macaques that soak themselves silly during the frigid winter months. As snowflakes flutter softly from leaden skies, scores of tiny red faces peep through the steam as you look on with green-eyed envy.

See the macaques during the winter months from December to February, when snowfall is heaviest. Get there from the nearby town of Karuizawa.

509 LANDMANNALAUGAR, ICELAND

Iceland crackles with volcanic voracity and natural pools abound. In the island's southern highlands, close to the brooding Hekla volcano, the tongue-twisting Landmannalaugar (meaning 'peoples' pools') marks the end of Iceland's greatest hike. Walkers arrive at the barren campsite after a four-day trek from Thórsmörk, passing lava fields and rhyolite rock formations – it's a stunning place to soothe aching feet. Hot and cold streams mingle to create the perfect bath – just slip in and shuffle around to find your perfect temperature.

If you don't fancy the hike, daily tours leave Reykjavik from mid-June to mid-September (www.bsi.is).

507 TROLL & JOTUN HOT SPRINGS, SVALBARD, NORWAY

Far, far away in the frozen Arctic north, all the way to the top of Norway and then halfway to the North Pole, you'll find the Svalbard archipelago, a collection of remote islands with seven national parks and 23 nature reserves. The Nordvest-Spitsbergen National Park is a haven for seabirds, arctic foxes, reindeer and polar bears, but there's something altogether more unusual in these frosty climes. The Troll and Jotun hot springs are the world's most northerly natural springs, at a latitude of 80°. The pools ain't that hot, around 24°C to 28°C, but in a land where summer highs peak at around 5°C, they're plenty warm enough.

Svalbard's summer is fleeting – June to August – but the midnight sun means days are endless. Fly from Oslo or Tromsø with SAS (www.flysas.com).

508 PAMUKKALE TERRACES, TURKEY

Stretching almost 3km along a mountain plateau and tumbling 160m into the vast Meander River valley, Turkey's Pamukkale Terraces are a geothermal wonder. Calcite-rich mineral springs formed by seismic activity stream down the hillside at a rate of 250L per minute. Over centuries, mounds of calcium carbonate and white limestone have solidified into crescent-shaped pools that make for perfect alfresco hot tubs with a view. Commonly known as 'Cotton Castle' and referred to as the eight wonder of the world by the Turkish people, Pamukkale has suffered at the hands of tourism over the years, but it's a natural wonder that remains one of the world's finest.

The terraces are located 10 minutes' drive from Denizli and are open from 8am to 6pm; tour buses run from most nearby towns. For information about the region visit www.pamukkaleturkey.com.

510 BLOOD POND HOT SPRING, BEPPU, JAPAN

If you haven't guessed, the water is so vividly red here that the locals named it Blood Pond. The vermilion colour comes from the high iron content, which oxidises when exposed to water. Iron oxide is rust, and who wants to sit in a pool of corrosion? But don't despair. Having feasted your eyes at Blood Pond, explore the rest of Beppu – this is Japan's leading spa town with the country's greatest concentration of springs.

Frequent trains connect Beppu with Tokyo (seven hours) and Fukuoka (2½ hours). The weather's best from October to May.

BEST NATURAL SPRINGS

STRANGEST OPTICAL ILLUSIONS & MIRAGES

Can you believe your eyes? When it comes to these head-twisters, chances are you can't.

511 FATA MORGANA, ANTARCTICA

Way up north (or way down south) the clear and pure air brings distant objects into sharp focus. Depth perception becomes impossible and the world takes on a strangely two-dimensional aspect. On maps and charts the early explorers meticulously laid down islands, headlands and mountain ranges that were never seen again. An amusing example of the phenomenon involves a Swedish explorer who was completing a description in his notebook of a craggy headland with two unusual symmetrical valley glaciers; he was actually looking at a walrus! Fata Morganas are caused by reflections off water, ice and snow, and when combined with temperature inversions, create the illusion of solid, well-defined features where there are none.

Touring the Antarctic? Look for a company that's a member of the International Association of Antarctic Tour Operators (www.iaato.org); it means they're into responsible tourism.

512 ST ELMO'S FIRE, EDINBURGH CASTLE, SCOTLAND

Herman Melville called it 'God's burning finger'. Caesar saw it on the javelins of his troops the night before battle. This spectacular effect (cause by the discharge of electricity from storm clouds to the earth) has always conjured thoughts of omens and divine intervention. It's often seen on the masts of ships during a storm; sailors would welcome the sight, as it usually comes at the point where a storm is quietening down. St Elmo was a protector of sailors, and it was seen as his calling card. The effect is frequently seen on the heights of Edinburgh's Castle Rock.

You can't miss the Castle, louring over the town from its volcanic perch. The Royal Mile will take you there.

513 POLAR LIGHTS, ALTA, NORWAY

A space spectacular, the polar lights are a dazzling Arctic and Antarctic display, their colourful sheets of light transforming the endless winter nights into natural lava-lamps. The polar lights – aka aurora borealis and aurora australis – form when solar particles, thrown out by explosions on the sun, are drawn by the earth's magnetic field towards the north and south poles, colliding with atmospheric gases to emit photons, or light particles. What results are brilliant sheets of green, red, white, purple or blue light.

With a latitude of N 69°, the Norwegian town of Alta is renowned as an excellent base to see the lights.

The polar lights – words simply fail to do them justice

The Brocken Spectre: travel into the next world?

514 BROCKEN SPECTRE, GOSLAR, GERMANY

For thousands of years anyone lucky enough to witness this extraordinary optical phenomenon probably thought they were in the presence of God or undergoing their own spiritual rebirth. That's because the spectator is confronted with an image of their shadow surrounded by a halo of light, usually around the head. The phenomenon mostly occurs near mountain peaks when the air is moist and the sun is low. The name owes its provenance to the Brocken, which at 1141m is the highest peak in the Harz Mountains straddling the German province of Saxony-Anhalt.

Berlin Linien Bus (www.berlinlinienbus.de) has a service to the Harz Mountain's gateway town of Goslar; the trip costs around €40.

515 GREEN FLASH, ST-JEAN DE LUZ, FRANCE

A favourite of those with romantic imaginations, the Green Flash (or Green Ray) seems to capture something of the ineffable and transitory nature of existence. It's an effect seen at the end of the sunset, when a green spot or a green ray seems to shoot out of the sun. The causes of the illusion are complex and have to do with the refraction of light, the thickness of the atmosphere and the curvature of the earth. Try for a glimpse of it in St-Jean de Luz, the town featured in Éric Rohmer's moody film *Le Rayon Vert*.

St-Jean de Luz is on the Basque coast, south of Biarritz; try some of its famous seafood while you're waiting for sunset.

516 NEW-GROWTH CONIFERS, MT ST HELENS, WASHINGTON, USA

This is one for a spring day. As you approach Mt St Helens, in Washington state, you'll see that the new, pale-green growth sprouting on the dark-green conifers forms an eye-bending pattern, almost like an op-art painting. Spread across the scale of the forest, the effect is startling. Mt St Helens erupted spectacularly in 1980, causing its north face to collapse in a shower of rocks and releasing a massive ash cloud. Fifty-seven people were killed and the landscape was instantly turned into a featureless moonscape. Since then, the area has been protected and allowed to regenerate.

Visit the Mt St Helens National Volcanic Monument website (www.fs.fed.us/gpnf/mshnvm) to check out the webcam and visitor details.

517 MAGNETIC HILL, LADAKH, INDIA

A land of high snowy passes and ancient gompas on the borderlands of Tibet, Ladakh is the kind of place where your imagination can run away with you. Here you can encounter the phenomenon of a magnetic hill, also known as a gravity hill, where vehicles left out of gear appear to roll uphill. This astounding effect has led to stories about how the magnetic force pulls planes off course. But in fact this is just a powerful illusion - the slope is actually slightly downhill, but the shape of the surrounding landscape and mountainous horizon mean that our usual reference points are obscured.

The hill can be found 30km from the historic capital of Leh along the Leh-Kargil-Baltic highway and is marked by a large sign.

518 DESERT MIRAGE, NULLARBOR, AUSTRALIA

This is a commonly observed phenomenon – a heat haze that makes the air shimmer and can make roads look wet. It's a mean trick, really. For exhausted travellers in brutal heat, the appearance of an illusory lake in the distance cruelly raises and then dashes hopes. On the other hand, if you're cruising comfortably along in a car with a mineral water to hand, the hazy refractions of light just add to the atmosphere of your road trip. Australia's Nullarbor Desert (its name means 'no trees') is the ultimate flat horizon. Driving along this seemingly endless road affords great opportunities for flirting with mirages.

Before attempting a Nullarbor crossing, make sure your vehicle is in excellent condition and you have plenty of water.

519 PAASSELKÄ DEVILS, LAKE PAASSELKÄ, FINLAND

In England they're called will-o'-the-wisps or jack-o'-lanterns. In America they're called spook lights. The Scots call them spunkies. The phenomenon they're referring to is a light that appears at night, often in marshy ground. If followed it will back off; it can also appear to follow you. Most cultures have seen such lights as evil spirits, luring travellers to doom, or harbingers of disaster. Finland's deep Lake Paasselkä is famous for mysterious balls of light; they've even been caught on film! In Finnish folklore, the lights are believed to mark the sites of treasure.

Traditionally, the Finns believed that early autumn was the best time to go looking for strange lights and the treasure below them.

520 SUN DOGS, TIMBUKTU, MALI

A sun dog (parhelion when it's being posh) is an effect seen around the sun. It looks like bright spots of light (or 'mock suns') sitting on either side of the sun itself. It can last for hours. In earlier times it was seen as a frightening omen of bad times ahead. But when you know it's just innocent ice crystals making prisms in the air it's a lot less threatening. You'll have the best chance of seeing one when the horizon is flat. Timbuktu's baked-sand vistas and ancient mud temples could make a good setting for a sighting.

In the dry season, battered 4WDs go from Mopti to Timbuktu almost every day. It will cost roughly $US20 for a seat.

STRANGEST OPTICAL ILLUSIONS & MIRAGES

MUST-SEE MASTERPIECES

This list could, of course, be considerably longer, but here's our pick of top-shelf canvases worth travelling to admire.

521 'THE PERSISTENCE OF MEMORY', MUSEUM OF MODERN ART (MOMA), NEW YORK, USA

Prolific painter, showman, shameless self-promoter or just plain oddball? Salvador Dalí was nothing if not a character. He called his surrealist paintings 'hand-painted dream photographs', and *The Persistence of Memory*, painted in 1931, gives you a glimpse inside one of the most fertile (or febrile) imaginations of the 20th century. In it, Dalí introduces the image of soft, melting pocket watches to the landscapes of his beloved native Catalonia. Melting watches became a recurring theme for Dalí, suggesting Einstein's theory that time is relative and not fixed. The painting, while big on reputation, is actually quite small – only 24cm by 33cm.

At the Museum of Modern Art (MoMa), dine in high style at Modern, a much-lauded foodie paradise of French-American cuisine; see www.the modernnyc.com.

522 'THE KISS', UPPER BELVEDERE, VIENNA, AUSTRIA

Sure, you've no doubt seen countless reproductions of this painting, but Gustav Klimt's sparkling original from 1908 will have you transfixed – by the shimmering swirls of gold, the geometrical patterns of the kissers ('manly' rectangles, 'girly' swirls), the tender detail in the hands. And, aaah, the kiss, and the joyful melding of two loved-up folks into one. The painting is characteristic of Klimt's work: erotically charged, dazzlingly embellished, rich in metallic tones. And let's give the museum its due – Schloss Belvedere is considered one of the world's finest baroque palaces. In other words, this is one for the romantics…

While visiting the Upper Belvedere, try to see the elaborately stuccoed and frescoed Marble Hall, offering superb views over the palace gardens and Vienna.

523 'BIRTH OF VENUS', UFFIZI GALLERY, FLORENCE, ITALY

In a gallery full of treasures, pride of place goes to Florence's home-grown maestros, including Sandro Botticelli (1445–1510). In the Sala di Botticelli, most gasps are directed towards the milky dreaminess of Botticelli's *Birth of Venus*. The artist took his inspiration from classical mythology that said Venus, goddess of love and beauty, emerged from the sea fully grown – and here she is, in all her curvy, luscious-locked glory, arriving at the seashore on a seashell, blown by the Zephyrs (symbols of spiritual passions). It's a masterpiece of ethereal loveliness.

To beat the enormous queues to the Uffizi, prebook your ticket via Firenze Musei (Florence Museums; www. firenzemusei.it).

524 'MONA LISA', LOUVRE, PARIS, FRANCE

The Louvre's star attraction, Leonardo da Vinci's *Mona Lisa*, resides behind a wooden railing and under bullet-proof glass – such is her undisputed pulling power. So much has been written about the painting yet so little is known of the lady behind that enigmatic smile. For centuries, admirers speculated that she might have been in love – or in bed – with her portraitist. The truth is more prosaic. The subject is thought to be Lisa Gherardini, wife of Florentine merchant Francesco del Giacondo, painted between 1503 and 1506. And that smile? It's at least 83% happy, according to 'emotion recognition' computer software.

Mona has quite an address: Room 6, 1st floor, Salle de la Joconde, Denon Wing, Musée du Louvre, Paris (www.louvre.fr).

525 'THE LAST SUPPER', CENACOLO VINCIANO, MILAN, ITALY

Finished with the earthly delights of Milan? Let the heavens provide a spiritual escape. Milan's most famous artwork is da Vinci's *The Last Supper*, depicting the moment Jesus utters the words 'One of you will betray me'. The mural decorates one wall of the Cenacolo Vinciano, the refectory adjoining the church of Santa Maria delle Grazie; it was painted in the late 15th century and travelled a rocky road to restoration. You'll find the baggage of dodgy reproductions and one dubious best-selling novel are shed once you're face to face with the work itself.

Viewings are limited to groups of 25 for a strictly timed 15 minutes (that's all). Bookings are essential: www
.cenacolovinciano.org.

526 SISTINE CHAPEL, VATICAN CITY

While 15th-century masterpieces flatter the Sistine Chapel's walls, it's Michelangelo's astounding ceiling and wall frescos that take the cake – picture sinners and prophets bursting out in 3D brilliance. His spectacularly detailed *Creation* frescos on the barrel-vaulted ceiling (painted from 1508 to 1512) are widely considered the high point of Western artistic achievement; he followed this up 24 years later with the dramatic *Last Judgment* on the end wall (1536 to 1541). For four difficult and solitary years, the reluctant artist painted the 800 sq metres of ceiling; 500 years on, the results will give you goosebumps.

The Sistine Chapel is part of the Vatican Museums; save time by purchasing tickets online: www.museivaticani.va.

527 'THE SCREAM', NASJONALGALLERIET, OSLO, NORWAY

The cliché of the tortured artist is only clichéd because it's true. It's fair to say that the megastars of the art world weren't all of sound mental health, and Edvard Munch (1863–1944) might just be their poster boy. Exhibit 1: *The Scream*, a haunting depiction of the inner torment of the Norwegian artist. Munch's family background explains some of the angst – his mother and elder sister died of tuberculosis and his younger sister suffered from mental illness. The painting's history is almost as tumultuous – it's been stolen (and recovered) *twice* since 1994.

View *The Scream* at Oslo's Nasjonalgalleriet (www.nasjonalmuseet.no), Universitetsgata 13. It's open Tuesday to Sunday; free admission.

528 'LUNCHEON OF THE BOATING PARTY', PHILLIPS COLLECTION, WASHINGTON, DC, USA

Is it just us, or do you want to hang out with the subjects of this painting too? No tortured artists here – this scene, painted by French impressionist Pierre-Auguste Renoir in 1881, sparkles with life and conveys pure *joie de vivre*. The painting captures an idyllic post-boozy-lunch atmosphere as Renoir's friends dine, drink, smoke and flirt overlooking the River Seine at the Maison Fournaise restaurant in Chatou (outside Paris). One of Renoir's favourite haunts, Parisians flocked here on weekends to rent rowing skiffs and enjoy a good meal.

Visit the Phillips Collection on weekdays (closed Monday), when admission is free; see www.phillipscollection.org.

529 'IRISES', GETTY CENTER, LOS ANGELES, USA

When Vincent van Gogh (1853–90) lived in the Netherlands and Belgium, his paintings were dark and heavy. Then he moved to France, and out went the gritty social realism and in came blazing flowers, portraits and wide-open spaces. In 1889, after episodes of self-mutilation and hospitalisation, van Gogh entered an asylum in Saint-Rémy, France. There, he created almost 130 paintings, including *Irises*. Vincent's brother Theo, an art dealer, described it as 'a beautiful study full of air and life', and he's not alone in his admiration – it's among the top 10 most expensive paintings ever sold.

Catch public transport to the Getty Center; it's served by Metro Rapid Line 761, which stops at the main gate on Sepulveda Boulevard.

530 'GUERNICA', CENTRO DE ARTE REINA SOFÍA, MADRID, SPAIN

Pablo Picasso's *Guernica* is a signature work of cubism, whose disfiguration of the human form became an eloquent symbol of the world's outrage at the horrors wrought upon the innocent by modern warfare. Making quite the impact in both theme and size (it measures 3.5m by 7.8m), *Guernica* was Picasso's protest against the German bombing of the Basque town of Gernika (Guernica) at the request of Franco during the Spanish Civil War in 1937; almost 2000 people died in the attack. Never has an artist's anger and a people's anguish been so movingly committed to canvas.

View *Guernica* at the Centro de Arte Reina Sofía (www.museoreinasofia.es), Callede Santa Isabel 52, Madrid.

MOST ICONIC TREES

National emblems, spiritual figureheads and works of art – discover the trees that are more than just roots, trunks, branches and leaves.

533 JŌMON SUGI, YAKUSHIMA, JAPAN

Plants aren't supposed to have faces, but this one has plenty. A truly antediluvian tree, this cryptomeria (a conifer related to the cypress) dates back at least 2000 years, probably much longer. Indeed, some estimates place it at over 7000 years old. Which explains how it got to be so knotted, gnarled and grizzled: extruding from its bulbous trunk are noses and chins and folds and wrinkles, like a geriatric troll's gurning visage. Of course, you might like to keep such thoughts to yourself – it's bigger than you (over 25m high, with a 16m girth), making it Japan's largest conifer.

The hike to the Jōmon Sugi takes four hours or more from the nearest roadhead along the Arakawa Trail.

531 CHÊNE CHAPELLE, ALLOUVILLE-BELLEFOSSE, FRANCE

Trees: useful for plenty beyond burning and building. Find one big enough, you can even put stuff (or people) inside: in Australia they've been used as jails, while in South Africa there's even a bar inside a tree, complete with dartboard. In 17th-century France, a more obvious inspiration for intra-arboreal construction was religion, so when an ancient oak in the small Normandy community of Allouville-Bellefosse had its trunk hollowed out by a lightning strike there was only one thing to do: stick a church in there. *Voila*: the Chêne Chapelle, housing the chapel of Notre Dame de la Paix (Our Lady of Peace).

Allouville-Bellefosse is 48km northeast of Rouen, at the junction of the D33, D34 and D110 roads. See www.discover vendee.com.

532 CEDARS OF GOD, LEBANON

People have been writing about, building with, making medicine from and simply admiring Lebanon cedars since history began: Phoenicians made ships with them, Egyptians mummified bodies with their resin, Solomon's first temple was built using cedars from Lebanon. Today, while a mighty cedar dominates Lebanon's national flag, the once-great stands of ancient trees are largely history. High in the mountains of the country's north, though, a precious grove – the Arz ar-Rab, or Cedars of God – loom above Bcharré. A handful of these are over a millennium old, all that remains of a vast forest that once blanketed the land.

Nearby Qadisha Valley is lined with caves that harboured early Christian monasteries; a visit can be combined with the cedars.

534 TANE MAHUTA ('LORD OF THE FOREST'), WAIPOUA FOREST, NEW ZEALAND

It's not often you get to meet a god. But in the titanic kauri forests of far north New Zealand it's easy to believe you're among deities: here, these truly colossal trees soar over 50m high, dwarfing those who delve between them. Two venerable trees dominate the Waipoua Forest: Te Matua Ngahere (Father of the Forest) presides over his own clearing, but a little further north, Tane Mahuta holds court. Named after the Maori god of the forest, the largest living kauri has stretched to 51m in height in his 1200-plus years. Hush, and be awed. As if you have a choice.

These beautiful trees are threatened by the kauri dieback disease; clean your shoes before and after visiting each forest.

'Avenue of the Gods' might be a more appropriate name for Madagascar's iconic baobab collection

535 AVENUE OF THE BAOBABS, MADAGASCAR

So much of the flora and fauna of this unique Indian Ocean island seems to have sprung straight from the imagination of Dr Seuss: hue-shifting chameleons with swivelling eyes, red-gold sifakas (lemurs) dancing across the sands, and of course the baobabs. These huge, bottle-shaped growths – called 'upside-down trees' because, well, they look like they've been turned upside down – grow across Africa and Australia, but it's in Madagascar that the tree hits peak form. Here, the mighty Grandidier's baobab looms over the landscape. Head to the island's centre-west, east of Morondava, to stroll among the giants of the self-explanatory Avenue of the Baobabs.

191

Avoid the crowds: arrive at dawn to see the massive trees glow burning red – ideal for photography.

GENERAL SHERMAN

Behold the living wonder that is General Sherman

536 GENERAL SHERMAN, SEQUOIA NATIONAL PARK, CALIFORNIA, USA

California does trees to the max. Consider Methuselah: this bristlecone pine germinated on the slopes of the White Mountains almost 5000 years ago, making it the world's oldest. Or whisk yourself to Redwood National Park to find the tallest – the coast redwood called Hyperion, soaring to over 115m. But the daddy – the biggest tree, which also makes it the largest single living thing on the planet – is a giant sequoia called General Sherman. It's 83.8m high, 11.1m in diameter, more than 2000 years old and has a volume of about 1500 cubic metres. And it's breathtaking – here, big really *is* beautiful.

The Sequoia Shuttle bus (US$15 return) serves the park from the city of Visalia from late May to early September (see www.sequoiashuttle.com).

539 EL ÁRBOL DEL TULE, SANTA MARÍA DEL TULE, MEXICO

You know how as you get older, it somehow seems less important to stay trim? Maybe that explains why this tree expanded to such a colossal size – it's wider than it is tall, with a girth of some 58m. The Árbol del Tule has been piling on the pounds for over 2000 years (some say a millennium longer than that), so it's no wonder this mammoth Montezuma cypress is no longer svelte. Now the centrepiece of a churchyard in this small town in Oaxaca state, the tree receives visitors who wonder at its 500-tonne mass.

Buses run from Oaxaca city, about 10km to the west of Santa María del Tule, about every 30 minutes.

537 SRI MAHA BODHI, ANURADHAPURA, SRI LANKA

Most of us come over all thoughtful in the presence of a nice tree. And Siddhartha Gautama was no exception. It was while pondering under a big old fig in what's now Bodhgaya, India, that he had a flash of inspiration: let's call it Enlightenment – after all, that's what everyone else called it once he became known as Buddha. The tree was revered as sacred – obviously – and when a cutting was planted in Anuradhapura by Princess Sangamitta in the 3rd century BC, that, too, became venerated. Today it's the centrepiece of a fascinating, ancient temple-and-palace complex.

Hire a bike to explore Anuradhapura's wealth of historic sites; a day's rental should cost about LKR150 to LKR200.

538 COTTON TREE, FREETOWN, SIERRA LEONE

A tree can be more than just a tree. As a symbol of a movement, a people or a country, something that seems so permanent, yet changeable and ultimately fragile, can express a spectrum of sentiments. So it is with the massive Cotton Tree, the main landmark of Sierra Leone's capital. In 1792, African-American slaves who'd won their freedom during the American War of Independence landed on the coast nearby; legend has it they hiked up to this same tree and gave thanks under its boughs. Today, especially after the brutal civil war that shredded the country, it's a potent symbol of hope.

Visit the Cotton Tree just before dusk to see its population of thousands of bats depart to feed each night.

540 MAJOR OAK, SHERWOOD FOREST, ENGLAND

In tales of old, the outlaw Robin Hood roamed the land, leading ye merrie men, robbing from rich, giving to poor and irritating the king (who may or may not have been bad King John). The Sherwood Forest of yore – which definitely *did* exist – remains, though much diminished, and in its midst stands the Major Oak. Legend has it that this 800-year-old tree harboured Robin and his men in its hollow trunk; true or not, its ancient, sagging branches are majestic nonetheless.

The Major Oak is a short walk from Sherwood Forest visitor centre near the village of Edwinstowe; it's accessible year round.

MOST ICONIC TREES

BEST DINOSAUR DIGS

They're old and rather dead, but still utterly fascinating. Get elbow-deep in prehistory at the following destinations.

541 FLAT ROCKS, AUSTRALIA

The Flat Rocks fossil site, southeast of Melbourne, has a special paleontological place in Australia – it was near to here that the first dinosaur bone in the country was found in 1903. More recently – since the discovery of bones at Flat Rocks in 1991 – it's become the scene of an annual dinosaur dig, with members of the public invited to spend a week hunting around the coastal rock platform for fossils. Each year, on average, around 700 bones are unearthed. Public digs take place in February.

Flat Rocks is near Inverloch, around 150km from Melbourne. For application details, see Monash University's Dinosaur Dreaming website (http://dinosaurdreaming.monash.edu).

Dinosaurs and the moon: lunar-like Ischigualasto

542 MUSEUM OF WESTERN COLORADO, USA

So you want to be the paleontologist, not the passenger? Then this museum in Grand Junction has the program for you. Sure, you can just wander among the bones at its Dinosaur Journey exhibit in Fruita, but you can also get your hands dirty by participating in a dinosaur dig in the deserts of western Colorado and Utah. Time in the field can be as short as half a day or as long as five days, and begins with field instruction before you get to poke about in the quarry searching for bones.

For details of digs, visit www .museumofwesternco.com and follow the 'Dinosaur Digs' link.

543 BAYANZAG, MONGOLIA

Commonly known as the 'Flaming Cliffs', this South Gobi area was first excavated in 1922, and is renowned for its number of dinosaur bones and eggs (view some in the Museum of Natural History in capital Ulaanbaatar). The landscape has an eerie beauty – a classic desert of rock, red sands, scrub, sun and awesome emptiness – and a treasury of bones. One of the most famous fossils is the 'Fighting Dinosaurs', the remarkable 80-million-year-old fossils of a protoceratops and velociraptor locked in mortal combat. It is thought that this and other fossilised snapshots were entombed by a violent sandstorm or by collapsing sand dunes.

Bayanzag is about 100km northwest of Dalanzadgad and 18km northeast of Bulgan. It can be surprisingly hard to find so take a driver or guide who's been there before.

544 BURGESS SHALE, CANADA

High in the Rocky Mountains, inside Yoho National Park, is a place that's something of an evolutionist's heaven. The Burgess Shale – described by Stephen Jay Gould as containing 'the world's most important animal fossils' – preserves the 515-million-year-old Cambrian fossils of marine creatures that were some of the oldest life forms on earth. In this small space there are hundreds of thousands – if not millions – of fossils that, when discovered in 1909, were the world's first-recorded soft-tissued fossils. You can join a guided walk through the park to the Shale, where you can poke about the rocks looking for fossils.

It's illegal to enter the Burgess Shale except on the sanctioned guided walks, which are operated by the Burgess Shale Geoscience Foundation (www.burgess -shale.bc.ca).

AARON MCCOY / LONELY PLANET IMAGES

545 PARQUE PROVINCIAL ISCHIGUALASTO, ARGENTINA

Also known as Valle de la Luna (Valley of the Moon), this park takes its name from the Diaguita word for land without life, which is only partly true. In this otherworldly landscape, there clearly was once life in abundance, as evidenced by the wealth of fossils, some dating as far back as 180 million years. Set into a desert valley between two sedimentary mountain ranges, the park's museum displays a variety of fossils, including the carnivorous *Herrerasaurus* (not unlike *Tyrannosaurus rex*) and the *Eoraptor lunensis* (the oldest-known predatory dinosaur).

Ischigualasto is about 80km north of San Agustín, and the only practical way here is by private vehicle. All visitors must go accompanied by a ranger; tours leave on the hour (more or less).

195

546 NEUQUÉN, ARGENTINA

The Argentine city of Neuquén is one of the earth's dinosaur hot spots. Three important paleontology sites – Plaza Huincul, Villa El Chocón and Centro Paleontológico Lago Barreales – lie within a couple of hours' drive of the city, featuring the bones of the world's largest known dinosaur (*Argentinosaurus huinculensis*) and the largest known carnivore, the 8-tonne *Giganotosaurus carolinii*. For true dino-freaks, there's the Centro Paleontológico Lago Barreales, where you can actually work – as in, get your hands dirty digging – on-site with paleontologists in one of the world's few fully-functioning dinosaur excavation sites open to the public.

The Centro Paleontológico Lago Barreales (www.proyectodino.com .ar) is 90km northwest of Neuquén.

547 KUGITANG NATURE RESERVE, TURKMENISTAN

The most impressive and pristine of Turkmenistan's nature reserves, Kugitang was created in 1986 to protect the Kugitang Mountain Range and the rare markhor mountain goat. It includes the country's highest peak (Airybaba, 3137m), several huge canyons, rich forests, mountain streams, the Karlyuk Caves and the amazing and unique Dinosaur Plateau. The plateau is presumed to be the bottom of a shallow lake that dried up, leaving dinosaur prints baking in the sun, after which a volcanic eruption sealed them in lava. There are 438 prints visible on a steep incline.

You'll need to organise a trip to the reserve through a local travel agent (the city of Turkmenabat is nearest to the reserve), who will get you a permit to visit and provide a driver.

548 DINOSAUR PROVINCIAL PARK, CANADA

Despite the theme-park-like name, Alberta's Dinosaur Provincial Park is serious dinosaur country. Set in the torn and twisted badlands east of Calgary, the 73-sq-km reserve has yielded more dinosaur bones (from more than 40 dinosaur species) than any other single location on earth. More than two-thirds of the park has been declared a 'natural preserve', an exclusion zone that can only be entered on ranger-led bus and walking tours. It's here that you'll find most of the bones, many of which lie scattered about the surface like gravel. Afterwards, head for the nearby town of Drumheller to visit the Royal Tyrrell Museum and its vast fossil collection.

Details of ranger-led trips into the natural preserve can be found on the park website at http://tpr.alberta.ca/parks/dinosaur.

549 MONTANA DINOSAUR TRAIL, USA

Most US states have a state fossil (alongside their state flower, bird, tree and even soil), but few have such a right to one as Montana. This northern state is rich in dinosaur bones (for the record, its state fossil is the duck-billed dinosaur), to the extent that it's created a Dinosaur Trail for visitors. The trail journeys between 15 dinosaur-related destinations, from museums to state parks to field stations. Highlights include

AARON MCCOY / LONELY PLANET IMAGES

'What you staring at, puny human?' With an attitude like that, no wonder this dinosaur became extinct

the Museum of the Rockies in Bozeman, which features the world's largest T-Rex skull among its massive collection; Makoshika State Park, where 10 species of dinosaur have been unearthed; and the Great Plains Dinosaur Museum and Field Station in the town of Malta, famously home to the mummified skeleton of a duck-billed dinosaur, said to be the best preserved dinosaur in the world.

Preview the Dinosaur Trail at http:// mtdinotrail.org.

550 LARK QUARRY, AUSTRALIA

About 95 million years ago, give or take a few million, when western Queensland was lush and tropical, a herd of small dinosaurs got spooked by a predator and scattered. The resulting stampede left more than 3000 footprints in the streambed, which nature remarkably conspired to fossilise and preserve. And there's more than just footprints in western Queensland: in 2005 the largest dinosaur bones ever found in Australia – from a titanosaurus –

were discovered near Eromanga; while to the north, Riversleigh is World Heritage listed for its fossils.

Lark Quarry can only be visited by guided tours, conducted at 10am, noon and 2pm daily. For further info see www.dinosaur trackways.com.au.

BEST DINOSAUR DIGS

MOST UNUSUAL FOUNTAINS

Dancing, spitting fire, eating children – these fountains are no ordinary players.

553 MUSICAL FOUNTAIN, XĪ'ĀN, CHINA

This all-singing, all-dancing fountain is kitsch in a way that only the Chinese can be – and utterly irresistible. The show takes place in the huge North Square in front of the thousand-year-old Big Wild Goose Pagoda, and it's really quite something – the largest musical fountain in Asia, no less. It has 22 different shapes ranging from straight-up jets of water to lotus flowers, and the jets are illuminated by coloured light. The display is choreographed to Chinese and classical music. If you don't mind a bit of a soaking you can wade right into the middle of it.

Bus 610 from the Bell Tower and bus 609 from the South Gate take you to the Big Wild Goose Pagoda.

551 CASCADE, CHATSWORTH, ENGLAND

The 43-hectare garden at Chatsworth, one of England's grandest homes, is famous for its waterworks. The cascade was added by the first duke as part of a baroque garden in the late 17th century. It runs from the Cascade House – a whimsical little baroque temple – down a series of stone steps. Every stone is cut slightly differently so that the water running over it gives a different tone. The garden also has a gravity-fed emperor fountain, a sea-horse fountain and a merry-japes willow tree fountain that squirts visitors from concealed jets as they approach.

198

All those fountains made you hungry? Drop by the Cavendish Rooms, Chatsworth's eatery, for a traditional English afternoon tea.

552 SWAROVSKI CRYSTAL WORLDS FOUNTAIN, WATTENS, AUSTRIA

The famous crystal manufacturers have made a kind of high-class, arty crystal theme park at their headquarters at Wattens, where you can have experiences like the Crystal Dome, a room of 590 faceted mirrors that sets up a shifting whirl of colour and reflection – all to the music of Brian Eno. The park is housed in a grass-covered mound topped by an immense stone head, a little Easter Island in feel, with eerily staring eyes. Grass covers the head so it appears as part of the mound. A fountain gushes from its open mouth.

The Crystal Worlds are just outside Innsbruck. By car, take the A12 and choose the Wattens exit. It's signposted from there.

554 FIRE & WATER FOUNTAIN, TEL AVIV, ISRAEL

The Fire and Water Fountain in the centre of Tel Aviv's Dizengoff Square is somehow appropriate as a symbol of this secular party city. Spinning crazily, spurting water at random moments and occasionally launching flames into the air, its outlandish behaviour continues into the night, largely ignored by the city's residents. It was designed by Ya'acov Agam, a leading Israeli artist known for his predilection for rainbow colour schemes. For the often derided and run-down Dizengoff Square (in the city's District 3), it's a much-needed burst of life.

Bus 18 will take you to Dizengoff Square. Nearby, the Gordon Inn (17 Gordon Street) combines the best of hostel and hotel living.

555 GRAND CASCADE, PETRODVORETS, ST PETERSBURG, RUSSIA

Also called Peterhof, this 'Russian Versailles', built by Peter the Great in the early 18th century, is lavishly blessed with fountains. There is one made in the shape of the sun, a chessboard fountain and trickster fountains that spray you when you step on a paving stone or take a seat. But the magnificent showpiece is the Grand Cascade, a system of 64 fountains that descend on a statue-lined course to the sea canal. The gilt figure of Samson subduing a lion forms a centrepiece. All the fountains at Petrodvorets are fed by springs and controlled by gravity.

The fountains are turned off in October, and turned on again at the end of May with great ceremony and merrymaking.

556 TREVI FOUNTAIN , ROME, ITALY

Immortalised by Anita Ekberg's dip in La Dolce Vita, the Trevi Fountain (Fontana di Trevi) was designed by Nicola Salvi in 1732. The flamboyant baroque creation depicts Neptune's chariot being led by Tritons with sea horses – one wild, one docile – representing the moods of the sea. The water comes from the aqua virgo, a 1st-century-BC underground aqueduct. The famous custom is to throw a coin into the fountain, thus ensuring your return to the Eternal City. In case you were wondering, the €3000 or so that is thrown away on an average day is hoovered up and donated to charity.

The Piazza di Trevi is usually crowded with tourists, but still has a magical atmosphere – especially if you go at night.

557 CROWN FOUNTAIN, CHICAGO, USA

This is possibly the world's first truly democratic fountain – in where else but the USA? Spanish artist Raume Plesa has taken the classical 'water spouting from the mouth of statue' element and turned it into a tribute to the people of Chicago. The fountain consists of a shallow black-granite reflecting pool (where people like to splash around and cool off) and two 15m-tall blocks with LED displays showing the faces of Chicago residents. When they purse their mouths, water spouts forth, seemingly from their lips. It's hypnotic and surprisingly touching.

You'll find the fountain at Millennium Park, on the corner of Monroe Street and Michigan Avenue.

558 BELLAGIO FOUNTAIN, LAS VEGAS, USA

Fountains are an essential part of the whole Vegas pageantry: it's something about the showy hubris of having all that lavish water in the middle of the desert, not to mention the super-size spectacle that many fountains are. The superest super-sized of them all is the fountain at the Bellagio hotel-casino. The Bellagio turns it on with Tuscan architecture, an 8m artificial lake, and a lobby sculpture composed of 2000 handblown, backlit flowers. The immense fountain outside gives its all in a choreographed show involving lights and show tunes. It performs on the half-hour from the afternoon until midnight.

For information on the Bellagio, hotel bookings and a glimpse of the fountain's schtick, visit www.bellagio.com.

559 EL GRIFO MÁGICO, CÁDIZ, SPAIN

Perhaps the best of several 'magic tap' fountains around the world, El Grifo Mágico is an amusing structure at the Aqualand water park in Cadiz. The huge tap, gushing a stream of water with no apparent source, appears to be suspended in mid-air. In fact a hidden pipe runs up the middle of the stream, sustaining the tap and circulating the water, but the illusion is still entrancing. Plus there is plenty more watery magic in the park's waterslides and wave pools

Aqualand Bahía de Cádiz is open June to September and entry costs €20.

560 KING FAHD'S FOUNTAIN, JEDDAH, SAUDI ARABIA

You can't miss this one – it's the world's tallest fountain, jetting over 300m into the air, spotlit at night, and visible from every point in the city. Jeddah is a wealthy commercial centre on the Red Sea, and the fountain, built in the 1980s, is the ultimate in conspicuous excess. Modelled on the Jet d'Eau of Geneva, it's a single plume shooting so high that the weight of the water in the air at any one time can exceed 18 tonnes. It sucks up seawater and was donated to the city by King Fahd.

Head to Al-Balad, Jeddah's crumbling old quarter, to get a feel for the city's history and see houses made of coral.

GOLDEN GREATS

Gaze at all that glitters – from big Buddhas to deserted beaches.

OK, it's actually copper (2700-plus tiles of gilded copper to be exact), but this striking canopy overlooking the Tyrolean city's central plaza certainly glitters like solid gold. Built in 1500 so that Maximilian I (the then Holy Roman Emperor) could watch tournaments and other 16th-century entertainments in the square below, the Golden Roof is now Innsbruck's most famous

Offer a slack-jawed prayer of wonder at the Shwedagon Paya, the pyramid of gold that is the Burma of old

landmark. It's actually a fine, three-storey balcony, decorated with coats of arms, figural reliefs and with Maximilian himself – the leader is diplomatically painted between his first and second wives (who hailed from different territories), to maintain international relations.

Innsbruck (www.innsbruck.com) has a cablecar and lift transport system; there is easy access to the ski-fields of Seefeld, Lizum and Stubai.

562 BALSA MUISCA, BOGOTÁ, COLOMBIA

A boat made of gold would be little real use. But a 19cm-long replica – well, that takes pride of place in Bogotá's Museo del Oro. The Gold Museum is a-shimmer with artefacts, but the Balsa Muisca is most precious. It represents the El Dorado legend that so tantalised the colonising Spanish, centred on the crater lake of Guatavita. Here the Muisca tribe launched *balsa* (rafts) laden with emeralds and gold, which they cast into the water as offerings to the gods. Many treasure-hunters have trawled the lake, with scant reward. But the Balsa Muisca, found miles distant, keeps the legend alive.

The Museo del Oro (www.banrep.gov.co/museo), in Santander Park, is open from Tuesday to Sunday; admission costs COP$3000 (free on Sunday).

563 GOLDEN BUDDHA, BANGKOK, THAILAND

It was a discovery that probably had temple-goers Thailand-wide reaching for their chisels: in 1957, while this formerly nondescript plaster Buddha was being lifted by crane into its new home, it was dropped; the plaster cracked and revealed the true treasure beneath – the world's biggest solid gold statue. The Buddha is around 700 years old, originally covered to hide its worth from the Burmese. Now displayed in Bangkok's Wat Traimit, it's 3m high and weighs over 5 tonnes. Fragments of the stucco in which the Golden Buddha was encased are also on show – perhaps to illustrate that it's what's inside that counts.

Wat Traimit is in Chinatown; from the temple, walk down Yaowarat Road, which is the centre of Thailand's gold trade.

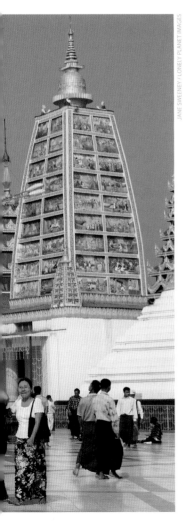

JANE SWEENEY / LONELY PLANET IMAGES

564 SHWEDAGON PAYA, YANGON, MYANMAR (BURMA)

You can't miss it – Shwedagon Paya, set on a hill overlooking Yangon, sticks out like a great, gold thumb. Among a collection of Buddhist shrines and statues, it's the main stupa that glitters greatest. Rising 98m, the huge bell dome is slathered in gold leaf and topped with a gemstone-encrusted spire – which, in turn, is topped with an orb of 4351 diamonds. What warrants such jewellery-box architecture? Somewhere under that ostentation is a casket containing eight of Buddha's hairs. When they were exposed once before, there was alleged tumult among men and spirits; Shwedagon Paya contains the chaos.

Myanmar is driest and coolest between November and February; Shwedagon Paya is best visited at sunrise and sunset.

201

565 GOLDEN TEMPLE, AMRITSAR, INDIA

It was officially renamed the Harmandir Sahib in 2005, but no one's going to stop calling this sparkling edifice the Golden Temple anytime soon. For one glaring reason: its main shrine is coated in 100kg of the stuff. This complex in northwest India – comprising sacred rooms, pilgrim dorms and a vast kitchen – is Sikhism's holiest site; the gilded Hari Mandir, afloat in the central sacred pool, is the show-stopper. However, the best thing here is that it's no dusty tourist site – this is a living temple, where the walls echo with Sikhs reciting verse, and where that enormous kitchen feeds 35,000 people daily.

Drinking alcohol, eating meat and smoking are prohibited in the temple; visitors must remove their shoes and cover their heads.

566 GOLDEN MUMMIES, WESTERN DESERT, EGYPT

In 1996 a donkey stumbled into a hole – and unwittingly made one of Egyptology's most important discoveries. Under the shifting sands of the Western Desert, near the down-and-out oasis town of Bahariyya, a subterranean necropolis had lain undisturbed for 2000 years. It was a vast repository of Greco-Roman history: wine jars, amulets and, it's thought, up to 10,000 preserved people. The bodies here aren't as well mummified as their Ancient Egyptian counterparts, but they're still lovingly decorated – some with lashings of gold. Visit Bahariyya's museum to see the best, which have gold masks, gold chest-plates and even gilded fingernails.

The oases of Bahariyya, Farafra, Dakhla and Kharga are linked by the 1000km Cairo–Luxor desert loop road.

567 BONANZA CREEK, DAWSON CITY, CANADA

Gold is a powerful thing throughout human history. In 1896 it turned moose pasture into metropolis virtually overnight as word spread that the yellow stuff had been found in Rabbit Creek (quickly renamed Bonanza Creek, for obvious reasons), 18km from what is now downtown Dawson. And so it was that Dawson burst into being as 30,000 prospectors, prostitutes, saloon-keepers and conmen all rushed to try their luck in the wilds of the Yukon; today you can do the same. Lay your cards down at Diamond Tooth Gertie's gambling hall, then pack your pan for Claim 6, the spot on the Bonanza that started it all, and where you could be lucky and find your fortune still.

Panning at Claim 6 is free; visitors can keep any gold they find. Pans can be rented in Dawson.

568 SUPER PIT, KALGOORLIE, AUSTRALIA

Who'd have thought a big hole could be so very interesting? But this is no trifling excavation: the manmade Super Pit at Kalgoorlie is 3.5km long, 1.5km wide and 370m deep – the scale is like an inverse Uluru. The reason for this great gash is, of course, gold. In 1893 some prospectors struck it lucky here; thousands followed, flocking to reputedly the richest patch of gold-bearing earth in the world – the Super Pit alone has produced 50 million ounces. Gaze from the Lookout and wonder how much more is yet to be found.

The Super Pit Lookout is off Outram Street; inquire at the visitor centre for times of the daily blasts.

Amritsar's gold-plated Sikh temple glitters in the middle of its holy pool like a giant bullion bar and is a magnet to millions of pilgrims

569 GOLDEN BEACH, KARPAS PENINSULA, CYPRUS

Places such as this are truly golden – not only is this beach in North Cyprus a glorious long sweep of sand, backed by rippling dunes, it must be the only beach of such size and perfection in the entire Mediterranean not to have had resorts built behind it. This shore near the tip of the Karpas Peninsula sees more donkeys than people; it's considered a nature reserve – because of the turtles that come here to nest – and the road to get here is slow and winding, further deterring mass tourism. Golden indeed.

Golden Beach is best reached by car; take the road north from Dipkarpaz towards the Monastery of Apostolos Andreas.

570 HAND OF FAITH, LAS VEGAS, NEVADA, USA

It seems fitting that a city of such glitz, where fortunes can be made (or lost) in a dice roll, should be home to one of the world's largest nuggets of gold. The fact that it was found by a man and his metal detector – not some big machine – makes the story even more Everyman. The 24kg Hand of Faith, named for its fingery shape, was unearthed in Australia but now resides in the foyer of the Golden Nugget casino, a million-dollar lucky charm for all who pass by.

The Golden Nugget casino (www .goldennugget.com) offers slots, baccarat, poker, blackjack and more; beginners can ask for free lessons.

GOLDEN GREATS

COOLEST
CAVES & GROTTOES

*Delve into the underworld to find religious relics,
dinosaur hideouts, hungry elephants and more.*

Kitum Cave: pachyderm paradise, but watch out for falling rocks

571 SELMA PLATEAU, OMAN

Once upon a time a brave shepherd girl called Selma was rewarded by God with a gift of seven stars, which fell to earth and formed seven deep shafts in a plateau in northern Oman. Heaven-sent indeed, today these subterranean supernova trails provide white-knuckle abseil-access to vast chambers below. One of these, the Cave of the Genies, is the largest cavern in the world, although it's off-limits at the time of writing while the Omani government screws in a viewing platform. However, Selma's other vertical gateways are open for exploration. If you've a head for heights, drop into Seventh Hole to explore the Canyon Room, stalactites and tunnels 120m down…

Muscat Diving and Adventure Centre (www.holiday-in-oman.com) runs abseiling tours into Seventh Hole, including pre-trip instruction and guides.

573 LÓNGMÉN CAVES, LUÒYÁNG, CHINA

This is the Chinese at their most exquisitely chisel-happy: a 1km stretch of limestone cliffs flanking the Yī River has been carved with 2345 grottoes and niches; in turn these have been filled with over 100,000 Buddhist sculptures – ranging from 2cm-tall icons to the 17m sitting Buddha in the Ancestor Worshipping Cave. The whole site is the handiwork of the Northern Wei dynasty, who began their artistic excavations around 500 AD; time, and the Cultural Revolution, have taken their toll – many of the religious artefacts have been pillaged or defaced over the years. But what remains is still a gob-smacking rock-cut gallery.

Visitors are not permitted inside the caves; walkways and staircases provide viewpoints from which to peer inside at the sculptures.

574 FAYE'S UNDERGROUND HOME, COOBER PEDY, AUSTRALIA

Few caves come with kitchen, billiard room and walk-in wardrobes. But then such is the need to escape the outback's 40°C heat that it can drive a woman to dig a home with all the trimmings. Coober Pedy, meaning 'white man's hole in the ground' in local Aboriginal dialect, is an inhospitable place. But since 1915 its opal riches have drawn prospectors nonetheless, many of whom have hewn dwellings, bars and even churches out of hillsides in search of cool retreats. Faye's is the finest: not a museum but an actual home, it shows how real people manage in the sun-baked back of beyond.

Coober Pedy is 846km from Adelaide, 685km from Alice Springs; there are Adelaide–Coober Pedy flights six days a week.

572 KITUM CAVE, MT ELGON NATIONAL PARK, KENYA

Mt Elgon Park straddles the Uganda–Kenya border, a little-visited surprise package of waterfalls, gorges, hot springs and caves. Kitum is a 180m-deep cavern, home to fruitbats – and probably the world's only spelunking elephants. Each night long processions of pachyderms plod into this black hole in Mt Elgon's eastern slopes to gorge on the salt-rich deposits inside. They scrape at the walls with their tusks (leaving gouges like abstract rock art), then pick up the fallen titbits with their trunks. An easy mineral fix – though a visible elephant skeleton, crushed by a rockfall, suggests it's not totally safe snacking.

Mt Elgon is 420km northwest of Nairobi; access is on sealed road via Kitale to Chorlim Gate.

575 BLUE GROTTO, CAPRI, ITALY

Some believed this to be a place where Sirens came to sleep, or where devils bewitched all who entered. There's certainly an enchanted air to this cavern on Capri, though the only fear felt by visitors now is for the safety of their heads. The Blue Grotto's entrance is just 1m high; getting in requires lying down in a rowboat, only big enough for two, and trusting your Italian oarsman to punt you through. But once inside, sit up: the cave expands and everything is illuminated, as sunlight filters through the sea below and flicks a switch on this Mediterranean marvel.

Visit on a sunny, calm day; sunlight enhances the blue, and boats can only enter if the water is still.

205

576 CENOTE DZITNUP, VALLADOLID, MEXICO

Mexico's Yucatán is a geological Swiss cheese. This Caribbean-lapped peninsula of easily eroded limestone is a soft touch for underground rivers, which have nibbled away to leave a series of *cenotes* (sinkholes) hidden under the jungle. Well, mostly hidden. Some, such as Cenote Dzitnup, have been discovered, and provide perfect natural swimming pools. At Dzitnup a tiny tunnel leads down into the domed cavern, dripping with stalactites and illuminated by a ray of sun through a hole in the craggy ceiling – nature's spotlight. The water beneath, a circle of icy turquoise, is the ultimate place to dive in with the fishes.

Cenote Dzitnup is 7km west of Valladolid; visit at midday to see the shaft of natural light at its brightest.

578 PAINSHILL PARK, ENGLAND

If Mother Nature hasn't done the job, have a go yourself. Or so thought garden-guru Charles Hamilton, who so liked the caves he'd seen on his Grand Tour of Europe he wanted to create his own. In 1738 he began to landscape Painshill Park; its centrepiece: a fake but fabulous grotto. Built of wood and brick, covered by 'stalactites' of gypsum crystals and skull-and-bones-lookalike limestone, it was a fairylike flight of fancy. After years of neglect, renovation is now under way, and part-restored, it's at its most interesting: a chance to see some of the grotto's glory, but also what trickery lies beneath.

Visit Painshill Park in November and December, when Father Christmas takes up residency in the Grotto.

580 MAMMOTH CAVE NATIONAL PARK, KENTUCKY, USA

Mammoth by name, mammoth by nature – this subterranean giant is the world's longest known cave. In fact, if you joined the planet's second- and third-longest systems together, Mammoth would *still* be the biggest: its 580km length – added to annually with each new exploration – easily outdoes any other. All that space isn't empty either: twisting helictites and gypsum flowers grow from the walls; fossils of sharks' teeth and gastropods lie in the rock; and more than 100 animal species – from Indiana bats and damp-loving salamanders to eyeless cave fish – thrive, a bounty of cavernicolous life.

Several cave tours are available. Most atmospheric, the Violet City and Great Onyx tours are lit by lantern only.

577 CUEVA DEL MILODÓN, PUERTO NATALES, CHILE

It doesn't taken a massive leap of imagination to picture 4m-tall dinosaurs roaming the wild landscapes of Patagonia – it's a pretty primordial place. Still, the Chileans have slapped a life-size plastic mylodon (giant sloth) in front of the entrance to this 70m-wide cave, just to make things easier. They've done this because a mylodon skeleton was unearthed here in the 1890s; the remains are long gone (to the British Museum) but the cavern, dripping with stalactites, still feels prehistoric. A short walk to the nearby lookout gives fine views over the mylodon's former stomping ground.

In Patagonia by Bruce Chatwin is recommended reading – the writer was inspired to visit the region by Milodón

579 DEER CAVE, GUNUNG MULU NATIONAL PARK, MALAYSIA

Super-sized and super smelly, Deer Cave doesn't do things by halves. This colossal karst cavern in the Borneo jungle is 2km long; its gaping mouth 174m wide by 122m high. And it's home to around two million wrinkle-lipped bats – and a whole heap of their guano. The ammonia stench is worth braving, however; a lantern-lit walkway delves into the huge hollow to reveal the unexpected: a light shaft illuminating a solitary patch of jungle. And, if you look carefully at the mouth of the south entrance, you'll see a rocky profile of Abe Lincoln keeping watch.

Bats emerge from Deer Cave between 5.30pm and 6.30pm most evenings; the mass exodus can be watched from the

Turqoise dreaming at Cenote Dzitnup

MOST AMAZING CATHEDRALS & CHURCHES

Praise be to someone, anyone, for the following collection of awe-inspiring, gob-stopping houses of worship.

581 CANTERBURY CATHEDRAL, ENGLAND

Canterbury is top of the pops when it comes to English cathedral cities, and is recognised as the spiritual heart of England. The World Heritage–listed cathedral, which dominates the town centre, is considered one of Europe's finest, and the town's medieval alleyways, riverside gardens and ancient city walls add plenty to the ye-olde atmosphere. Nonbelievers may find themselves converted inside the extraordinary early-Gothic cathedral, filled with enthralling stories, striking architecture and a real and enduring sense of spirituality. There are also intriguing whispers of violence and bloodshed – the cathedral has attracted pilgrims since the murder here of Archbishop Thomas Becket in 1170.

History: tick. Location: tick. Atmosphere: tick. The 15th-century Cathedral Gate Hotel (www.cathgate.co.uk) adjoins the spectacular cathedral gate.

582 BASILICA DI SAN MARCO, VENICE, ITALY

In the heart of *La Serenissima*, Piazza San Marco (St Mark's Square) beautifully encapsulates the splendour of Venice's past and its tourism-fuelled present – it's filled for much of the day with competing flocks of sightseers and pigeons. But it's to the sigh-inducing St Mark's Basilica that all eyes are drawn. You won't mind the exorbitant prices charged at the square's cafes, so long as you can linger to feast your eyes on this architectural mishmash of spangled spires, Byzantine domes, mosaics and marble. Inside, the soaring stone structure still sets standards for razzle-dazzle, from the intricate geometry of 12th-century polychrome marble floors to the 11th- to 15th-century mosaic domes glittering with millions of gilt-glass tiles.

You'll need to be dressed modestly (ie knees and shoulders covered) to enter the basilica.

583 LALIBELA, ETHIOPIA

In the remote town of Lalibela, you need to look below your feet to see one of Christendom's great moments in architecture. Here, 11 churches have been carved out of the volcanic bedrock, earning the town the working title of 'Africa's Petra'. Supposedly chiselled out by King Lalibela by day and angels by night, the 800-year-old churches are like buildings frozen in stone, carved from the top down into some of the most remarkable churches on the planet. They form two clusters in the middle of town, with the *coup de grâce* – the cruciform-shaped Bet Giyorgis – set slightly, almost reverentially, apart.

Ethiopian Airlines flies to Lalibela from Addis Ababa and Gonder, or you can brave the two-day bus journey from Addis.

584 METEORA, GREECE

The forest of rock at Meteora is a favourite with rock climbers, but long before ropes and carabiners, monks established a series of monasteries atop the rock spires, built in what Unesco in its World Heritage listing has described as 'impossible conditions'. Six of these monasteries remain (at one time there were 24) atop the rocks that thrust up to 400m above the Thessaly Plain. Where once the only access was in nets pulled up hundreds of metres (an approach still favoured by the most pious of visiting monks), steps now lead tourists onto the rocks and into the monasteries.

The town of Kalambaka is huddled at the foot of the Meteora rock spires. Kalambaka can be accessed by bus and train from Athens and Thessaloniki.

585 BASILIQUE DE NOTRE DAME DE LA PAIX, YAMOUSSOUKRO, CÔTE D'IVOIRE

The Ivory Coast isn't a world-beater in many things, but it does have what is regularly claimed to be the largest church in the world. The basilica in the capital city of Yamoussoukro is one of West Africa's most astonishing sites. Completed in 1989, it was built in three years by a labour force of 1500, working day and night in great secrecy. It bears a striking and deliberate resemblance to St Peter's in Rome and each of its 7000 seats is individually air-conditioned. There's 7400 sq metres of stained-glass windows, a 3-hectare plaza… and yet just one million Catholics in the whole country.

English-speaking guides are on duty in the basilica; bring your passport, which a guard will hold until you leave.

586 BASILIQUE DU SACRÉ COEUR DE MONTMARTRE, PARIS, FRANCE

To the north of the River Seine and the heart of Paris sits Montmartre, a romantic neighbourhood of cobbled streets, sleepy cafes and ivy-covered balconies. Overlooking it all is the magnificent 19th-century travertine stone Basilique du Sacré Coeur (Basilica of the Sacred Heart). On long summer evenings, lovers litter the steps leading to the city's highest landmark. Buskers sing of revolution, street artists perform and red wine flows. Below them all unfolds the most spine-tingling of Parisian vistas. What could be more atmospheric?

Arrive on the first Friday of each month to take part in a spiritual day retreat; see www.sacre-coeur-montmartre.com for details.

587 TEMPPELIAUKIO CHURCH, HELSINKI, FINLAND

Hewn into solid rock, this modern church was designed by Timo and Tuomo Suomalainen in 1969 and remains one of Helsinki's foremost visitor attractions. The church symbolises the modern innovativeness of Finnish religious architecture and features a stunning 24m-diameter roof covered in 22km of copper stripping. From the outside, the church dome protrudes from the bedrock like a giant, copper-topped cairn; from the inside sun pours in through the beamed walls, lighting the interior in tiger stripes. The church has great acoustics and holds regular concerts.

The church is on Lutherinkatu, with the entrance at the northern end of Fredrikinkatu.

588 ST BASIL'S CATHEDRAL, MOSCOW, RUSSIA

No picture can prepare you for the dramatic impact of the crazy confusion of colours, shapes and ice-cream-like swirls of Moscow's St Basil's Cathedral. This ultimate Russian symbol was created between 1555 and 1561 (replacing an existing church on the site) to celebrate the capture of Kazan by Ivan the Terrible. The cathedral's apparent anarchy of shapes hides a comprehensible plan of nine main chapels: the tall, tent-roofed one in the centre; four big, octagonal-towered ones, topped with the four biggest domes; and four smaller ones located in between.

The cathedral is at one end of Red Square, alongside the walls of the Kremlin, and the interior is open daily except Tuesday.

589 BORGUND STAVE CHURCH, NORWAY

Medieval stave churches are a peculiarly Norwegian phenomenon that evolved from Viking wooden palisade construction methods. Borgund is one of the best-known, most-photographed and certainly the best-preserved examples. Dedicated to St Andrew, it was constructed in the 12th century beside one of the major trade routes between eastern and western Norway. Next door to it is the only freestanding medieval wooden bell tower still standing in Norway. If you enjoy walking, be sure to build in time to undertake the two-hour circular hike on ancient paths and tracks that starts and ends at the church.

The church is located 30km southeast of Lærdalsøyri along the E16.

590 BASILICA DI SAN PIETRO, VATICAN CITY

No list of great cathedrals would be complete without St Peter's, Italy's biggest, richest and most spectacular church and the home of Catholicism. It owes much of its glory to Michelangelo, who took over the design of the basilica in 1547 at the age of 72. He was responsible for the great 136m-high dome, and the hauntingly beautiful *Pietà* (the only work he ever signed) just inside the Porta Santa (Holy Door). Excavations beneath the basilica have uncovered part of the original church and what archaeologists believe is the tomb of St Peter, one of the Twelve Apostles.

Free English-language guided tours of the basilica are run from the Vatican tourist office at 9.45am Tuesday and Thursday, and at 2.15pm every afternoon from Monday to Friday.

MOST
COLOSSAL CROWDS

From festivals to football stadiums, get lost among the globe's biggest gatherings.

'Lemme see a sea of hands! I wanna see a sea of hands out there!' – the awesome pomp of North Korea's Mass Games

591 SUNDAY MARKET, KASHGAR, CHINA

A contender for most ancient crowd: there's been a gathering at this Chinese outpost since the first ever travellers hefted backpacks. This is Silk Road Central, the historic point at which traders plodding between east and west hawked their wares before continuing on their epic journeys. That it's central to anything is astonishing – Kashgar is in the middle of the middle of nowhere, on the edge of a desert so fierce its name (Taklamakan) translates as 'go in, never come out'. But come the weekend, Kashgar's venerable market throngs with Uighurs, Tajiks, tourists, goats, pickpockets: seemingly the whole world congregated at world's end.

To reach Kashgar by road takes 24 hours from Ürümqi (China), two days from Sost (Pakistan), two days from Osh (Kyrgyzstan).

593 GLASTONBURY FESTIVAL, ENGLAND

A measly 1500 people showed up to the first Glastonbury Festival back in 1970; the entrance ticket included free milk from the Worthy Farm cows. A few decades on and attendance at this party-hosting patch of green in rural Somerset is around 135,000. The music is supplemented by everything from comedians to cabaret, and the festival-goers now tend to prefer more potent beverages. The scale and spread of entertainment is mind-boggling – 80 stages, 700-plus performers – as is negotiating your way around the site, between the global food stalls, hippie fields, quagmires of mud and 134,999 other fun-seeking souls.

Glastonbury (www.glastonburyfestivals .co.uk) is held in June; tickets go on sale the previous autumn and usually sell out immediately.

594 GRAND CENTRAL STATION, NEW YORK, USA

Funny that the world's biggest station by number of platforms (44) can be found in a nation wedded to the car. But then New York's Grand Central is much more than a terminus – half the people wandering its theatrical concourse probably have no intention of boarding a train at all: the building, renovated in 1998, is a sight in its own right. The beaux arts interior is garnished with opulent chandeliers, grand staircases, an iconic marble-and-brass clock and an astronomical ceiling, painted with golden constellations. For the 750,000 people who pass through daily it makes for a glamorous commute.

Free walking tours of Grand Central and its environs run every Friday at 12.30pm, starting from the Whitney Museum entrance (www.grandcentralterminal.com).

592 MASS GAMES, PYONGYANG, NORTH KOREA

Scary and spectacular in equal measure, North Korea's Mass Games personify its totalitarian politics. Ranks of meticulously organised dancers and gymnasts – around 100,000 in all – create a visual display not of personal skill but of perfect synchronicity; the marvel is in the masses working together. They perform (following months of rigorous rehearsal) stories of nationhood and tributes to their Dear Leader, as well as mixing in plenty of 'ain't our government great?' propaganda via innovative means: 20,000 participants sitting on one side of Pyongyang's May Day Stadium hold up coloured cards to make intricate pictures, mostly with a pro-regime theme.

The Mass Games are held mid-August to mid-October. September to October is less humid and more pleasant than summer in North Korea.

595 KUMBH MELA, INDIA

When the Hindu forces of good and evil had a fight over a *kumbh* (pitcher) of sacred nectar, four dollops spilled onto the earth below: at Allahabad, Haridwar, Nasik and Ujjain. Deemed holy hubs because of it, these cities now witness a mass human messiness as they take it in turns to host the Kumbh Mela festival – the biggest religious gathering on the planet. Up to 70 million people join this party: participants – young and old, plus plenty of naked sadhus – gather to dunk in the cities' rivers, essentially a colossal communal bath.

Kumbh Mela (www.kumbhamela.net) is held four times every 12 years; each Mela lasts several weeks, with designated key bathing dates.

211

596 HAJ, MECCA, SAUDI ARABIA

Not everyone's invited to join this humongous congregation – the haj is for Muslims only, though this restriction doesn't stop numbers swelling to up to two million a year. All Muslims who are sane and able must make the haj at least once in their lives – it's one of the Five Pillars of Islam. Hence the hordes descending on Mecca annually for four days of religious observance: dressed in white, pilgrims perform en masse counter-clockwise circuits of the Kaaba building, drink from the Zamzam Well, praise Allah from the shadeless slopes of Mt Arafat and commune with fellow Muslims from across the globe.

The dates of the haj change annually; 2011's haj is from 4 to 7 November; 2012's is from 24 to 27 October.

597 SHIBUYA CROSSING, TOKYO, JAPAN

That something as, well, pedestrian as a pedestrian crossing can be considered an ultimate sight is testament to the overwhelming hurly-burly of humanity that scuttles across this Japanese junction. The nexus of a trendy shopping district – all fashion stores and TV-screen bling – Shibuya Crossing is in front of Shibuya Station, one of Tokyo's (and the world's) busiest. Also, it's a 'scramble crossing' – the many, *many* traffic lights turn red at the same time, prompting what feels like every citizen in the city to spill out onto the junction and make a simultaneous mass dash for the other side.

Watch Shibuya Crossing from the 2nd-floor window of the Starbucks in the Tsutaya building on the crossing's north side.

598 CAMP NOU, BARCELONA, SPAIN

Not only a huge crowd but perhaps one of the most passionate – the 98,787 souls that can cram into FC Barcelona's goliath of a stadium on match days are not fans, they're pilgrims. This football club transcends simple sport; it is a Catalan cause, a force behind which the patriots of this autonomous enclave of Spain amass. And never is this fervour expressed more vociferously than when Barca hosts arch-rivals Real Madrid. When the capital's big boys come to town for football, Camp Nou's three vertiginous tiers – packed to the lofty rafters – erupt in a frenzy of soccer appreciation and regional rivalry.

The Camp Nou Experience includes a visit to parts of the stadium, the museum and multimedia zone; tickets cost €19. See www.fcbarcelona.com.

599 KEJETIA MARKET, KUMASI, GHANA

There are great crowds of everything at Kejetia. People, yes – variously shopping for foodstuffs and funeral gifts, carrying overflowing baskets on their heads, having their hair braided, touting tat. But there are also crowds of *things*: live (and dried) chameleons, Ashanti sandals, voodoo trinkets, soap and shampoo, plastic toys and locally woven Kente cloth. Kejetia is one of the biggest markets in Africa, a township of commerce whose sea of corrugated-iron roofs shades jacks-

NABIL MOUNZER / CORBIS

The haj: two million Muslims per year can't be wrong

of-all-trades and the locals who rely on them. It's hot and hassling; it's vast and fascinating: it's all of Ghana in vivid microcosm.

Kumasi is a four-hour bus ride inland from Accra; the market, just east of the city centre, is held daily.

600 CARNAVAL, SALVADOR, BRAZIL

Shhh – don't tell Rio, but word on the street is that Salvador's Carnaval is actually better… OK,

Rio's samba extravaganza attracts a slightly bigger crowd, but the two-million-strong shimmying and shaking souls that head to Salvador instead don't seem to mind and just get on with the serious business of having fun. Carnaval is markedly different here – these super-sized parade-parties are heavily influenced by the city's Afro-Brazilian heritage: *trios elétricos* (trucks with loudspeakers) blast out Afrobeats, bands wielding thunderous drums beat tribal rhythms, and the traditions of the Candomblé religion filter through

the theatrics. Ultimately though, this is an awful lot of people having an awfully good time.

To join the parade you need to be affiliated to one of the groups *(blocos)* by purchasing the relevant *abadá* (T-shirt).

MOST COLOSSAL CROWDS

BEST SIGHTS FROM ABOVE

Get up high for an angel's-eye view of these breathtakers.

601 THE WORLD ARCHIPELAGO, DUBAI, UNITED ARAB EMIRATES

Only in Dubai. This vast engineering project sought to replicate the globe as a series of artificial islands. The thinking was that the islands would be bought for use as resorts and playgrounds for the rich. The lowering clouds of the global financial crisis put the brakes on construction, and the project has lost momentum, although reports that the islands were sinking back into the sea are apparently unfounded. From the air it's an impressive sight, albeit a wacky one. It's as if a Bond villain has turned his megalomania to more benign schemes.

The World ('A Vision Made Real') has a glossy website (www.theworld.ae) where you can check out pictures and learn more about the scheme.

602 FORBIDDEN CITY, BEIJING, CHINA

Beijing's Forbidden City was home to the emperors of the Ming and Qing dynasties, and closed to the outside world for 500 years. The emperors rarely left the confines of their pleasure dome – everything they desired was there within its walls. The scale is quite something to get your head around. There are over 800 buildings and close to 1000 rooms. The courtyard overlooked by the Gate of Supreme Harmony is so massive that it could hold an imperial audience of up to 100,000 people. It takes at least a day to see the complex, but to get a sense of the extent of it, it's best seen from above.

Nearby Jingshan Park has a series of five hills topped with pavilions. From the highest you can get a good view of the Forbidden City.

603 DEAN'S BLUE HOLE, BAHAMAS

Blue holes seem made to be viewed from the air. They're sinkholes formed by erosion, and their depth gives them a darkness that stands out in the paler blue of the surrounding water. From above they look like a brilliant eye open in the sea. Dean's Blue Hole is the world's deepest sea-filled sinkhole, a vast vertical cave plunging 203m deep. As well as being spectacular from above, Dean's is a stunner from within. It has one of the world's largest underwater cave rooms, and with unusually clear and calm seas the visibility is great.

Dean's Blue Hole is on Long Island, about 5km west of Clarence Town.

604 PURNULULU NATIONAL PARK, AUSTRALIA

Until the release of aerial photos in the early 1980s, this remote wilderness in Western Australia was all but unknown to the outside world. Traditionally used by the Kija Aborigines during the wet season, the rugged web of gullies, cliffs, gorges, domes and ridges holds many Aboriginal art and burial sites within its extraordinary landforms. Over a period of 20 million years, the sandstone mounds of the park's Bungle Bungle Range were eroded into beehive shapes. Today, these surreal cones with eye-catching orange and grey stripes speckle this immense natural labyrinth in the Australian outback.

June to August is cool but busy; May is less crowded but hot (30°C-plus days). The visitor centre is open from 8am to noon and 1pm to 4pm.

605 FRANZ JOSEF GLACIER, NEW ZEALAND

The early Maori knew Franz Joseph as Ka Roimata o Hine Hukatere ('Tears of the Avalanche Girl'). Legend tells of a girl losing her lover when he fell from the local peaks, and her flood of tears freezing into the glacier. From above it's a breathtaking river of ice shouldering through stern mountains. Local tour operators run helicopter jaunts that take you on a scenic flight and then land you on the glacier so you can get a close-up look at the undulating blue-ice terrain. You can also ice hike and swim in heated pools fed by glacier water.

The Franz Josef Glacier is on the west coast of New Zealand's South Island. The terminal face is a 40-minute walk from the car park.

215

The majesty of the Franz Josef Glacier

Smithson's Spiral Jetty: timeless art in harmony with nature

606 'SPIRAL JETTY', UTAH, USA

Of all the earthworks of the 1970s (and beyond), *Spiral Jetty* is the most famous and beloved. A stunningly simple spiral of basalt rocks placed in Utah's Great Salt Lake, *Jetty* is the masterwork of artist Robert Smithson. It extends 460m from the shore of the lake in a counterclockwise curve. Since its creation, nature has taken over as resident artist. Smithson made the jetty in a time of drought, but when normal weather patterns returned the work was submerged for three decades. It continues to come and go, its original black turned to white by salt encrustation.

The *Jetty* is in the Golden Spike National Historic Site. There are no restrictions on your visit; you're free to walk right out on it.

607 BAGAN, MYANMAR

Situated on the banks of the mighty Ayeyarwady River, ancient Bagan is one of Southeast Asia's most memorable sights. The sheer number of temples, monasteries and stupas (about 4400) demands that you get up above them for the wonderful collective views of stupa upon stupa dotting the plain. Climbing to a temple lookout for sunset is an important part of the Bagan experience, but the best scene is from a hot-air balloon at dawn. You coast over the temples and enjoy a bird's eye view of local traffic (bicycles and bullock carts predominate) and morning market activities.

Book ahead for Balloons over Bagan's popular morning sorties, which operate in the October to March dry season.

608 CAPPADOCIA, TURKEY

The unearthly landscape of Cappadocia in central Turkey just begs you to take the long view. Almost treeless, this vast canvas for changing light is filled with rose- and honey-tinted gorges, soft cliffs riddled with pigeons' nests, rock monasteries and fairy chimneys, the whimsical shapes left by erosion. It's hardly surprising that this is one of the world's great ballooning centres. On a fine morning in the town of Göreme, you'll see crowds of balloons taking to the sky. Join one for a dawn flight and float over pinnacles resembling castles, lions and penises.

Kapadokya Balloons (www .kapadokyaballoons.com) was the first ballooning company established in Göreme, and its pilots and safety standards are first-rate.

609 PIAZZA SAN PIETRO, VATICAN CITY

One of the world's great public spaces, Bernini's piazza was laid out between 1656 and 1667 for Pope Alexander VII. Seen from above, it resembles a giant keyhole with two semicircular colonnades, each consisting of four rows of Doric columns, encircling a giant ellipse that straightens out to funnel believers into the basilica. The effect was deliberate – Bernini described the colonnades as representing 'the motherly arms of the church'. The scale of the piazza is dazzling: at its largest it measures 340m by 240m; there are 284 columns and, on top of the colonnades, 140 saints.

You can get a marvellous view of the piazza from the dome of St Peter's Basilica.

610 UFFINGTON WHITE HORSE, ENGLAND

Britain has a number of ancient hill figures – large shapes etched into hillsides and filled with packed chalk – but this is by far the oldest, dating back 3000 years. Opinions differ as to its meaning; some have questioned whether it is actually a horse at all. The shape is certainly quite abstract, with an almost feline curve to it, but accounts from medieval times refer to it as a horse and it's quite similar to horses on Iron Age coins. It may have been associated with the Celtic horse goddess Epona. The horse must be scoured regularly or the shape is quickly lost; it almost disappeared altogether in the 19th century.

The horse is in Oxfordshire. The best views of it are from the Vale of the White Horse. You can also see it from nearby Dragon Hill.

BEST SIGHTS FROM ABOVE

BEST ROCK FORMATIONS

Nature built them to be admired, so get yourself to these bizarre hunks of stone.

613 MOERAKI BOULDERS, NEW ZEALAND

Stretching north from the fishing village of Moeraki, Koekohe Beach might easily be mistaken as a bowling alley for the gods. Scattered about its sands is a collection of large, remarkably spherical boulders, which Maori legend says are the remains of eel baskets, kumaras and calabashes washed ashore from the wreck of a legendary canoe. Geologists opt for the simpler idea that they are harder remnants left behind as the mudstone cliffs at the back of the beach eroded away. The largest of the dozens of boulders are up to 3m in diameter.

InterCity buses between Christchurch and Dunedin stop at the turn-off to Moeraki. Try to time your visit with low tide.

611 TORRES DEL PAINE, CHILE

Soaring almost vertically more than 2000m above the Patagonian steppe, the granite pillars of Torres del Paine dominate the landscape of what may be South America's finest national park. Resembling a fistful of broken fingers, the craggy peaks form one of the most abstract mountain skylines in the world. Most visitors come here to hike the extraordinarily popular W trek, taking in the classic panoramas of the spires, while hardier souls hike a full circuit around the mountains, taking at least a week. If you're rushed, you can hike up to the Torres del Paine lookout, directly beneath the towers, in one long day from Laguna Amarga.

Buses for Parque Nacional Torres del Paine depart from the city of Puerto Natales, usually around 7am, 8am and 2.30pm.

612 CAPPADOCIA, TURKEY

So bizarre and inhospitable are these lunar landscapes in the heart of Turkey that early dwellers went underground, building houses, churches and monasteries into the soft cliffs. Entire subterranean cities sprang up, which enabled early Christians to hide from the Romans. Above ground, in terrain that was sculpted by erosion and volcanic eruptions some nine million years ago, rose-tinted pillars, honeycomb cliffs, strange rock formations, volcanic cones known as 'fairy chimneys', and dramatic gorges combine to create unique scenery. The ancient monastic centre of Göreme is Cappadocia's highlight, with its rock-hewn churches and Byzantine frescoes.

Try a bird's-eye view with a hot-air balloon tour; for details visit www.cappadociaturkey.net.

614 MT AUGUSTUS, AUSTRALIA

Australia has one headlining monolith – Uluru – but it is another rock, the little-visited and remote Mt Augustus in Western Australia, that actually lays claim to the title of world's largest. Twice the size of Uluru (about 8km long and covering an area of almost 48 sq km), it's buried beneath a fuzz of vegetation and struggles to fit inside the lens of a camera, placing it far from most tourists' agendas. If you make the long trip to this Gascoyne landmark (it's a 380km drive from the nearest large town, Meekatharra) it's a 12km return walk to the mountain summit, 1105m above sea level.

There's no camping in Mt Augustus National Park, but there's accommodation nearby at Cobra Station and Mt Augustus Outback Tourist Resort.

615 SHÍLÍN (STONE FOREST), CHINA

A conglomeration of utterly bizarre but stunning karst geology, the Stone Forest of Yúnnán province is a natural wonderland. A massive collection of grey limestone pillars split and eroded by wind and rain (the tallest reaches 30m high), the place was, according to legend, created by immortals who smashed a mountain into a labyrinth for lovers seeking privacy. You won't get much privacy now with the hordes of tourists, but idyllic, secluded walks are within 2km of the centre, and by sunset or moonlight Shílín becomes otherworldly.

Shílín is about 120km southeast of Kūnmíng and can easily be visited as a day trip by local bus.

616 TWELVE APOSTLES, AUSTRALIA

OK, so there aren't 12 of them and they aren't really Apostles, but the centrepiece of Australia's Great Ocean Road – one of the most spectacular coast roads in the world – is definitely a place worthy of a little biblical big-noting. Outliers of the coastal limestone cliffs behind them, these rock stacks rise up to 45m from the furious Southern Ocean in an array of shapes. By nature, the soft limestone is under constant attack from wave erosion – in 2005 one of the stacks succumbed to the constant slaps from the sea, collapsing and leaving just eight 'apostles' still standing.

The Twelve Apostles are suitably 12km east of Port Campbell; discover more about them and their surrounds at www .greatoceanrd.org.au.

617 HALF DOME, CALIFORNIA, USA

Rising more than 1400m above the eastern end of Yosemite Valley, and looking like a wave about to crash into the valley, the granite monolith of Half Dome is an iconic bit of rock. By far Yosemite's most distinctive natural feature, it has a 93% vertical grade, making it the sheerest cliff in North America. Climbers come from around the world to grapple with its legendary north face, but good hikers can reach its summit along a 27km round-trip trail from Yosemite Valley; the final slog up the rock summit is assisted by a cable handrail.

For information about Half Dome, visit the Yosemite National Park website (www.nps.gov/yose).

618 WAVE ROCK, AUSTRALIA

Large granite outcrops dot the wheatbelts around Perth, Western Australia, and the most famous is the perfectly shaped, multicoloured cresting wave of Wave Rock. Formed some 60 million years ago by weathering and water erosion, Wave Rock's streaks of colour were created by run-off from local mineral springs. To get the most out of Wave Rock, you need to wander around the many walking trails, especially the one leading to the superb Mulkas Cave, an important indigenous rock-art site with over 450 stencils and handprints.

Grab the walking trails brochure from the visitor centre (www.waverock.com.au), open 9am to 5pm daily). Wave Rock is 350km east of Perth.

619 BALANCED ROCK, UTAH, USA

Utah's Arches National Park is all about bizarre rock formations – arches, bridges, fins, mesas, buttes – but the most striking must surely be the simply titled Balanced Rock. Looking like an overblown lollipop, it's a 3244-tonne boulder teetering precariously atop a leaning 17m-high pedestal, while the rock rises another 21m. The pedestal is made of soft mudstone, which erodes faster than the rock above, so eventually it will snap, and the boulder will come crashing down.

From the Arches National Park Scenic Drive, a 500m wheelchair-accessible walk loops around Balanced Rock.

620 PETRA, JORDAN

Hewn from towering rock walls, the imposing facades of the great temples and tombs of Petra represent a city carved by the Nabataeans – Arabs who controlled the frankincense routes of the region in pre-Roman times – in a hidden valley concealed from the outside world. You approach Petra through a narrow 1.2km defile known as the Siq. Just as you start to think there's no end to the Siq, you catch a glimpse ahead of Petra's most impressive sight, the Al-Khazneh (Treasury). From here, passages lead to an array of other buildings; you really need two full days to do Petra justice.

Minibuses run daily between Petra and Amman and Wadi Rum. Petra's ticket office is in the visitor centre, where you can buy one-, two- or three-day passes.

MEDIEVAL SIGHTS

Fairytale castles, fortified cities, fearsome tyrants and stomach-turning torture – Europe's rich medieval past is a historian's dream.

621 DUNSTANBURGH CASTLE, NORTHUMBERLAND, ENGLAND

The English county of Northumberland is famous for striking medieval castles – Bamburgh and Alnwick draw the biggest crowds, but for isolated beauty it's hard to beat Dunstanburgh. This 14th-century fortress hugs the exposed North Sea coastline between the tiny villages of Craster and Embleton. It's wonderfully ruinous – only the main gatehouse remains,

Carcassonne: enduring symbol of medieval France

together with a crumbling tower and sections of the squat defensive wall. But the location is dramatic. Accessible only on foot, and best approached in the soft dusk light of a summer evening, it's easy to see why the landscape artist Turner loved to paint here.

The castle is operated by the National Trust (www.nationaltrust.org.uk), which charges an entrance fee, but you'll see it best by walking the stunning coastal path, and beaches, from Beadnell to Craster (10km).

IZZET KERIBAR / LONELY PLANET IMAGES

622 HER MAJESTY'S ROYAL PALACE & FORTRESS, LONDON, ENGLAND

In a country rich in muscular strongholds, nowhere embodies medieval England better than this 11th-century fortified palace. This former royal residence is a mix of private quarters, grand communal spaces and ostentatious pomp, but it's the palace's more macabre history that visitors love most. Commonly known as the Tower of London, the castle is most famous for the 15th-century incarceration of two young princes, Edward V of England and his brother, Richard of Shrewsbury, who are believed to have died here after being interned as illegitimate sons of Edward IV. The prisoners are long gone but the medieval mystery endures.

The Tower of London (www.hrp.org.uk/toweroflondon) is centrally located; get here on buses 15, 42, 78, 100, RV1, or take the tube to Tower Hill.

624 ÁVILA, SPAIN

A short hop from Madrid brings you to Ávila, a World Heritage site and one of Europe's finest medieval towns. Walking the walls is the thing to do here. Punctuated by 88 fortified towers and with six gates, these 2.5km-long 11th-century fortifications completely encircle the town and were built by King Alfonso VI as protection during the Christian Reconquista. Ávila is Spain's highest city, at 1130m above sea level, and following the southern perimeter leads the eye to a distant mountain vista unchanged over the centuries. Inside the walls, Romanesque churches and convents, Renaissance palaces and Castilian mansions are beautifully preserved amid the atmospheric cobbled streets.

Ávila is 110km west of Madrid – frequent trains (www.renfe.com) and buses (www.lasepulvedana.es) run to the city in about 1½ hours.

623 CARCASSONNE, FRANCE

Sometimes, if you want the best, you have to deal with the crowds. So it is at Carcassonne. France's picture-postcard 13th-century medieval jewel is a day-tripper's dream, but look past the throng and you'll see they're all here for a reason. Few fortified cities are as fantastic. A double-ring of ramparts shields a soaring castle with a central keep, protected by a series of 52 towers and a deep moat bearing a classic drawbridge; impregnable and foreboding. Just plan to visit early or late in the day to see the town at its uncrowded best.

From the end of June to August, Carcassonne Festival (www.festivaldecarcassonne.fr) puts on more than 100 shows in opera, theatre and music, including performances at the medieval Roman Theatre.

625 CASTLE OF THE MOORS, SINTRA, PORTUGAL

For centuries Islamic Moors and Christian Europeans battled for control of the Iberian Peninsula. And between 711 and 1492 it was the Moors who had the upper hand, stamping their mark across the land we now recognise as modern-day Portugal and Spain. The Portuguese town of Sintra has the best-preserved relics: the splendidly decrepit Moorish castle – Castelo dos Mouros – is in a forest outside town, overlooking the town and beyond to the vast blue expanse of the Atlantic Ocean. The castle's rundown state makes this one of the more genuine medieval experiences possible.

Sintra comes to life during the annual Festival of Music and Dance (www .festivaldesintra.pt), with events held in some of the old town's wonderfully atmospheric venues.

626 RHODES, GREECE

Think of the Greek islands and you'll be dreaming of white beaches and the blue Aegean. What you might not imagine is a medieval old town of such importance it has been a World Heritage site since 1988. Variously occupied in the Middle Ages by Christian and Muslim rulers, the town of Rhodes exhibits a disparate mix of architectural and religious styles. From the Palace of the Grand Masters in the Upper Town to the Ottoman mosques and *hammam* (bathhouses) of the Lower Town, Rhodes attracts just as many culture vultures as it does beach bums.

During May and June Rhodes hosts the annual Medieval Rose Festival (www .medievalfestival.gr), with events such as guided moat tours and dragon chases through the old town.

627 YORK MINSTER, ENGLAND

In the walled city of York, 320km north of London, construction of the continent's greatest Gothic cathedral began in 1220 and would last for a staggering 250 years. It was worth the wait. Built to a classic cruciform design, the Minster towers above York's famously narrow alleys and stout city walls. With intricate decor, spooky subterranean crypts and enormous chiming 10-tonne bells, this is cathedral design on steroids. But it's the windows that tourists love most – some date to the 12th century and the 23m-tall Great East Window is the world's largest piece of medieval stained glass.

York is crowded during the high-season summer months – an autumn visit (from September to October) can still provide warm days but with a fraction of the crowds.

628 VISBY, GOTLAND, SWEDEN

At the height of the medieval Baltic Sea trade, Visby boomed. Situated on the Swedish island of Gotland, the city thrived with wealthy merchants and became one of Europe's key strategic locations, acquiring the status symbols – cathedrals, churches and mansion houses – that defined a successful medieval settlement. It also drew envious glances from Denmark and wasted no time in throwing up a muscular defensive wall. Today Visby is a hot destination for partying Swedes, but it's also listed by Unesco as one of Scandinavia's finest preserved medieval towns. Indeed, anywhere with a fortified bastion called 'Gunpowder Tower' has to be worth a visit.

Jousting, jesters and jocularity – the Swedes know how to make merry and Medieval Week (www.medeltidsveckan .se) rocks Visby every August in a 600-year-old kind of way.

629 ELTZ CASTLE, WIERSCHEM, GERMANY

Castles: nothing says 'medieval' better than a stout stone edifice topped with towering turrets. In a continent blessed with more than its fair share, 12th-century Eltz Castle is one of Europe's finest. Romanesque and baroque in style, Eltz's fantastical design is the perfect vision of a classic fairytale castle. The sheer walls soar an impressive eight storeys from a 70m-high cliff above the Elzbach River, whilst the eight lofty towers conjure images of Rapunzel's coils of golden hair. Owned by the same family for 33 generations and furnished almost exactly as it was 500 years ago, Eltz offers a fascinating insight into the life of the wealthy medieval elite.

Eltz Castle (www.burg-eltz.de) is 25km from the city of Koblenz; take a train to Moselkern or Karden and pick up one of the marked hiking trails.

York Minster: two-and-a-half centuries in the making

630 CASTLE POENARI, TRANSYLVANIA, ROMANIA

On an exposed cliff in Romania's Argeş River valley, close to the beautiful Făgăraş Mountains, stands a ruined castle said to be the inspiration for Bram Stoker's *Dracula*. Remote and inaccessible, this 13th-century fortress was commissioned by local leaders but abandoned after 200 years. Enter Vlad the Impaler. Good old Vlad rescued the castle from dereliction, making it one of his primary bases for practising his trademark of death by impalement. Poenari is said to be one of the most haunted places in the world and you can visit the ruins if you fancy tackling 1480 steps from the valley bottom.

Curtea de Argeş is a lovely town about 25km from Castle Poenari, with good accommodation and entertainment options.

MEDIEVAL SIGHTS

MOST UNUSUAL BEACHES

Candy sands, disappearing waves, transformed trolls –
if life's a beach, these are its strangest days.

631 BOWLING BALL BEACH, CALIFORNIA, USA

Compared to green sand or vanishing tides, 'round rocks' don't initially sound like reason enough to visit this Californian beach. And yet, when you get down there and see the 'bowling balls' sitting like some tidy giant's game on the sand, you can't help but get a thrill. Best seen at low tide, the rocks are freakily round and freakily regular, and clustered together as if they've been placed there. The truth is, they're stubborn. The softer rock around them washed away, but these tough customers withstood the waves.

If you're driving, take Highway 1. The Bowling Balls are on the Mendocino Coast; take the Schooner Gulch Road off the highway.

632 HARBOUR ISLAND, BAHAMAS

Blink your eyes. Are you in some kind of Lucy-in-the-Sky, fairy-floss and cream-pie hallucination? Or is that sand really…pink? Yep, it is. The colour is caused by tiny particles of coral mixing in with the white sand. Pink-sand beaches occur all along the east coast of Harbour Island. As if that's not enough to make it your new favourite island ever, you'll also find the classic sighing, lucid, blue Bahamas seas. You can leave the rose-coloured glasses at home for this one.

Afternoon cocktails on your private balcony looking out onto the petal-coloured sands? Lash out at Pink Sands Resort (www.pinksandsresort.com).

633 GLASS BEACH, CALIFORNIA, USA

This beach is a testament to nature's amazing ability to turn trash into treasure. Overlooked by cliffs, this place was once seen as just a convenient dumping ground for Fort Braggs' garbage. Up until the late 1960s, folks would hurl their refuse – including old cars and appliances – straight over the cliffs and into the oceans. Finally the authorities put a stop to it. Over the ensuing decades, the sea performed a remarkable conjuring act, acting like a huge tumbler to winnow out the glass and turn it smooth. These days the beach resembles a gem shop. People used to collect the glass, but that's now forbidden.

Follow Fort Bragg's Elm Street to its end and then hike down the dirt trail to the beach. Take care, the path can be treacherous.

634 PRINCE WILLIAM SOUND, ALASKA, USA

This close to the northernmost point of the Gulf of Alaska is where beaches get truly otherworldly. Tidewater glaciers spilling into the sea. Cold clear air. Mountain peaks reflected in the pure waters. And black sand framed by green hills and blue ice. That's before you even get to the wildlife of the region – harbour seals, sea otters, whales, eagles and bears, to name but a few. It's no wonder this is heaven for kayakers.

If kayaking around a calving glacier sounds a little hair-raising for you, consider a glacier cruise (www.princewilliamsound.com) instead.

635   PAPAKŌLEA, HAWAII, USA

When it comes to beaches, the volcanic islands of Hawaii aren't content to leave it at sugar-white. They mix it up with ebony black, Mars red – and green! Papakōlea's not exactly blazing emerald, but it does have a distinct green tint from olivine crystals deposited on the beach by a volcanic explosion about 10,000 years ago. These crystals are heavier than the rest of the volcanic materials, so as the water washes the rest away, the beach gets greener. Eventually the olivine will run out and the beach will be grey, but not any time soon in human terms.

Papakōlea is in the Ka'u district. You'll have to hike in and climb down the cinder cone. But hey, it's green!

When it comes to Papakōlea, the rest of the world's beaches are green with envy

'One small step for a giant, one giant leap for mankind...' The Giant's Causeway: bringing mythical beings closer together

636 CHANDIPUR, INDIA

The sea here has a magic trick – it disappears! At low tide it waves goodbye and heads out for some 5km (yes, that's unusually far; when you see it happen you'll know how freaky it is). That in itself may not be enough to draw you here, but while you're waiting for the sea to come sloshing back in with a 'just kidding!' you'll be able to explore the seabed, complete with shells, driftwood and little red crabs. And when you're in Orissa, why not check out some of its other off-the-tourist-trail beaches?

While you're at it, visit the Orissan town of Puri in June or July for the stunning Rath Yatra festival (www.rathyatra.net).

637 PERISSA, SANTORINI, GREECE

Don't expect to get this one to yourself – with a beach this famous, you have to share. Perissa is probably the most beautiful of Santorini's black-sand beaches, overlooked by the huge rock Mesa Vouno, which is lit up at night. The beach is long so you won't be too squashed in with

GARETH MCCORMACK / LONELY PLANET IMAGES

638 GIANT'S CAUSEWAY, NORTHERN IRELAND

It's easy to see how legends grew up around this masterwork. Volcanic eruption has shaped thousands of basalt columns into precise hexagonal shapes, grouped together like organ pipes. It's almost impossible to believe that they haven't been carved by human hands. The mythology of the place has the famed warrior Finn McCool swapping shouted threats with a Scottish giant over the sea. They started to make a causeway so they could get their hands on each other. (Geology supports the myth: there are similar structures on the Scottish side of the sea.) Don't miss particularly sculptural structures like the Giant's Boot and the Chimney Stacks.

The Causeway is near Bushmills in County Antrim. Ulsterbus 252 goes on a circular path from Belfast to the Antrim Glens.

639 RAINBOW BEACH, AUSTRALIA

Not content with merely taking on an unusual colour like red or green, Rainbow Beach takes on a myriad. On Fraser Island (the world's largest sand island) off Australia's east coast, the beach is backed by exquisite cliffs where you can see the rainbow colours most clearly in edible-looking striations of nougat, rose, honey and cream. Aboriginal legend has it that a spirit personified in the rainbow dived into the cliffs during a fight over a woman, staining them with his colours. The sand looks gold from a distance but scoop up a handful and you'll see the rainbow.

Get up early to hand-feed wild dolphins at nearby Tin Can Bay. There is only one feeding a day, at 8am sharp.

640 VÍK BEACH, ICELAND

The little town of Vík has three distinctions. One, it's Iceland's southernmost point. Two, it's the rainiest place on the island. And three, it has one of the most beautiful beaches in the world. Obviously it's for looking at, rather than swimming in… White waves wash up on jet-black sands, like a beach seen in negative. The cliffs above glow green from all that rain. And strange basalt figures stand here and there like sculptures. They're traditionally believed to be ill-fated trolls that got caught out in the sun.

Accommodation in Vik is limited. Try the hostel (www.hostel.is/hostels/vik).

the hordes, but if you do feel like some time out, the ruins of Thira, an ancient city, are just a sprightly hike away. Bring flip-flops to this beach – the black sand holds the heat.

Stay close to the action at Stelios Place (www.steliosplace.com), just metres from the beach; it has white balconies, a pool and good breakfasts.

MOST UNUSUAL BEACHES

GREATEST BOOKSHOPS

The best spots to browse, buy, hang out, find sanctuary among the shelves, rave about your favourite writers and meet book-loving characters.

643 LIVRARIA LELLO, PORTO, PORTUGAL

A little over 100 years old, this art nouveau gem in Portugal's second city remains one of the world's most stunning shops. Competing for attention with the books are wraparound, neo-Gothic shelves, featuring panels carved with Portuguese literary figures. A track, used by the staff for transporting stock in a cart, leads from the entrance to the red staircase, which winds up to the first floor like an exotic flower. Books are available in English as well as Portuguese, and there's a small cafe beneath the stained-glass skylight.

You can continue the art nouveau tour of Porto at Café Majestic and streets such as Rua Galeria de Paris.

641 ANOTHER COUNTRY, BERLIN, GERMANY

The commendably eccentric Another Country is a hub for everyone from Berlin's expat community to indie bands. The Kreuzberg institution is more of a library than a conventional bookshop: you can pay for the book, return it when you've read it, and get your money back – minus €1.50. In addition to some 20,000 books, the sprawling shop-cum-club offers much-loved events, including the Tuesday-night film club, Thursday TV night and Friday dinner. In the finest tradition of left-field bookstores, Another Country inspires as well as sells creative efforts, and its website features a comic and a story about the shop.

Located at Riemannstrasse 7, Another Country (www.anothercountry.de) is open Tuesday to Friday 11am to 8pm and weekends from noon to 4pm. The film and TV nights start at 8pm; the dinner at 9pm.

642 SHAKESPEARE & COMPANY, PARIS, FRANCE

Where did the American beat poets go to share cigarettes and profundities when they were in Europe? Shakespeare & Company of course – located in Paris' Latin Quarter, a tome's throw from Notre Dame Cathedral. George Whitman, the eccentric American bibliophile who opened the cosy store in 1951, has handed the reins to his daughter as he approaches 100. Nonetheless, much of Shakespeare & Co's creative, chaotic spirit remains. It's still a prime spot to fill your rucksack with paperbacks, hang with the Left Bank literati, and admire the packed shelves, wooden beams and poetic posters.

Nearby transport links include St-Michel (metro line 4) and St-Michel Notre Dame (RER lines B and C). Visit http://shakespeareandcompany.com for more information.

644 SELEXYZ DOMINICANEN, MAASTRICHT, THE NETHERLANDS

Occupying a 13th-century Dominican church – which the Dutch city's cyclists had appropriated for bike storage – Selexyz Dominicanen consists of a steel bookstack rising towards the heavens. Cunningly, this both leaves the nave's grandeur intact and creates 1200 sq metres of selling space – despite the 750-sq-metre floor area. Staircases and a lift lead to the top of the three-storey stack, where you can eyeball 14th-century ceiling paintings. The altar has been superseded by a cafe, with a halo of lights hanging above a cruciform table. It's an award-winning architectural triumph and a peaceful haven for page-thumbing.

Close to both Liège in Belgium and Aachen in Germany, Maastricht is connected to Amsterdam, some 220km northwest, by train.

645 BOOKÀBAR, ROME, ITALY

Just the thought of big, sexy art books makes us consider diverting our travel dollars to collecting coffee-table beauties. It's rash talk, but even hardened travellers might agree when they ogle the arty tomes in Bookàbar. With a curvy ceiling and long, smooth shelves, the shop's coolly contemporary, snow-white interior hoards books, catalogues, CDs, DVDs and merchandise. It looks like a space station staffed by extremely well-read astronauts. The neighbours certainly don't lower the tone, as it's part of the Palazzo delle Esposizioni exhibition centre. Bookàbar's adjoining cafe serves dishes inspired by the centre's exhibitions.

Palazzo delle Esposizioni, which normally has a few exhibitions covering various art forms, is near the junction of Via Nazionale and Via Milano.

646 THE BOOKWORM, BEIJING, CHINA

The Bookworm does everything a good bookshop should do – which is a lot more than sell books. The Beijing mothership, which has spawned branches in Sūzhōu and Chéngdū, has played a huge role in promoting both local and foreign literature. Not only is it one of the few places in China where you can pick up books that are banned in the country, it has a lending library with 16,000-plus titles. The library is also the setting for a healthy program of events, from gigs to an annual literary festival. There's even a whisky bar and monthly wine club.

The Bookworm International Literary Festival takes place in Beijing, Sūzhōu and Chéngdū over two weeks in mid-March; see www.chinabookworm.com.

647 DAUNT BOOKS, LONDON, ENGLAND

London is an armchair explorer's dream, offering high-quality, travel-focused book dens such as Stanford's and The Travel Bookshop. Our favourite is Daunt Books. The mini-chain stocks a lot more than guides and maps, and everything – from biographies to fiction – is handily arranged by country. The green Daunt Books sign is found in five well-heeled enclaves of London, but the Marylebone branch is the original and best. Occupying an Edwardian bookshop, its long oak galleries with polished floors and shelves, graceful skylights and William Morris prints create a peaceful atmosphere.

The branches at 83 Marylebone High Street, Chelsea, Holland Park, Hampstead and Belsize Park open seven days a week; visit www.dauntbooks.co.uk.

648 POWELL'S CITY OF BOOKS, PORTLAND, OREGON, USA

The aptly named City of Books is the largest independent bookstore in the US. The flagship store is four storeys high and takes up an entire city block, and you can genuinely get lost wandering its many rooms. With more than a million new and used books in stock, a rare books room with autographed first editions, regular art exhibits and author events, and a coffee shop to keep your energy levels up, this place is dangerously addictive. Bank on your quick one-hour 'browse' turning into a whole day. Locals love the laid-back attitude and personal service that normally belong to a smaller store.

Located at 1005 W Burnside, Powell's is in the Pearl District of Portland, known for high-end galleries and boutiques.

649 ATLANTIS BOOKS, SANTORINI, GREECE

In an age when independent bookshops are being replaced by chains and websites, a gang of American and European university graduates realised the dream of opening one – on a Greek island. 'We found an empty building facing the sunset, drank some whiskey and signed a lease,' explains the shop's website, though we suspect it was more of a mission than that. The shop occupies the basement of a whitewashed, cliff-top villa, which the communally minded staff also call home. The terrace overlooking the Aegean hosts cultural happenings, and inside are more cult novels and quality books than you can shake a quill at.

Santorini is to linked to Athens by Blue Star Ferries, Hellas Flying Dolphins ferries, Olympic Air and Aegean Airlines.

650 LIBRERÍA EL ATENEO GRAND SPLENDID, BUENOS AIRES, ARGENTINA

It's grand, it's splendid, it's a strong contender to be the world's most beautiful bookshop. Occupying a 1920s theatre in downtown BA, El Ateneo has kept the sumptuous auditorium's original furnishings – and added books. Beneath the painted ceiling, shelves have been built into the spectator balconies. When you've finished gawping at the ornate carvings, the former theatre boxes are now intimate reading rooms. There's a cafe on the stage, between red velvet curtains, and the final firework in the literary spectacle is the round-the-clock opening hours.

Librería El Ateneo Grand Splendid is located on the south side of Ave Santa Fe, 50m west of Ave Callao.

20TH CENTURY'S DARKEST HISTORY

Sombre places where you can learn history's terrible lessons, pay your respects to the fallen and vow that these horrors must never happen again.

A scene of remembrance enacted at Hiroshima's Peace Memorial Park

LOU JONES / LONELY PLANET IMAGES

651 BERLIN WALL, GERMANY

It's ironic that Berlin's most popular tourist attraction is one that no longer exists. For 28 years the Berlin Wall, the most potent symbol of the Cold War, divided not only the city but the world. Built in 1961, the Wall was a 155km-long symbol of oppression that turned West Berlin into an island of democracy within a sea of socialism. Continually reinforced and refined over time, it eventually grew into a complex border security system that included a 'death strip' made up of trenches, floodlights, patrol roads, attack dogs, electrified fences and watchtowers staffed by trigger-happy guards.

The Berlin Wall Memorial (Bernauer Strasse 111) includes a section of the original wall, a documentation centre, chapel, art installation and outdoor gallery.

653 AUSCHWITZ-BIRKENAU, POLAND

In 1940, on the outskirts of the small town of Oświęcim, the Nazis established a concentration camp that was to become history's largest experiment in genocide. Most commonly known by its German name, Auschwitz originally held Polish political prisoners. It was later designated for the extermination of Jews, and a larger facility was constructed at nearby Birkenau. It has been estimated that around 1.5 million people of 27 nationalities, including 1.1 million Jews, were murdered here. Both camps have been preserved as the Auschwitz-Birkenau State Museum; a visit is both harrowing and deeply moving.

For most visitors, the jump-off point for Oświęcim is Krakow, 40km east. Up to 10 buses run daily to the museum entrance.

652 HIROSHIMA PEACE MEMORIAL PARK, JAPAN

On 6 August 1945, the world's first atomic bomb was dropped on Hiroshima, with 90,000 civilian deaths. Three days later it was followed by a second atomic bomb, dropped on Nagasaki, with a further 75,000 deaths. Both cities are now home to poignant monuments and museums outlining the horrors of those events, and honouring the victims. The Hiroshima Peace Memorial Park is dotted with memorials and stands across the river from the Unesco-protected A-Bomb Dome, perhaps the starkest reminder of the destruction visited upon the city. Built in 1915, it was one of very few buildings left standing near the bomb's epicentre, and today serves as a powerful symbol of the city's tragic past.

Nagasaki's monuments are no less moving; both cities hold deeply affecting memorial services on the anniversaries of the bombings.

231

654 WORLD TRADE CENTER SITE, NEW YORK, USA

True, 9/11 falls outside the 20th century by a matter of months, but its inclusion is warranted. On 11 September 2001, terrorists flew hijacked planes into the World Trade Center's Twin Towers, turning the whole complex into dust and rubble and killing nearly 2800 people. Many ideas for renewal and a memorial at the site have been bandied around, but consensus (and construction) has been slow. The memorial plaza, honouring 9/11 victims and rescuers, consists of a forested park with two square pools where the Twin Towers once stood; it is scheduled to open on the 10th anniversary of the tragedy.

The entire National September 11 Memorial & Museum should be open by 2012; read about the design and progress of the site at www.wtc.com.

655 KILLING FIELDS OF CHOEUNG EK, CAMBODIA

Between 1975 and 1978, some 17,000 Cambodians who had been detained and tortured by the Khmer Rouge were transported to the extermination camp of Choeung Ek, where they were often bludgeoned to death to avoid wasting bullets. In 1980, the remains of 8985 people were exhumed from mass graves; 43 of the 129 communal graves here have been left untouched. More than 8000 skulls, arranged by sex and age, are visible behind the glass panels of the Memorial Stupa, erected in 1988. It's a grim, confronting place, but essential for understanding just how far Cambodia has come in little over three decades.

The Killing Fields are 15km from central Phnom Penh; most people arrive by bicycle, moto (motorcycle taxi) or taxi.

656 KIGALI MEMORIAL CENTRE, RWANDA

The horrific events that unfolded in Rwanda in 1994 have been etched into the world's consciousness as one of the most savage genocides in history. What happened is beyond belief – an estimated 800,000 Rwandans were killed in just three months, mostly by gangs of youths armed with machetes and guns – but the country has taken great strides towards recovery. The profoundly moving Kigali Memorial Centre is a must for visitors to Rwanda. Downstairs is dedicated to the 1994 genocide and its victims; upstairs covers other genocides around the world. Buried in the memorial gardens are the remains of 250,000 victims, gathered here as a final resting place.

In Kigali, stay at the Hôtel des Mille Collines (www.millecollines.net), the hotel where horror and hope collided, as outlined in the movie Hotel Rwanda.

657 PERM-36, RUSSIA

Perm-36 is about 25km from the town of Chusovoy, itself 100km east of the city of Perm in Russia's Ural Mountains. Remote, in other words. Which suited its purpose: Perm-36 was one of the infamous Soviet forced-labour camps of the Gulag Archipelago, where many dissidents were persecuted. Stalin ordered the camp built in 1946; countless artists, scientists and intellectuals spent years in the cold, damp cells, many in solitary confinement. Before the first prisoners arrived, the surrounding trees were destroyed so that inmates couldn't determine where in Russia they had landed. Today Perm-36 is a fascinating museum and moving memorial to the victims of political repression.

The Perm-36 museum office in Perm can arrange a taxi and translator for visitors; see www.perm36.ru.

658 APARTHEID MUSEUM, JOHANNESBURG, SOUTH AFRICA

During the apartheid era (1948 to 1990), the South African government attempted to categorise everyone into one of four groups: African, coloured (mixed race), Asian or white. These classifications were then used to regulate where and how people could live and work. Opposition to the system was met with government-sanctioned violence. Johannesburg's evocative Apartheid Museum brilliantly illustrates the rise and fall of South Africa's era of segregation and oppression. Particularly chilling is a small chamber in which hang 131 nooses, representative of the 131 government opponents who were executed under antiterrorism laws.

Further explore the apartheid era at the excellent Hector Pieterson Museum in Soweto, southwest of the Jo'burg city centre.

Rwanda's Kigali Memorial Centre

659 SREBRENICA-POTOČARI MEMORIAL CENTER, BOSNIA & HERCEGOVINA

Winston Churchill once commented that 'the Balkans produce more history than they consume', and the 1990s saw much tragic history being made in the region. As Yugoslavia imploded, ethnic tensions were heightened. The state of Bosnia and Hercegovina declared independence in 1991, but over the next three years a brutal and extraordinarily complex civil war raged. In July 1995, Dutch peacekeepers could only watch as the starved, supposedly 'safe area' of Srebrenica fell to a Bosnian Serb force. An estimated 8000 Muslim men and boys were subsequently slaughtered in Europe's worst mass killings since WWII. Today, the massacre is commemorated by a large cemetery and open-air modernist mosque at Potočari, some 8km northwest of the town.

The Srebrenica-Potočari Memorial Center was opened in 2003 at the former UN base; see http://sru.potocarimc.ba.

660 TSITSERNAKABERD, YEREVAN, ARMENIA

In one of the 20th century's lesser-known tragedies, an estimated 1.5 million Armenians died during the death throes of the Ottoman Empire (from 1915 to 1923), thanks to state-sponsored massacres or deportations of virtually all of the Armenian population within the empire. Deportation meant forced marches into the Syrian deserts, under conditions designed to kill the deportees. Commemorating the agony of this era, the Armenian Genocide Museum and its accompanying memorial create a moving experience. The underground museum houses large photographs that tell the story of the genocide simply and baldly. Outside there's a magnificent view of Mt Ararat, the symbol of Armenia 40km inside modern Turkish territory.

The memorial is set on Tsitsernakaberd Hill across the Hradzan Gorge from central Yerevan; a taxi is the easiest option. See www.genocide-museum.am/eng.

20TH CENTURY'S DARKEST HISTORY

MOST ENDANGERED SIGHTS

Tourism, political instability and urban development threaten some of our greatest natural and cultural history – do your bit for preservation and consider some cool alternatives.

661 ABU MENA, EGYPT

Rising groundwater, urban growth and agricultural development threaten the archaeological site of Abu Mena, 45km southwest of Alexandria. The consequences for this early Christian settlement are startling – the clay soil liquefies with excess water and immense cavities open under large areas of the complex, forcing authorities to underpin endangered buildings with sand in an attempt to prevent further damage. A great alternative involves heading underground to Alexandria's Catacombs of Kom el Shoqafa, a rabbit warren of early Egyptian sarcophagi that's claimed to be one of the seven wonders of the medieval world.

Egyptians flock to Alexandria in summer and hotels become scarce; head there in the still-warm winter (December to February) to get the eerie catacombs to yourself…and the deceased.

The Bagrati Cathedral, a location that provides great views out over Tbilisi – and onto Georgian history

662 MEDIEVAL MONUMENTS, KOSOVO

Synonymous with conflict and destruction, Kosovo hides a rich seam of Byzantine-Romanesque ecclesiastical architecture and a medieval history many people are unaware of. Four forlornly beautiful relics – the 13th- and 14th-century monasteries of Dečani, Patriarchate of Peć and Gračanica, and the Church of the Virgin of Ljeviša – form the collective known as the Medieval Monuments. Ornately decorated with wall paintings, the sites remain endangered due to political instability. By contrast, the capital city of Priština is embracing the modern world – simply hang out in buzzing bars and cafes in this confident nation crackling with fierce pride and independent spirit.

The airport is 17km west of Priština; a taxi ride is the only way into the city and will set you back around €25.

664 BELIZE BARRIER REEF RESERVE SYSTEM, BELIZE

Sandwiched as they are between the Pacific Ocean and Caribbean Sea, all Central American countries have strong aquatic diversity. Belize, nuzzling Mexico's far southeast corner, offers 386km of idyllic coastline and the largest barrier reef in the northern hemisphere. Pristine atolls, lagoons and corals, plus iconic sights like the 124m-deep Great Blue Hole, attract divers from across the globe. But excessive mangrove cutting and ongoing coastal development are threatening the fragile balance of the ecosystem. Instead of diving, head upwards to the Maya Mountains, home to Belize's highest peaks and a number of ancient Maya ruins.

At 1124m, Doyle's Delight is Belize's highest peak; Lubaantun is a ruined Maya city dating from around 800 AD.

665 TOMBS OF BUGANDA KINGS, KASUBI, UGANDA

When fire tore through the Tombs of the Buganda Kings in March 2010, a national scandal erupted. Constructed in the late 19th century, the Unesco-protected tombs celebrate four kings of the Buganda kingdom, a sub-national kingdom within Uganda. With the cause of the fire unknown, looting and rioting broke out, as the relationship between the Buganda tribespeople and the government grew increasingly tense. Both sides have vowed to reconstruct the sacred site, but unrest remains. In the meantime, take a look at Namugongo Martyrs Shrine, a memorial to over 30 Buganda victims of the 1886 religious massacre that occurred here.

Namugongo Martyrs Shrine is 12km northeast of the Ugandan capital, Kampala. Frequent tours run from the city.

663 BAGRATI CATHEDRAL & GELATI MONASTERY, GEORGIA

Back in the 3rd century, Georgia became one of the first countries to adopt Christianity and it seems they've been building churches, cathedrals and monasteries ever since. Most famous is the site at Bagrati. The 11th-century cathedral is a Christian religious masterpiece, while the Gelati Monastery is richly adorned with frescos and wall paintings. Ruined during the Ottoman Empire, restoration began in 1952. Today, concerns surround the method of reconstruction, which is believed to be endangering the entire site. For a different religious fix, stick to the capital, Tbilisi – the city has dozens of churches, many of Georgian and Armenian heritage and rich in cultural significance.

The 12th-century Metekhi Church in Tbilisi stands on a cliff overlooking the Mtkvari River and is a great viewpoint to look out over the city.

666 CORO, VENEZUELA

On Venezuela's central northern coast is the Spanish colonial city of Coro, dating from the early 16th century and a principal example of Caribbean earthen architecture. Some 602 historic buildings, mostly 18th- and 19th-century churches and merchants' quarters, form the city's core. A strong Dutch influence can also be seen. The site was added to Unesco's endangered list in 2005 as a consequence of climate-change-induced rain damage and insensitive development plans. As an alternative, consider a trip to nearby Médanos de Coro National Park, where you can explore constantly shifting sand dunes that reach 40m in height.

235

The national park is open from 9am to 6pm (www.losmedanos.com, in Spanish).

The Everglades: everlasting wonder

667 RICE TERRACES, CORDILLERAS, PHILIPPINES

Rice farming defines Asian civilisation and the terraces of the Philippine Cordilleras, on the northern island of Luzon, are a 2000-year-old icon of agricultural heritage. Known as the 'eighth wonder of the world', the manmade terraces cling to impossibly steep valleys and meld seamlessly with nature's verdant backdrop. Symbolic of sacred folklore and ingenuity, many terraces are now neglected as the modern world lures young farmers to the city, and the site is ill-equipped for large numbers of visitors. The Cordilleras Mountains are home to Mt Pulag, the Philippine's second-highest peak (2992m), which makes a great alternative to visiting the terraces.

Permits for climbing Mt Pulag are available from the offices of Mt Pulag National Park at Ambangeg, a 250km drive north from Manila.

668 RAINFORESTS OF THE ATSINANANA, MADAGASCAR

Around 60 million years of geographic isolation have afforded Madagascar a unique ecosystem, so unusual that scientists call this 'the eighth continent'. Most animal species are endemic and while lemurs are the star attraction, you'll also find curious creatures such as the tenrec, fanaloka or aye-aye. The Rainforests of the Atsinanana are six national parks

JIM WARK / LONELY PLANET IMAGES

669 EVERGLADES NATIONAL PARK, FLORIDA, USA

It's not every day that the USA appears on the world's 'at risk' radar, but this isn't the first time the Everglades have been under threat. Containing the western hemisphere's largest mangrove ecosystem, the park is struggling with reduced water flow and increased nutrient pollution, which are degrading the aquatic network and damaging marine species. While the government works to correct the problem, try Biscayne National Park as an alternative. Downtown Miami might be on the near horizon, but here you can swim, snorkel and kayak to your heart's content, or simply pitch a tent and gaze at the view.

Allow 60 to 90 minutes to drive from Miami to Biscayne National Park; check out the park's website (www.nps.gov/bisc/) for fees, access instructions and suggested activities.

670 WALLED CITY, SHIRVANSHAH'S PALACE & MAIDEN TOWER, BAKU, AZERBAIJAN

To many people, Baku means industrial wastelands and oil dollars, but there's a cultural history here that is more valuable than the countless wellheads. The 12th-century Walled City of Baku, in an area first settled in the Palaeolithic period, exudes the history of empires including the Arabic, Persian and Ottoman. Spectacular highlights include the Maiden Tower, a 12th-century bastion and symbol of national identity, and the ornate 15th-century Shirvanshah's Palace. These and other sites are priceless examples of iconic architecture but are threatened by the continued spread of modern development. Less threatened is the Gobustan Rock Art Cultural Landscape in the semidesert of central Azerbaijan, a collection of 6000 rock engravings that chart ancient human settlement.

You can visit the rock art as a day trip from Baku; fly in on Azerbaijan Airlines (www.azal.az).

in the island's east, supporting rare and endangered species. But illegal logging is threatening the forests, leading to international anxiety and calls for strict embargoes. Avoid exacerbating the situation by heading to a less troubled corner – the isle of Nosy Komba offers hidden coves and great high-altitude trekking.

Boats to Nosy Komba run at 9am daily from Hell-Ville on Nosy Be; the trip costs MGA5000.

MOST ENDANGERED SIGHTS

SACRED SITES

Make your own pilgrimage to some of the world's great spiritual places.

673 MEĐUGORJE, BOSNIA & HERCEGOVINA

On 28 June 1981, six youths in the Bosnian mountain village of Međugorje claimed to have seen an apparition of the Virgin Mary. Instantly, a place of pilgrimage was born, complete with bus tours and an unholy number of souvenir stands. The Virgin is said to still appear at Međugorje, bringing messages to the world, delivering them through the original six 'visionaries' – three of them see the apparition daily. For a Međugorje vision of your own, begin in the famed bridge town of Mostar; Međugorje is about 30 mountainous kilometres away.

After your devotions, sample the region's best wines at the delightful ivy-draped Stankela winery nearby.

671 SOURCE OF THE GANGES, INDIA

The River Ganges is Hinduism's holiest river, beginning in the Himalayan peaks of Uttar Pradesh and spilling out into the Bay of Bengal more than 2000km later. For Hindus, the source of the Ganges is a holy of holies, and many thousands make the pilgrimage to the spot near Gangotri. To join them requires a trek of 24km from Gangotri, threading through Himalayan valleys to Gaumukh, where you'll find the trickle of water that will flow on to become one of Asia's major rivers. Pilgrims perform *darshans* (offerings) as near as possible to the point where water flows from the ice wall beneath the terminal moraine.

Pilgrimage season is from April to November. Religious tourism is big business and numerous buses, share 4WDs, porters and ponies are on hand for transport.

672 THE 88 TEMPLE CIRCUIT, JAPAN

On the Japanese island of Shikoku there are 88 temples, a number equal to the evil human passions as defined by the Buddhist doctrine. If you want to free yourself from every one of these passions in a single hit, you can do so by completing the 88 Temple Circuit. Traditionally the 1500km route was walked, even though there's more than 100km between a couple of the temples. In modern times, however, it's become just as acceptable to complete the 88 Temple Circuit by tour bus – who said the gods don't move with the times? The circuit begins in Tokushima and most pilgrims go clockwise.

Spring and autumn are the best times to visit Shikoku – summers can be stiflingly hot, and typhoons frequently pound the Pacific coast from June until October.

674 CAMINO DE SANTIAGO, SPAIN

One of the great Christian pilgrimages is to the tomb of the apostle St James in the Spanish city of Santiago de Compostela. It's a journey of such spiritual note that it's considered to be Europe's premier cultural itinerary and is also listed on the Unesco World Heritage register. The Camino begins in Roncesvalles, on the French border, and covers 783km to the Atlantic coast. Cycling and horseback are considered appropriate forms of pilgrim transport, but most people walk the route, wandering between an extensive system of *albergues* (refuges), spending around one month as a modern pilgrim.

Hundreds of Camino-related websites offer fascinating history, practical advice and personal experiences: try www .pilgrimage-to-santiago.com for starters.

675 ADAM'S PEAK, SRI LANKA

In the highlands of Sri Lanka there's a mountain that's all things to all religions. Depending on your spiritual persuasion, the indent on the summit of Adam's Peak (Sri Pada) is either the place where Adam first set foot on earth, or a footprint left by Buddha, Shiva or St Thomas. Small wonder the track to the summit is like an ant trail in the pilgrimage season (December to May). Secular pilgrims will find the view alone worthy of the journey. On a clear day it stretches to the Sri Lankan capital, Colombo, 65km away.

The climb is up steps most of the way. A 2.30am start will easily get you there for a spectacular sunrise – unless throngs of pilgrims slow your pace.

676 MT KAILASH, TIBET

As the source of several of Asia's mightiest rivers, including the Ganges, Karnali and Indus, it's little surprise that the Tibetan peak of Mt Kailash is revered in a number of religions. To circuit holy Kailash is a pilgrimage for Buddhists, Hindus, Bonpos, Jains and, more recently, trekkers. The most ardent pilgrims walk the 52km circuit in a day, while the truly pious prostrate themselves around the mountain, lying down with arms outstretched, then standing and lying down again at the point that their hands reached. The journey to Kailash is itself an epic worthy of being called a pilgrimage, so allow time for this remarkable trek.

The festival of Saga Dawa in May/June is the most popular time to visit the mountain. Some find the pilgrim atmosphere a highlight; others find the large numbers of tourists off-putting.

677 MASHHAD, IRAN

With a name that translates as 'the place of martyrdom', Mashhad is sacred to Shiites as the place where the eighth imam and direct descendant of the Prophet Mohammed, Imam Reza, died in 817. Each year, more than 15 million Shiite pilgrims visit this city in eastern Iran, which literally radiates out from Haram-e Razavi, the site of the Holy Shrine. The busiest pilgrimage times are around the Iranian New Year (21 March) and a dedicated pilgrim season from mid-June to late July. Non-Muslims are not permitted into the Holy Shrine itself, though there are three attached museums that can be visited.

Be aware that during major pilgrim seasons, almost all accommodation and transport will be booked out months in advance

678 SANCTUAIRES NOTRE DAME DE LOURDES, FRANCE

Lourdes has become one of the world's most important Christian pilgrimage sites since 1858, when 14-year-old Bernadette Soubirous saw the Virgin Mary in a series of 18 visions. There are four sanctuaries at the site, the most revered being the Cave of the Apparitions; its walls, worn smooth by millions of hands, shine in the glow of candles. Adjacent are 19 baths where volunteers will dip you into the seriously icy stream water for a few seconds. The baths are often used by invalids seeking cures but are open to all comers (of any or no religious affiliation).

You can enter the grounds around the clock via the Entrée des Lacets (rue Monseigneur Theas).

679 SHASHEMENE, ETHIOPIA

With the Rastafari movement founded on the belief that Ethiopian emperor Haile Selassie is an African Messiah, it's unsurprising that a Rasta community has taken root in Ethiopia. Around 240km from Addis Ababa, Selassie himself granted land in the town of Shashemene to Jamaican Rastafarians in the 1960s. It was first settled by 12 Jamaicans but the community has now grown to number hundreds. In the late 1970s the most famous Rasta of all, Bob Marley, visited Shashemene, and in recent years his widow has talked of relocating his remains here, which would indeed turn this southern town into a site of music and Rasta pilgrimage.

The Rasta community straddles the main road just north of town. It is readily distinguished by its tri-coloured buildings and dreadlocked inhabitants.

680 MT ATHOS, GREECE

Known as the Holy Mountain, Mt Athos is a self-governing community of 20 Eastern Orthodox monasteries sprinkled around the slopes of 2033m-high Mt Athos on Greece's Halkidiki Peninsula. A strict entry-permit system applies: only 100 Orthodox pilgrims and 10 non-Orthodox visitors are allowed in at a time; only men over 18 years of age can visit; permit applications from non-Orthodox visitors must be made at least six months ahead; and *diamonitiria* (permits) usually allow stays of just four days.

The Holy Mountain is reached by boat, and you then walk between monasteries, each of which contains a guesthouse.

BEST HORSE-LOVERS' SIGHTS

If you're equine by nature, the world is your pony at the following events and places.

681 MELBOURNE CUP, AUSTRALIA

They call it the race that stops a nation, and in the state of Victoria it even warrants a public holiday. Held on the first Tuesday in November, the Melbourne Cup is one of the world's great sporting events, a 3200m race that pits together 24 of the nation's – and the world's – finest thoroughbreds. First run in 1861, it's the richest two-mile handicap race in the world (the winner receives more than A$3 million), drawing more than 100,000 spectators into Flemington racecourse in a fashion frenzy that ranges from fine frocks to the foolish. Across the nation it's a betting bonanza – in 2010 Australians wagered more than A$100 million on the race.

Suburban trains run from Melbourne's city stations to Flemington, on the western fringe of the city centre.

682 IL PALIO, SIENA, ITALY

This heart-stopping event revolves around a bone-crunching, bareback horse race run around Siena's Piazza del Campo; it lasts 90 seconds although the rest of the day is taken up with major-league carousing. The frequently violent race features jockeys from Siena's 17 neighbourhoods, all traditional rivals (intermarriage is often forbidden). Expect to see riders thudding to the ground with alarming regularity (this truly is a no-holds-barred event) and don't be surprised to be offered a baby bottle of wine when it's all over – for the neighbourhoods, a win means rebirth.

Siena is 1¼ hours from Florence by bus or three hours from Rome. The race is held on 2 July and 16 August each year.

683 CALGARY STAMPEDE, CANADA

For 10 days each July, Calgary – known colloquially as 'Cowtown' – dons its spurs for the self-proclaimed 'greatest outdoor show on earth'. Headlined by one of the richest rodeos on earth, offering more than C$2 million in prize money, it's an invite-only affair for the world's greatest and toughest cowboys. There are 10 events spread across 10 days, culminating in Showdown Sunday – the winner of each Showdown event saunters away with C$100,000. Evenings at Stampede Park are given over to the uniquely Albertan event of chuckwagon racing, the 'half-mile of hell' that sees four chuckwagons and outriders hurtle around a racing track at around 60km/h – think Ben Hur meets Ascot.

Ticketing and information can be found at the event website: http://cs.calgarystampede.com.

Yee-haa! In Cowtown, a hard-as-nails cowboy won't kowtow to this bucking bronco

Vienna's Spanish Riding School – an equine extravaganza *nonpareil*

684 SPANISCHE HOFREITSCHULE, VIENNA, AUSTRIA

The world-famous Spanish Riding School is an unequalled equestrian show performed by Lipizzaner stallions, a crossbreeding of Spanish, Arab and Berber horses. These graceful stallions perform an equine ballet to a program of classical music while chandeliers shimmer from above. With tickets booked out months in advance, training or movement programs are open to the public at various times. The most regular is the 'Morgenarbeit' (morning training) session. For these, tickets can be bought the same day at gate 2, Josefsplatz in the Hofburg. Queues are very long early in the day, but most people have disappeared by around 11am, when you can often get in quickly.

Tickets can be ordered through the website (www.srs.at), with unclaimed tickets resold about two hours before performances.

685 VICTORIAN HIGH COUNTRY, AUSTRALIA

The Australian bush is full of legends, and few are bigger than *The Man from Snowy River*, 'Banjo' Paterson's poetic figure who rides through the High Country in pursuit of a runaway horse. It's a tale that's drawn people into these mountains on horseback ever since. If you want to ride the true *Man from Snowy River* slopes, head for Corryong, near the headwaters of the Murray River. Most Snowy River wannabes, however, beeline for Mansfield, for easy access to the cliff face that featured in the 1982 film, and to Craig's Hut, the cattlemen's hut purpose-built for the movie.

Follow the 'High Country' and 'Adventure' links at the Tourism Victoria website (www.visitvictoria.com) for a list of horseback operators.

686 ASCOT RACES, ENGLAND

This most famous of racecourses celebrates its 300th anniversary in 2011, though the first incarnation of the Royal Ascot races emerged with a four-day horse race in 1768. This grew into the internationally renowned five-day event we know today: a flurry of jockeys in silk and elegant horses, hats, frocks and suits. The Royal Procession tradition began in 1825, when coaches carrying royalty drove up the centre of the racecourse. The iconic Ascot Racecourse has a capacity of 80,000.

Royal Ascot races are run in mid-June, with other race events throughout the year. For more details visit www.ascot .co.uk.

687 FERIA DEL CABALLO, JEREZ, SPAIN

Held three weeks after Semana Santa (the week leading up to Easter Sunday), Jerez de la Frontera's Horse Fair is one of Andalucía's biggest festivals and a celebration of all things equine. The fair attracts more than one million visitors and past the music, dancing and bullfights are all kind of horse competitions, from dressage through to polo. Each day there's a colourful parade featuring hundreds of horses passing through the Parque González Hontoria fairgrounds, with the aristocratic-looking male riders decked out in flat-topped hats and frilly white shirts, and their female *crupera* (sideways pillion) partners in flamenco-inspired dresses.

Information about the fair can be obtained from the Jerez tourist office (www.turismojerez.com).

688 MONUMENT VALLEY, ARIZONA/UTAH, USA

Saddle up your inner cowboy and head for the land that's outshone actors in dozens of Westerns. With its fiery red spindles, sheer-walled mesas and grand buttes, Monument Valley has long been a darling of film-makers, turning it into the ultimate cowboy destination. It's part of the Navajo tribal lands, so tourism is kept on a pretty tight rein in the valley – visitors are pretty much confined to the road – but one of the few ways to throw off the bridle is to join one of the Navajo-led horseback tours.

Horseback tours start from US$40. Outfitters in Kayenta and at Goulding's Lodge offer tours.

689 CAMARGUE, FRANCE

Just south of Arles, the Camargue is France's equivalent of an outback, a bleached, flat, marshy wild place, famous for both its teeming birdlife (especially pink flamingos) and its small white horses. If you see brown horses, don't despair; Camargue horses are born brown and don't turn white until maturity. The mellow disposition of the horses, which have been roaming wild here for centuries, makes horseback riding the ideal way to explore the region's patchwork of salt pans, rice fields, and meadows dotted with grazing bulls.

Check out farms along the D570 to Arles for horse-riding opportunities.

690 MUSÉE VIVANT DU CHEVAL, FRANCE

The Grand Stables of the Château de Chantilly house the Living Horse Museum, where 30 pampered equines live in luxurious wooden stalls built by Louis Henri de Bourbon, who was convinced he would be reincarnated as a horse (hence the extraordinary grandeur). Displays cover everything from riding equipment and horse toys to portraits, drawings and sculptures of famous nags. Every visitor will be mesmerised by the 30-minute Présentation Équestre Pédagogique (Introduction to Dressage) – a Chantilly must-do included in the admission price. Even more magical and sought-after are the handful of equestrian shows performed in the stables each year; tickets are like gold dust and can be reserved online (www.museevivantducheval.fr).

The chateau is just over 2km east of the Chantilly train station: the most direct route from there is to walk along avenue de la Plaine des Aigles through a section of the Forêt de Chantilly.

BEST HORSE-LOVERS' SIGHTS

BEST SUNRISES & SUNSETS

It's the planet's great conjuring trick: Sun appears! Sun vanishes! And in such a blaze of glory, too.

691 MONKEY TEMPLE, KATHMANDU, NEPAL

The 360-degree views from Swayambhunath (affectionately known as the 'Monkey Temple' for its resident troupe of cheeky macaques) are worth the stairs. Legend has it that the Kathmandu Valley was once a lake and that the hill on which Swayambhunath stands was 'self-arisen' *(swayambhu)* like a lotus leaf from the waters. It still appears to float above the smog and noise of the city in its own serene bubble. The sun comes up all pink and hazy, bells ring, voices raise in devotional song, prayer wheels and pigeon wings clatter, monkeys croon. Top off a circuit of the stupa with a morning at the temple's tea shop.

You might want to take the short taxi ride to the temple. Your guesthouse should be able to arrange pick-up and a good price.

RICHARD I'ANSON / LONELY PLANET IMAGES

692 GRAND CANYON, ARIZONA, USA

There are the kind of sunsets where you look at the sky, and then there are the kind where you look at what's going on around you. It's hard to imagine a finer canvas for the sinking sun's lightshow than the nougat, lavender and ochre striations of this spectacular gorge. Linger beyond sunset to see the last of the sky's colours reflect off the pinnacles and the clear stars coming out. Hopi Point is a popular (and crowded) point; Yaki Point is also spectacular and may afford you a more meditative experience.

The easiest way to get to your perfect sunset position is to use the extensive (and free) shuttle-bus system.

693 MT KILIMANJARO, TANZANIA

A mountain on the equator topped with snow and written about by Hemingway – even without offering the chance to climb to the top of Africa, Kilimanjaro packs plenty of allure. Add in sunrise over the shimmering plains and the chance to spot sunbirds and colobus monkeys, and you're hooked. Your climb up Africa's highest peak takes you through farmlands, lush rainforest, alpine meadows and the harsh lunar landscape of the peaks. Although many people are attracted to the Kili climb because you can do it without equipment, it can be extremely dangerous and you need to pick your guides carefully.

Don't want to summit? Try the easy-to-follow footpaths that link the towns on Kilimanjaro's lower slopes.

694 ANGKOR WAT, CAMBODIA

This sumptuous blend of lotus-shaped towers and sky, carved with celestial nymphs and reflected in the lake below it, is a temple complex built early in the 12th century by a succession of Khmer kings to honour the god Vishnu. It was abandoned in the 15th century and many of its structures disappeared under the grasp of giant banyan roots and luscious forest. It's perhaps best seen at sunset, when the whole sacred city turns gold, but it's also a magical place for sunrise, with the towers emerging into the light and the lake taking soft dawn colours.

If you wait around after sunrise, many of the tour groups go back to Siem Reap for breakfast, leaving Angkor Wat pretty much deserted.

Looks good enough to eat: the Grand Canyon suffused in the golden glow of sunset

CABLE BEACH, BROOME, AUSTRALIA

Red from the *pindan* (the rust-coloured dirt), the aquamarine of Roebuck Bay and the pearl white of Cable Beach's sands – this improbable combination of colours makes Broome's landscape one you'll never forget. Drowsing on this beach and watching the sun set over the Indian Ocean is one of life's great treats. There's generally a crowd for the sunset show but with 22km of beach to choose from, you won't have to try hard to find your own private vantage point. It's hard to beat lying on those silky sands but if you want to mix it up, try sunset from the back of a camel.

The luscious, Zen-styled Cable Beach Resort (www.cablebeachclub.com) has the best address in town – it's right on the beach.

STONEHENGE, ENGLAND

Who dragged these 50-tonne stones up from south Wales (it would have taken 600 people to move one stone more than half an inch), and why? These famed rocks, set atop each other in a ring and inner horseshoe, never fail to exert a fascination, even with half of Europe's pottiest pagans swaying and drumming and moaning around them. The wizard-in-cloak factor is highest on the summer solstice, but if you can stomach that, this really is the most magical time to see sun break through the stone ring. The heel stone aligns with the rising sun, fuelling speculation that Stonehenge is some kind of celestial timepiece.

Stonehenge is on Salisbury Plain in Wiltshire, west of Amesbury. It's preserved by the National Trust (www.nationaltrust.org.uk).

WADI RUM, JORD

They call it 'the Valley of the Moon', but it's equally tuned to the sun. This most romantic of desert landscapes was lodged in the Western imagination by TE Lawrence (Lawrence of Arabia), who based his subversive military operations here and wrote lyrically of it in his *Seven Pillars of Wisdom*. David Lean, in his biopic about Lawrence, did much of his filming in these narrow valleys. Overlooked by towering sandstone mountains, Wadi Rum is a sublime theatre for changing light. Watching the sunrise transform this austere landscape is an experience that will sink into your bones.

Public transport to Rum village is limited. Most visitors come on tours arranged from Wadi Musa or Aqaba.

698 SUN GATE, MACHU PICCHU, PERU

Picture this: you're high in the Andes, breaking camp in the small hours on the Inca Trail to time your arrival to Intipunku (the Sun Gate) with dawn. You make it and walk through to find the lost city of the Incas spread below you on the verdant terraced plain, with the craggy peak of Huayna Picchu looming over it all. You make out the ruins of palaces, baths and temples, among them those devoted to the worship of the sun god, Inti. The strengthening light brings out the brilliance of the green and picks out the detail of the city. It's a good morning.

Numbers on the Inca Trail are severely limited. You'll need to apply for a permit at least six months in advance.

699 OIA, SANTORINI, GREECE

You have to work pretty hard to upstage volcanic Santorini, with its black-sand beaches and white higgledy-piggledy houses spilling from the steep slopes to the luminous blue sea. In fact, the only thing that can reduce the island to a supporting role is the sun setting into the Mediterranean Sea. Oia beach is the classic place for a Santorini sunset as it affords an uninterrupted view of the horizon and you get to see the show right to the end. But if you want to avoid the sometimes feverish crowds, head further down south along the caldera's edge.

In summer buses leave every half-hour for Oia. The last one leaves at 11.20pm.

700 SVALBARD, NORWAY

The northernmost tip of Europe is a chilly wonderland of glaciers, icebergs, whales, reindeer and polar bears. For a whole four months during winter it's plunged into darkness, but the flipside of that is the white nights of summer (between late April and late August), when the midnight sun reigns in the sky. The sun never dips below the horizon, but it still follows an arc and generates some incredible colours in the glacial air. Midnight sunset may be best combined with a glacier walk or a kayaking trip.

Svalbard doesn't come cheap: you'll have to fly nearly 1000km from the nearest airport and budget accommodation is thin on the ground.

BEST SUNRISES & SUNSETS

BEST RECORD-BREAKING SPECTACLES

A primal instinct urges human beings to be competitive: run faster, jump higher, push harder and, er, eat more hot dogs. The following record-breaking feats cause quite a scene.

701 FREEDIVING, DEAN'S BLUE HOLE, LONG ISLAND, BAHAMAS

Competitive freediving, or competitive apnea as the sport is sometimes known, involves competitors attempting to dive to great depths, achieve great distances or stay underwater for a significant amount of time, all on a single breath. One of the most popular places for freedivers to attempt to break records is at Dean's Blue Hole, off Long Island in the Bahamas. At a depth of 203m, it is the deepest known seawater blue hole. It was here in December 2010 that William Trubridge set the record for the longest dive without fins, holding his breath for four minutes and 10 seconds as he plunged to a depth of 100m and back.

Dean's Blue Hole is in a bay west of Clarence Town off Long Island. The closest major airport is on the Turks and Caicos Islands from where a plane can be chartered to fly to Deadman's Cay, the local airport on Long Island.

702 WORLD'S HIGHEST TIGHTROPE WALK, ZUGSPITZE MOUNTAIN, GERMANY

Tightrope walking, or funambulism, is the practice of walking along a wire or rope suspended from two opposite points, usually at a great height. Walkers may use a pole for balance or extend their arms from their sides at a 90-degree angle. In 1974 Frenchman Philippe Petit famously crossed the 60m void between the towers of New York's World Trade Center on a highwire, without a safety net or harness. In 2009 professional tightrope walker Freddy Nock set a world record for highest tightrope walk when he ascended the wire of the aerial tram up Germany's highest mountain, the Zugspitze, finishing at a death-defying 2943m.

The Zugspitze Mountain, part of the Bavarian Alps, is in southern Germany near the Austrian border. It's possible to ride the aerial tramway from the German village of Eibsee.

703 CHRISTIE'S AUCTION HOUSE

The world's premier auction house for fine art, Asian art, jewellery, photographs and wine, Christie's continually breaks world records when it comes to the extraordinary prices people are prepared to pay for coveted works of art or pieces of jewellery. In 2010 Pablo Picasso's *Nude, Green Leaves and Bust* sold for the tidy sum of US$106.5 million, the most paid for any artwork at auction. Christie's has salerooms all over the world – New York, London, Paris, Amsterdam, Geneva, Milan, Zurich, Dubai and Hong Kong – but the most amazing sales are so exclusive (and expensive) they generally happen out of the public eye.

If you happen to have a lazy few hundred thousand dollars lying around, check www.christies.com for a list of sale items.

704 WORLD'S STRONGEST MAN

Looking like oversized plastic action figures, the contestants in the World's Strongest Man competition flex their basketball-sized biceps in a contest to see who can pull a plane, toss a keg, carry a boulder, lift a giant log and run with two huge fridges slung over their shoulders (among other extraordinary feats of strength). The comp is often staged in settings as over the top as the strongmen themselves; in 2010 it was held at South Africa's sprawling Sun City resort and in 2009 the strongmen strutted their stuff on the island of Malta.

A gruelling schedule of qualifying comps is conducted throughout the year before the big daddy of events, usually held in December. See www.theworldsstrongestman.com.

705 CLIMBING 'THE NOSE', EL CAPITAN, YOSEMITE NATIONAL PARK, CALIFORNIA, USA

In 1958 three men made the first ascent of the brow of the imposing 910m-high El Capitan. It took them a total of 47 days. An impressive feat considering 'the Nose', as the rock face is known, was once considered impossible to climb. These days, however, climbers make the ascent in around four to five days and the really good (or crazy) climbers try to outdo one another in getting to the top in around 2½ hours. Yes, 2½ hours! Free climbers ('look Mum, no ropes') have ascended the face in under 12 hours.

Yosemite is a three- to four-hour drive from San Francisco and about six hours from Los Angeles. El Capitan is on the north side of Yosemite Valley.

706 SPENCER TUNICK ARTWORKS

If getting naked with a few thousand of your closest friends is on your list of things to do, then Spencer Tunick's large-scale human art installations are an artistically sanctioned way to get your kit off in public. Tunick's early works often featured single nudes but by the late 1990s his celebration of the nude form had become more ambitious. He has taken pictures of nudes in New York's Grand Central Station and on the Aletsch Glacier in Switzerland. In 2007 Tunick shot approximately 18,000 nudes in Mexico's main square, breaking his own record of 7000 nudes set in Barcelona in 2003.

To be notified of upcoming shoots and the chance to be involved, provide your details at www.spencertunick.com.

707 WAITERS' RACE, BRUSSELS, BELGIUM

Conducted around the world in various locations (Hong Kong, Russia, Finland, Germany and France to name a few), waiters' races have become somewhat of an international phenomenon. One of the oldest and most popular is conducted every September on the Esplanade du Cinquantenaire in Brussels. Contestants carry a bottle of liquor and three full glasses for 2.5km to the finish line. In order to be crowned victorious, not a single drop can be spilt from either glass or bottle. The race is accompanied by a mini festival of sorts, with market stalls, brass bands and wine tasting.

It's free to enter the race but you must be a professional waiter. For info on the race in Brussels as well as other races worldwide check out www.waitersrace.com.

708 LAND SPEED RECORD, BONNEVILLE SALT FLATS, UTAH, USA

The 30,000 acres of hard, white salt crust at Bonneville are a freak of nature. The area is 20km long and 8km wide, and the salt is up to 1.5m thick in places and perfectly flat. Dazzling and surreal, this moonscape-like setting is where freaks of speed come to test their mettle and to have a shot at shattering the land speed record. Every August the Flats host 'Speed Week', where hundreds of drivers compete to set records in a mind-boggling array of categories too numerous to list. Suffice to say vehicles range from the two-wheeled variety to those that resemble horizontal rockets.

Info on the Flats and on Speed Week can be found at www.utah.com/playgrounds/bonneville_salt.htm.

709 RACE TO THE TOP OF THE EMPIRE STATE BUILDING, NEW YORK, USA

The Empire State Building Run-Up has been an annual tradition since 1978. Each February runners jostle each other through the building's narrow stairwell, up 1576 stairs from the lobby to the finish line on the 86th-floor Observation Deck. The race is open to men and women but the starts are staggered, with the women setting off five minutes before the men. The men's record time of nine minutes and 33 seconds was set in 2003. The women's record, set in 2007, stands at 13 minutes and 12 seconds.

Entrants must prove their athletic credentials and be approved by the New York Road Runners Club in order to compete. The Empire State Building is on 5th Avenue at 34th Street in Manhattan.

710 HOT DOG EATING, CONEY ISLAND, NEW YORK, USA

As legend has it, the world's most famous hot dog eating competition was sparked on 4 July 1916, when four immigrant Americans challenged one another to a hot dog eating contest to determine who was the most patriotic. Over the years the contest has grown such that 2010 saw over 40,000 competitive-eating fans descend on Coney Island to see eaters duke it out. Champion for 2010, Joey Chestnut took home the coveted mustard-coloured belt and a tidy US$10,000 after downing 54 dogs in 10 minutes.

The competition happens every 4 July and is sponsored by Nathan's Restaurant, Coney Island, Brooklyn. See the website www.nathansfamous.com for details.

MOST STUNNING GARDENS

Why have so many cultures envisaged paradise as a garden?
Take a wander through these Edens and see for yourself.

711 GENERALIFE GARDENS, GRANADA, SPAIN

The beauty of the Alhambra is its use of water – in Islamic culture, the purity of water was a symbol of paradise. Built on the hill above the famous fort, the Generalife was a summer palace, a place where the emirs would retreat with their harems for a bit of R&R. Its gardens are a tranquil wonderland where rows of curved fountains fall into oblong pools and water trickles down staircases. The long views are framed by cypress trees, hedges, flower gardens and cascading vines. From the ivy-covered terrace you can see down into the valley below.

A ticket to the Alhambra costs €12, but you can visit the Generalife only for €6. It's best to buy your tickets in advance.

712 SUMMER PALACE, BEIJING, CHINA

The 'Gardens of Nurtured Harmony' began life as a retreat for royalty sick of the hothouse atmosphere of the Forbidden City. Today, they're a park for Beijing's city dwellers and a popular tourist magnet. Their central feature is Longevity Hill, which was built from earth excavated to make the lake. On the edge of the lake sits a marble boat, one of the projects of Empress Dowager Cixi, who made herself highly unpopular by grabbing money meant for the navy to fund her fantasies. The garden is a classic example of Chinese landscaping, with rockeries, pavilions, temples and pools.

The summer palace is about a half-hour taxi ride from Beijing, or you can take the subway to Wudaokou.

713 MONET'S GARDEN, GIVERNY, FRANCE

The village of Giverny is a mecca for Monet fans and devotees of the impressionist school. Claude Monet lived here from 1883 until his death in 1926, in a rambling house surrounded by flower-filled gardens. The northern part of the estate is the Clos Normand, where Monet's pastel-pink house and Water Lily studio stand. But, more than anywhere, it's in the Jardin d'Eau (Water Garden) that you can see where artistic inspiration struck. This is where Monet created his trademark lily pond, as well as the famous Japanese bridge. The light, the colour, the heady scents – it's enough to inspire you to pick up a paintbrush yourself.

Want to stay the night? Monet is said to have tucked up beneath the crisp sheets of 19th-century La Musardière (www.lamusardiere.fr).

714 RYOAN-JI, KYOTO, JAPAN

The gardens of the Unesco-listed 'Temple of the Peaceful Dragon' are filled with pleasant features (a lake with islands, a teahouse, blossom in season), but its fame is drawn from the 'dry garden', a classic Zen affair of punctiliously raked gravel and moss-covered stones. There are 15 stones, but they're arranged so you can never see more than 14 at a time – until you reach enlightenment, that is. While you wait, admire the placement of the rocks, and pay special attention to the space between them: for the garden's many aficionados, this is where the magic happens.

Crowds pack the viewing platform, which may take the edge off your Buddhist buzz. Try visiting in the early morning on a weekday.

Bulbalicious! The many-splendoured delights of Keukenhof

715 KIRSTENBOSCH NATIONAL BOTANICAL GARDEN, CAPE TOWN, SOUTH AFRICA

What sets Kirstenbosch aside from other botanical gardens is its setting at the foot of Table Mountain and its (nearly) all-indigenous collection. It was the first botanic garden in the world to concentrate on a country's native flora. Today it has over 7000 species both in the open air and in conservatories. It's renowned for its fynbos and protea exhibits, and there's also a permanent exhibition of stone sculptures in the Zimbabwean style. If you're in the mood for a bit of wilderness after all that cultivation, take one of the many paths that lead you around and up the mountain.

The garden is open daily: 8am to 7pm in summer, 8am to 6pm in winter.

716 KEUKENHOF, LISSE, THE NETHERLANDS

You have to time your visit to this garden carefully: it's only open for a brief period between March and May. Why? Because it's all about the glory of spring, as expressed through lovingly designed bulb plantings. Spread over 32 hectares and featuring sculptures, a lake, woodland, 4.5 million tulips and a carillon, it's a wonderfully kitsch, crayon-bright, quintessentially Dutch extravaganza. Along with all those tulips, you'll see daffodils and hyacinths, as well as bluebells, which are often planted in undulating beds between banks of other flowers so that they look like streams of water. After a long winter, this place is a tonic.

Get the exact dates of opening and find the easiest way to get to Lisse from Amsterdam at www.keukenhof.nl.

251

Ah, Versailles! All the beauty of a bygone age...

717 ISOLA BELLA, LAGO MAGGIORE, ITALY

In 1632, a count of the Borromeo family set about transforming this little hunk of rock into a fantasy dedicated to his wife Isabella. The fishermen who used to live here wouldn't recognise the place now – a baroque villa dominates the island, with luscious gardens spilling down in terraces from a central unicorn figure. Long statue-lined vistas end in views of lake and mountains, and camellias, magnolias, azaleas and rhododendrons riot down to the waterside. And just when you're wondering if you've somehow wandered into one of those divine kitsch paintings of the '50s, a white peacock struts into view.

The ferry ride to Isola Bella, with the whole impossible confection floating before you, is part of the fun. Catch it from Stresa.

718 SISSINGHURST CASTLE GARDEN, ENGLAND

Sissinghurst was the labour of love for Vita Sackville-West, a poet who knocked around with the Bloomsbury Group in the 1930s, and her husband Harold Nicolson. The garden is a series of intimate spaces or 'rooms', separated by hedges, with the remains of a medieval castle forming a focal point. Each 'room' has its own character and colour, with the

ANN CECIL / LONELY PLANET IMAGES

719 VERSAILLES, FRANCE

All the profligate grandeur of the *Ancien Régime* is embodied in the magnificent gardens of the palace at Versailles. And their extreme order – all manicured lawns, raked gravel, hedges and parterres – is no accident: the gardens were understood as a symbol of the king's power and its civilising order. But although the gardens may be a bit stark, they never fail to impress. Loads of fountains (including the central one of Apollo and his chariot, another symbol of the king), a whole Olympus of classical statuary, a splendid orangery and a system of boskets (miniature groves) entertain the eye.

On weekends from April to October you can see the Grandes Eaux, musical spectacles accompanied by gushing fountains and waterfalls.

720 HUNTINGTON BOTANICAL GARDENS, LOS ANGELES, CALIFORNIA, USA

Business tycoon Henry E Huntington put his wealth to good use. The Huntington, in the San Gabriel Valley, is a stellar research library and art collection. But the treasures don't end there. Outside is the botanical garden that Huntington had built in 1903, converting an existing ranch. With over 14,000 species and 14 separate gardens, it's one of the USA's most impressive collections. A jungle garden with orchids and a strawberry snowball tree, a Shakespeare garden containing plants mentioned in the plays, a Japanese garden, a desert garden, and a system of lily ponds are just some of the highlights.

Browse the gardens, pick up little-known facts about the plant species and plan your visit at www.huntington.org.

most famous being the trend-setting all-white garden. The place is crammed with romantic features: an orchard, a rose garden, a nuttery, a moat. Oh, and if you eat at the restaurant, you'll be dining on food grown in the vegetable garden.

The village of Sissinghurst is on the Biddenden Road, near Cranbook in Kent. It's a 20-minute walk from the bus stop so you may want to drive.

MOST STUNNING GARDENS

MOST VERTIGO-INDUCING CLIFFS

Dare to look down from these walls – be they wave-bashed, snow-covered or absolutely ancient.

Vestmanna: a natural wonderland

GRANT DIXON / LONELY PLANET IMAGES

721 BANDIAGARA ESCARPMENT, MALI

The Bandiagara Escarpment is not just a cliff, it's a home. People have lived on, under and actually inside this 150km-long ridge for centuries. First it was the Tellem, who somehow carved tombs and dwellings into the rock's most inaccessible reaches; now it's the Dogon, who tend to place their settlements on top of the 500m escarpment, or on the sandy plains below it. Exploring is an adventure – village-to-village walks involve negotiating ancient steps hewn into the sandstone, nosing into cliff-face granaries and exploring the culture – the animist beliefs, fetish objects and exuberant mask ceremonies – of the Dogon themselves.

When meeting hogons (Dogon spiritual leaders) take a gift; wait for instructions on where to stand to avoid disturbing sacred sites.

722 KALAUPAPA, MOLOKA'I, HAWAII, USA

For the outcast leprosy sufferers of Hawaii it was, at least, a splendid isolation. Following local diagnosis of the disease in the 19th century, victims were banished to remote Kalaupapa Peninsula, an ancient ooze of solidified lava jutting into the Pacific, backed by the world's highest sea cliffs. Rising up to 1000m, these *pali* (cliffs) made a formidable fence, trapping patients in the colony below. Today, Kalaupapa is a Historical Park, and people actually *want* to enter: the 1400-step descent from lofty lookout to leprosy settlement reveals the landscape's natural grandeur and the human tragedy it quarantined for so long.

Access to Kalaupapa (www.nps.gov/kala) is by guided trip with Damien Tours only; Moloka'i Mule Tours offers rides down the cliff.

723 VESTMANNA, FAROE ISLANDS

It might look like a harsh, primeval landscape, permanently ruffled by angry southwesterlies and lashed by an Atlantic that has raged unhindered all the way from North America. But the cliffs of Vestmanna, the most dramatic sea defences of the Faroe Islands – an isolated archipelago anchored betwixt Scotland and Iceland – are full of life. Fulmars, kittiwakes, guillemots and puffins all squawk, dive, nest and nurture on these 500m-high bastions of basalt, flitting amid the sea stacks and eerie grottoes. Get up close to the action by boat, sailing alongside the sheer-rising rock and into the caves – just don't forget your binoculars.

Boat trips from Vestmanna village to the cliffs run year-round, weather permitting; mid-May to mid-August is best for birdwatching.

255

Beachy Head: mind the gap...

724 BEACHY HEAD & THE SEVEN SISTERS, ENGLAND

Boundary fences don't come more glaring. This seemingly impervious wall of white rock, guarding a section of England's English Channel coast, must have looked a forbidding impediment to would-be invaders from continental Europe. The South Downs uplands of the Seven Sisters undulate for several kilometres before rising to the ultimate natural barrier: Beachy Head, at 162m the highest chalk cliff in the country. Sadly this accolade has led to another type of notoriety – since the 17th century unhappy souls have gravitated towards its dangerous vantage, making it one of the world's most popular, if scenic, suicide spots.

The last 13km of the South Downs Way (Exceat to Eastbourne) takes in the Seven Sisters and Beachy Head. See www.nationaltrail.co.uk/southdowns.

725 CABO GIRÃO, MADEIRA

Since the 1930s a Chapel of Our Lady of Fátima has stood on top of Cabo Girão. You may want a little divine protection looking down from this cape: at 570m high, these are some of the highest cliffs in Europe, plunging dangerously into the Atlantic below. It's typical of Madeira – the Portuguese island is a volcanic burp, essentially the peak of a huge underwater range that reared its head around five million years ago. The island doesn't do gently pretty; this is nature at its most raw – with Cabo Girão the literal face of all that dramatic geology.

Visit in April and May, before the summer rains and when the island's profuse geraniums, bougainvilleas and hydrangeas start to bloom.

726 AMPHITHEATRE, DRAKENSBERG MOUNTAINS, SOUTH AFRICA

It's the geological equivalent of a Zulu strike-force, warriors made from rock. Indeed, the Zulu call the Drakensberg Mountains 'Quathlamba', or 'Battlement of Spears' – especially appropriate for the 8km-long cirque of stone known as the Amphitheatre. Theatrical it is, a horseshoe wall of sheer cliff, soaring 1000m above the valley floor, and tickled by waterfalls. Tugela, one of the world's tallest waterfalls, tumbles in five tiers from escarpment top to bottom, while the Khubedu, which springs from the Amphitheatre's Mont-aux-Sources, eventually turns into the Orange River and pours into the Atlantic 2000km away.

The five-hour return hike to Mont-aux-Sources starts from Sentinel car park, near Witsieshoek; the summit is reached via two chain ladders.

727 ACAPULCO, MEXICO

It's not your own vertigo that's of chief concern here. It's the daredevil/downright crazy *clavadistas* – cliff divers – that will make you shudder. Young men have been hurling themselves off the 35m-high crags of La Quebrada for years, saying their prayers at the shrine at the top before making their graceful plunge. The height of the leap is impressive enough, but it's the timing that's so crucial – if the dive into the narrow gulch isn't performed at the precise moment, to coincide with an incoming wave, then a very shallow rocky landing awaits…

Cliff-diving is performed daily at 1pm, 7.30pm, 8.30pm, 9.30pm and 10.30pm; the best vantage is from the designated viewing platform.

728 GREAT AUSTRALIAN BIGHT, AUSTRALIA

Cliff upon cliff upon cliff upon cliff… Looking east from the frontier-feel town of Eucla along Australia's barren south coast there seems no end to this monster sea wall: variously 60m- to 120m-high jags of pale sedimentary rock, the Great Bight stretches largely uninterrupted for over 1000km of emptiness. Well, empty-ish. Though few humans frequent this lonely place (backed by the equally lonely Nullarbor Plain), a surprising diversity of life has evolved to handle the hostile conditions. Australian sea lions flop on the beaches, leafy sea dragons camouflage themselves in the kelp-rich water, and platoons of southern right whales overwinter offshore.

Visit the Head of Bight lookout, 78km west of Yalata (South Australia), from July to September to watch southern right whales from the coast.

729 FLAMING CLIFFS, GOBI DESERT, MONGOLIA

The vertigo induced by these blazing rocks in the otherwise fairly empty Gobi Desert is more chronological than physical. These cliffs aren't very high but they are dramatic, being blood-orange and in the middle of nowhere. The mind-bending thing about Bayanzag – Mongolia's Flaming Cliffs – is the history discovered here. In the 1920s the first dinosaur eggs ever unearthed were found; many fossils followed, including the bones of a hornless rhinoceros, one of the largest mammals that ever lived. Small cliffs, maybe – massive history.

Bayanzag is 120km northwest of Dalanzadgad; travel in the Gobi requires a 4WD, a knowledgeable guide and long drives.

730 NANGA PARBAT, PAKISTAN

The best place to view colossal Nanga Parbat is from a bucolic spot (think grassy knolls and polo-playing locals) called Fairy Meadow. Which sounds misleadingly whimsical for anything related to this terrifying peak in the westernmost Himalaya, keeper of the biggest cliffs. Nanga Parbat – known, chillingly, as Killer Mountain – is the world's ninth-highest summit; the sheer 4600m drop of its Rupal Face is the world's highest cliff. A cold stone wall of immense proportions, frequently rumbled by rockfalls and avalanches, it looks as deadly as its moniker suggests. Best remain with the fairies and admire from a safe distance.

The trailhead for the four-hour hike to Fairy Meadow is accessed by jeep from Raikot Bridge on the Karakoram Highway.

MOST VERTIGO-INDUCING CLIFFS

TALLEST STRUCTURES

Get some elevation, and perhaps a little vertigo, in these temples to tall and towering construction.

733 CN TOWER, CANADA

For those who care about such distinctions – and apparently some people do – Toronto's 553m-high CN Tower has never ranked among the world's tallest buildings because it doesn't have floors and is thus technically not a building. Instead, it gets the honour of being the world's tallest tower. Its primary function is radio and TV communications, but relieving tourists of as much cash as possible is another priority. Glass elevators whisk you up the outside to observation decks at the top where, for extra thrills, one deck has a glass floor. On a clear day, you can see for about 160km.

Check out the array of visitor possibilities at www.cntower.ca.

731 PETRONAS TOWERS, MALAYSIA

Anchoring the huge Kuala Lumpur City Centre urban development, these iconic steel-clad twin towers opened in 1998 and rise through 88 storeys to a height of 452m. Designed by Argentine architect Cesar Pelli, the floor plan is based on an eight-sided star that echoes arabesque patterns. Islamic influences are also evident in each tower's five tiers (representing the five pillars of Islam) and in the 63m masts that crown them, calling to mind the minarets of a mosque and the Islamic star. The highest you can go as a visitor is the 41st-floor Skybridge connecting the two towers, a modest 170m above ground.

Only 1640 free tickets are issued to the Skybridge daily, so be at the ticket counter in the basement as soon as you can after it opens at 8.30am.

732 TAIPEI 101, TAIWAN

Before Dubai's Burj Khalifa went silly and skyward, this monster in the Taiwanese capital stood proud as the world's tallest building. Named for its number of storeys, the skyscraper is 508m high and impossible to miss, towering above the city like the gigantic bamboo stalk it was designed to resemble. Construction began in 1997 and the exterior was completed in 2003. Though it's been dwarfed by Burj Khalifa, is does retain the record for the world's fastest elevator: the pressure-controlled lift travels at 1010m per minute and takes 40 seconds to get from ground level to the 89th-floor observation deck.

Taipei 101 is in the city's Xinyi district. The photo on the tower's homepage (www .taipei-101.com.tw) will give you some idea of its skyline domination.

734 RYUGYONG HOTEL, NORTH KOREA

North Korea has had a lot of overinflated ambitions, and prime among them is the Ryugyong Hotel. Begun in 1987, even then with a plan to make it the world's tallest hotel, it is yet to be completed, with construction having stood idle for 16 years after 1992. Dubbed the 'worst building in the history of mankind' by *Esquire* magazine, it's pyramid-meet-rocket structure stands 330m high (105 storeys) – completely dominating the Pyongyang skyline. When construction resumed in 2008 the building was freshened up with exterior glass panels, diluting some of the leaden Soviet appearance. Work is projected to be completed in 2012.

The hotel is in the North Korean capital, Pyongyang. To find it, just look up.

735 KVLY-TV MAST, NORTH DAKOTA, USA

For a long time, the tallest structure on earth was this TV tower in the otherwise unheralded town of Blanchard in North Dakota. Built in 1963, it rises needle-thin to a height of 628.8m – more than 170m higher than the Petronas Towers. It was the tallest structure on earth until Warsaw erected its 646m radio mast seven years later – a structure so perilous it collapsed in 1991, leaving the KVLY-TV mast to reclaim the honour, at least until 2010 when it was superseded by Burj Khalifa. If you need another reason to visit, Blanchard is near to Fargo, the town immortalised by the Coen brothers' movie of the same name.

Blanchard is beside the Minnesota border, 80km south of Grand Forks.

736 BURJ KHALIFA, DUBAI, UNITED ARAB EMIRATES

Call it impressive or preposterous, there's no denying that Burj Khalifa is a ground-breaking feat of architecture and engineering. The world's tallest building – all 162 storeys of it – pierces the Dubai sky at 828m (more than twice the height of the Empire State Building) and opened on 4 January 2010, only six years after excavations began. Up to 13,000 workers toiled day and night, at times putting up a new floor in as little as three days. For visitors, the main attraction is the observation deck 'At the Top' on the 124th floor, a lofty 442m above the ground.

Reserved, time-stamped tickets for At the Top are available at the ticket office and online (www.burjkhalifa.ae).

737 MILLAU VIADUCT, FRANCE

Bridges are normally celebrated for their length, but in the south of France comes a bridge noteworthy for its height: at 343m the Millau Viaduct is the tallest bridge in the world. Around 20m higher than the Eiffel Tower, it spans the Tarn River south of its source in the Massif Central. The bridge opened in December 2004 and was designed by British architect Norman Foster, whose other works include the Swiss Re Building (aka The Gherkin) in London and New York's Hearst Tower. For double measure, it's also the world's longest cable-stayed deck.

Millau is around 110km north of Montpellier; buses (a two-hour journey) connect the pair.

738 Q1, AUSTRALIA

Towering over Australia's most famous beach at Surfers Paradise, the construction of Q1 in 2005 made the already high-rise skyline of the Gold Coast look rather dwarfish. The building steeples to a height of 322m, aided and abetted by a 97m-high spire at the top. It is billed as the tallest residential tower in the world, with 526 apartments staring over the country's holiday and theme-park capital. For visitors, there's the 43-second elevator ride to observation levels 77 and 78, at the base of the spire, for views that extend to Brisbane and Byron Bay.

If you're in the market for an apartment, try www.q1.com.au; if you're in the market for a view, try www.qdeck.com.au.

739 SINGAPORE FLYER, SINGAPORE

Getting high in tightly corseted Singapore is as simple as stepping aboard the largest Ferris wheel in the world. Spinning up to a height of 165m – the equivalent of a 42-storey building – this wheel is so large it takes more than half an hour to complete a single rotation. It has 28 capsules, each holding 28 people, and while it originally turned in an anticlockwise direction, it was soon reversed on the advice of feng shui masters, who said it was going against the sun and taking fortune away from Singapore. So now you get a good view, and Singapore gets good feng shui. Win-win.

The wheel (www.singaporeflyer.com) is at 30 Raffles Street, a five-minute walk from the MRT's Promenade station.

740 KINGDA KA, NEW JERSEY, USA

If vertigo alone isn't enough to get your heart going, try adding the elements of speed and disorientation on the world's highest roller coaster. Standing tall at the Six Flags Great Adventure in Jackson, New Jersey, Kingda Ka reaches a height of 139m (about the same height as the Great Pyramid of Giza) and fairly whips along. So much so that, before the construction of Formula Rossa in Abu Dhabi, Kingda Ka was also the world's fastest roller coaster, accelerating to 206km/h in 3.5 seconds.

Take an online ride first at www.sixflags .com/greatadventure/rides/kingdaka.aspx.

MOST SPECTACULAR FIREWORKS DISPLAYS

The best places to see the night light up and go snap-crackle-pop!

741 EDINBURGH INTERNATIONAL FESTIVAL, SCOTLAND

This event's all about atmosphere and setting. It comes at the climax of the International Festival, which every summer transforms the city into one big theatre, with an audience by turns enchanted, exhausted and sozzled. With Edinburgh Castle looking down from its volcanic perch at the Georgian townhouses and Gothic closes, the spectacle and the feeling of the festival's final moments are always going to sweep you away. The display is staged in Princes Street Garden and held to music from the Scottish Chamber Orchestra. The concert lasts for about an hour.

You can buy a ticket to jostle with the Princes Street crowds, but it might be more salubrious up on nearby Calton Hill.

742 NEW YEAR'S EVE, SYDNEY, AUSTRALIA

It seems like the whole city turns out for this one, spilling into parks, onto rooftops and down to the harbourside. There's pre-show entertainment galore, but everyone's really just waiting to see what 'bridge effect' the pyrotechnics will come up with to light up the Harbour Bridge. After a much-adored, much-remembered millennium display and the 2000 Olympics, the bar is high. But whatever comes, it always looks good reflected in the waters of Sydney's photogenic harbour and in the pearly white flanks of the Opera House. There are two waves of fireworks, the big one at 9pm and a smaller one at midnight.

Book into the Observatory Hotel (www.observatoryhotel.com.au) for a swanky dinner and a perfect view from Observatory Hill.

743 FEAST OF THE REDEEMER, VENICE, ITALY

Firework light flickering in the water between illuminated gondolas and behind the city's famous spires, domes and bell towers – sublime. And this is no flash-in-the-pan display: the fireworks go on for an hour. Considering they're to celebrate the salvation of the city by Christ (during the dreadful time of the 16th-century plague that wiped out a third of the city's population), you'd expect something out of the ordinary. As opposed to Carnivale, which is a bit of a tourist circus, this is a genuinely local festival, with Venetians decorating their houses and turning out in force for the fireworks.

The Feast takes place on the third weekend in July – stick around after Saturday's fireworks for Sunday's gondola regatta.

Redeem your soul, and all your senses, at the Feast of the Redeemer

Guy Fawkes Night: blowing up the skies, not the king…

744 OLD YEAR'S EVE, AMSTERDAM, THE NETHERLANDS

The Dutch have it right when it comes to New Year's Eve. Firstly, far more appropriately and neatly, they call it Oudejaarsdag (Old Year's Day) or Oudejaarsavond (Old Year's Eve), or sometimes even Oude en Nieuw (Old and New). And none of that messy 'I'll see you on New Year's Eve Day…' Secondly, they take it as an excuse to crack out the crackers, big time. Amsterdam is the epicentre of the parties, with its famous clubs gearing up for a monumental night, but the firework scene is largely a street-based thing, with everyone joining in.

Nieuwmarkt, a square in Centraal, is a particularly lively place to bid farewell to the Old Year. Watch out for stray rockets.

745 MACY'S 4TH OF JULY DISPLAY, NEW YORK, USA

No one goes crazy for fireworks like the USA on the 4th of July, and no one goes crazy for the 4th of July like the New York department store Macy's, which stages America's biggest Independence Day display. Six barges line up to detonate the mother of all 4th celebrations, featuring the trademark Macy's golden mile, a cascade of sparks stretching for a mile across the river. The display, which is more about size than duration (it usually clocks in at not much over a half-hour) is accompanied by performances from A-list music stars.

If you can't be there in person or don't want to brave the crowds, catch NBC's live coverage on TV.

746 POORAM, THRISSUR, INDIA

Pooram is the elephant procession to end all elephant processions, held in Kerala's festival hot spot, and it ends with a jumbo-sized fireworks display that lasts for up to four hours. While you're waiting for the show you'll be entertained by the parade, in which two teams of beautifully caparisoned elephants face off across the temple grounds. On each elephant's back a man holds a parasol taller than the elephant itself, while another waves a yak-tail fan like a feather boa. As the temple orchestra plays, the parasols are exchanged among the elephants' riders. The drumming goes all day.

Pooram is held in the Malayalam month of Medam, in April or May. The festivities go for 36 rowdy hours, so bank some sleep.

747 BONFIRE NIGHT, LONDON, ENGLAND

This is fireworks with a history, and a rather nasty history at that. Guy Fawkes Night or Bonfire Night, held on 5 November, commemorates the foiling of the Gunpowder Plot in 1605. Fawkes and a group of Catholic conspirators had planned to assassinate King James; Fawkes was discovered with explosives under Westminster Palace, and the crisis was averted. On Bonfire Night the hapless Fawkes is burnt in effigy all over England to the accompaniment of thousands of backyard and large-scale fireworks displays. It used to be a children's festival, but in these more-careful times it's the adults who set the fuses.

In London, each district will have a firework display. One of the best is at Battersea Park.

750 YAMAYAKI, NARA, JAPAN

This whiz-bang display on Nara's Mt Wakakusa owes its existence to a centuries-old Buddhist feud. There used to be two rival temples on this mountain, and mediation between the monks went so badly that the 342m mountain ended up being torched. Today, in commemoration, monks light sacred fire at the Kasuga Shrine, carry it to the mountain, and set it ablaze. It generally burns for a half-hour or so, followed by fireworks as only the Japanese can do them. The best viewing spot is Nara Park, on the east side of the city; arrive early to get a good position.

Yamayaki takes place on the second Sunday in January. It's bitterly cold, so rug up.

748 CHINESE NEW YEAR, SHANGHAI, CHINA

There's just something about spending Chinese New Year – observed around the world in various Chinatowns – in a *real* Chinese city, and Shanghai has one of the best celebrations. It's essentially an occasion for family and friends more than tourists, but if you're hungry for fireworks you won't be disappointed. There's an explosion of them at midnight to welcome in the New Year and ward off bad spirits, and then a barrage of firecrackers on the fifth day of the New Year to herald the arrival of the God of Wealth. The New Year follows the lunar calendar, and falls somewhere in January or February.

The Chinese take this time to visit relatives, so accommodation is booked solid and many businesses shut. Plan well in advance.

749 INTERNATIONAL FIREWORKS FESTIVAL, MONTRÉAL, CANADA

Summer is fireworks season in Montréal. Every Wednesday and Saturday night from June through August, crowds pack La Ronde, the city's amusement park, to watch the cream of the profession duke it out in 30-minute musical sets. This is no case of just throwing your biggest and brightest bangers up in the air: the sets must be intricately choreographed and in harmony with the music. That's not to say you won't see some spectacular fusillades and sheer show-offy magic. The pyrotechnicians are playing to a highly educated audience, and this is the biggest fireworks festival on earth, so they crack out their best.

You can buy tickets to sit in La Ronde, but thousands choose to see it for free from nearby vantage points.

MOST SPECTACULAR FIREWORKS DISPLAYS

MIGHTIEST RIVERS

Adrenaline kicks, natural wonders, engineering phenomena or religious pilgrimage – take your pick from these spectacular river-related sights.

The world's largest religious celebration and the biggest single gathering of humanity – that's the Kumbh Mela. Once every three years, Hindus from across the world make the pilgrimage to bathe in the sacred water of the River Ganges for a festival that lasts weeks and sees impromptu tent cities spring up on the riverbanks. Washing in the river is said to purify the inner self, as unique planetary positions medicate

'Hey, buddy! Grab an oar and do some work!' On the Colorado River, the guy up front gets to relax and enjoy the ride

the waters with cleansing nectar. The 2010 event attracted 40 million devotees, including rare public sightings of Himalayan saints such as sages, seers, sadhus and yogis.

Various forms of the Kumbh Mela are celebrated at regular intervals, rotating around four venues. The next takes place in Allahabad from 27 January to 25 February 2013. Allahabad has no airport, but trains, including express services, link to major cities including Kolkata, Delhi and Mumbai.

JOHN ELK III / LONELY PLANET IMAGES

752 KENAI RIVER SALMON RUN, ALASKA, USA

Each summer, from May to September, the rivers of Alaska play host to one of nature's most spectacular migrations, as thousands of salmon battle their way upstream to ancient spawning grounds. Some of the finest runs are on the Kenai River, which is rich in the king, red, silver and pink species. And it's not just quantity; these fellows are super-sized – the world-record king salmon was landed here at a rod-snapping 44kg. Whether you want to cast a line, watch the grizzlies fishing or cast your lens towards moose or multifarious bird species, this is the place to be.

The biggest fish are in the river's 'lower' section, running 34km from the town of Soldotna – a three-hour drive from Anchorage – to the mouth at Cook Inlet.

753 CONFLUENCE OF NILE RIVER, KHARTOUM, SUDAN

Mark Twain said of the world's longest river, 'If you should rear a duck in the heart of the Sahara, no doubt it would swim if you brought it to the Nile.' It's a cute way of saying the 6650km-long Nile breathes life to northern Africa's parched land; annual floods are the lifeblood that fertilise arid plains. If you can't stretch to a multiday cruise, take a trip to Khartoum. In the Sudanese capital, the river's two major tributaries converge. The fast-flowing Blue Nile and languid White Nile mix in a silty swirl before flowing on to the distant shores of Egypt's coast.

See the confluence from the old White Nile Bridge, but snap no photos – the crossing is considered 'strategic' so shutterbugs beware.

754 RAFTING THE COLORADO RIVER, GRAND CANYON, ARIZONA, USA

One of the fiercest debates over the Grand Canyon is whether it's best viewed from the top or bottom. Native Hualapai Indians argue that their nerve-jangling glass skywalk offers the ultimate experience, but 1100m below on the Colorado River, intrepid rafters think otherwise. On a multiday trip you'll eat, sleep and breathe the canyon, gliding along the river, exploring secret crevasses and camping under canvas. You don't get any of that on a skywalk. There's only one drawback: tumbling along through some serious rapids, so thrilling is the ride that you might just forget to look up at the view.

Flagstaff-based Rivers & Oceans (www.rivers-oceans.com) is a no-fee booking agent that will scour the market and find you the best deal for the trip you want.

265

Trekking the frozen Zanskar River

755 ZANSKAR RIVER ICE TREKKING, CHADAR, INDIA

Rivers – perfect for a spot of rafting, cooling tired feet or maybe casting a few lines. Not in Chadar. High in the remote Himalayan passes and isolated valleys of Ladakh, the Zanskar River serves up an altogether frostier experience. For a few short weeks at the end of January, the water ices over and affords locals a direct but fleeting means of travelling through the Zanskar region. For them it's a precious lifeline. For hard-core trekkers, this five- to eight-day route – known as the Chadar Ice Trek – means panoramic mountain views, secret monasteries and sleeping in caves through nights of -30ºC.

Project Himalaya (www.project-himalaya.com) is a small operator specialising in adventure trips in the Himalaya. Its 21-day Chadar trek itinerary includes transfers through Delhi.

756 YANGTZE RIVER & THREE GORGES DAM, CHINA

China's Three Gorges project was controversial on many levels – environmental impact, human displacement, lost cultural heritage – but the resulting dam on the Yangtze River is a wonder of the modern world. The stats are mind-boggling: 2335m wide and 185m high, the dam has stemmed the mighty Yangtze and formed a reservoir that stretches 650km upstream; that's what you get for a cool US$40 billion. It may be hard to accept that 1200 settlements and 1300 archaeological sites have been lost forever, but this is the thrusting face of modern China and the embodiment of development raging throughout the country.

The huge city of Chóngqìng is on the upper reaches of the Yangtze, 20 hours' sailing from the Three Gorges and the starting point for many cruises.

757 SHOTOVER RIVER BY SPEEDBOAT, QUEENSTOWN, NEW ZEALAND

In the land of adventure sports (think bungy, canyon swinging or zorbing) thrill-seekers in Queenstown can get the ultimate ride. For kicks with a bit more horsepower, strap yourself in for the ultimate jet-boat ride along the Shotover River. As the throttle opens and the scenery blurs by, the sheer canyon walls come startlingly close as you pull out of another 360-degree spin. Crawl back to land, regain your balance and relax – now you can absorb the full glory of the surroundings.

Shotover Jet (www.shotoverjet.com) is the original speedboat operator – find them 7km from Queenstown along Gorge Road. Rides cost NZ$119.

758 RIVER MERSEY FERRY, LIVERPOOL, ENGLAND

Liverpool's skyline inspired the greatest pop music of the 1960s, and also influenced architectural design as far away as China. While the likes of the Beatles and Gerry & the Pacemakers propelled this industrial city to global prominence, Western settlers in China drew inspiration at the beginning of the 20th century. Shanghai's iconic Bund – now dwarfed by the explosion of dazzling towers on Pudong – is redolent of the Custom House and Pier Head buildings of Liverpool's waterfront. You'll see fewer flashing lights and soaring skyscrapers on the Mersey, but the fabled river crossing remains a nostalgic river journey.

Ferry cross the Mersey? You can make it happen with a 50-minute guided tour from Mersey Ferries (www.merseyferries.co.uk); prices from £6.50.

759 GREAT RIVER AMAZON RAFT RACE, IQUITOS, PERU

What started as a bit of fun in 1999, when a handful of crews cobbled together rafts for a 20km race, is now an ever-growing event pulling competitors from around the globe. Following the Peruvian Amazon for 180km from Nauta to Iquitos, teams paddle for three days (or 12 hours and 19 minutes for the record-holders), through remote jungle and piranha-infested waters. To join them you'll need a sense of adventure and a knack for crafting a balsa-wood raft. Sound too dangerous? Then head to Iquitos instead to catch the finale.

Iquitos is unreachable by road – you can fly from Lima but it's better to take a boat (cargo or cruiser) from any other Amazon port city.

760 SUMIDA RIVER FIREWORKS FESTIVAL, TOKYO, JAPAN

Every year upwards of one million Japanese pack the banks of Tokyo's Sumida River, with many camping out for weeks in advance to pin down the best spots – and it's all in the name of pyrotechnics. The Sumida River Fireworks Festival is the oldest fireworks display in Japan, dating from 1732 when a shogun arranged a water ceremony to commemorate victims of a famine and locals ignited rockets and crackers to mark the occasion. Nowadays it's all about competition – biggest, loudest and brightest is definitely best. Squeeze in among the crowds and watch the river skyline blaze into the night.

The annual festival occurs each July. The focus is around Asakusa Station but covers two parts of the city, from Sakurabashi Bridge to Kototoibashi Bridge, and Komagatabashi Bridge to Umayabashi Bridge.

MIGHTIEST RIVERS

BIG THINGS OF AUSTRALIA

If you thought things were big in Texas, wait until you discover Australia's fascination for all things elephantine and concrete.

761 GOLDEN GUMBOOT, QUEENSLAND

In a dry, brown country, it's an unlikely slanging match: is Tully or Babinda the wettest town in Australia? The two north Queensland towns vie publicly to be known as the soggiest spot, right down to an annual Golden Gumboot Festival celebrating the rivalry. In Tully they've gone a step further, erecting a large Golden Gumboot (with a green tree frog scaling its side) as a monument to the town's 150 days of rain each year. It's a battle only half won, however, with rumour long suggesting that Babinda has plans to build a Big Umbrella.

For the record, Tully has recorded Australia's highest annual rainfall: 7.9m in 1950. The Golden Gumboot Festival is held each May.

762 BIG PENGUIN, TASMANIA

By Australian standards, the island state of Tasmania is small but it does have the Big Penguin, in a town named Penguin where, true to the name, penguins come ashore each night. The Big Penguin stands on the Penguin foreshore, among penguin-shaped rubbish bins and stores filled with such things as inflatable waving penguins. Even the fire station is decked out in penguins. If you've travelled all this way to see a concrete and fibreglass penguin, you'll probably want to stick around to see the prototypes. They shuffle ashore between about September and March at – yes – Penguin Point. Talk about obsession.

Penguin is midway between Burnie and Devonport on Tasmania's north coast.

763 BIG LOBSTER, SOUTH AUSTRALIA

They catch some pretty big lobsters along South Australia's southeast coast, but nothing in the league of the steel and fibreglass lobster that lords it over the seaside town of Kingston. Built in the 1970s (by the same man responsible for the landmark big bagpiper on Scotty's Motel in Adelaide), this critter's antennae rise to a height of 17m and, unlike some of Australia's big things, it actually looks like the animal it represents. Inside the structure known locally as Larry is a restaurant where, naturally, you can slurp down a lobster for dinner.

The Big Lobster is so big it has its own website: www.thebiglobster.com.au.

764 BIG SUBMARINE, NEW SOUTH WALES

Finally, a big something with some semblance of meaning, even if no sense of direction. Surfacing in Holbrook, midway between Sydney and Melbourne, on the country's busiest highway, hundreds of kilometres from the nearest port, is this 90m-long submarine with an unusual backstory. Before WWI, Holbrook was known as Germanton, but following a daring submarine attack in the Dardanelles, guided by English commander Norman Holbrook, the town's title was de-Germanised and the lieutenant's name adopted instead. Holbrook (the town) went a step further in 1997, purchasing the decommissioned submarine HMAS *Otway* and displaying it in a park.

The town is on the Hume Highway, around 400km from Melbourne and 500km from Sydney.

765 BIG PINEAPPLE, QUEENSLAND

If Australia has a patriarch of 'big things', it is the Big Pineapple in Woombye. Once said to be the second-most-visited tourist attraction in the country (behind the Sydney Opera House), it was famously part of the 1983 royal tour by Prince Charles and Princess Diana. Rising 16m above the pineapple fields of the Sunshine Coast hinterland, it's been a family favourite for decades, even earning a place on the heritage register. After going into receivership in 2009, the Big Pineapple has recently been touted as the possible site of a motor-racing museum.

The Big Pineapple is 7km south of the Sunshine Coast town of Nambour, near the Bruce Highway.

269

The Big Pineapple: if it's good enough for the royals, it's good enough for you

As if Australian crocs aren't scary enough, now they've taken up the 'sweet science'

766 BIG BOXING CROCODILE, NORTHERN TERRITORY

Not content just to have a silly name, the town of Humpty Doo upped the ante by erecting one of the country's silliest big things. Most visitors pass the 8m-high Big Croc on the drive between Darwin and Kakadu National Park. It can be seen wearing a grin – and boxing gloves. The town itself is a testament to overly ambitious thought, having been established with a postwar plan to turn the surrounding floodplain into a sea of rice fields. It failed. So the town cheered itself up with a very large crocodile.

Humpty Doo is 40km from Darwin. Turn off the Stuart Highway onto the Arnhem Highway and it's just ahead.

767 BIG BANANA, NEW SOUTH WALES

The original, and perhaps still the best. At a bend of its own in the Pacific Highway in Coffs Harbour, the Big Banana was unpeeled to the public in 1964. Since then it's stopped millions of travellers on one of Australia's busiest highways, even if it was once voted the 'most bizarre and grotesque tourist attraction in the world'. If it's so much as brushed past a banana it can be purchased inside the Big Banana complex: banana milkshakes, bunches of bananas, banana jam, banana stubby holders. Not to be mistaken for the other Big Banana in Carnarvon on Australia's west coast.

The Big Banana is on the Pacific Highway, just north of Coffs' city centre.

768 BIG ROCKING HORSE, SOUTH AUSTRALIA

Yes, almost all of Australia's native animals have been immortalised as big things, but so too has an 'animal' as obscure as the rocking horse. High in the Adelaide Hills, in the town of Gumeracha, it's the showpiece for a local wooden toy factory. Visitors can climb through the horse to three vantage points: one on the rockers, one on the saddle, and one atop the horse's head. It is impressively large, weighing 25 tonnes, set into 80 tonnes of concrete and rising more than 18m above the ground. But, no, it doesn't rock.

Check out the rocking horse (and the wooden toys) at www.thetoyfactory.com.au.

769 BIG GALAH, SOUTH AUSTRALIA

If you've taken the time to drive halfway across Australia, you can probably be excused for thinking that you're hallucinating. But that pink bird by the petrol station in the small highway town of Kimba really is an 8m-high galah, that most raucous and iconic of Australian bush birds. Why it's here is anybody's guess, and whether it's really the halfway point across the country is another guess, but it's been perched here for almost 30 years so just go with the flow… big things sometimes come with big claims.

Kimba is 1700km west of Sydney and 2200km east of Perth: apparently halfway across…

770 GLOUCESTER TREE, WESTERN AUSTRALIA

After all the manufactured kitsch, how about a natural high in the endemic karri forests of southern WA? Growing to 90m, karris are among the tallest trees in the world and a number of them once served as fire lookout towers. Today, three have been converted into 'climbing trees', with visitors ascending their trunks on metal spikes to platforms built into their canopies. The most popular climbing tree is the Gloucester Tree, at the edge of the town of Pemberton, with its platform 60m above the forest floor. Even higher, at 75m, is the Dave Evans Bicentennial Tree.

Head out of Pemberton on central Ellis Street, turning left onto Kennedy Street and then right onto Johnston Street; the tree is 3km out of town.

BIG THINGS OF AUSTRALIA

BEST HISTORICAL RE-ENACTMENTS

There's nothing like standing at a historic site and seeing its history dramatically re-enacted, via a colourful fair or noisy simulated battle.

773 INTI RAYMI, SAQSAYWAMÁN, PERU

Before the Spanish conquest of South America toppled the Inca empire, the annual festival of Inti Raymi was one of its most important observances. Held annually on the southern hemisphere's winter solstice, it honoured the sun god. Inti Raymi fell out of observance in the 16th century, but since the 1940s has been re-enacted each year at the Inca ruins at Saqsaywamán, on the outskirts of Cuzco. High priests and nobles walk along streets strewn with flowers to an old fortress, where they enact ceremonies based on ancient Inca traditions.

Inti Raymi (www.cusco.net/articulos/intiraymi.htm) takes place on 24 June each year, and is free to view.

771 BRISTOL RENAISSANCE FAIRE, WISCONSIN, USA

It's nowhere near Bristol (it's not even in England) but this annual fair does a good job of imitating the British port in the year 1574. That was when Queen Elizabeth I paid her visit to Bristol, so the event faithfully recreates the look and feel of Renaissance England. There's a great deal of theatre involved, with actors roaming the streets in costume, speaking Elizabethan English, brandishing swords and interacting with visitors. There are also a lot of diverting shops and rides if you tire of the historically correct.

The Bristol Renaissance Faire (www.renfair.com/bristol) takes place at 12550 120th Ave, Kenosha, Wisconsin, from 10am to 7pm on weekends between early July and early September. Adult entry is US$18.95.

772 SOVEREIGN HILL, AUSTRALIA

The most tumultuous period of Australia's colonial history was the gold-rush era of the 1850s, when prospectors from around the world descended on the enormously rich goldfields of Ballarat, Victoria. The era lives on at Sovereign Hill, an outdoor museum, with an unsealed main street lined with replica shops and pubs, and diggings along a stream whose bed has been salted with gold dust. Costumed residents stroll the streets, with outbreaks of staged re-enactments from actors playing 19th-century soldiers, miners, businessman and the scandalous courtesan Lola Montez.

Sovereign Hill (www.sovereignhill.com.au) is in Bradshaw St, Ballarat, and adult entry is A$41. A daily train from Melbourne, the Goldrush Special, connects with a bus from Ballarat station to the site.

774 SIEGE OF MALBORK, POLAND

In the Polish town of Malbork sits a huge red-brick castle that seems way out of proportion to the village below. This is Malbork Castle, which was once known as Marienburg. In medieval times it was the headquarters of the Teutonic Knights, Germanic warrior-monks who established an empire in this part of Central Europe. It's one of the largest castles in the world, and each July it hosts the Siege of Malbork, a re-creation of the 15th-century siege of Marienburg by Polish forces. It's a lively three-day event with costumed soldiers on horseback, sound-and-light effects, night-time attacks and lots of big swords.

The Siege of Malbork (www.visitmalbork.pl) takes place in late July each year. Malbork is easily accessible by regular trains from Gdańsk (45 minutes).

775 RAPSKA FJERA, RAB, CROATIA

St Christopher is well known for being the patron saint of travellers, but he's also the patron saint of the island of Rab, Croatia. Which is a good reason to travel all the way there to take part in this annual fair involving a big dose of historical re-enactment. First held in 1364, the celebrations have a long pedigree. As they did all those years ago, they still culminate in a crossbow tournament. Before that event, you can amuse yourself by taking in displays of traditional crafts, a re-creation of a medieval household and a vibrant costume parade.

Rapska Fjera (www.rab-croatia.com/fjera/efjera.htm) takes place annually from 25 to 27 July. Ferries from the mainland port of Jablanac head to Rab all year round.

776 INTERNATIONAL LIVING HISTORY FAIR, ENGLAND

For some people, historical re-enactment is a casual spectator sport, something to pep up the visit to a historic location. For others, it's a lifestyle. Attend this annual re-enactors' market and be amazed at the breadth of the products on sale by historically themed traders from across Europe, and by the skills of the artisans and craftworkers who create them. Many re-enactment societies also promote themselves at the fair. Could you too be seduced by the appeal of slipping on some chain-mail and stepping a few centuries back in time?

The International Living History Fair (www.livinghistoryfairs.com) is held in February and October each year at the Warwickshire Exhibition Centre in Leamington Spa. Adult entry is £3.50.

777 BATTLE OF WATERLOO, BELGIUM

This climactic battle of the Napoleonic wars would have been famous even if Swedish supergroup ABBA hadn't used it as the theme for their Eurovision-winning song 'Waterloo' in 1974. Fought on Sunday 18 June 1815 near the town of the same name in Belgium, it ended with the defeat of the French by the allied forces commanded by the British Duke of Wellington and the Prussian Gebhard von Blücher. Nearly two centuries later, the battle is re-enacted in June each year, a spectacular sight for onlookers.

The Waterloo Battlefield (www.waterloo1815.be) is at Route du Lion 315, 20 minutes' drive from Brussels. The regular Battlefield Tour costs €5.50.

778 BATTLE OF HASTINGS, ENGLAND

This pivotal battle in 1066 deposed England's existing monarchy and brought Norman rule across the English Channel by way of William the Conqueror. As such, it changed England's course dramatically, making it the most-remembered armed conflict in British history. Every year at Battle Abbey in the aptly named Battle, East Sussex, the Battle of Hastings is restaged, with thousands of participants and spectators from around the world. In addition to the clash of arms, living history encampments recreate 11th-century life.

The battle re-enactment (www.english-heritage.org.uk) occurs on the weekend either before or after 14 October. Adult entry is £11. Phone 0870 333 1181 for more details.

779 CIVIL WAR REMEMBRANCE, MICHIGAN, USA

The American Civil War tore the US apart in the 1860s, dividing the north from the south over issues of slavery and states' rights. It's so recent, historically speaking, that it can still be a controversial subject today – right down to how best the war should be commemorated. Each year during the Memorial Day weekend in late May, Greenfield Village in Michigan hosts a Civil War Remembrance weekend. Re-enactors dressed as soldiers from each side, civilians, musicians and presenters all bring to life this period of conflict.

Greenfield Village (www.thehenryford.org/village) is located at The Henry Ford, 20900 Oakwood Blvd, Dearborn. Adult entry is US$22.

780 JIDAI MATSURI, JAPAN

One of three major festivals held in Kyoto each year, the Jidai Matsuri's most popular aspect is its historical re-enactment parade. This colourful procession includes figures dressed in authentic costumes from various eras of Japanese history, aptly reflecting Kyoto's former role as the imperial capital. The parade includes members dressed as samurai, soldiers, workers, villagers and members of the royal court.

Jidai Matsuri (www.jnto.go.jp) takes place on 22 October each year. The procession departs from Kyoto Imperial Palace at noon, progressing to the Heian Jingu Shrine.

MOST UNUSUAL LAKES

Some are high, some are sacred, some are jam-packed with jellyfish –
all are spectacular.

The underwater glories of Jellyfish Lake

781 LAKE TITICACA, PERU/BOLIVIA

Few lakes can claim to be the birthplace of a whole civilisation. But the Inca believed it was from the high-altitude waters of Lake Titicaca that creator-god Viracocha brought forth the sun, moon and man himself; two of the lake's 40-plus atolls, Isla del Sol and Isla de la Luna, bear remains of the resulting Inca shrines. The lake is still sacred to Andeans today: to the Uros of Titicaca's reed-woven Islas Flotantes; to the Quechua, who graze alpaca on Amantaní island; to the poncho-wearing fishermen working the ethereal blue; and to the many shore-dwelling Aymara, whose vibrant *folklórico* fiestas celebrate lakeside living.

Titicaca's hub towns are Puno (Peru) and Copacabana (Bolivia); travellers can cross the border overland via Yunguyo or Desaguadero.

782 CRATER LAKE, OREGON, USA

A violent eruption, almost unfathomable depths, Klamath Native American folklore and a 100-year-old tree that refuses to sink – there's strangeness to the beauty of Oregon's Crater Lake. Depending on who you talk to, this circle of purest blue formed 7700 years ago, due to either a volcanic super-explosion or a battle between the gods of sky and the underworld. It's nearly 600m deep, and a mountain-ringed stunner. Which is perhaps why the Old Man of the Lake doesn't want to leave – first noted in 1896, this weather-bleached hemlock trunk continues to bob vertically in the water, floating up to 6km a day, like a coastguard patrol.

Crater Lake is open year-round. Snow can close some areas between October and June; the visitor centres are only open May to September. See www.nps.gov/crla.

CASEY & ASTRID MAHANEY / LONELY PLANET IMAGES

783 JELLYFISH LAKE, PALAU

Think of this paradisaical salt lake as a sort of giant turquoise soup – in which the ingredients are very much alive… In the island nation of Palau, a scatter of mushroomy outcrops far-flung in the North Pacific, there's a tropical lagoon that pulsates with millions – tens of millions – of gelatinous jellyfish. These graceful sea gobbets pirouette through the water like an endless chorus-line of translucent ballerinas – and you get to swim with them. Millions of years of isolation and evolution have rendered the stings of these jellies virtually harmless, so careful snorkellers can safely join their delicate dance.

275

Jellyfish Lake is on Eil Malk Island, a 45-minute boat ride from Koror; a permit (US$35) is required.

784 LAKE NICARAGUA, NICARAGUA

The local Nahua didn't mince words when they named the largest island in Central America's largest lake: Ometepe ('two hills') comprises a pair of matching volcanoes, rising from the depths of Lake Nicaragua. These connected cones – the larger, 1610m Concepción is still active and smoking – are home to some 30,000 people plus quirky pre-Columbian petroglyphs and forests full of monkeys. In the lake itself, there's more wildlife: previously thought to be the world's only freshwater sharks, the lake's unique fish are actually bull sharks that have adapted to swim upriver from the salty Caribbean so they can fin around under the volcanoes.

Regular ferries cross the lake, connecting mainland San Jorge with Moyogalpa; the crossing takes an hour.

785 LAKE MÝVATN, ICELAND

In the late 1960s, NASA sent the *Apollo 11* crew to the lava fields of northern Iceland to train for their moon walks. Not a surprising choice – the shallow Lake Mývatn, Iceland's fourth largest at about 37 sq km, is just like a moonscape. Dotted with volcanic islets and lined with stark shores of salient craters, volcanic cones, towering lava pillars, boiling mud pits and bubbling hot springs, this geologically active area dazzles the eye in a very sci-fi way. If it weren't for the ducks that roam the sandbars, it could just as well be another planet.

276

Base yourself at either Reykjahlid on the lake's northeastern shore or smaller Skútustadir on the south side; hardcore hikers should note the road around the lake is 36km.

786 LAKE MANASAROVAR, TIBET

Expanses of water don't get holier than Lake Manasarovar. Rippling at a suitably heavenly 4556m, high up in the Tibetan Himalaya, this sapphire pool is sacred to both Hindus and Buddhists. The former believe creation-god Brahma begat it as a place of worship, the latter believe that this is where Buddha was conceived. Both trek to its shores, to wash away their sins in the icy water and walk around its 88km circumference. Colossal Mt Kailash – even holier still, being revered by four religions – overlooks this lonely lake. Save some monastic remains and a few hardy yaks, the peak is the pilgrims' only companion.

Treks around Kailash and Manasarovar are accessed from Darchen (30km south), a four- to five-day jeep ride from Lhasa.

787 LLYN Y FAN FACH, WALES

This isolated drop of blue, beneath a cirque of raw Welsh hills, is enchanting – and enchanted. The story goes that in the 13th century a farmer grazing cattle on the nearby slopes spotted the most beautiful woman he'd ever seen. She was a fairy maiden, who agreed to marry him on one proviso – he must not hit her more than twice. In time, the inevitable happened – three strikes, and the otherworldly wife disappeared back into the lake, taking her magic cows with her. Today the valley is rich in medicinal herbs and bog plants, perhaps the mistreated fairy maiden's healing legacy.

Llyn y Fan Fach is 12km southeast of Llandovery; park near Blaenau Farmhouse to follow the trail to the lake.

788 LAKE TOBA, SUMATRA, INDONESIA

The eruption of Mt Toba around 75,000 years ago scored a Volcanic Explosivity Index rating of eight. Know nothing of such indexes? Suffice to say, that's top of the scale – the planet's biggest ever ka-boom. Unsurprising, then, that it left behind the world's largest crater lake, a 100km by 30km flooded caldera, punched into the wilds of northern Sumatra. Lake Toba has been part of traveller folklore for decades and is a picturesque but risky spot – that super-volcano is still very much active. The fun-loving Batak people live here anyway, and offer a warm welcome (and a palm wine or two) to those visiting their precarious home.

Boats leave from Parapat for Pulau Samosir, the island in Lake Toba; stay in Tuk Tuk, the island's main village.

789 LAKE EYRE, AUSTRALIA

Eyre is sometimes Australia's biggest lake. But sometimes it's not there at all. Such are the fluctuations of this (potentially) massive, flooded – or parched – salt pan in northern South Australia. Covering an area of 9690 sq km – roughly the size of the Netherlands – Lake Eyre is usually dry and crusty, an epic emptiness. But when it rains, this outback wilderness comes alive: a blue tongue of water oozes across the desert, migratory birds stop off for a drink, tiny brine shrimp materialise, and the stalwart if rarely satisfied members of Lake Eyre Yacht Club get to have a sail.

The best way to view Lake Eyre is by plane; flights leave from William Creek, Marree and Coober Pedy.

The Devil's Garden? No, this is heaven; Plitvice Lakes

790 PLITVICE LAKES, CROATIA

Croatia's precious network of 16 lakes interlinked with waterfalls is acknowledged on the Unesco World Heritage list. The Plitvice Lakes are also known as the Devil's Garden, which refers to the associated tale of the area being flooded by the Black Queen after a long drought and countless prayers. Limestone and travertine caves pock the surrounding landscape, with dense forests crowding around the rims of the upper lakes.

Snow lovers should visit anytime from November to March; in December and January the lakes are frozen. The lakes are open daily all year from about 8am to 7pm.

MOST UNUSUAL LAKES

MOST SURREAL GHOST TOWNS

Get a dose of spooky and ponder the past in these eerie abandoned places.

791 PRYPYAT, UKRAINE

That Ferris wheel looming gloomily over a derelict city. Those dodgem cars with weeds growing through them. Houses leaking and peeling. Rusted cars and abandoned trains. Yes, you're in the 'Alienation Zone', the area around the site of the Chornobyl nuclear disaster. Prypyat, once a Soviet show city of wide boulevards and symmetrical corners, was built for workers at the Chornobyl plant and had a population of 50,000. It was evacuated in two days after a reactor at the plant exploded in 1986, sending a shower of radioactive material into the surrounding areas. If you're game, you can take a tour of the abandoned city.

The cost of a tour of Chornobyl and Prypyat is approximately US$250 for two people, less per person for a group.

792 PYRAMIDEN, SVALBARD, NORWAY

As ghosts towns go, it's hard to beat one where you might meet a polar bear or a reindeer roaming the empty streets, not to mention one that has the world's northernmost grand piano. Pyramiden was sold by Sweden (which then owned it) to a Russian mining community in 1927 and developed into a model Soviet town. When the coal began to run out in the 1990s, the company pulled out hastily – so hastily that much of the town was left behind. There are still books on library shelves and swings in playgrounds. Because of the extreme cold, this time-frozen town will remain as it is for years.

You can reach Pyramiden by boat; you'll need a guide with a gun to scare off polar bears.

793 PLYMOUTH, MONTSERRAT, LESSER ANTILLES

In years gone by Montserrat was a picture-postcard Caribbean haven – clear waters, golden beaches and a carefree vibe that drew travellers from around the globe. Then, in the summer of 1995, the long-dormant Soufrière Hills volcano blew its top and obliterated the tourist trade in one monstrous, gassy blast. Plymouth, the island's capital, disappeared under a sea of ash, becoming an instant ghost town. Plymouth remains lost but the island continues to offer world-class diving and sailing, as well as the chance to survey the town now known as the 'modern Pompeii'.

Before you visit, check out the Montserrat Volcano Observatory's website (www .mvo.ms) for the latest volcano alert level.

794 SILVERTON, AUSTRALIA

In the 1880s Silverton was a booming little silver-mining community with its own football team, newspaper and jockey club, but it was done for by the opening of new mines in nearby Broken Hill. Most of the residents moved on and took most of the town (literally; their houses) with them. What remains today is a fraction of the original, but there are some significant buildings like the hotel and jail left. Surrounded by stark red land, it's a dream for location scouts and has featured in many movies, including *Mad Max 2* and *The Adventures of Priscilla, Queen of the Desert.*

Silverton's not quite a ghost town – a tiny resident population runs a tourism industry; see www.silverton.org.au.

795

CRACO, ITALY

'Build not your house upon the clay' – that's the moral of Craco, a derelict medieval hill town in southern Italy. Although, to be fair, it did survive for centuries before its foundations were rocked by earthquakes. Its population had been depleted anyway by war and migration, but in the mid-20th century earthquakes exacerbated the problems of its clay-based foundations, a quickly built retaining wall retained mainly water which made the clay wetter, landslides ensued, and the whole thing got too rickety for habitation. The townsfolk moved down into the valley, leaving Craco a forlorn, crumbling sentinel above.

Craco is found in southern Basilicata. You can also see it in the background of Mel Gibson's film *The Passion of Christ*.

Craco, and a lesson for the ages: don't build on clay

Bodie, California, is so spooky even the buildings seem to wink at you...

796 BELCHITE, SPAIN

This village located in the Zaragoza region of Spain was destroyed during a battle between fascist and communist forces in 1937. Afterwards, a new village was built alongside it, but the remains of the old one were left to serve as a war memorial. The levelled town complete with its bullet-pocked ruins is dominated by the skeleton of the church. Visitors can see inside the hollowed shell, although many areas are closed off as being unsafe. A wander through this carcass of a town is a poignant reminder of the Spanish Civil War and its destruction of ordinary lives.

Old Belchite is about 20 minutes away from the new Belchite on foot. You can get a bus to the new Belchite from the city of Zaragoza.

797 GRYTVIKEN, ANTARCTICA

South Georgia Island, hunkering in the brutal seas of the southern Atlantic Ocean near Antarctica, doesn't seem like a great place to set up shop. And yet, it's seen a number of population waves. The first sealers, in the 19th century, sealed until they could seal no more, then abandoned base. In the early 20th century, a whaling community

DOUGLAS STEARKLEY / LONELY PLANET IMAGES

798 BODIE, CALIFORNIA, USA

This is a bustling little ghost town, with annual visitors numbering in the hundreds of thousands. It's a pretty bandbox version of the genre as well, its buildings in a state of 'arrested decay' – it's been looked after by caretakers since the 1940s, so it's never been ravaged by vandalism. Bodie was left high and dry after the Californian gold-rush wave receded. It was once a thriving spot with a population of more than 10,000 people, but when the mines started to dry out, folk started leaving. Today you can wander through this 'Wild West' time capsule with its preserved interiors.

Bodie is located high in the eastern Sierra Nevada Ranges, and the road is often closed in winter.

799 REAL DE CATORCE, MEXICO

Real de Catorce means 'the Eagle's Nest' – a little catchier than its original handle, 'Royal Mines of Our Lady of Conception of Guadalupe of the Fourteen Poplars'. This stunningly located almost-ghost town sits on the fringes of the Sierra Madre Oriental. It was a wealthy silver-mining community until early last century. Not long ago, it was nearly deserted, its streets lined with crumbling buildings, its mint a wreck. In the 1970s it became known for its peyote and was visited by acid pilgrims. These days the population is creeping up again, so if you want to see its last ghost-town moment, complete with ruins, abandoned buildings and doors creaking in the breeze, you'd better be quick.

Get dinner and a bed at Mesón de la Abundancia (www.mesonabundancia .com), in the restored 19th-century building of the town's former treasury.

800 SEWELL, CHILE

This 'City of Stairs' high in the Andes, with its vertiginous streets, pastel buildings and art deco school, looks so pretty you almost want to move in. It was built in 1905 to house workers at the El Teniente copper mine and was named after an executive of the US mining company. When the boom days were over, the company started relocating the population down to the valley. By the late 1970s it was game over for Sewell as a living community. The site was put on Unesco's World Heritage list in 2006.

It's easy to arrange a tour to Sewell. The official website (www.sewell.cl) is a good starting point.

established itself at Grytviken, and again killed the goose that laid the golden egg. Whales were hunted almost to extinction, and the station was abandoned in the 1960s. You can visit the rusty remains (and Shackleton's grave) by ship.

There's a tiny museum (http://sgmuseum .gs) near the old whaling station maintained by the British administration. Drop in for a chat.

MOST SURREAL GHOST TOWNS

MOST IMPRESSIVE STEPS & STAIRCASES

From haunted spirals to staircases-cum-calendars, the world is full of fun ways of rising to the top.

801 HOUSE OF SLAVES, ILE DE GORÉE, SENEGAL

Never was there greater discrepancy between the fates of those above and below stairs. On an Atlantic-battered island in the sea just off the Senegalese capital of Dakar, the unassuming steps of this crumbling Dutch-colonial house separated the traders from the slaves beneath. The privileged could look down from their vantage on the incarcerated men, women and children – kept 20 to a 2.6-sq-metre cell – and select which they'd wrench away to foreign lands for a life of servitude. In the dark, fetid bowels below, the charges were led down a passage direct to the ocean: the 'door of no return'.

Gorée's museums and sites are closed on Monday; for a virtual visit, go to http://webworld.unesco.org/goree/en/index.shtml.

RICHARD I'ANSON / LONELY PLANET IMAGES

The holy ghats: where life can thrive…and end

802 POTEMKIN STAIRS, ODESSA, UKRAINE

Leading from the grand squares of this self-proclaimed City of Heroes to its Black Sea harbour, this stolid staircase is far more than a thoroughfare. For starters it's an optical illusion – look up from below at the 192 steps and the whole flight seems to lengthen, a quirk of architectural perspective. But more, it's a symbol: in 1905 a battle between tsarists and mutinying sailors ravaged the Ukrainian city, and the subsequent silent film *The Battleship Potemkin* placed its re-creation of the death and devastation here. The moving black-and-white images – bodies falling, babies tumbling – is considered a seminal moment in cinematic history.

Odessa is a seven- to eight-hour bus journey from Ukrainian capital Kyiv; trains take longer (around nine to 12 hours).

803 SPANISH STEPS, ROME, ITALY

A Spanish staircase leading to a French church in the Italian capital, flanked by the deathbed of an English poet – this fine fan of 137 steps, hewn in the 18th century, has always been a place for cultures to mingle. And still today: the majestic Piazza di Spagna throngs with international touts, and tourists flipping coins into the Barcaccia Fountain, nosing into the Keats-Shelley House (Keats's last resting place, now a museum), climbing to the Renaissance splendour of the Trinità dei Monti church, or lolling on the steps themselves. Just don't pack a picnic: eating on this superlative staircase is strictly forbidden.

Visit in spring to see the steps decorated with pink azaleas. The Keats-Shelley House (www.keats-shelley-house.org) is open from Monday to Saturday; entrance is €4.

805 MIRABELL GARDENS, SALZBURG, AUSTRIA

Venus, Vesta, Minerva, Juno… Liesl, Marta and Fraulein Maria – this glorious baroque garden in Austria has them all, in spirit at least. For while graceful statues of god and goddess mingle with the flowerbeds of this finely pruned park, it's *The Sound of Music* magic that leads Julie Andrews wannabes to Mirabell's short, creamy staircase for a quick recreation of 'Do-Re-Mi'. After a step-jumping singalong, lose yourself in the hedge maze and visit the Dwarf Garden, a cluster of grisly and grotesque statues from the 18th century – allegedly based on unfortunate real-life people.

Mirabell Gardens are open year-round, from around 6am until dusk; visit in summer to see the flowers in full bloom

806 STAIRCASE TO THE MOON, BROOME, WESTERN AUSTRALIA

When the full moon rises over the glistening mudflats of Roebuck Bay, a gateway to the heavens appears… At least that's how it seems as the pearly glow, reflected on the exposed low-tide shore, shimmers in an apparent staircase to the sky. This occurs three nights a month from March to October. When Mother Nature plays tricks with the light, a full-moon food market springs up to feed the onlookers, while the bay itself feeds other visitors: 150,000 birds stop off at Roebuck each year, making this beach one of the most important avian sites in the world.

Broome is 2415km north of Perth. Broome Bird Observatory (www .broomebirdobservatory.com) offers tours and a range of accommodation.

804 HOLY GHATS, VARANASI, INDIA

Varanasi is one of the most colourful, chaotic places on earth – it's not for the faint-hearted. Devotees performing *puja* (prayers), kids throwing cricket balls, old men chewing blood-red betelnut and ladies washing vibrant saris: the ghats of Varanasi – the 80-odd sets of waterfront steps leading down into the River Ganges – are where all life happens in Hinduism's holiest city. They give bathers access to the water, lead up into palaces and temples, and play host to raucous festivals. But they're also where life ends: some of the ghats are solemn spots, reserved for funerals, where bodies burn outside on wooden pyres – a macabre scene, perhaps, but the most auspicious Hindu send-off.

Local boatmen offer waterbound tours along the ghats; haggle hard for a fair price. Sunset and sunrise are the most atmospheric times.

283

The Tulip Stairs: fit for kings and queens…and ghosts

807 EL CASTILLO, CHICHÉN ITZÁ, MEXICO

No understated desk calendar for the Maya – they liked their astronomical time-telling devices large and lairy. The temple of Kukulcán – often referred to as El Castillo, the Castle – is 24m of pyramidical steps, topped with a temple and nestled into Mexico's jungly Yucatán. With a total of 365 steps (one for each day of the year) on its four sides, this is a stone-made diary, which comes into its own each equinox: with its cunningly calculated size, slope and orientation, these two dates see the sun cast a shaft of squiggly light on the staircase, like a serpent slithering to the top.

Equinoxes (21 March and 22 September) are busy; note, the phenomena are almost as good during the preceding and following weeks.

808 PHILADELPHIA MUSEUM OF ART, PENNSYLVANIA, USA

Not so much a simple staircase as a metaphor for the triumph of the underdog, the sweep leading up to Philadelphia's Romanesque repository of art was immortalised by a sweaty Sylvester Stallone. As the tracksuited Rocky Balboa slogged up the steps to punch the air in glory, so now do legions of fans.

NEIL SETCHFIELD / LONELY PLANET IMAGES

809 TULIP STAIRS, LONDON, ENGLAND

Fit for a queen that didn't live to ascend them, this swirl of steps, fringed by a flowery iron balustrade, is one of the remaining original features of the Queen's House in Greenwich. Begun in the early 17th century for the wife of James I, it was designed by Inigo Jones, freshly inspired by his European wanderings to install the first geometric self-supporting spiral staircase in the country. Today, however, its intrigue is more supernatural than structural: a fuzzy snap taken in the 1960s appeared to show a ghostly figure climbing the flight. A haunted escalator? Or a bad photo? The mystery remains.

The Queen's House, now an art gallery, is part of the National Maritime Museum (www.nmm.ac.uk); it's open daily from 10am to 5pm.

810 INCA STAIRCASE, HUAYNA PICCHU, PERU

Health and safety regulations didn't trouble the Inca any. Yes, their top-notch mortarless engineering resulted in many a fine structure, but the ancient stone steps snaking up the sides of 2700m Huayna Picchu – the iconic pointy peak that rears up in the background of every Machu Picchu postcard – are for the brave only. In places this staircase is practically vertical, the steps narrow and shallow, with plunges into a mountain abyss beside. It's a tough, hair-raising slog to the top, 350m above the ruins themselves, but the reward is the best view of the ultimate lost city.

Only 400 permits per day are issued for the Huayna Picchu climb; arrive by sunrise and queue at the trailhead.

After jogging up, take in the view of city skyscrapers and enter the museum, which houses one of the best collections in the US. To meet the man himself, stay at the bottom: here a bronze of the boxer – a prop from *Rocky III* – is on free display.

The museum (www.philamuseum.org) is open from Tuesday to Sunday. Admission costs US$16; first Sunday of the month is 'pay what you wish' day.

MOST IMPRESSIVE STEPS & STAIRCASES

KITSCHIEST SIGHTS

The best of the dazzlingly crass, bright as a brass band, all-stops-out tacky and sublimely unashamed.

811 LEDERHOSEN, GERMANY/ AUSTRIA

To many folk outside the German-speaking nations, the idea that *lederhosen* (short leather trousers) are a symbol of masculine virility is greeted with considerable scepticism. These smartly embroidered three-quarter trousers, usually fashioned from the hide of an elk, goat, calf or pig, were first donned during the 18th century, being the favoured attire of butch Bavarian mountain men who had an additional penchant for leather suspenders, or braces, to hold the trousers up. Old photographs from the period reveal that *lederhosen* could indeed look rather fetching but this was largely due to the athleticism of the models. Nowadays *lederhosen* retailers sell calf implants to make customers' legs seem manlier.

Pick up a pair at Salzburg's Miracle's Wax Museum, on Getriedegasse – and perhaps some Mozart eau de toilette to go with them.

812 BLACKPOOL ILLUMINATIONS, ENGLAND

The queen bee of England's fun-by-the-sea-type resorts is unquestionably Blackpool. It's unashamedly bold and brazen in its efforts to cement its position as the country's second-most visited town after London. Tacky, trashy and, in recent years, a little bit tawdry, Blackpool doesn't care because 16 million people a year don't either. The town is famous for its tower, its three piers, its Pleasure Beach and its Illuminations, a successful ploy to extend the brief summer holiday season. From early September to early November, 8km of the Promenade are illuminated with thousands of electric and neon lights. Tripping the light fantastic down its length is guaranteed to make you smile.

There are direct trains to Blackpool from Manchester and Liverpool; most other arrivals change in Preston.

813 COSPLAY PUBS, TOKYO, JAPAN

If dressing as a schoolgirl, a *Dragon Ball* character or Hello Kitty is your bag, head to Tokyo for a spot of fancy dress in one of numerous cosplay (short for 'costume play') pubs, where stars of manga, graphic novels, video games and anime come to life in intricate, elaborately detailed costumes. The Akihabara district is your best bet for entering a world where blue-haired, silver-clad, stern-expressioned cartoon warriors sip beer and attempt to out-manga each other, while sugar-cute girls play little-girl games and bat their Bambi eyelashes.

Akihabara (often shortened to Akiba) is in central Tokyo. You'll know you're there when you see all the electronics shops.

814 BOLLYWOOD POSTERS, MUMBAI, INDIA

Not only is India's exuberant film industry the world's oldest and largest, it's also responsible for some of the most audacious, bizarre, and charmingly kitsch moments ever captured on celluloid. Naturally, the posters promoting Bollywood films tend to reflect the grandiose weirdness of the industry's conventions. Up until a few years ago posters were hand-painted in every city by local artists with varying degrees of artistic integrity, which sometimes resulted in the movie's stars being unrecognisable. With the introduction of digital artwork these hand-painted posters have been reappraised as works of art, appearing in exhibitions from London to Milan.

Where else to pick up the best examples of the breed but in Mumbai, capital of the Bollywood industry.

815 RUSSIAN KITSCH RESTAURANT, ST PETERSBURG, RUSSIA

Exquisite faux luxuriance exudes from every comical inch of Russia's priceless epicurean nod to the kitsch and famous. Green marble, polished gilded bronzes, garlands of flowers, hand-painted ceiling murals, divine sofas and a gallery adorned with naked busts – if you could dream it up after a night at an opium den, chances are the Russian Kitsch Restaurant has it in spades. Despite its tasteless opulence, the vibe is totally relaxed and the only thing that's stiff is the vodka. The menu reflects the decor's absurdity with mismatched food, such as herring pickled in pistachio, adding to the fun flavour.

Dress in your Eurotrash best and head on down. The Russian Kitsch Restaurant is situated on Vasilievsky Island in St Petersburg.

816 DUOMO, SIENA, ITALY

There's no question that Siena's duomo is sublime. Its vaulted roofs, painted blue with gold stars to mimic the heavens, are charming and the Donatello sculpture of John the Baptist is exquisite. It's just that it's a little…loud. A zebra motif of striped black and white marble is continued from the exterior to the interior columns. There's a hysterically ornate marble-and-porphyry pulpit by Pisano (drop a coin in a slot to see it light up!) and a decorated marble floor. It's marvellously hectic, but after a while you may find yourself wanting to rest your eyes. Look up to those heavens.

Try pici, the traditional Sienese pasta, at the classy Al Marsili on the Via del Castoro.

817 TIKI TI, LOS ANGELES, CALIFORNIA, USA

What kitsch list is complete without a tiki bar? And this pocket-sized version in LA has got to be the ultimate example of the genre. It's got tikis and tiki memorabilia everywhere. It's got a drinks wheel you can spin if you can't decide what to have. It's got a menu of 92 tropical drinks. And it's got two generations of tiki bartenders: the owner, Ray Buhen, opened it in 1961, and now his son and grandson run the bar. Squeeze in and try their concoctions. If you order the Uga Buga, the whole room will yell 'Uga Buga' at you. Try it. It's fun.

The bar usually opens at 4pm. Check the website (http://www.tiki-ti.com) before you visit; sometimes the owners close Tiki Ti to go on vacation.

818 GRUTAS PARK, DRUSKININKAI, LITHUANIA

Also known as 'Stalin World', Grutas Park is a blackly humorous, deeply ironic museum-cum-theme park dedicated to the Soviet occupation of Lithuania, featuring a sculpture garden with statues of former Soviet identities, plus re-creations of gulags including electrified fencing and wooden guard towers. There were plans to herd visitors in via a cattle truck on a railway station, but this was defeated after fierce public disapproval. There are occasional re-enactments of Stalin giving speeches, Soviet pioneers singing about the glory of work and Lenin sitting on a bank fishing.

Got your Pioneer uniform? You're ready to go. Visit www.grutoparkas.lt for information on pricing, location and how to get there.

819 MAO MEMORABILIA, SHANGHAI, CHINA

The father of the Cultural Revolution turns up everywhere, and on everything, in contemporary China. He's on keyrings. He's on ashtrays. He's on wrist watches and rings. He's on cigarette lighters and thermometers and towels and yo-yos. He's a figurine. He's glow-in-the-dark. A bit of Mao tack makes a great souvenir (hey, which of your friends back home is going to say no to a Mao yo-yo?), but show a little sensitivity about flaunting your purchases around in China – there are still deeply rooted feelings concerning Mao, both reverent and traumatised.

A good place to pick up your Mao-based gimcrackery is the French Concession in Shanghai.

820 GROTTENBAHN, LINZ, AUSTRIA

Gnomes are the quintessence of kitsch, and Grottenbahn, at the summit of Pöstlingberg mountain in Linz, has a tonne of 'em. This odd little theme park packs you into a dragon train and trundles you past cavorting gnomes, twinkling stalactites, woodland creatures and Grimm's fairytale characters. Once off the train, it's more Grimm's, with (kind of motheaten) tableaux from the stories. It all has a slightly uneasy air to it (is it the stuffed cats?) and won't be making any 'Austria's prime attractions' lists any time soon, but if it's gnomes and fairylights (and stuffed cats) your soul craves, this one's for you.

Grottenbahn is open from 10am to 5pm. From June through August it stays open until 6pm.

MOST EYE-OPENING WORKPLACES

Take a holiday to watch others work – from super salt miners to the men who make car-shaped coffins.

They may look colourful, but Fès's tanneries stink to high heaven

821 COLCHANI, SALAR DE UYUNI, BOLIVIA

The *campesinos* (farmers) of Colchani are the salt of the earth. Or rather, salt *is* their earth, as they toil on the dazzlingly mind-bending, seemingly never-ending pans of the high-altitude Salar de Uyuni. The parched bed of an ancient lake, this is the world's biggest salt expanse. Here, locals make a living extracting the white stuff, scraping it into small, pyramidical piles before it's removed for processing, or bartered for wool and meat. The more artistic of the excavators can be seen at Bloques de Sal, a small cooperative nearby where ingenious statues and even furniture have been shaped from sparkling saline blocks.

The Hotel de Sal (www.hosteldesal.com), a hotel built from salt blocks, is located in Colchani, 30 minutes from hub-town Uyuni.

822 TOBACCO FIELDS, VIÑALES, CUBA

Smoking cigars might be a dirty habit, but their production is far more attractive. Arguably the world's best dark tobacco originates from verdant Viñales valley – a flashback workplace of neat fields, ox-pulled ploughs and simple farmhouses scattered amid the limestone outcrops of western Cuba. Visits to plantations are easily arranged from local *casas particulares* (private rooms in local houses) – strike out between the leafy greens by shonky bicycle, or hike local tracks during the winter/spring harvest to see the pickers in action. Nearby Pinar del Río's Francisco Donatien factory showcases the production process, from the unbundling of leaves to the rolled, pressed and boxed finished cigars.

Viazul buses (www.viazul.com) regularly connect Havana to Viñales, via Pinar del Río; the journey time is 3¼ hours.

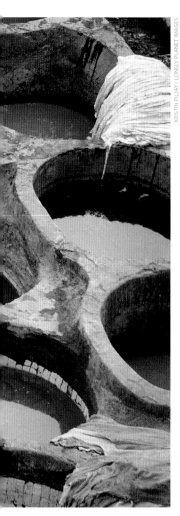

KRISTIN PILAY / LONELY PLANET IMAGES

823 TANNERIES, FÈS, MOROCCO

The first challenge is to find this fascinating workplace – the ancient medina of Fès is a spaghetti of 9400 alleyways of ever-increasing narrowness and convolution: getting lost is a given. Follow your nose, though, and you will eventually unearth the tanneries. Here, men make leather the same way it's been made for 7000 years, dipping animal skins into an artist's palette of mud-brick dye vats to produce the pouffes, bags and babouches that proliferate the souks. But this is definitely a stinky business – cow urine, pigeon poo and fish oils are just some of the ingredients added to the mix.

The leather shops by the tanneries have views down onto the vats; sprigs of mint are offered to mask the smell.

289

824 TSUKIJI FISH MARKET, TOKYO, JAPAN

Rise and shine – it's the early bird that catches the fish at Tsukiji, Tokyo's 250-sq-metre marine market. At 5.30am in this cluster of old warehouses, the tuna auction begins, touting to serious buyers who scrutinise the wares, perhaps trying a tiny morsel before bidding fiercely for prime pieces – the best fetch US$60,000 a hunk. In the wholesale area, tanks of many-tentacled and slimy species await purchase by the restaurateurs able to identify them; the less fish-savvy, however, should head for the outer market where small snack bars serve up – unsurprisingly – the world's freshest sushi breakfasts.

Only 140 visitors may visit the tuna auction per day; visitors are prohibited from the wholesale area before 9am.

825 TESHI HIGH ST, ACCRA, GHANA

Baseball boots, cocoa beans, pineapples and planes – all around human-size and fashioned from wood – line Teshi high street, a dusty suburb of capital Accra. This motley collection – add in cola bottles, Cadillacs, brogues, Bibles – has a macabre purpose: these are fantasy coffins, designed to transport the deceased into the next life, in the style of their past one. A seamstress might have a sewing machine casket; a journalist could be buried in a biro. The trend began in the 1950s, and a peek into Teshi's workshops shows there's nothing the carpenters can't create to ensure a truly original send-off.

Accra has a cheap, efficient transport system of tros-tros (minivans) and taxis; Nkrumah Circle is the main hub.

826 BONDI BEACH, SYDNEY, AUSTRALIA

As Aussie as a can of Foster's, the red-yellow skull caps of Australia's surf lifesavers are indisputable icons of the country. It all began in 1907 on Sydney's Bondi Beach. Or was it at nearby Bronte? The two city sand-strips squabble over the 'World's First Surf Lifesavers' title, but outsiders don't care – they're just grateful these finely honed lifeguards are patrolling the crashing Pacific. What a place to work, though – Bronte is an idyll of Norfolk Island pines and sandstone headlands, while Bondi is undisputed beach-king: big, brash, dotted with bars and beautiful people, it's as iconic as the lifesavers themselves.

A 2.5km coast walk links Bondi Pavilion to Bronte Cliffs, passing Aboriginal rock carvings and Tamarama beach.

827 HAT WORKSHOPS, CUENCA, ECUADOR

Ecuador's hatmakers have every right to be peeved. The so-called 'Panama hat' is not Panamanian at all, but the skilled handiwork of weavers further south, where the special straw that is used in their manufacture is grown. The town of Montecristi twines the finest 'Panamas', but Unesco-listed Cuenca, in the highlands, produces the most number of hats – and is a comelier spot. In this cluster of colonial mansions and dazzling churches, you can find the workshops of master craftsmen: they work early morning and late afternoon, when the straw is more pliable, to create superfinos – hats that are so well woven they can be rolled up to pass through a wedding ring, and emerge without a crease.

Panama-hatmaker Homero Ortega's 'The Magic of the Hat' museum is at its Cuenca base. See www.homeroortega.com.

828 GLASS WORKSHOPS, MURANO, VENICE, ITALY

The furnace roar, the chink of tools, the fierce-red glow of glass being moulded by expert hands… The canalside workshops of Murano are literal hotbeds of activity – activity that's changed little over centuries. The foundries of this island, a spin in a vaporetto (motorboat) away from Venice, have been blowing glass since 1291; now Murano's wares are considered the world's best. Smalto (enamelled glass), millefiori (multicoloured glass), beads, bowls, vases, horses – all trademarked 'Vetro Artistico Murano' – are produced here. The shops are full of delicate objects, but a better option is to watch as a blower transforms molten blob to thing of beauty.

Murano's Glass Museum runs guided Glass In Action tours (Tuesday and Thursday at 2.30pm), which include glass-blowing demonstrations. See www.musei civiciveneziani.it.

Surf's up at Bondi Beach

829 DHOW YARDS, SUR, OMAN

The city of Sur has always relied on the sea. During the 18th and 19th centuries more than 150 vessels docked here daily, while ships loaded with cargo left for India and East Africa. Many of those craft would have been dhows, graceful wooden boats flying large triangular sails. Today, though they've been usurped, and the sound of outboard motors whines about the harbour, carpenters do still make traditional dhows. Stroll down to the shipyard in the early morning, when the skeletons of the half-built boats – at this, Arabia's easternmost point – are set aglow by the region's first sunrise.

Visit Sur between September and November for cooler temperatures and to watch turtles hatch at nearby Ras al-Jinz.

830 RAILWAY WORKSHOP ROAD, RAWALPINDI, PAKISTAN

The heavy-goods vehicles that ply Pakistan are not simple trucks – they're automotive works of art, the trussed-up chorus line of the Karakoram Highway. This epic road north to Kashgar, China, would be distinctly less colourful were it not for the craftsmen of Railway Workshop Road, a hub for truck decoration garages. The craftsmen here take a basic Bedford and weld on ornate extras; they daub flowers, ladies and Islamic texts, and apply as many jangly bits as the chassis will bear. It can cost a year's wages to spruce-up one truck – but it announces to the world you're good to go.

Buses leave for Hunza, on the Karakoram Highway, from Rawalpindi's Pir Wadhai station; sit on the right for the best views.

MOST EYE-OPENING WORKPLACES

BEST SPORTY SIGHTS

You've heard about them in hushed, reverential tones, now check out the spots that set sporting pulses racing.

831 ANCIENT OLYMPIA, GREECE

The Olympic Games trace their ancestry back to Ancient Olympia on Greece's Peloponnese peninsula, where they were held every four years for at least a thousand years until their abolition by killjoy Emperor Theodosius I in 394 AD. The World Heritage site, once home to the 12m-high Statue of Zeus (one of the original Seven Wonders of the World) is still a recognisable complex of temples, priests' dwellings and public buildings. The stadium, which could seat at least 45,000 men (no women were allowed), is entered through an archway. The start and finish lines of the 120m sprint track and the judges' seats still survive.

From Olympia, there are buses to Tripoli and Dimitsana. There are no direct buses to Athens; connections go through Pyrgos.

832 BEACH VOLLEYBALL, RIO DE JANEIRO, BRAZIL

Buff men in bathing suits and babes in bikinis playing volleyball on the sand became a regular sight on the beaches of Ipanema and Copacabana in the heady '80s. It's little wonder the sport enjoyed a meteoric rise in popularity (particularly among spectators) after debuting as an official Olympic sport at the 1996 Atlanta Games – where the Brazilian women won gold and silver. The first international beach volleyball exhibition was held in Rio de Janeiro in 1986.

January to February is the time for Rio's annual Beach Volleyball Competition at Ipanema beach.

292

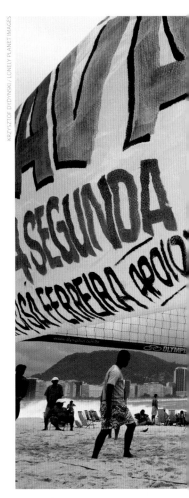

KRZYSZTOF DYDYNSKI / LONELY PLANET IMAGES

833 MONT VENTOUX, FRANCE

It's arguably the most famous climb in the world's most famous bicycle race. Known as the 'Giant of Provence' and taking its name from the French word for 'wind', Mont Ventoux is an imposing and daunting peak that's become a beacon for almost any cyclist in France because of its Tour de France fame. The Tour has crossed Mont Ventoux 14 times, and legions of cyclists have tested their legs against its gradients – it averages around 7.5% over the 22km climb from Bedoin, which ascends more than 1600m. The record for the climb is 55 minutes 51 seconds, set by Spaniard Iban Mayo in 2004.

The route for the Tour de France changes yearly; for updates on the route, visit the tour website at www.letour.com.

834 PIPELINE, HAWAII, USA

On the north shore of the Hawaiian island of O'ahu, the glassy tubes of Banzai Pipeline roar ashore to create the unofficial world mecca of surfing. Winter swells bring in towering 10m waves, creating conditions that can be insane – these waves have claimed more lives than any others on earth. The waves break onto a dangerously shallow reef, while equally hazardous currents pull at the surfers who crowd the sea. The Billabong Pipe Masters – the surf contest to end all surf contests – rounds out the pro surf tour here each year.

To find the Pipeline, head for Ehukai Beach Park and, facing the ocean, walk about 100m to the left.

293

Rio scene: babes, bikinis, buff bods and beach volleyball

The contradiction that is *muay thai* – a graceful ballet of bone-crunching intensity

835 ST ANDREWS, SCOTLAND

Golf's Holy Grail, the oldest and most esteemed course on the planet: golf has been played here since the 15th century, and by 1457 it was apparently so popular that James II had to ban it because it was interfering with his troops' archery practice. Anyone can play the Old Course, since it's a public course, though getting a tee-off time is – literally – something of a lottery. Unless you book months in advance, the only chance you have of playing here is by entering a ballot before 2pm on the day before you wish to play.

Enter the Old Course ballot at www .standrews.org.uk.

836 SUPER BOWL, USA

America's National Football League (NFL) championship, the Super Bowl, is the pinnacle of American football. It's played at a different stadium each year, with no NFL team ever having played on its home turf. Held on the last Sunday in January or the first Sunday in February, it's estimated that 60% of America's TVs tune in to the event. As such, the telecast is also known for extravagantly expensive high-concept advertising, with a 30-second spot costing around US$3 million in 2010.

The venue changes each year; get amped at www.nfl.com. Book accommodation now, if you're lucky you'll find a room in the host city.

837 MUAY THAI, BANGKOK, THAILAND

High kicks and high jinks are all part of the Thai boxing (*muay thai*) spectacle, with wild musical accompaniment to the ceremonial beginning of each match and frenzied betting throughout the stadium. Bouts are limited to five three-minute rounds separated with two-minute breaks. Common blows include high kicks to the neck, elbow thrusts to the face and head, knee hooks to the ribs and low crescent kicks to the calf. Early accounts of Thai boxing date to the 15th century, when it was used in warfare between Myanmar (Burma) and Thailand.

Get ringside at Lumpini stadium on Rama IV Road, Bangkok; book tickets through your hotel. Fight nights are Tuesday, Friday and Saturday.

calls for the 'art' of bullfighting to be left permanently on the shelf. Aficionados see past the lack of competition inherent in each bull being physically impaired before a performance and being pitted against a team of spear-wielding humans, preferring to focus on the skill and bravery presented by a matador's fancy footwork. There are 400 bullrings throughout Spain – testament to this enduring tradition.

Bullfighting season is from March to October; Madrid's Plaza de Toros is a classic bullring. Note that bullfighting has been banned in the Catalonia region from 2012.

838 AUSTRALIAN FOOTBALL LEAGUE GRAND FINAL, MELBOURNE, AUSTRALIA

Melbourne becomes mayhem for that 'one day in September' (usually the last Saturday) when the two best sides slug it out for the Australian Football League (AFL) premiership. The nation's most-watched sport was given the go-ahead in 1858 by the then dominant cricket faculty; it was introduced as a way to keep cricketers fit in the off-season. The final is fought on the hallowed turf of the Melbourne Cricket Ground (MCG) from where every move, play and umpiring decision is televised around the globe.

Melbourne is the home of AFL; for all the info see www.afl.com.au.

839 MONTE CARLO, MONACO

Along some of the most moneyed streets in Europe come some of the richest and most familiar sights in motor sport.

On the streets of this principality, nestled into France's uberchic Côte d'Azur, the all-singing, all-revving Formula One show makes its most glamorous annual appearance, racing along the waterfront as those on multi-million-dollar yachts watch from the Mediterranean shores. Wander the city for familiar Grand Prix scenes, such as the marina or casino, or time your visit (and budget) to be here when the beautiful people and cars are in town in May.

Tickets for the Grand Prix can be purchased online from the Automobile Club of Monaco (www.formula1monaco.com).

840 BULLFIGHTING, MADRID, SPAIN

It's been going on since the middle of the 18th century, which guarantees it a place on the 'culturally significant' shelf, but there are increasingly vociferous

BEST SPORTY SIGHTS

FINEST FLORAL PHENOMENA

Spring blossoms, floral artworks, carpets of wildflowers – all bloomin' marvellous!

841 CHERRY BLOSSOM, KYOTO, JAPAN

It's enough to move you to write a haiku – the delicate beauty of Japan's cherry tree blooms could make poets of us all as it turns city parks and rural hillsides countrywide into petal-fluttered fairylands. But this isn't just a floral phenomenon – it's a cultural one, too: the springtime *sakura* (blossoming) causes this fast-paced nation to slow down for a while, to appreciate the beauty of nature. Witness it best in Kyoto's Maruyama-koen: this park, home to a resplendent weeping cherry tree, bustles with Japanese enjoying *hanami* – blossom-viewing picnics – where they spread their blue tarpaulins and bento boxes under nature's prettiest canopy.

Japan's first blossoms bud on the southern Okinawan Islands from January; Kyoto/Tokyo bloom March/April; Hokkaido's trees bloom in May.

842 GIANT WATER LILIES, RUPUNUNI, GUYANA

Giant green tea trays afloat on inky waters, the *Victoria Amazonica*'s 3m-wide lily pad is strong enough to support a baby. But it's the plant's brief but beautiful flower that impresses most. The lily blossoms at dusk, a bright white bloom with a powerful scent designed to attract – and trap – passing beetles. The next night it buds again, an odourless pink, letting the now pollen-coated bugs escape, before it sinks beneath the surface, job done. Deep in Guyana's rainforests, see wattled jacanas hop about the lilies – the country's national flower – before sunset sparks the flower's fragrant show.

Stay at Rupununi Savannah's Karanambu Ranch (www.karanambu.com), home to a giant otter rehabilitation program, to see spectacular lily ponds.

843 WILDFLOWERS, NAMAQUALAND, SOUTH AFRICA

South Africa's outback is usually a pretty barren place. Stretching up the North Cape to the Namibian border, this is a land of harsh beauty and apparent emptiness. That is, until it rains. Winter downpours initiate one of the world's great transformations, and suddenly the plains erupt with 4000 species of technicolour wildflowers: daisies, herbs, aloes; orange, yellow, pink, purple – a blanket of floral finery. It's an unpredictable display – the intensity and timing of the blooms depend on rainfall and sunshine (for instance, the buds might not open on cloudy days). But, with luck, you'll see Mother Nature at her flowery finest.

Flowers tend to bloom from August to October. Drive the N7 highway between Garies and Springbok for a good chance of flower viewing.

844 LAVENDER FIELDS, PROVENCE, FRANCE

No amount of purple prose does justice to this spectacle in the south of France. Come summertime the fields of Provence are awash with lavender – row upon fragrant row of the stuff, mingling with the golden wheat and yellow sunflowers. Lavender used to grow wild in the region's rocky limestone soil, but by the 20th century man had taken over, ordering it into pleasingly neat ranks to better reap its precious perfume. Now it's made into a range of products, best sampled at local fêtes around the Luberon massifs or on the plateaux of Salut, where villagers celebrate their precious purple harvest.

Visit from mid-June to early August, when the scent is strongest and the colour deepest; July–August is best for sunflowers.

845 KITULO NATIONAL PARK, TANZANIA

Welcome to the Garden of God. Or the Serengeti of Flowers. Take your pick of local nicknames, both are equally applicable to this little-known national park in the Southern Highlands of Tanzania. Hiking here – over montane grassland, 3000m up – is good year-round, but during the rains something special happens: 45 species of orchid, as well as red-hot pokers, honey-peas, proteas, giant lobelias, lilies, and a botanist's lottery-win of other species inflames the plains. Better still, hundred of butterflies and birds –from the rare Denham's bustard to endangered blue swallows – are drawn to this floral fireworks display.

Visit during the rainy season (December to April) for the best blooms; September to November is better for hiking.

846 'PUPPY', GUGGENHEIM, BILBAO, SPAIN

High art and horticulture make an unlikely but uplifting union at Bilbao's iconic Guggenheim Museum. Sitting outside the entrance is a 12m-tall pooch made of marigolds, petunias, begonias and other bedding plants, mounted on a steel frame to create a multicoloured, continually growing floral fur. This West Highland terrier-made-topiary is the brainchild of Jeff Koons, a modern artist preoccupied with the proliferation of advertising and mass entertainment in our media-saturated times. As such, *Puppy* can be read as an 'allegory of contemporary culture', cleverly 'juxtaposing cultural references'. Or you might just think a giant flowery dog is really cute.

The Guggenheim (www.guggenheim -bilbao.es) is open 10am to 8pm Tuesday to Sunday (open Monday in July and August); the admission price includes an audio guide.

847 FLOWER CARPET, BRUSSELS, BELGIUM

Did you know that Belgium cultivates 60 million begonias every year? And to look at Brussels' huge biennial Flower Carpet display you'd think every one of them was there, decorating the capital's Grand Place in fine floral fashion. They're not, but it takes around 750,000 of these hardy but beautiful blooms to make what has to be the world's most fragrant tapestry. Every two years a team of 100 gardeners spends months designing a new 'picture' made up of many-hued begonias; then, in just four hours, they transform a 77m by 24m expanse of city paving into a piece of petalled art.

The next carpet will be laid on 15 August 2012; visit at night, when light shows illuminate the flowers. For more, see www.flowercarpet.be.

848 FLORES DE MAYO, PHILIPPINES

In May, the Philippines pongs. In a good way. At this time of year sees the month-long Flowers of May festival, when the scents of ylang-ylang, hibiscus, calachuchi and sampaguita fill the air. This is the start of the wet season and, as the rains arrive, a bounty of thirsty flowers begins to blossom. To say thanks, this predominantly Catholic nation makes offerings to the Virgin Mary throughout the month, with girls dressed in white laying petals down in churches and the Santacruzan (Holy Cross) procession seeing a carnival king and queen parade the streets under a canopy of blooms.

The *habagat* (southwest monsoon) hits the Philippines from May to October; the dry season for most of the country is from November to April.

849 BLOEMENCORSO, ZUNDERT, THE NETHERLANDS

Flower parades are held throughout the bloom-loving Netherlands, but one of the biggest is the Bloemencorso of Zundert. Each spring, gorgeously decorated, multicoloured floats in the shape of animals and fantastical creatures pass through the streets of the town near the Belgian border, each one of them constructed entirely from flowers. The floats are accompanied by marching bands, costumed performers and thousands of spectators. Teams of designers spend months on their amazing creations, using something like 500,000 dahlias in each float, and vying for coveted prizes as the town is taken over by 'flower fever'.

Bloemencorso takes place on the first Sunday in September. Check out the memorials to Vincent Van Gogh while you're there - this is his home town.

850 CHELSEA FLOWER SHOW, LONDON, ENGLAND

Touting itself as the world's most famous flower show, the Chelsea Flower Show has been described as the horticulturalist's Mt Everest. Extraordinary floral displays and gardens by international landscape artists draw visitors from all over the world in a colourful and sweetly-scented extravaganza. Flowers that have never been seen before are often unveiled. The prestigious event run by the Royal Horticultural Society has nearly a century of tradition behind it and garners huge media attention, so get in quick if you don't want to miss out on tickets.

The show is held over five days in late May on the grounds of the Royal Hospital, London.

MOST MAGNIFICENT MOSQUES

From pure golden domes to dry mud walls and converted cathedrals – Muslim places of worship take many forms. Make your pilgrimage to some of the most stunning.

851 KUBAH MAS MOSQUE, DEPOK, INDONESIA

Throughout history, religious architecture has been flamboyant and overstated. Cathedrals, temples and synagogues form some of our richest architectural heritage, designed to win hearts and minds with shows of lavish wealth and unrivalled levels of craftsmanship. Islam can certainly hold its own in this game and Indonesia is home to one of the world's flashiest examples. Known as the 'Golden Dome' mosque, Kubah Mas was constructed in 2001 and funded entirely by a private benefactor. It features floors of the finest Italian granite, crystal chandeliers and domes of 24-carat gold – to some this mosque might have a touch of the emperor's new clothes about it, but the effect is breathtaking nonetheless.

Although not part of Jakarta, urban sprawl means it's hard to tell where the capital ends and Depok begins. Trains from Jakarta take 30 to 60 minutes.

852 LALA MUSTAFA PAŞA MOSQUE, FAMAGUSTA, CYPRUS

Cyprus is a land of contrasts, torn between Greek and Turkish lineage. This 14th-century mosque is actually in Turkish Famagusta, known locally as Gazimağusa, and it used to be a cathedral. Consecrated as St Nicholas' in 1328, at first glance this seems like a classical French structure with ornate design and rich tracery detail. But what's this? Look to the sky and something's missing. The soaring limestone towers that once graced the western elevation are no longer – destroyed during the Ottoman Empire and subsequently replaced with a single incongruous minaret. Little original decor remains, save a solitary stained-glass window high in the front facade.

If you're lucky enough to find the mosque-keeper, ask him to show you the hidden stone slab etched with a medieval depiction of St Nicholas.

853 AL-HARAM MOSQUE, MECCA, SAUDI ARABIA

This is the big one. Every year millions of Muslims travel to Saudi Arabia in the world's largest gathering of humanity. The haj, Islam's sacred pilgrimage, defines the city of Mecca and the Al-Haram Mosque is like no other on earth. The name simply means 'The Great Mosque', and it's almost unimaginably large – the complex accommodates 800,000 worshippers on a regular basis and up to four million during haj. Centrally located is the Kaaba, the sacred building towards which all Muslims pray and around which devotees process hypnotically at the peak of the pilgrimage.

Mecca is in eastern Saudi Arabia, 75km inland from the Red Sea city of Jeddah. Regular flights connect Mecca to the capital, Riyadh (www.saudiairlines.com).

854 GREAT OMARI MOSQUE, GAZA, PALESTINIAN TERRITORIES

Life is hard in the world's most hotly disputed territory, and the Great Omari Mosque has had a tough life. The oldest Islamic place of worship in Gaza, the mosque has been pushed and pulled asunder as successive empires stamped their authority on this ancient site. Modest by modern standards, the beautiful sandstone edifice wears its influences with grace. The symmetrical arches of the main fascia resonate with ecclesiastical style, while some of the internal columns are believed to be of ancient synagogue origin.

Great Omari Mosque is on Omar Mukhtar Street in the Old City area of Gaza. Seek consular assistance for up-to-date travel and visa advice.

855 DJENNÉ MOSQUE, MALI

The mosque in the island-bound Mali town of Djenné seduces travellers with the mud-brick hue of its fortress-like exterior and the large supporting cast of wooden beams that protrude through the walls into the brilliance of the African sun. So captivating is this earthen marvel, the world's largest mud-brick structure, that it'll make little difference to your experience to learn that the current building only dates from 1907. It was modelled on the Grande Mosquée erected on the same site in 1280; the original building fell into ruin in the 19th century.

Technically, non-Muslims are not allowed inside but locals will offer to take you in for a price to be negotiated; remember to cover up.

Mud-brick seduction: Djenné mosque, Mali

300

İstanbul's wonderful Aya Sofya

856 AYA SOFYA, İSTANBUL, TURKEY

No, it doesn't honour some saintly Sophia – this astonishing construction was named for divine wisdom ('sophos' in Greek). The name is apt: the incredible beauty of this ancient building, created by the Byzantine Emperor Justinian in 537 AD, is due to the cunning of the innovative architects who perched its vast, seemingly floating 30m dome on pendentives and hidden pillars. Converted to a mosque after the Ottoman invasion of 1453, Aya Sofya is now a secular monument – but when shafts of sunlight strike the gold mosaics of its cavernous interior, you might be forgiven for experiencing a religious moment.

The mosque is in Sultanahmet, İstanbul's main historic district, which is best explored on foot. Opening times are from 9am to 4pm daily except Monday.

857 SHAH FAISAL MOSQUE, ISLAMABAD, PAKISTAN

This mosque was designed in the form of a Bedouin's tent – but no desert nomad ever slept under a canvas like this. Pinned at each corner by four needle-like minarets that soar 90m, the pyramid-shaped prayer hall appears to hover serenely on an elevated plateau overlooking the city. For such a huge structure – the mosque is Pakistan's largest and can accommodate upwards of 250,000 worshippers – the effect is mesmeric, especially at night or during festivals such as Eid, when the illumination is spectacular. The interior is no less impressive, covered in striking white marble and decorated with mosaics and an elaborate Turkish-style chandelier.

Islamabad is surrounded by hills and therefore has a relatively moderate climate. Summers can be oppressive, so the cooler months (October to December) are a good time to visit.

858 GREAT MOSQUE OF XĪ'ĀN, CHINA

The Silk Road trade routes brought more to China than mere commercial gain. In the 7th century merchants from Persia and Afghanistan also brought their religion and those who settled became the forefathers of the country's Muslim community. Built in 742, under the Tang dynasty, the Great Mosque of Xī'ān is truly unique and as beguiling as the city's more famous Terracotta Warriors. Despite this being a holy Muslim site, there's nothing remotely Islamic about the design. With ornate arched pergolas, verdant landscaped gardens and nary a minaret in sight, the untrained eye would be forgiven for thinking this is a classic Chinese temple.

This is the only Chinese mosque to accept visitors, daily from 8am to 7.30pm – its location near the famous Bell Tower makes it easy to find.

859 SULTAN MOSQUE, SINGAPORE

The British statesman Sir Stamford Raffles, founder of Singapore, funded the original construction of this iconic mosque with a S$3000 grant in 1824. As the island's Muslim community grew, the number of worshippers increased and by the time the mosque celebrated its centenary it was in need of expansion. In keeping with Singapore's diversity the new plans mixed classical Moorish, Turkish and Persian themes, topped off with an ornate golden dome that crowns the 5000-capacity prayer hall.

Take the MRT to Bugis to find Sultan Mosque. You're also just a short walk from the Sikh temples of Little India.

860 IMAM MOSQUE, IRAN

Headlining beside one of the world's largest squares, Esfahan's Imam Mosque is a tiled wonder. Completely covered, inside and out, with pale blue and yellow ceramic tiles (an Esfahan trademark), it's a stunning 17th-century mosque, with its tiles seemingly changing colour depending on the light conditions. The main dome is 54m high and intricately patterned in a stylised floral mosaic, while the magnificent 30m-high portal is a supreme example of architectural styles from the Safavid period (1502 to 1772).

There are daily flights to Esfahan from Tehran and Mashhad. Once there the easiest way to get around is by bus.

MOST MAGNIFICENT MOSQUES

UGLIEST BEASTS

True, beauty is in the eye of the beholder – but some of these creatures might leave you looking the other way...

'Hey, human – you're no oil painting yourself!' An aye-aye lays down the law

861 PROBOSCIS MONKEY, SUNGAI KINABATANGAN, MALAYSIAN BORNEO

The ugliest by a nose? Well, not if you're a female proboscis. In the riverine forests of Malaysian Borneo, it's the males with the hugest hooters that have most luck with the ladies. Only the boys of this unmistakable monkey species boast such fine olfactory organs; bulbous, and drooping obscenely from their rosy pink faces, these snouts are thought to play a part in both sexual selection and howling volume. But mostly they just make the proboscis look odd – and gave rise to their original Malay name, *orang belanda* or 'Dutchman', a none-too-PC nod to the region's first, apparently big-nosed colonisers.

Arrange a trip into the Kinabatangan region from Sandakan or Kota Kinabalu. Wet season, when travel is harder, is from October to March.

862 MANATEE, CRYSTAL RIVER, FLORIDA, USA

That these fat and wrinkly sea cows were once mistaken for mermaids seems barely believable – the sailors responsible had clearly been tucking into the rum, or celibate at sea too long. But that's the myth surrounding the lumbering manatee – more tuskless walrus crossed with aquatic elephant than seductive marine maiden. These 400kg, 3m-long creatures with stumpy flippers and a sizeable girth possess limited obvious beauty, though there's something endearing about their sorrowful eyes. To decide for yourself, head to the brackish waters of Florida's Crystal River, where you can come face to whiskered snout with the West Indian subspecies.

If you swim with manatee, obey interaction guidelines: snorkel rather than dive, keep your distance and do not touch.

863 AYE-AYE, AYE-AYE ISLAND, MADAGASCAR

If you wanted to see an aye-aye, you'd think Aye-Aye Island would be the place to go. But sightings of this frankly terrifying-looking lemur aren't guaranteed even here – which might be no bad thing. Madagascans believe the aye-aye is an augury of evil, and it certainly looks the part: this gremlin primate has orange bug eyes, leathery ears and skeletal black fingers, its middle digit extending, old-crone-like, longer than the rest. The aye-aye uses this gruesome tool to tap-tap on bark, then scrape out the bugs it detects within. Is it a bad omen? Probably not. But is it creepy? Yes indeed.

Aye-Aye Island is privately owned; visits are arranged via the Chez Roger Hotel in nearby Mananara.

303

864 PLATYPUS, EUNGELLA NATIONAL PARK, AUSTRALIA

OK, so we think it's cute now, but time was when this hodgepodge critter seemed a quite unnatural sight. The first platypus skin arrived at the British Museum in 1798 – and the experts there thought it a hoax: surely some joker had just sewn together bits of other creatures? But no, this Australian oddity is very much real. Warm-blooded like a mammal, egg-laying like a reptile, it has venom strong enough to kill a dog and uses electricity to snuffle out food. In short, the tutti-frutti ice cream of the animal world – mixed up, weird, but rather lovely for it.

The viewing platform at Broken River, in Queensland's Eungella National Park, offers good sightings; visit at dawn and dusk.

865 NARCISSE SNAKE PITS, MANITOBA, CANADA

There are uglier snakes than the red-sided garter. But still, 10,000 of them in one hole, writhing around in a massive, sinuous squirm, is enough to induce an onset of ophidiophobia. The snakes like the limestone by the shores of Lake Winnipeg – dens in the bedrock provide warmth over winter. But come spring it's time to copulate: in April/May the herptiles-on-heat emerge into the pits for a mating frenzy. With a dangerous dash across Highway 17 they disperse for the summer, before regrouping in autumn to huddle down again. Simply, it's an incredible wildlife spectacle – *and* the stuff of nightmares.

The Snake Pits are on Highway 17, 6km north of Narcisse, and a two-hour drive from Winnipeg.

866 STAR-NOSED MOLE, EASTERN USA/CANADA

Mother Nature has produced some oddballs, but the star-nosed mole could just take the biscuit. In body it's a fairly bog-standard mole – velvety fur, feet designed for digging. But in face, it's more science-fiction. Forget cutesy snuffling nostrils; here instead sit 22 bright-pink tentacles, exploding like a tropical flower – or man-eating triffid… It's alarming to say the least, but useful if you're a star-nosed mole – these unsightly, unlikely protrusions are the most sensitive appendages in the mammalian world, allowing the critter to sense, search out and consume up to 12 separate foodstuffs a second. A very snappy (if not pretty) schnozz.

Star-nosed moles are found in North America, from Georgia to Newfoundland; look for their hills in wet lowlands and marshes.

867 BALD UAKARI, YAVARI RIVER, PERU/BRAZIL

Well, wouldn't you be embarrassed if you looked like this? The permanent blush of the bald uakari is an alarming sight; its red head and hairless scalp make it look badly sunburned – and explain why locals dubbed it the 'English monkey'. But these attributes are actually a sign of good health; indeed, the redder the head the better! Sadly the species isn't in such great shape – confined to a small patch of Amazonian forest, bald uakaris are highly endangered. But sail around Lago Preto, a conservation concession set up largely to protect them, and you might spot a crimson critter.

Travellers can join expeditions to Lago Preto Conservation Concession to observe wild red uakaris with environmental charity Earthwatch (www.earthwatch.org).

868 ELEPHANT SEAL, SOUTH GEORGIA

In polite circles it's considered rude to comment on someone's weight – but, come on, this is one obese beast. The elephant seal is the world's largest fin-footed mammal; the males particularly flop about on land like Jabba the Hutts – only with much bigger noses. It's this flabby proboscis that lends the species its name, and enables it to produce such thundering roars when after female attention. So imagine the scene in South Georgia come mating season: the South Atlantic isle is home to around 113,000 breeding pairs, the beaches packed with cantankerous Lotharios fighting loudly over who gets to be the main, massive man.

Some cruises from Ushuaia, Argentina, sail to Antarctica via South Georgia; trips run November to March and take around two weeks.

'You sure this is my home planet?' A star-nosed mole seeks directions

869 MARABOU STORK, LUANGWA VALLEY, ZAMBIA

An unattractive bird, with even less attractive habits, the marabou doesn't do itself any favours – particularly in the wildlife-profuse Luangwa Valley, where innumerable prettier creatures roam. This 1.5m stork has a psoriatic scalp, bald bar a few tufts – like a turkey improperly plucked. Then there's the pendulous sack dangling from its throat, equally off-putting whether inflated for courtship or sagging like an unfilled sausage. These 'undertaker birds' carry a whiff of death, their feathers like a black cape, their diet largely carrion. The fact that they defecate on their own legs –

a noisome cooling mechanism – completes an already unpleasant picture.

Visit the Luangwa Valley during the dry season (May to August) for good game viewing; marabous prefer dry, arid conditions.

870 YAK, THE HIMALAYA

Those big, hairy bovines are undoubtedly the signature beasts of the Himalaya; you'll encounter them in Tibet, Nepal, Bhutan and the mountain regions of India. Well, more correctly you might encounter a *nak* or a *dri* (a female yak) or a *dzokpyo* or a *dzum* (a more easily domesticated yak-cow crossbreed).

Whatever the name, you're not likely to find them until you're high in the mountains: yaks aren't happy below 3000m. Trekking in Tibet you may find a yak train toting your group's camping gear, but if you don't get into the mountains you may still find yak on your restaurant table, as yak burger.

Yak burgers, yak steaks and other yak dishes feature on many Kathmandu menus, but Lhasa in Tibet is undoubtedly the yak cuisine capital.

UGLIEST BEASTS

BEST PLACES OF REST

Above ground or six feet under, these are prime spots for both the living and the dead.

873 CITY OF THE DEAD, CAIRO, EGYPT

This is the most curious cemetery in the world: it's not only a city of the dead, but of the living. Chronic housing shortages in Cairo have driven families to live in tombs in the large cemeteries on the city's outskirts. Traditionally, Egyptians buried their dead surrounded by rooms, so that relatives could live in them during the long mourning period. These are now occupied by squatters – often large families – who use the gravestones as tables, and dry their laundry on lines between tombstones.

It's known more properly as the Northern Cemetery (Al-Qarafa). It's an easy walk heading east from Midan al-Hussein along Sharia al-Azhar.

871 HOLLYWOOD FOREVER CEMETERY, LOS ANGELES, CALIFORNIA, USA

These immaculate lawns and stately memorials are the final picture for much of Hollywood royalty. The glamorous graves at the back of Paramount studios are a veritable Milky Way of departed glitterati, including Rudolph Valentino, Fay Wray, Douglas Fairbanks, Harvey Henderson Wilcox (who founded Hollywood, on his ranch), Mel Blanc (the voice of Bugs Bunny; his tombstone reads 'That's all folks') and cenotaphs to Jayne Mansfield and Johnny Ramone, among others. In summer, Angelenos come armed with deckchairs and picnics to watch old movies projected onto a wall. So, it's weird – this *is* LA.

In true over-the-top Hollywood style the cemetery has touch-screen consoles, meaning the dead can truly speak from beyond the grave.

872 PÈRE LACHAISE CEMETERY, PARIS, FRANCE

The world's most-visited cemetery has a star-studded afterlife gathering, with residents as diverse as Edith Piaf, Marcel Proust, Oscar Wilde, Honore de Balzac and Isadora Duncan. It was founded in 1804, but languished until the management had the bright marketing plan of moving the remains of famous people here, such as Molière, to attract business. Follow the graffiti and crowds to the most notorious tomb, that of Jim Morrison – lead singer of the Doors, who died in Paris in 1971. A security guard is posted to prevent excessively rock-and-roll tributes (previously, fans would take drugs and even have sex on the tomb).

Strapped for time or not actually in Paris? Then avail yourself of the official website's virtual tour (www.pere-lachaise.com).

874 HARTSDALE PET CEMETERY, NEW YORK, USA

In 1896 Dr Samuel Johnson, a vet, offered his apple orchard to a bereaved friend as the burial place for his dog. Today Hartsdale, in New York, has 70,000 graves, including those of some famous war dogs, and a memorial to the Red Cross dogs that served during WWI. Famous owners who have had their pooches interred here include Mariah Carey and Diana Ross. The headstones make fascinating reading ('Sport: Born a dog, died a gentleman'). Among the endlessly entertaining names are Bum, Grumpy, Jerk, J Edna Hoover, and a surprising number of pets called Peggy.

No personal mutt to mourn? Worry not; Hartsdale holds an annual War Dog Memorial Celebration (June) and Blessing of the Animals (September).

875 TOMB OF PACAL, MEXICO

In the foothills of the Chiapas mountains lie the remains of the ancient Mayan city of Palenque, set in a tangle of jungle. It's a place of cinematic splendour, complete with rolling mist and thick undergrowth. The city's most famous monument is the Tomb of Pacal (Pacal was the city's 7th-century founder-king). The secret opening to the tomb was discovered, by chance, within the glorious Temple of the Inscriptions, a steep, stepped pyramid. Inside is a limestone sarcophagus, sealed with a lid weighing more than 5 tonnes, inscribed with the now-famous Mayan depictions of Pacal falling into the underworld.

December and January are the best months to visit, in the height of the dry season. Avoid June to August, when the rains are heaviest.

876 TAJ MAHAL, AGRA, INDIA

The Taj Mahal in Agra is surely the world's most beautiful place in which to push up daisies. The 17th-century Mughal emperor Shah Jahan built the mausoleum in memory of his favourite wife, Mumtaz Mahal, using white marble from Rajasthan, crystal from China, turquoise from Tibet and sapphire from Sri Lanka. It's a monument to love, one of the world's most famous buildings and represents the pinnacle of Mughal architecture. But such beauty came at a price: the mammoth cost helped lead to the fall of Shah Jahan and the Mughal empire.

The Taj exudes beauty in the golden dawn light, so an early start provides the most atmospheric visit.

877 NON-CATHOLIC CEMETERY, ROME, ITALY

This overgrown garden in a busy corner of Rome is a surprise. Romantic poets Keats – who died at the unripe age of 26 – and Shelley are buried here. The garden's dominated by a sharp-tipped pyramid: the fanciful tomb of a Roman general with a penchant for Egyptology. The evocative, lushly verdant cemetery is usually deserted, and there seems no more fitting spot for Romantic poets. Seek them out, read the inscription on Keat's grave – 'Here lies one whose name was writ on water' – and weep.

Entry to the cemetery is free but donations are welcomed. It's open Monday to Saturday from 9am to 5pm, and Sunday from 9am to 1pm.

878 CATACOMBS OF ROME, ITALY

Ancient Roman law forbade burial within Rome city limits. Most Romans were cremated, but early Christians were buried in a series of endless, echoing, underground tunnels, out near the old Roman road, the Via Appia. This underground death complex is Rome's most haunting sight – now empty of bodies but retaining early Christian frescos, altars and icons. Three sets of catacombs are open. The largest, di San Callisto, has over 29km of tunnels, and once housed St Cecilia, the patron saint of music, while the martyr St Sebastian was buried in his eponymous catacombs.

Tour-o-phobes look away – visits are escorted and follow a pre-determined route. But hey, do you really want to get lost down there?

879 PYRAMIDS OF GIZA, CAIRO, EGYPT

These pyramids on the outskirts of Cairo may be ancient (dating to around 3200 BC) but they're as space-age as tombs get. They pierce the sky, unperturbed by crowds of hustlers, camels and camcorder-toting tourists. An estimated 20,000 to 30,000 workers built the pyramids, the largest of which is constructed from over two million blocks. Once covered in white limestone, they would have gleamed dazzling white. Inside, the pharaohs were equipped with everything from mummified cats to boats to ferry them into the afterlife.

The pyramids are a 16km cab ride west of Cairo. They're visible from afar, so you'll know if the driver's taking you for a ride.

880 DOGON TOMBS, MALI

A craggy mass rears up from the sun-bleached plain, one of West Africa's most stunning sights. The Bandiagara Escarpment is where the remote Dogon tribe lives. Most extraordinary in this extraordinary place are the tombs. These are tiny buildings set into the cliffs, often halfway up, with no discernible method of approach. They look like they were built by aliens, but were constructed by the Tellem tribe, who lived here before being driven away by the Dogon. Now the Dogon use the inaccessible structures to house their dead, hauling the bodies up on ropes.

Bandiagara is 63km from the bustling town of Sévaré, where there is ample bush-taxi and minibus transport.

GREATEST VIKING SIGHTS

The Viking reign spread fear across Europe for more than 300 years. Want to catch a glimpse of it yourself? Knock back that drinking horn, grab your favourite axe and let's go pillaging.

881 LINNDUCHAILL FORTRESS, ANNAGASSAN, IRELAND

When Vikings spent the winter of 841 in Ireland, two settlements were established. Totally self-sufficient, the projects represented a marked step forward from the usual smash-and-grab raids. But the two forts suffered differing fates. One was abandoned and lost to the land, while the other flourished and became a major city. You've probably heard of it – it's called Dublin. Now the long-lost twin has been found. In 2010 archaeologists began excavations near Annagassan in the northeastern county of Louth. The extensive site has already given up human remains, tools and jewellery and is expected to become of one Europe's most significant Viking discoveries.

Locals have long known of Annagassan's Viking roots – now they celebrate their heritage with an annual festival each August, marked by battle recreations and traditional food.

882 ALTHING, THINGVELLIR NATIONAL PARK, ICELAND

Viking spirit smoulders intensely in Iceland, through fjords, snowfields and deep glacial valleys, but nowhere more so than at the Althing (Alþingi in Icelandic). This is the island's ancient parliament, established in 930 as the annual meeting point where representatives from across the country forged democracy in an attempt to resolve conflict and distribute power. For many, the journey was perilous – up to two weeks through the inhospitable interior, crossing glaciers and fording swollen rivers. Today's trips are somewhat shorter. Day trippers come to this World Heritage site in the Thingvellir National Park to see not only the Althing but also a verdant landscape cleaved asunder by the Mid-Atlantic Ridge faultline.

Tours to Thingvellir can be arranged year-round, but the short summer season (June to August) is the best time to visit, when days are longer.

883 BIRKA & HOVGÅRDEN, BJÖRKÖ ISLAND, SWEDEN

To depict Vikings as mere perpetrators of rape and pillage would be to tell only half the story. Yes, they were fierce and they sure could be brutal, but they also pioneered political and economic expansion in northern Europe and beyond. Sweden's Birka and Hovgården archaeological site has uncovered the most complete Viking trading settlement yet discovered. Located 30km west of Stockholm, 8th-century Birka is Sweden's oldest town and excavations date the Viking occupation to the 9th and 10th centuries. Once of world importance, the town is now reduced to fragmented traces of stone forts, ramparts and jetties, together with the museum that has its own reconstructed settlement.

Why not make like a Viking and head to Birka by boat? Boats depart from Stadshusbron near Stockholm's main train station (see www.stromma.se).

Sophisticated barbarians: the wonders of the Viking Ship Musuem

884 VIKING SHIP MUSEUM, OSLO, NORWAY

What do you do when excavations uncover a Viking ship entombed within a burial mound? It can't just be left in situ, exposed to the elements and liable to rot. So when your country reveals several such finds, the natural thing to do is bring them together under one roof. Oslo's Viking Ship Museum houses two of the finest examples ever uncovered – the *Oseberg* and *Gokstad* – together with fragmentary remains of the *Tune*. The beautifully sleek, oak-built ships were used as burial chambers for nobility, whence they were loaded with all sorts of finery to accompany the Viking leaders to the afterlife.

309

The museum is curated by the University of Oslo and is close to the centre of town. From Jernbanetorget, by the train station, take bus 30 to Bygdøy.

L'Anse aux Meadows: a long way from home for the Norsemen

885 JELLING MOUNDS, RUNIC STONES & CHURCH, DENMARK

In the 10th century Denmark was ruled by Viking King Gorm and his wife, Queen Thyre, and Jelling was their royal manor. Like all good monarchs, they appreciated grand acts of symbolism and the complex is remarkable for flat-topped burial mounds – 70m wide and 10m high – and runic stones that stand in their memory. Thyre's memorial came first, built by Gorm upon her death. Their son, the wonderfully named Harald Bluetooth, would later honour his father and add his own stamp by building a wooden church to mark his introduction of Christianity to Denmark. Today's church dates from the 12th century and contains the country's earliest murals.

Kongernes Jelling (www.kongernesjelling .dk) is the museum and information centre that tells the story of this extensive complex – admission is free.

886 ISLE OF MAN

Iceland claims to have the world's oldest democratic parliament but the Isle of Man, plonked in the middle of the sea between England and Ireland, has a title every bit as impressive. This tiny but beautiful island of 80,000 people has boasted a *continuous* democratic parliament – known as the Tynwald – since 979 (Iceland's governmental rule was discontinued between 1799 and 1844). The island's Viking-era attractions include burial grounds, runic crosses and castles founded during the invasions. The Manx people love this history – so much so that they have a Viking association, annual festival and 'Tynwald Day' celebration to mark the yearly meeting of parliament.

Tynwald Day and the Viking Festival both take place in early July – the Isle of Man Steam Packet (www.steam-packet.com) operates ferries from the UK mainland.

887 L'ANSE AUX MEADOWS, NEWFOUNDLAND, CANADA

OK, it's got a very un-Viking-like French name (translated into English as Meadow Cove), but make no mistake; hard-as-nails Norsemen once prowled these shores. And they would have felt right at home, so similar to northern Europe's landscapes are the craggy coves, inlets and beaches of Newfoundland. L'Anse aux Meadows is the only known Viking village in North America, making it the earliest European presence on American soil. The remains of three sod-roofed timber longhouses and five smaller buildings were discovered at the 11th-century settlement – beautifully reconstructed for modern visitors – and the site was awarded Unesco World Heritage status in 1978.

L'Anse aux Meadows is 430km north of the town of Deer Lake, so you'll need a place to stay. Break the journey and bed down at the suitably named Valhalla Lodge (www.valhalla-lodge.com).

888 JOMSVIKINGS, EUROPE

The world's largest Viking re-enactment society (yep, there is such a thing) is a macho and hairy bunch that rampages orgiastically around various parts of Europe. Going under the grandiose banner of the 'Viking Age Elite Brotherhood', these robust chaps offer the perfect opportunity to haul out your warrior regalia. The group's adventures are based on the capers of the original Jomsvikings, a 10th-century Baltic military brotherhood. Most current 'warriors' have over a decade of so-called fighting experience beneath their, um, heavily-studded belts. Novices can join the scene at festivals, markets and general bludgeonings across the continent.

Is nowhere safe? Vikings have invaded the web! See where they'll be in real life by checking the events calendar at www.jomsvikings.com.

889 SHETLAND ISLANDS, SCOTLAND

As rampaging Viking conquests go, Scotland made for easy pickings. Nordic raiders made merry on the gnarly shores of the North Sea coast, close to home and similar in terrain. Lying 320km from western Norway – little more than a day's sailing – the Shetland Islands were a stepping stone to Iceland, Greenland and America. Take your pick from sights such as more than 30 longhouse discoveries on the island of Unst or the extensive remains of the Jarlshof settlement. The best sight happens once a year, when locals celebrate their heritage by burning a replica longship in the raucous Up-Helly-Aa festival.

Up-Helly-Aa takes place annually, on the last Tuesday of January. Get to Shetland by ferry (www.northlinkferries.co.uk) or plane (www.loganair.co.uk).

890 LOFOTR VIKING MUSEUM, BORG, NORWAY

In Norway's distant northern climes, on the remote Lofoten archipelago within the Arctic Circle, you can play at being a Viking in a land unchanged for thousands of years. The soaring sea cliffs, sweeping green pastures and snowcapped mountains are far removed from modern life, but are the ideal backdrop for the Lofotr Viking Museum. This former Iron Age farm is the site of the largest known Viking building, the beautifully recreated 83m-long chieftain's longhouse, together with a working blacksmith's forge and real-life, rowable ship. Yes, it's a long journey to get there, but that never deterred the real Vikings – what are you waiting for?

Fly from Oslo to Harstad/Narvik or Bodø, from where you can take another flight, use a ferry or travel the road bridge to Lofoten.

GREATEST VIKING SIGHTS

MOST CLASSIC ART DECO BUILDINGS

Streamlined, swish and deco fabulous – these are the buildings that put the style on the map.

891 PALACIO SALVO, MONTEVIDEO, URUGUAY

In its day the Palacio Salvo was the tallest building in South America, and it's still got an air of grandeur about it. That looming tower is a symbol of Montevideo and appears on hundreds of postcards. It was built as a hotel in 1928, but these days it's given over to apartments and offices. It may not play any public role in the city's life but the 100m-tall building still captures the imagination. Plus, from some angles it looks like a surprised elephant robot, and you can't get cooler than that.

You'll find the Palacio Salvo on the Plaza Independencia, the city's main square.

892 BILTMORE HOTEL, MIAMI, FLORIDA, USA

This magnificent edifice – butter-yellow, with arches, palm trees and a high white cupola lending a Moorish feel – once housed a speakeasy run by Al Capone. Inside it's an extravaganza of marble, mahogany, leadlight and hand-painted frescos. The hotel was built in the Jazz Age and in its heyday counted Ginger Rogers, Bing Crosby, Judy Garland and the Duke and Duchess of Windsor among its regulars. Its spectacularly huge pool saved the hotel's bacon during the Great Depression by hosting popular aquatic shows with alligator wrestling and water nymphs; Johnny Weissmuller, the most famous screen Tarzan, was once a swimming instructor here.

Book or just have a look at www.biltmorehotel.com. If a room's out of your reach, consider dropping by for afternoon tea or a guided tour.

RICHARD CUMMINS / LONELY PLANET IMAGES

893 RADIO CITY MUSIC HALL, NEW YORK, USA

John D Rockefeller Jnr had Radio City built as a symbol of hope and renewal in the midst of Great Depression gloom. And what a symbol it is. The largest indoor theatre in the world, an art deco fantasia with a proscenium arch like a huge sun, an immense Wurlitzer organ and a gold curtain (the biggest theatre curtain in the world), the Music Hall can even make its own weather using its original mechanisms. And all that's before the Rockettes come on stage. You'd have to be pretty depressed to resist its magic.

If you're in New York at Christmas, you just have to catch the lighting of the Christmas tree at Radio City Music Hall. Guaranteed to melt a Grinch.

894 CHRYSLER BUILDING, NEW YORK, USA

Architect William van Alen planned the dramatic unveiling of the Chrysler Building's ornate tower by assembling it inside the building. Made of stainless steel and modelled on the hubcaps used on Chrysler cars of the late 1920s, the completed spire was hoisted into position in 1½ hours. Completed in 1930, the art deco building's 77 floors and ornamental top made it the world's highest structure – not just scraping the sky but piercing it at 319m.

The Chrysler is best viewed from the Empire State Building's observation deck; visit day and night to get the full effect of the changing skies over New York City.

313

Miami's Biltmore is such an iconic piece of architecture it's easy to forget its original purpose: as a hotel, and a grand one at that

Disguised beneath 50 years of revolutionary dust, Havana hides some of the most quintessential art deco monuments on the planet

895 MUNICIPAL THEATRE, NAPIER, NEW ZEALAND

The Napier of today is the silver lining of the dark cloud that was New Zealand's worst natural disaster. Rebuilt after the 1931 earthquake in the popular styles of the time, the city retains a unique concentration of art deco buildings. Architecture obsessives flock here from all over the world, and the city even holds a deco festival. One of the prime spots on aficionados' lists is the restored Municipal Theatre with its deco signage, domed foyer, decorative seats and space-station light fittings. The theatre holds performances and hosts functions.

The theatre is on Tennyson Street, as is Café Ujazi with its excellent coffee. Try the *rewana* special, a big breakfast on traditional Maori bread.

896 BACARDI BUILDING, HAVANA, CUBA

Finished in 1929, the magnificent Edificio Bacardí, topped with the Bacardi bat, is a triumph of art deco architecture with a whole host of lavish fittings that somehow manage to make kitschy look cool. The way it's hemmed in by other buildings makes it hard to get a full kaleidoscopic view of the structure from street level, though the opulent bell tower can be glimpsed from all over Havana. It's even more satisfying to look at when you know that the gold and white tiles are supposed to represent the colours of the company's rums. There's a bar in the lobby, natch.

You'll find the building on the Avenue de las Misiones.

897 WILTERN THEATER, LOS ANGELES, CALIFORNIA, USA

Like a visitor from Emerald City, the Wiltern sits on the corner of Wilshire and Western (get it?) in a pale glory of turquoise glazed tiling. It was once the Warner Brothers Theater and opened in 1931, but its first run, dogged by the Great Depression, was cut short after only a year. Its mixed fortunes continued and it limped along before being renovated in the '80s. And thank goodness for that, as the interior is a gem, with a sunburst roof, terrazzo floors, murals, decorative tiles and a vast organ.

These days the Wiltern hosts a great selection of indie music. It's run by Live Nation – check out www.livenation.com for what's coming up.

898 REGAL CINEMA, MUMBAI, INDIA

It might seem like an odd match – the hectic pace and colour of Bollywood and all-singing, all-dancing Indian filmgoers combined with the cool streamlined outlines of an art deco cinema. But because this is Mumbai, a film-obsessed, confident city that loves to mix eclectic elements into a just-right whole, it works. And because the Regal is in Colaba, where peeling pastel deco sits happily amid the palm trees and steamy air, it seems right at home. Its sleek lemon exterior leads to a charming pale-blue interior with classical relief sculptures and geometric patterns.

Drop into Bade Miya, a much-loved street stall on Tulloch Road, for a post-show snack.

899 MAISON GUERLAIN, PARIS, FRANCE

Deco was born in Paris, and although it's not a particularly deco city, there are still some *exquise* examples of the style lurking around. One of these is the swish Guerlain boutique on the Champs-Élysées. Guerlain is Paris' most famous parfumerie, and its shop is one of the most beautiful in the city. With its shimmering mirror-and-marble and wrought-iron deco interior, it's a reminder of the former glory days of the Champs-Élysées, when you could have walked a boulevard lined with these treasures. Treat your eyes as well as your pulse points.

Cool your shop-sore heels in the Piscine Pontoise, an airy deco swimming pool in the Latin Quarter.

900 HOTEL LOCARNO, ROME, ITALY

Exuding the raffish charm of a well-to-do rogue, the Locarno resembles an art deco film set. In fact in 1978 it starred in its own film, *Hotel Locarno*. It was built in 1925 and it's a very lush, gold-and-wrought-iron, Italian version of deco, almost harking back to nouveau, with its stained glass and birdcage lift. But those rooms papered in elaborate gold fabric and fitted with pale wooden beds are pure deco. There's a divine little courtyard where you can relax on wrought-iron chairs with a cocktail.

The Locarno is in the Campo Marzio neighbourhood, which puts it near the Spanish Steps, Piazza del Popolo and the Villa Borghese.

MOST CLASSIC ART DECO BUILDINGS

SOARING SPIRES & NEEDLES

Historic, artistic or just really, really tall – look up at the world's best sky-piercers.

903 CAPTAIN COOK OBELISK, BOTANY BAY, AUSTRALIA

It's not a big monument – which is odd considering the size of the discovery it commemorates. In the nondescript town of Kurnell, on the edge of Botany Bay National Park, sits a diminutive white spire marking the spot where James Cook first landed in 1770, thus 'finding' Australia. The immediate landscape is little changed since the Captain's day: rugged coast, woodlands of wattle and eucalypt, sandstone cliffs, crashing waves. Life for the Aborigines, however – who Cook first met right here – has altered beyond recognition. Walks from the obelisk, leading around the park, show the bay's natural and historical legacy.

The 1.1km Burrawang Loop walking trail leads from the park's visitor centre to the Cook Obelisk with interpretive signs en route.

901 ROME STELE, AKSUM, ETHIOPIA

With ploughshares negotiating obelisks and women doing laundry in the Queen of Sheba's Bath, it's hard to picture today's Aksum – a dusty town in far north Ethiopia – as a one-time world heavyweight. Aksum dominated Red Sea trade routes from 400 BC; as such it's littered with treasures, including fields of ancient stelae. There are more than 100 of these engraved-granite obelisks, grand monuments that once announced the city's stature. Most notable is the 24m Rome Stele – pinched on the orders of Mussolini and erected in the Italian capital, it wasn't until 2008 that it was restored to its rightful place.

Visit during one of Aksum's religious festivals, such as Timkat (January) or the celebration of Maryam of Zion (late November).

902 OXFORD UNIVERSITY, ENGLAND

Ah, those dreaming spires, the air of antiquated academia, boats being punted down the languid Thames… Oxford is quintessential England: set on the banks of the country's most famous river, its oldest university (teaching has taken place here since 1096) has retained an astonishing architectural harmony – best seen from above. Ascend the 124 steps to the top of the Church of St Mary the Virgin – itself boasting a spectacular spire – to look over the surrounding turrets, towers and gargoyles. Or leave the city centre for nearby Boars Hills, where a full panorama – dreamy indeed – is revealed.

Visit Oxford Tuesday to Friday – weekends are busy with tourists and shoppers, and the Ashmolean Museum is closed on Monday.

904 FERNSEHTURM, BERLIN, GERMANY

Want to prove socialism can be a success? Then build a 368m aerial with a big silver blob on top. That was the thinking in the German Democratic Republic in 1969, when it unveiled the Fernsehturm (TV Tower) on the eastern side of the Berlin Wall. This oversized symbol told the world: life behind the Iron Curtain is grand, thanks. It was a shame for this secular government, then, that when the sun shines on that silver gobstopper – today home to a revolving restaurant – it reflects in the shape of a crucifix: to this day Berliners call it the 'pope's revenge'.

The tower entrance is opposite Alexanderplatz S-Bahn station; lifts take 40 seconds to reach the viewing area, at 204m. For more, see www.tv-turm.de.

905 VISHWANATH TEMPLE, VARANASI, INDIA

The most important Shivaite temple in a city devoted to god Shiva – indeed, in the holiest city in India – is bound to be a bit special. Thus it's unsurprising to learn that the dome-spire of Varanasi's Vishwanath Temple, tucked just inland from the River Ganges, is coated in 820kg of pure gold. There's been a shrine here for 1000 years, and millions of Hindus visit each year. Non-Hindus are forbidden from the temple's sacred insides – but can still appreciate the bling and spiritual significance. The Udai Silk Shop across the street offers glittering views from its 2nd-floor window.

Visit Varanasi during the Shivaratri Festival (February/March), which celebrates Shiva's marriage, and sees immense crowds bathing in the Ganges.

907 THE LIGHTNING FIELD, NEW MEXICO, USA

Not one needle but a whole pin cushion! 'The Lightning Field' art installation by sculptor Walter De Maria is an incongruous grid of poles piercing the New Mexican desert. Picture 400, 6m-high poles, arranged in a grid one mile by one kilometre. Why? Why not? It's a piece to be walked amid and contemplated, the solitude and silence of this otherwise empty plain as affecting as the needles themselves. Nature plays its part – sunset and sunrise inflame the steel pylons, and if you happen to see lightning (storms typically roll through between July and August) you're in for quite a show.

The site is near Quemado (128km from Albuquerque). Overnight stays are permitted from May to October; advance booking is required.

909 MINARET OF JAM, AFGHANISTAN

Forgotten by the outside world until the mid-20th century, the Minaret of Jam remains a holy grail for many travellers to Afghanistan. The first view of the minaret as it looms suddenly and unexpectedly from the folds of the mountains is worth all the rough roads it takes to get there. Reaching a dizzying height of 65m, the tower is covered in intricate brick decoration and text from the Quran. For many years, archaeologists were mystified as to its purpose in this isolated location. Jam is now recognised to be the site of the lost city of Firuzkoh, the capital of the medieval Ghorid empire, destroyed by the Mongols.

It's possible to climb the minaret and the views are amazing. The steps are narrow and dark; bring a torch.

906 TELLO OBELISK, CHAVÍN DE HUÁNTAR, PERU

The enigmatic Tello Obelisk – long resident in Lima – was moved in 2008 to take prime place in the Chavín National Museum. It's almost home, because this 2.5m stele used to stand in the nearby 3000-year-old temple-complex of Chavín de Huántar – the only remaining evidence of one of the oldest civilisations in the Americas. The obelisk is a riddle-in-granite, carved by the Chavín with the whole gamut of Peruvian ecology – caiman, eagles, big cats – for who-knows-what reason. After the museum, visit the site itself, a maze of tunnels and chambers, to better understand these ancient architects.

Chavín is a two-hour drive from regional hub-town Huaraz; this scenic route crosses the Cordillera Blanca.

908 ST VITUS CATHEDRAL, PRAGUE, CZECH REPUBLIC

In a place lauded as the 'City of a Thousand Spires', how do you pick just one? Perhaps the turrets atop the Charles Bridge's Staré Mesto Tower, for centuries one of the city's key defensive structures? Maybe the twin Gothic steeples of the Church of Our Lady before Tyn? Or how about the Old Town Hall, from which you get fine views over the other rooftops? No, first prize goes to St Vitus Cathedral, looming from within Prague Castle, which has spires to spare – from the pinnacles atop the graceful flying buttresses to the top of the Bell Tower, a 287-step lookout.

St Vitus Cathedral is open 9am to 4pm daily (till 6pm April to October); entry to the western side is free.

910 MUD SKYSCRAPERS OF SHIBAM, YEMEN

As you approach Wadi Hadramawt from the sun-blasted plains, the heat haze lifts and you realise that city skyline on the horizon is not a mirage. It's Shibam, a 2500-year-old city of seven- and eight-storey tower blocks built entirely out of mud and faith. These ancient but still inhabited skyscrapers are about 500 years old, and have given the town the nickname 'Manhattan of the Desert'. Unlike Manhattan, the narrow streets between the buildings are devoid of traffic and eerily quiet, while the city rises from fields of date palms. The sight will leave you breathless.

There is a curfew for tourists at night and a police escort is compulsory at all times.

FINEST FORTS

Some are circled by polar bears, others by pounding oceans –
all are spectacular strongholds.

The fort of Jaisalmer is a breathtaking sight: a massive sandcastle rising from the sandy plains like a mirage from a bygone era

911 FORT CANNING, SINGAPORE

A fort reborn, Singapore's most strategic spot has had a varied history, resulting in a park that combines cannons and concerts, bunkers and bromeliads. A Malay settlement was centred on this gentle hill in 1300, but it was the Brits who made a military mark in 1861, building a bastion to protect their interests in the region. The chunky fort gate and sally port access tunnel can still be seen, and the former barracks now house the Singapore Dance Theatre. This is typical of Fort Canning today, a mixture of heritage trails and heavy artillery, all infused with the Spice Garden's heady scent.

Fort Canning (see www.nparks.gov.sg) is within walking distance of City Hall, Clarke Quay and Dhoby Ghaut MRT stations.

912 CITÉ DE CARCASSONNE, FRANCE

It would be unsurprising to find a beautiful princess holed up in one of the 52 towers of Carcassonne's medieval citadel, such is the fairytale aspect of the place. It's not one monument but a cluster, with 3km of battlements encircling the Gothic Basilica of St Nazaire, the moated and drawbridged Château Comtal, and no small number of craftshops and eateries – plenty of people still live and do business inside the ancient walls. Unbelievably the place was nearly pulled down in the 1840s, but a vociferous campaign and painstaking restoration by architect Viollet-le-Duc saved the day – a suitably fairytale ending.

The medieval city is free to enter; access to the Château and ramparts costs €8.50 (http://carcassonne.monuments -nationaux.fr/en/).

913 JAISALMER, RAJASTHAN, INDIA

It's either a mirage, or a really, *really* big sandcastle… This might reasonably be your summation as the hulking mass of Jaisalmer Fort looms up from the nothingness of the great Thar Desert. This Rajasthani outpost is huge – built in the 12th century atop an 80m hill, the fort has 99 bulging bastions, three layers of walls and a series of monstrous gates, designed to keep out invaders. The gates admit many these days, though: a large proportion of Jaisalmer's washerwomen, spice sellers, clock menders and other inhabitants live within this sandstone behemoth, making this historic relic a breathing, vibrant, vital home.

Jaisalmer is 300km from Jodhpur; buses and trains connect the two. Every February the Desert Festival is held near Jaisalmer.

319

RICHARD I'ANSON / LONELY PLANET IMAGES

914 FORT SÃO SEBASTIÃO, ILHA DE MOÇAMBIQUE, MOZAMBIQUE

As the former capital of Portuguese East Africa, Ilha de Moçambique clearly deserved some decent protection. So in 1558, on the northern tip of this offshore island, construction began on Fort São Sebastião – making it the oldest surviving fort in sub-Saharan Africa. Its position is domineering, jutting out into the turquoise of the Indian Ocean, but it's the continuity of the architecture across the tiny island that impresses. The colonial masters eventually outgrew the Manueline chapel, the Governor's House and the old fort itself, and no one has seen fit to change the place since.

Ilha de Moçambique is 2000km north of capital Maputo. Guides can be arranged at the tourist information centre.

915 PRINCE OF WALES FORT, CHURCHILL, CANADA

It's not so much the cannons you should fear at Prince of Wales Fort. Indeed, the heavy artillery here, usually found chilling under a layer of snow, has never fired a shot: the fort was surrendered to the French in 1782 by an undersized British garrison that was never trained to use its big guns. No, it's the polar bears you need to look out for, a sizeable number of which patrol the Manitoban shores of Hudson Bay, looking for seal snacks. It's easy for them to hide around the star-shaped walls; tour guides come armed with knowledge *and* loaded rifles.

Prince of Wales Fort is 1.5km from Churchill; tours are available upon request in July and August (see www.pc.gc.ca).

916 PORTOBELO, PANAMA

Poor Portobelo. Today it's a sleepy town of fishermen and farmers, but once, what glories! Back in the day, unimaginable riches passed through this Caribbean port, en route from Lima, Peru to Spain: it's estimated 45 fleets of galleons sailed between 1574 and 1702, each carrying at least 30 million pesos of booty. All that wealth needed protection, so a series of forts were constructed. Still standing today are the cut-coral walls of Fuerte Santiago, the crumbling remains of Fuerte San Fernando, and Fuerte San Jerónimo, whose cannon embrasures still sit as the Spanish – who departed in 1821 – left them.

Portobelo is a 1½-hour drive from Panama City. Visit on 21 October for the Festival de Cristo Negro, one of Panama's liveliest celebrations.

917 JABRIN FORT, OMAN

Fort-o-philes are spoiled for choice in Oman: the Arabian enclave is home to 500 of them, desert redoubts of all shapes and sizes. But it is the mountain backdrop that makes Jabrin perhaps the most impressive. Built around 1670 by the Imam Bil'arab bin Sultan, it combines the beauty of a palace – lattice windows, trellised balconies, intricate frescos and Islamic calligraphy – with sturdy defences: lookout turrets, arrow-holes, 360-degree rooftop views and a special Imam Protection Room, designed with secret hideouts underneath, so soldiers could leap to the defence of their master should he be attacked by a conniving guest.

Jabrin is 240km southwest of Muscat. The best time to visit is October to April, when temperatures average 25°C to 30°C.

918 CARTAGENA, COLOMBIA

When a city's this pretty, there's only one thing for it – surround it by 12km of impregnable stone, to keep your pastel-hued mansions safe from pirates and the encroachment of modernity. So it came to pass that the Colombian port of Cartagena, founded by the Spanish in 1533, is so encircled. While a new metropolis sprawls outside, the Old Town sits, little changed, within Las Murallas – its protective fortifications. Explore on foot: wend from the Puerta del Reloj gateway to beautiful Plaza de Bolívar and to Las Bóvedas (former dungeons, now souvenir shops), all the while feeling safe as houses.

Cartagena airport is 3km northeast of the Old Town; buses to the capital Bogotá take around 20 hours.

919 GOLUBAC FORTRESS, SERBIA

Built to dominate a strategic stretch of the River Danube, tumbledown Golubac Fortress is now being consumed by it. A hydroelectric dam on the Iron Gate Gorge has raised water levels hereabouts, and the lower reaches of this 14th-century stronghold have been flooded as a consequence. It's still an imposing sight, however: a hill-rambling bastion of nine sturdy towers and irregular 3m-thick walls. You can see what the Turks, Hungarians, Serbs and Austrians – who spent centuries battling over Golubac's ownership – were fighting for. Now a road carved right through the fortress's surviving battlements means you can visit without so much fuss.

Golubac Fort is 4km downstream from Golubac town; to get there, catch a bus from Belgrade in the direction of Kladovo.

In recent years the population of Aït Benhaddou has dwindled, giving the place the eerie feeling of a deserted stage-set around sunset

920 AÏT BENHADDOU, MOROCCO

Look familiar? You don't need to have crossed the fringes of the Sahara to have seen Aït Benhaddou before – this sun-baked kasbah has made many movie appearances, ranging from *Lawrence of Arabia* to *Gladiator*. It is, in the fortress world, indisputably A-list. Unsurprising, as it's picture-perfect: a hillside jumble of scorched-red mud-brick houses, dotted with the odd palm tree and carpet seller. In its day it was a key stop-off on the caravan route north to Marrakesh; today most locals have moved into the new village over the river, though there'll be a few on hand to lead you through this citadel superstar.

Aït Benhaddou is 9km off the main Ouarzazate–Marrakesh road; there are no direct buses – charter a taxi from Ouarzazate (32km away).

FINEST FORTS

MOST INTERESTING GATEWAYS & ARCHES

Cross the thresholds of these fine, fun and fearsome entrances and archways.

If anything rivals the Eiffel Tower as the symbol of Paris, it's this magnificent monument to Napoleon's 1805 victory at Austerlitz

921 WAGAH, INDIA/PAKISTAN

Two sets of metal gates, one orange-white-green, the other bearing a crescent moon and star, stand equidistant over a line on the tarmac – the only road crossing between India and Pakistan. Traced after partition in 1947, the border dissects the village of Wagah – which has subsequently become host to an unusual spectacle. Every evening the guards of both nations, resplendent as cockerels in high-plumed hats, act out a gate-closing ceremony of pomp and patriotism. Foot-stamping, goose-stepping, unbridled machismo – it's a chance for uneasy neighbours to gain theatrical one-upmanship, while crowds of Indians and Pakistanis cheer, metres apart but utterly divided.

Wagah is 28km from Amritsar, 20km from Lahore. The ceremony occurs at sunset every day and lasts around 45 minutes.

922 UGAB RIVER GATE, SKELETON COAST, NAMIBIA

It's not the most inviting of gateways – the barrier at Namibia's Ugab River bears two ghoulish skull-and-crossbones, a stark warning to all who enter. It's a warning worth heeding: these gates open into the wilder reaches of the Skeleton Coast, a hostile strip of rusting shipwrecks, thumping Atlantic – and not a lot else – running up to Angola. It's divided into three sections: the first, Henties Bay to Ugab, passes stinky Cape Cross Seal Reserve; the second, via Ugab's gate to Terrace Bay, is a starkly stunning lair of surprisingly abundant wildlife; the third, from Terrace Bay, sees the road simply die altogether…

Permits are required to enter Skeleton Coast Park at Ugab. Driving beyond Terrace Bay is prohibited; access is by fly-in safari only.

924 GATEWAY OF INDIA, MUMBAI, INDIA

Built to commemorate King George V's 1911 visit to India, it looks like a half-size version of Paris' Arc de Triomphe, but with Islamic flourishes. Right on the waterfront it's a major meeting point in Bollywood, as India's movie and business capital is fondly nicknamed. Completed in 1924, it only served as the entrance to Britain's colonial jewel for 24 years – the last colonial regiment marched away from the gateway in 1948. The finest views of the Indian icon don't come cheap – you need a room in the adjacent and very pricey Taj Mahal Palace & Tower Hotel to enjoy them.

If your budget doesn't stretch to the Taj Hotel the boats from the gateway's wharfs to Elephanta Island offer fine views.

925 BABYLONIAN ISHTAR GATE, BERLIN, GERMANY

An Aladdin's cave of treasures, Berlin's Pergamon Museum opens a fascinating window onto the ancient world. One of the stars of the show is the reconstructed Ishtar Gate, from Babylon during the reign of King Nebuchadnezzar II. It's impossible not to be awed by the huge gate, the Processional Way leading up to it and the facade of the king's throne hall. All are sheathed in glazed bricks glistening in radiant blue and ochre. The strutting lions, horses and dragons, which represent major Babylonian gods, are so striking that you can almost hear the roaring and fanfare.

Budget at least two hours for the other attractions at this amazing museum and be sure to pick up the free and excellent audioguide.

923 ARC DE TRIOMPHE, PARIS, FRANCE

The terrifying 12-exit roundabout encircling the Arc de Triomphe is perhaps not what Napoleon had in mind when he commissioned it in 1806. But then he also planned to win all his battles and have this victory monolith completed sooner than 1836. No matter, it's finished now, and is the epicentre of Paris. Wide boulevards (including the Champs-Élysées) radiate from its base. Views from its stocky, 50m top are sweeping: southeast to the Louvre, south to the Eiffel Tower, northwest to the Grand Arche de la Défense – a hulking white-marble monument, almost deserving of a list entry of its own.

The Arc de Triomphe is open daily from 10am to 10.30pm (until 11pm from April to September). Take Métro lines 1, 2 or 6 to Charles de Gaulle–Étoile station.

926 ITSUKUSHIMA-JINJA, MIYAJIMA, JAPAN

This is one of the best vistas in Japan. Fact. In the 17th century, Confucian scholar Shunsai Hayashi travelled Japan and listed what he believed to be its *nihon sankei* – three best views. This seemingly floating red *torii* (traditional gate) and accompanying shrine on Miyajima, near Hiroshima, was one of them. The island has long been a place of worship; indeed, people come here to worship the island itself. It certainly looks heavenly, a small outcrop of rugged maple forest, temples and tranquillity amid the Seto Sea – with the iconic, waterbound Itsukushima-jinja providing a striking entrance.

Visit Miyajima on 17 June for the Kangensai Festival, when musicians on boats serenade the shrine (www.nihonsankei.sakura.ne.jp).

927 DELICATE ARCH, ARCHES NATIONAL PARK, UTAH, USA

Arch-lovers are spoilt for choice in this protected piece of Utah high desert – as you might surmise from its name. There's the graceful curves of Double Arch; tucked away Tower Arch; or the 91m-long span of Landscape Arch, one of the world's largest. In all, over 2000 of these varied sandstone erosions have been recorded within the national park. But it's Delicate Arch that adorns all the postcards – and has become the symbol of the state. Standing 52m tall and alone on a Mars-red bluff, it's best seen late afternoon, when the dying sun seems to set it on fire.

The 2.4km walk from Wolfe Ranch to Delicate Arch takes 30 to 45 minutes. Drivers should head for Delicate Arch Viewpoint (www.nps.gov/arch/index.htm).

928 DURDLE DOOR, ENGLAND

There's something primordial about this place: perhaps it's the fact it's on Dorset's Jurassic Coast; perhaps it's the Old English name (meaning to bore or drill); or maybe it's just the eternal crashing of the sea. Whatever it is, the naturally eroded rock arch of Durdle Door feels strangely timeless, even as the constantly gnawing English Channel knows otherwise – one day this rock span will collapse, leaving a solitary sea stack in its wake. Until then, walk the cliff path for the ultimate views, taking in millennia of fossils, gracefully curved coves and the might of Durdle Door itself.

View Durdle Door while walking the 23km Ferrybridge–Lulworth Cove section of the long-distance South West Coast Path (www.southwestcoastpath.com).

929 BRANDENBURG GATE, BERLIN, GERMANY

The Brandenburger Tor has, it seems, always been a symbol of something. Built by Carl Gotthard Langhans in 1791 as a monument to peace, it was ironically bomb-battered during WWII. During Berlin's divided years, it stood for the separation of the city – built as a thoroughfare, this gate was blocked by the infamous Wall, which ran right past its pillars. But when the Wall came down in 1989 it was at

WIBOWO RUSLI / LONELY PLANET IMAGES

The vermilion *torii* (shrine gate) of Miyajima's Itsukushima-jinja is one of the most photographed sites in Japan

this icon that crowds of East and West Berliners gathered – now the Brandenburg Gate is a symbol of unity and harmony once more.

The gate is on Pariser Platz, Mitte; take the U-Bahn U2 line to Mohrenstrasse or the train to Brandenburger Tor.

930 BAB SHARQI, DAMASCUS, SYRIA

St Paul's Road to Damascus may have led him through this ancient opening. Bab Sharqi – one of seven great gates allowing access to the walled Syrian capital – is located at the eastern end of Straight Street, the avenue to which God directed the Christian convert. It's the only remaining entry to the Old City to retain its Roman plan, though 2000 years have taken their toll – only fragments of the original stonework still remain. It still forms a grand entry, though: from here you plunge into a warren of alleys, spicy souks and secretive Damascene houses that time has left almost untouched.

Spring and autumn are the best times to visit; check the dates of Ramadan – restaurants may be closed during the day.

MOST INTERESTING GATEWAYS & ARCHES

MOST FASCINATING ARTISTS' GARDENS

One-off imaginations have turned these gardens into offbeat wonderlands.

931 LAS POZAS, MEXICO

Edward James was born to a fabulously wealthy family and for years lived it up as a patron of the arts, sponsoring many of the surrealists and helping found the New York City Ballet. But a yearning for Eden saw him give it all away and head for Mexico in search of his perfect garden. He spent the rest of his life transforming Las Pozas (in the northern mountains, named for the descending river pools on the property) into his dream jungle paradise, and making immense concrete surrealist sculptures and follies to adorn it.

Stay at the romantic El Castillo (www .junglegossip.com/castillo.html) – it's walking distance from Las Pozas.

932 WILLIAM RICKETTS SANCTUARY, AUSTRALIA

Head up to green Mt Dandenong, near Melbourne, to find this whimsical sculpture garden. It's the work of William Ricketts, an Australian artist with a before-his-time bent for environmental and Indigenous issues. He spent a lot of his life living in Aboriginal communities in central Australia before settling in the Dandenongs. Some think his sculptures of Aboriginal people as spirits of the land are twee, but set among the ferns and mountain ash they have a tranquillity and power, seeming to grow right out of their surroundings. Ricketts lived here into his 90s, sculpting to the last.

The park is open from 10am to 4.30pm daily, with the exception of Christmas Day.

933 CHANDIGARH ROCK GARDEN, INDIA

From little things… Nek Chand, a government official, was clearing himself a small garden and used the rubble to make a wall and a couple of sculptures. It seems he was hooked: over the ensuing years, working at night and in his spare time, he fashioned a fantastic edifice of found-object mosaics. It was eventually discovered by authorities, who liked it so much they not only spared it, but gave Chand a salary and helpers to keep building. Today it's a junk Alhambra, with waterfalls and thousands of sculptures of animals and dancing girls set in arched mosaic courtyards.

It's a three-hour train journey from Delhi to Chandigarh (if you catch the fast train). The garden is in Sector 1 of the city.

934 GIARDINO DEI TAROCCHI, ITALY

When you think 'Tuscan garden', you probably don't think this. Niki de Saint Phalle, an autodidact artist and sculptor (and, in her day, actor and model) created it over years, basing it around the figures of the tarot cards. As you'd expect from someone who as a girl painted the fig leaves on the school statues red, the sculpture garden is a larger-than-life riot of joyous, bulbous figures. Highlights are the Magician with his gaping mouth and mirrored face, the exuberant Sun, the Moon upheld by crabs and dogs, and the massive pink High Priestess.

The Tarot Garden's website (www .nikidesaintphalle.com) has detailed directions from Siena, Rome and the Leonardo da Vinci airport.

935 TILFORD COTTAGE GARDEN, ENGLAND

Artist Rod Burn and his wife Pamela, a holistic therapist, created this garden around their 17th-century cottage in Surrey, and at first glance it seems like a typical charming English concoction, with a bog garden, a wild garden and a Victorian knot garden. But that's before you spot the (steel) giraffe looming out of the trees or notice the (topiary) figure falling head-first into a hedge. Or the tree with its bole painted gold. Or the apple orchard growing parallel to the ground. As well as sculptures and visual gags scattered around the place, the plants themselves have been tweaked out of the usual: check out the birch trees twisted into a screen.

The garden is open to groups of six or more. It's best to make a reservation (01252 795423).

936 OWL GARDEN, SOUTH AFRICA

Miss Helen, who created a private world of her own in her house and garden, is a classic example of an outsider artist. She was a recluse in the conservative village of Nieu Bethesda; she shunned company and was regarded with suspicion. She decorated her house with lovely, outlandish murals made from coloured glass. In 1964 she hired a sheepshearer, Koos Malgas, to help her construct a sculpture garden of camels, shepherds, donkeys and sheep, all facing east. The owl was her totem figure and she used it over and over again. At the end of her life, fearing she was going blind, she killed herself – by ingesting crushed glass.

Give the Owl House a call on 049 8411 733 to arrange your visit.

937 JARDIN ROSA MIR, FRANCE

Something like a homemade Parc Güell, the Jardin Rosa Mir in Lyon is the creation of Jules Senis, a Spanish tiler who dreamed up the garden and vowed to make it a reality while he was in hospital battling cancer. The garden is named after his mother. It's not large, but makes up for that by being crowded with found materials (rocks, shells, coral, even snail shells) that make elaborate mosaics on walls and pillars. Teamed with lemon trees, succulents, ivy and geraniums, the effect is surprisingly charming.

The Jardin Rosa Mir is on Grand Rue de la Croix Rousse in the 4th arrondissement of Lyon; admission is free.

939 PHILADELPHIA'S MAGIC GARDENS, PENNSYLVANIA, USA

Isaiah and Julia Zagar are mosaic evangelists. They moved to Philly's South Street neighbourhood in the 1960s, took a look around, and evidently thought 'this place could use some colour!'. At the time the district was in decline, and the couple were able to buy several derelict buildings. They did them up with bright mosaics inside and out. Isaiah Zagar's biggest work is the Magic Gardens, which he built on a vacant lot near his house – a mammoth mosaic labyrinth incorporating local trash, mirrors and tiles. It depicts events from his own life and world history. When the owners tried to sell the site, the community rallied to save the Gardens.

For visitor information and to get a glimpse of the mosaics, visit http://www .phillymagicgardens.org.

939 MILLESGÅRDEN, SWEDEN

This is a dreamy space outside Stockholm, something like a Swedish Isola Bella. The home of Carl and Olga Milles, both artists, it was created by them and Carl's architect half-brother Evert. It transforms a rocky slope into a series of terraces gracefully leading the eye downwards and littered with architectural finds like the marble archway from a hotel. Milles' sculptures – immense saints, gods and angels held aloft on pillars – hold sway on the lower terraces. The most touching part of the garden is Little Austria, a loving recreation of Olga's much-missed homeland.

The garden features white urns designed by Milles. You can buy flowerpots based on them in the Millesgården shop.

940 HOWARD FINSTER'S PARADISE GARDENS, GEORGIA, USA

This one's a gift from god. Finster was a Southern preacher who received a vision telling him to make art, and, untrained as he was, that was what he went ahead and did. His paintings are done in a naive style, often with text; for Finster, the art was all about the message. The Paradise Gardens are a jumble of mosaic materials (bottles, mirrors) and found objects: everything *and* the kitchen sink, and the bathtub, too. There's a chapel and a folk art gallery. It might not be everyone's idea of paradise, but you're sure to find something you like.

Just before Finster died, he put up a note in the Gardens asking that they be preserved. If you'd like to donate, visit www.finstersparadisegardens.org.

BEST CELEBRITY SIGHTS

Try the celebrity lifestyle on for size at the following hang-outs of the rich and famous.

You can't escape the Fab Four in Liverpool, so stop by the Cavern Club to check the scene of their earliest gigs

941 CHELSEA HOTEL, NEW YORK, USA

If the walls of the Chelsea Hotel could talk they'd probably just mumble incoherently before passing out. A haunt of legendary writers, musicians, playwrights, radical intellectuals and other associated booze-hounds, the Chelsea still stands as a bohemian beacon drawing in interested artists and tourists alike. Not a great deal has changed since Jimi Hendrix, Janis Joplin, Bob Dylan, Patti Smith and Leonard Cohen all cooled their heels here during the '60s. The ramshackle grandeur of the building still enchants and the artworks by renowned residents are worth a look, even if you aren't planning on sleeping off a hangover in one of the rooms.

The hotel is in the heart of Chelsea on West 23rd Street between 7th and 8th Avenues. A standard double room will set you back around US$120.

943 KODAK THEATRE, LOS ANGELES, CALIFORNIA, USA

Every year celebrity self-congratulation goes into overdrive as the stars don the most expensive and most glamorous designer suits and gowns and pose their way down the red carpet at the Academy Awards. The Kodak Theatre was purpose-built in 2001 to give the Oscars a permanent home and it's possible to get a glimpse inside on one of the theatre's 30-minute tours. For a chance to be blinded by the stars at their most bright on Hollywood's night of nights you can put your name into a lottery to score tickets in the bleachers overlooking the red carpet.

The theatre is in the heart of Hollywood on the northwest corner of Hollywood Boulevard and Highland Avenue. For a shot at bleacher seats go online in early September at www.oscars.org/bleachers.

944 SUNDANCE FILM FESTIVAL, PARK CITY, UTAH, USA

It might be -20°C but Sundance is 'so hot right now'. What began as a festival to showcase the work of low-budget, independent film-makers has turned into a spectacle of Hollywood stars. Each January, fans and film stars descend on the frozen streets of Park City, Utah to witness the unveiling of the next big thing in independent cinema. However, despite the recent rush of movie megastars to Sundance, the festival maintains its indie cred. In 2010 the festival instituted a new category called 'NEXT' to showcase extremely low-budget films.

See the festival's official website (www.sundance.org) for everything you need to know, including where to stay, what to see and even how to volunteer.

945 HOLLYWOOD HILLS, LOS ANGELES, CALIFORNIA, USA

When the stars aren't away sunning themselves in St Barts or St Tropez many of them call the Hollywood Hills home. An extremely affluent neighbourhood in Los Angeles, the Hills are known for exclusivity and residential privacy. Winding roads and leafy aspects set the neighbourhood apart from the flat expanse that is central LA. It's possible to tour the Hills and have the homes of the stars pointed out but it's just as fun to cruise around on your own for a sneak peek at how the other half lives.

The Hills are bordered by Laurel Canyon Boulevard to the west, Vermont Avenue to the east, Mulholland Drive to the north, and Sunset Boulevard to the south.

942 CAVERN CLUB, LIVERPOOL, ENGLAND

If you happened to be in the audience at the Cavern Club during John Lennon's debut performance in 1957, you would most likely have booed him off the stage. A jazz club in the late 1950s, the Cavern was strictly anti-rock-and-roll. It is said that Lennon's rendition of Elvis Presley's 'Don't Be Cruel' was not well received. In the early 1960s the club changed hands and between 1961 and 1963 the Beatles appeared on stage more than 290 times. Six months after their last performance, the Beatles headed off on their first tour of the USA. The rest, as they say, is history.

The club is at 10 Mathew Street in the centre of Liverpool. Opening hours are 11am to 8pm Monday to Wednesday, 11am to 2am Thursday to Saturday and 11am to 12.30am Sunday. Entry during the day is free.

From million-dollar real estate to harbours full of mega-cruisers, there's no disputing the glitz and glamour of the French Riviera

946 MADAME TUSSAUDS, LONDON, ENGLAND

For more than 200 years Madame Tussauds has been immortalising sporting heroes, politicians, pop stars, royalty and more. Pick a celebrity, any celebrity, and chances are that their waxy counterpart is here. Once you get over the creepiness of being in a room full of cold, lifeless, silent statues that look *exactly* like human beings, it's a thrill to get up close and personal to your idols.

Madame Tussauds is on Marylebone Road, two minutes' walk from Baker Street tube station. Opening hours are usually 9am to 5.30pm; entry is from £25 per adult.

947 SUN STUDIO, MEMPHIS, TENNESSEE, USA

The birthplace of rock and roll, the Memphis Recording Service, as it was known in the early '50s, was where blues and country music came together to produce what we know now as rock and roll. With the sound came the legends: Johnny Cash, Elvis Presley, Roy Orbison and Jerry Lee

LAURENT GIRAUDOU / PHOTOLIBRARY

948 ST TROPEZ, FRENCH RIVIERA

Bring your boat and your Bulgari dahling. What was once a tiny fishing village is now *the* place to be seen on the Riviera. Swanky nightclubs, bars, restaurants, boutique shops and beaches are festooned with the uber-rich and famous. During summer, space on some of the most beautiful and popular beaches needs to be booked in advance. It costs nothing to walk to the citadel overlooking the town, however, from where you can celebrity spot to your heart's content.

Park your private plane in the local airport or drive the 100km from Nice.

949 ED SULLIVAN THEATER, NEW YORK, USA

As the long-time home of the variety program *The Ed Sullivan Show,* this Broadway theatre saw stars such as Elvis Presley, the Beatles, the Rolling Stones and the major stars of Motown grace its stage. In more recent times, as the host of the *Late Show with David Letterman,* a steady stream of Hollywood A-listers, world leaders and sporting stars have come through the theatre's doors. Guests have included Johnny Depp, Jerry Seinfeld, Jay-Z, Matt Damon and Rihanna.

The theatre is at 1697 Broadway between West 53rd and West 54th Streets; take the subway to 7th Avenue. For tickets to the *Late Show* visit www.cbs.com/late_night/late_show/tickets.

backwater. That was until the 20th century, when tourism came to town. Now stars and spendthrifts vie for space on the sand or in the numerous high-end restaurants and designer stores. With an area of only 21 sq km and a population of barely 8500, the odds of eyeing off a member of the glitterati are good.

Twin Otter aircraft is the most popular way to arrive on the island, unless you own your own private jet, of course. Ferries make the trip from St Martin but the crossing is often rough.

Lewis were just a few of those who recorded here in the early years. The original building, now known as Sun Studios, still functions as a recording venue and tourist attraction.

The studio is at 706 Union Avenue, east of downtown Memphis at the intersection of Union and Marshall Streets. It's open year-round.

950 ST BARTS, FRENCH WEST INDIES

Handballed from France to Sweden and back to France from 1648 to 1878, the tiny island of St Barthélemy was once considered a Caribbean

BEST CELEBRITY SIGHTS

MOST VISIONARY ARCHITECTS & THEIR WORKS

They came, they saw, they made their mark – the world's master builders have left quite a legacy.

Stand in awe of German history – and modern architecture – at Berlin's Reichstag

MARTIN MOOS / LONELY PLANET IMAGES

951 EDWIN LUTYENS & NEW DELHI, INDIA

When you're a busy colonising power and you need to shift your administrative capital, simply bring in a man to design a new one. Such was the task set Edwin Lutyens when the British Empire shifted HQ from Calcutta to Delhi. The plans were begun in 1912: Lutyens envisaged 'New Delhi' as all grand official buildings and wide boulevards, combining classical architecture with subcontinental flair. Rajpath (the King's Way) is the showpiece: the monumental India Gate marks its eastern end; Rashtrapati Bhavan marks the west – a 340-room palace, built for an imperial viceroy but now home to the president of an independent nation.

Rashtrapati Bhavan is generally closed to the public, but the gardens are opened each February; security is very tight.

952 ALVAR AALTO & THE FINLANDIA HALL, HELSINKI, FINLAND

Fine Finnish form and function combine on the banks of Töölö Bay, thanks to Alvar Aalto's bold concert house. It was supposed to be part of a grander plan – in 1961 the architect proposed a swath of buildings to revitalise Helsinki. It didn't happen, but this marble-clad monolith hints at the bigger picture, and showcases Aalto's trademark style: modernist lines, asymmetricity, an avoidance of right angles and a dash of Mediterranean flavour. The sound's a bit off – the inclined roof, designed to provide the acoustics of a high church, didn't quite work. But as a physical monument it's a resounding success.

Finlandia Hall (www.finlandiatalo.fi) can only be visited on a guided tour on set dates; tours cost €10.50.

953 NORMAN FOSTER & THE REICHSTAG, BERLIN, GERMANY

The seat of the German parliament has witnessed some torrid times. First completed in 1894, the Reichstag has seen the declaration of a Republic and the rise of the Nazis, been mysteriously burned out, and then bombed to bits, left to ruin, unhappily restored and marooned in a Wall-divided city. But following the reunification of Germany in 1990, British architect Norman Foster stepped in. The Reichstag was transformed: a marriage of old and new – Soviet graffiti can still be seen on the original walls and a dazzlingly modern cupola of steel and glass symbolises the forward-thinking attitude of the nation.

333

The dome of the Reichstag (see www.bundestag.de) is open from 8am to midnight (last admission is 10pm); arrive early to avoid long queues.

Everyone knows about *the* Pyramids, but did you know about the *other* pyramids? Saqqara was the forerunner of them all

954 IMHOTEP & SAQQARA, EGYPT

The world's first master architect? Born around 3000 BC, and one of the few non-royals to attain god-like status, Imhotep was a legend in Ancient Egypt, and a rampant overachiever: a doctor, a vizier, a poet, an astrologer – and a dab hand at building pyramids. He designed the stepped structure at Saqqara, an inconceivably enormous pile for the time and the planet's first cut-stone monument (previously, temples were made of perishable materials). Believing the incumbent pharaoh Zoser required a fancy tomb to facilitate his rise to the heavens, Imhotep erected for him this six-tiered, 62m-high pyramid, which became the blueprint for all that followed – and which is somehow still standing today.

Saqqara is 30km south of Cairo; there is a new Imhotep Museum on site, on the right side of the car park.

955 FRANK LLOYD WRIGHT & TALIESIN WEST, SCOTTSDALE, ARIZONA, USA

'A building is not just a place to be. It is a way to be.' So said Frank Lloyd Wright, who dedicated his life to redesigning and improving housing and public spaces. Wright designed 1141 buildings; only a handful are open to the public, one of which is his own winter home. Taliesin West typifies Wright's style – low ceilings, open-plan living, indoors seguing into outdoors – while connecting with the natural world beyond. Window aspects and tiny trails connect the house to the foothills of the Sonoran Desert, Wright's inspiration.

Taliesin West (www.franklloydwright.org) is in Scottsdale, Arizona; a range of public tours (one to three hours) is available daily from 9am to 4pm.

956 ANTONI GAUDÍ & THE SAGRADA FAMÍLIA, BARCELONA, SPAIN

Never has one man's vision so completely captured the essence of a city. Antoni Gaudí *is* Barcelona: his fluid structures are playful yet solid, devout yet fun, full of colour and utterly unique – like the Catalan capital itself. Gaudí lived from 1852 to 1926 and in that time dotted Barcelona with fantastical buildings – the fairytale Park Güell, curvaceous Casa Milà, the sea-inspired Casa Batlló. But it's his unfinished masterpiece, the Sagrada Família, that impresses most – even if this controversial church is part stone symphony to god, part building site. As arguments continue over Gaudí's final wishes, it looks set to remain this way for quite some time to come.

Sagrada Família (www.sagradafamilia.cat) is open daily from 9am to 6pm (to 8pm from April to September); entrance costs €12.50. Lifts run up two of the towers (€2.50).

957 JØRN UTZON & THE SYDNEY OPERA HOUSE, AUSTRALIA

It is, in fact, a Danish architect who's responsible for this most Australian of icons. The brilliant-white shells of Sydney's Opera House – a design nod, perhaps, to the Aboriginal midden that once occupied Bennelong Point – was conjured by Jørn Utzon in 1957 in response to a competition. It's near impossible to believe the design was almost discarded by the judging panel, so perfectly do the concert carapaces sit within their harbour setting: Botanic Gardens behind, city skyscrapers nearby, 'Old Coathanger' bridge a constant companion. Indeed, to

catch the ferry into adjacent Circular Quay is one of the world's most satisfying arrivals.

The Sydney Opera House (www.sydneyoperahouse.com) offers a range of tours; the two-hour Backstage access-all-areas tour costs A$155.

958 CHARLES GARNIER & THE PARIS OPERA, FRANCE

Understated, *moi?* Not likely. Paris' Palais Garnier opera house is as flamboyant as you'd expect from a theatrical institution in the heart of this beautiful city. Having won a competition to design a new concert hall in 1860, Paris-born Garnier let loose his sense of showmanship – picked up from tours of Greece and Rome – to create a glittering stage for the arts. The sweeping double staircase of multicoloured marble; the opulent, chandelier-hung auditorium; the mosaic-and-gold foyer: all scream drama, yet are supported by a pragmatic steel framework, strong enough (just) to support all that ostentation.

Palais Garnier (www.operadeparis.fr), on the corner of rue Scribe and rue Auber, is open daily from 10am to 5pm (to 1pm on days with a matinee).

959 NICHOLAS HAWKSMOOR & THE LONDON CHURCHES, ENGLAND

Christopher Wren left his mark on London – the dome of St Paul's Cathedral remains one of the capital's most enduring symbols. But he also gave the city another legacy: Nicholas Hawksmoor. Wren's apprentice constructed six imposing churches – a handful of the 50 proposed, though never realised, by a 1711 act of Parliament – with

Gothic spires that would define the skyline for centuries. Perhaps finest is his immense Christ Church in Spitalfields, a sturdy Georgian baroque box with a towering steeple – grander in scale than many a cathedral, and a prime example of Hawksmoor's vision.

Christ Church (www.christchurch spitalfields.org) is open Monday to Friday (11am to 4pm) and Sunday (1pm to 4pm); free lunchtime concerts are held on the first Friday of the month.

960 KENZO TANGE & THE PEACE CENTER, HIROSHIMA, JAPAN

To rebuild in a city that had suffered the most horrific, era-defining destruction – that was the challenge faced by Japanese architect Kenzo Tange as he embarked on the most poignant of projects. Central Hiroshima was flattened by an atomic bomb on 6 August 1945; by 1954 a memorial park was open, a place of remembrance and an appeal for world peace. Tange's no-nonsense buildings were key to that sentiment. Constructed from plain concrete with no fripperies to distract from the exhibits inside, his museum offers a framed view to the dilapidated A-Bomb Dome, the sole building to survive the nuclear attack.

From JR Hiroshima Station take a red bus bound for Yoshijima and get off at Heiwa Kinen Koen (Peace Park). See www.pcf .city.hiroshima.jp for more details.

MOST VISIONARY ARCHITECTS & THEIR WORKS

BEST PLACES TO SEE RED

'Workers of the world, unite!' Communist ideologies may have faded 20 years ago, but there are still places where comrades can explore their proletarian roots.

963 LA COMANDANCIA DE LA PLANTA, CUBA

Tourists flock to Cuba for its retro '50s chic, late-night salsa bars and revolutionary social history. Yet few get further than hitting the rum, shaking their thing and bagging an iconic Che T-shirt. So what else is there? High in the Sierra Maestra Mountains lies La Comandancia de la Planta, the secret base where Castro commanded his troops in the guerrilla war against Batista control. Well hidden, the camp is pretty much unchanged from Fidel's day and can only be reached by a vertiginous 4WD track and strenuous hike from the village of Santo Domingo.

Santo Domingo is remote – from Santiago take a bus to Bayamo (two hours) and then grab a taxi for another two-hour ride to the village.

961 ALL-RUSSIA EXHIBITION CENTRE, MOSCOW, RUSSIA

The USSR's communist cogs ground to a halt in 1991 and Moscow has progressed apace in recent years. True enough, the suburbs are scarred with scores of dour housing blocks but few other signs remain in a city that's embracing capitalism. So what of all the relics? Fear not, comrades, for the All-Russia Exhibition Centre offers a true Stalinist experience. The 200-hectare site has a fascinating collection of purposeful-looking statues, ornate fountains and fresco-rich pavilions, celebrating the power of workers and the strength of the union. There's even a 100m-high statue of a spaceship and an original Vostok rocket – proud memorials to an era when communism conquered outer space.

Take the short metro ride on line 6 from the centre of Moscow, alighting at station VDNKh (www.vvcentre.ru/eng).

962 DIEFENBUNKER, CARP, ONTARIO, CANADA

Americans weren't the only ones to take budget-draining measures to safeguard their citizens (namely political leaders) against possible nuclear attacks. In Canada, the government set up a constellation of disaster-proof 'diefenbunkers' (named for John Diefenbaker, the prime minister who commissioned their construction) across the nation. The largest one, just a few kilometres beyond the nation's capital, measures over 9300 sq metres and contains a radio station, an expansive ops centre and a giant vault to store the Bank of Canada's entire gold-bar supply. Today, spirited tour guides lead visitors through the city-sized shelter, which is now known as Canada's Cold War Museum.

Tours costing C$14 are available year-round. Check out www.diefenbunker.ca for additional details.

964 KAROSTA PRISON, LIEPAJA, LATVIA

If you're craving some serious punishment, or just want to brag that you've spent the night in a Soviet jail, then sign up to become a detainee for an evening at grungy Karosta Prison, a former detention facility for disobedient soldiers. You'll be subjected to regular bed checks, verbal abuse by guards in period garb and forced to relieve yourself in the world's most disgusting latrine (seriously). Try booking the night in cell 26 (solitary confinement) – you won't be bothered, but the pitch-blackness will undoubtedly drive you off the edge. Those only wanting a pinch of masochism can visit the facility on a guided tour.

Guided tours cost LVL2 and are available daily from 10am to 6pm between May and September, other times on request (see www.karostascietums.lv).

965 798 SPACE, BEIJING, CHINA

You can't get more communist than a 1950s East German–built military factory in the suburbs of Beijing, named after factory unit 798. It was reborn as a sanctuary for the city's contemporary art community, which was pushed from pillar to post by disapproving authorities; galleries sprouted here in the late 1990s and today the complex is a bustling hive of modernist installations and studio space. The sober ambience of the cavernous workshops complements the artworks impeccably. Vivid Maoist slogans can still be seen daubed on the high ceilings, while defunct factory machinery and statues of rugged workers imbibe the factory's former proletarian spirit.

798 Space is located at 4 Jiuxianqiao Lu in Cháoyáng District. Explore the numerous galleries then kick back in one of the tranquil cafes.

966 PENSION, LĪGATNE, LATVIA

Tucked deep within the pines of Gauja National Park is a dreary rehabilitation centre. But this is no ordinary hospital; beneath the bland '60s architecture lies a top-secret Soviet bunker, known by its code name: the Pension. When Latvia was part of the USSR, the Pension was one of the most important hideouts during a time of nuclear threat. Its location was so tightly guarded that it remained classified information until 2003. Today, visitors can wander through the bunker's iron-clad halls – the 2000-sq-metre shelter still looks as it did when it was in operation some 40 years ago.

To organise your LVL4 visit of the Pension, check out www.bunkurs.lv.

967 SOVIET SCULPTURES, MINSK, BELARUS

After the collapse of the Soviet Union, liberated locals began tearing down the looming statues of their deposed despots. But in Belarus, Soviet ideals are still alive and kickin'! In fact, most sculpted homages to commanding comrades still stand tall among the city's streets. A stroll through the city centre is like stepping through a time machine: Lenin proudly perches over a podium in front of the House of Government, the bust of Felix Dzerzhinsky, founder of the KGB, watches over pedestrians along Independence Avenue, and Mikhail Kalinin, noted Soviet revolutionary, stands guard in his eponymous square.

If you're visiting Belarus, be sure to apply for your tourist visa at least two weeks ahead of time to avoid any logistical snags.

968 TRABI SAFARI, BERLIN, GERMANY

Europe's Eastern Bloc once chugged along to the tumultuous tone of communism's iconic car, the Trabant. Unsurprisingly for a vehicle that was originally intended to be a three-wheel motorcycle, the little Trabi isn't the world's cutest car. Nevertheless, more than three million units rolled off the production line and spent many happy years pottering around Europe's furthest outposts. Today the Trabi has cult status, with owners' clubs spread far and wide. You might not get to own one, but you can hop behind the wheel of a restored model and take a guided tour of Berlin's communist-era relics.

One-hour tours cost from €30 per person, starting at the BallonGarten near Checkpoint Charlie; check www.trabi -safari.de.

969 MUSEUM OF GENOCIDE VICTIMS, VILNIUS, LITHUANIA

Lithuania's battle for independence is portrayed in Vilnius' Museum of Genocide Victims, otherwise known as the KGB museum, housed in the former headquarters of the Soviet operation. From 1940 to 1991 thousands of resistance fighters were arrested and incarcerated here, many en route to exile in Siberia. Today the relic-filled galleries tell the graphic story of the conflict. Most sobering are the isolation chambers, torture rooms and padded cells of the dungeons. The names of many of the dead are carved into the building's exterior walls.

The museum is best taken in with an English-speaking guide (reserve one in advance) or headphone audio tour.

970 THE GREENBRIER WHITE SULPHUR SPRINGS, WEST VIRGINIA, USA

Fearing the wrath of the missile-wielding Soviets, the US government sprung into action in the late '50s and commissioned 'Project Greek Island' on the grounds of a posh hotel. It appeared as if the estate was adding another wing of rooms, but this was a cover-up for the construction of a massive emergency relocation centre underground. The 10,000-sq-metre bunker was meant to house the American Congress during a nuclear attack, and featured living quarters, a hospital and a broadcast centre with a fake backdrop of the Capitol! After the collapse of the Soviet Union, all was revealed in the *Washington Post*.

Daily 90-minute tours of the relocation bunker are on offer for US$30. See www.greenbrier.com/bunker to make reservations.

SPOOKIEST BUILDINGS

Buildings around the world guaranteed to send a shiver down your spine.

SEDLEC OSSUARY, KUTNÁ HORA, CZECH REPUBLIC

By the mid-1800s, the crypt at the Sedlec monastery had been a popular burial site for centuries, with plague outbreaks and Hussite Wars contributing thousands of remains. In the 1870s a local woodcarver was hired to make creative use of the bones that had been piling up in the crypt. This was no minor task: the ossuary contains the remains of over 40,000 people,

Most Thai temples have centuries of history, but this spiky sanctuary in Chiang Rai was only begun in 1997

many of which were used to decorate the chapel. The effect is as beautiful as it is macabre: elaborate light fixtures, arrays of bells, furnishings, splashy wall treatments and coats of arms are all loving recreated from skulls and bones of all sizes. Is that chandelier staring back at you?

To reach the monastery, drag your bones 800m south from Kutná Hora's main train station. More gory details are at www .kostnice.cz.

972 RYUGYONG HOTEL, PYONGYANG, NORTH KOREA

Under construction since 1987, the massive and still unfinished 105-storey Ryugyong Hotel in Pyongyang looks like a luxury hotel designed for Mordor. Nicknamed the 'Hotel of Doom' and described as 'the worst building in the history of mankind' by *Esquire*, its construction was halted due to lack of funding, and the partially completed building stood windowless and looming ominously over the city for 16 years before work resumed in 2008. It was strikingly modern when first designed, but time has not been kind to the building, which now looks simultaneously menacing, dated, and unconscionably extravagant relative to the impoverished populace.

Once granted a visa, visitors to North Korea have little choice in where they are allowed to visit or photograph, but at 105 storeys, the Ryugyong Hotel is hard to miss from anywhere in the capital.

973 DŌNGYUÈ TEMPLE, BEIJING, CHINA

Beijing's most morbid shrine, the operating Taoist shrine of Dōngyuè Temple is an unsettling but fascinating place to visit. Stepping through the entrance you find yourself in Taoist Hades, where tormented spirits reflect on their wrongdoings. The 'Life and Death Department' is a spiritual place to ponder your eventual demise, the 'Department for Wandering Ghosts' and the 'Department for Implementing 15 Kinds of Violent Death' have slightly less inviting names, while the ill might seek out the 'Deep-Rooted Disease Department'. Other halls are less morbid, but no less interesting. Visit during the Chinese New Year or the mid-autumn festival to see the temple at its most vibrant.

Paying the extra yuan for a guide can be helpful for interpreting the aspects of the temple that might otherwise defy explanation.

974 WAT RONG KHUN, CHIANG RAI, THAILAND

Still under construction, Chiang Rai's controversial modern temple is part traditional Buddhist temple, part white-frosted wedding cake, and part avant-garde art with a disturbing penchant for pointiness. Visitors must cross a bridge to the temple over a field of fangs and hundreds of pleading white arms and suffering faces of statues reaching up from hell. While stark whiteness predominates, the inside and other parts of the temple compound (including the toilets) are sparkling gold.

Wat Rong Khun is open daily; the White Temple is a short drive from Chiang Rai.

339

The compellingly creepy Catacombe dei Cappuccini hold the mummified bodies of thousands of locals

975 CATACOMBE DEI CAPPUCCINI, PALERMO, ITALY

All of the inhabitants of the catacombs below Palermo's Capuchin Monastery are decked out in their Sunday best. Unfortunately, that Sunday was several hundred years ago, and the outfits have fared significantly better that the wearers. The mummified bodies and skeletons of some 8000 Palermitans from the 1600s through to the 1800s are kept in the catacombs for all to see, some so well preserved that they look eerily lifelike. Men and women occupy separate corridors, and within the women's area there's a special virgin-only section. Spooky for adults, probably terrifying for the kiddies – be warned.

The catacombs are a 15-minute walk from Palermo's Piazza Independenza along Via Cappuccini, or a short bus ride.

976 LEMP MANSION, ST LOUIS, USA

Reputed to be one of the country's most haunted houses (if there are degrees of hauntedness), St Louis' Lemp Mansion has a long history of odd occurrences. Charles Lemp committed suicide in the house in 1949 and, ever since, strange things have taken place here, including doors that swing open spontaneously, glasses that leap off tables and break, and a tragically short-lived reality TV show. Today, the mansion operates as a restaurant and inn that seek to capitalise on the morbid fame through murder mystery dinner theatre, Halloween parties and weekly tours by a noted 'paranormal investigator'. Stay the night if you dare.

The mansion can be found just off Interstate 55, south of the Anheuser-Busch Brewery. Find more information on spooky events and reservations at www .lempmansion.com.

977 SCOTT MONUMENT, EDINBURGH, SCOTLAND

A spiky Gothic fantasy with more than a passing resemblance to a Thai temple, the monument to Sir Walter Scott is a beloved fixture of the Edinburgh skyline. Just 61m high, the climb to the top doesn't sound daunting until you find yourself wedged into the preposterously tiny spiral staircase. The final curve is so notoriously tight that squeezing yourself out the final doorway requires the flexibility of a spelunker. Edinburgh mystery writer Ian Rankin once set the scene of the crime at the top of the Scott Monument, with much of the story focusing on the physics of getting a stiff cadaver

down the twisty staircase. Not a claustrophobe? This might make you think otherwise.

For history and seasonal visiting hours, see www.edinburghmuseums.org.uk.

978 CHORNOBYL REACTOR #4, UKRAINE

Famously the site of the world's biggest nuclear disaster in 1986, the 30km-radius exclusion zone is mostly uninhabited today, but limited tours have been available since 2002 for travellers who are curious enough to get a glimpse of the industrial ghost town and aren't put off by the ominous click of a Geiger counter. Factories, homes, schools, and a particularly creepy abandoned amusement park stand decaying and choked with weeds, but remain much as they looked at the time of disaster. The Ukrainian government has indicated that the exclusion zone will be increasingly open to travellers in the coming years. Just don't step on the radioactive moss.

The best way to visit Chornobyl is to use one of the several Kyiv-based agencies such as Solo East (www.tourkiev.com) or New Logic (www.newlogic.com.ua).

979 OTTAWA JAIL HOSTEL, CANADA

Want to spend the night in the slammer? Why not make it a jail haunted by the spirits of former inmates and deemed unsuitable for prisoners in the early 1970s due to appalling conditions? Opened in 1862, the Carleton County Gaol was in operation for over a century, but it was hardly a hit with the prisoners, who complained of cramped conditions and sanitation problems.

It might not have been suitable for prisoners at the time, but if you're a traveller on a tight budget and don't mind that your room happens to be a prison cell and your bunkmate might be spectral, it's perfect. As a 'prisoner' today, your punishment includes parking, wifi and a games lounge.

To get yourself locked up for the night in the Canadian capital, book through Hostelling International at www .hihostels.ca.

980 WHITE ALICE, ALASKA, USA

A gold-rush town a century ago and the finishing line for the Iditarod dog-sled race today, Nome is the perfect example of a honky-tonk, almost-at-the-Arctic-Circle frontier town. Overlooking the town and the Bering Straits from the top of Anvil Mountain is White Alice, a weird Cold War relic. From down in the town it looks like a bizarre space-age Stonehenge, closer up it could be a film set for a shoot of the Victorian-era *War of the Worlds*. The four strange corrugated-iron sound reflector structures were intended for listening to suspicious Soviet activity.

For a real Alaskan experience visit White Alice during the midnight sun: Nome and the Bering Straits at your feet, the Arctic Circle just to the north and Siberia not far west.

SPOOKIEST BUILDINGS

MOST RISQUÉ SITES

Avert your eyes now – from giant phalluses to saucy showgirls, the world goes X-rated.

From the first bars of music to the last high kick it's a whirl of fantastical costumes, sets, choreography and champagne at Paris' iconic Moulin Rouge

981 KHAJURAHO, MADHYA PRADESH, INDIA

That the Chandellas, the dynasty behind Khajuraho, chose to build their cultural capital on a remote and dusty plain is perplexing, but fortunate – the unappealing location kept their risqué repository safe from the disapproving eyes of Muslim invaders. And disapprove they would've: Khajuraho's temples are dominated by erotica, a Kama Sutra made stone, carved in a frenzy of artistic aphrodisia from 950 to 1050 AD. Seductive apsaras (heavenly nymphs), couples copulating in athletic poses, full-on orgies, a little bestiality...all are reproduced in sandstone. Why, no one quite knows, but it seems this ancient civilisation was extremely comfortable with its sexuality.

Khajuraho is a 10-hour bus ride from Agra, 14 hours from Varanasi; the quickest option is to fly there from Varanasi.

982 CHIMI LHAKHANG, NEAR PUNAKHA, BHUTAN

Lama Drukpa Kunley – the Divine Madman – wasn't your conventional saint. He peed on religious pictures, drank, womanised and generally acted scandalously until his death in 1529. But there was method behind this Madman – he used outrageousness to better teach Buddhism to the people. His subduing of the Dochu La demoness by use of his 'magic thunderbolt' has particularly captured the Bhutanese imagination: many houses are decorated with Kunley's 'flying phallus' to ward off evil. At Chimi Lhakhang, a remote monastery dedicated to the saint, childless women visit in the hope that some of the Madman's virility might rub off.

Chimi Lhakhang is a 20-minute walk from the road. It can be slippery after rain; the best time to visit is spring/autumn.

BRUCE YUAN-YUE BI / LONELY PLANET IMAGES

983 MOULIN ROUGE, PARIS, FRANCE

Frilled and fabulous, the Moulin Rouge was once the epitome of Parisian *joie de vivre*. The infamous nightspot first opened its doors in 1889 in the seedy district of Pigalle; here, low-lifes fraternised with arty types, and the emphasis was on creativity and fun. It was under the Moulin Rouge's namesake red windmill that the can-can was first kicked, a dance through which courtesans could seduce by showing acrobatic acumen and a bit of skin. Today it's all a little less debauched – showgirls dance to dining tourists. Those in need of an immodesty fix should try the Musée de l'erotisme next door.

There are two Moulin Rouge showtimes each night (9pm and 11pm); the show only costs from €80, dinner and show combos cost from €150.

343

984 CERNE ABBAS GIANT, ENGLAND

A man with no insecurity issues, the naked Cerne Abbas Giant stands proud (in every way) on a hillside in rural Dorset. He's around 400 years old, 55m tall and carries a 37m-long club – but it's his, er, other weapon that grabs the attention. His body is outlined by a trench cut through the grass to the chalk below, so he needs regular maintenance – rock replacement and a bit of weeding. It also means he's easy to alter – scientists think he once carried a cloak, now overgrown, while the puritanical Victorians let the grass grow over his manhood.

The National Trust car park offers the best views; from here it's a 250m walk to the Giant.

985 CHINESE SEX CULTURE MUSEUM GARDEN, TÓNGLǏ, CHINA

It's odd that in anything-goes Shanghai – once dubbed the 'Whore of the Orient' – the authorities took such dislike to Liu Dalin's museum. A collection of 9000 years of Eastern erotica, the Chinese Sex Culture Museum was the sociology professor's labour of love. But due to lack of support from the city (he wasn't allowed to write the symbol for 'sex' on his sign, for starters), Dalin moved his chastity belts and lascivious landscape paintings to the town of Tónglǐ. Now, his 1200 artefacts are back on show, with the addition of a saucy statue garden, where sexuality and shrubbery combine.

344

Picturesque Tónglǐ, 80km west of Shanghai, gets busy with weekend day trippers; stay overnight at traditional guesthouse Zhèngfú Cǎotáng.

986 MARDIS GRAS, SYDNEY, AUSTRALIA

Showgirls and cowgirls, leopard-skin and lifeguard trunks, men dressed like pharaohs, in fishnets, in almost nothing at all – this is no ordinary fashion parade: Sydney Mardis Gras is a colossal, camp, sequined and saucy celebration of lesbian, gay, bisexual and transgender liberation in Australia, and across the world. Today's party atmosphere belies more troubled roots – Sydney's first such march for homosexual rights in 1978 ended in police violence. It's a sign of the increasingly liberated times that now people of all persuasions – and in any state of feathered dress or political T-shirt – can get together for a raucously 'peaceful' knees-up.

The parade, held every February, starts around 7.45pm; the best viewing spots are along Oxford and Flinders Streets.

987 RED LIGHT DISTRICT, AMSTERDAM, THE NETHERLANDS

It's no surprise that the oldest part of Amsterdam is where you find the 'world's oldest profession' – the sex industry here dates back to the 14th century, when sailors docked – and then looked for a place to drop anchor… What this does mean is that Amsterdam's Red Light District is really rather lovely – tall gabled buildings hugging narrow canals, criss-crossed by bridges. Plus around 250 windows where ladies in undies display their wares. It's a curious mix of scenic and seedy, and the best place to get an insight is the Prostitution Information Centre, from where an ex sex-worker leads eye-opening tours.

The Prostitution Information Centre provides info and advice; it runs an hour-long walking tour every Saturday at 5pm (€12.50).

988 KANAMARA MATSURI, KAWASAKI, JAPAN

Prudes should look away now – you can't escape the male member in Kawasaki come April. The annual Kanamara Matsuri (Festival of the Steel Phallus) originated in the 17th century, when local prostitutes began to pray for protection from sexually transmitted diseases at the Kanamara Shrine. Now the celebration is open to anyone who wishes to attend (but perhaps not the easily offended). A 2.5m pink phallus is paraded through streets lined with locals, tourists and transvestites; vegetables are carved into suggestive shapes then auctioned off to the highest bidders; and there's no end to the penis-themed paraphernalia on sale, ranging from lollipops to lucky charms.

The festival's main event is held on the first Sunday in April; the parade of the penis starts around noon.

(Un)dress to impress and have a gay old time at Sydney's saucy Mardi Gras

989 ICELANDIC PHALLOLOGICAL MUSEUM, HÚSAVÍK, ICELAND

How do you pick a favourite in a museum of 270 members? It's not easy: this museum of penises is a phallologist's fantasy, containing specimens from almost all of Iceland's native species, plus some foreign extras. Museum founder Sigurdur Hjartarson, who's been collecting since 1974, has accrued appendages from sperm whales (1.7m long) and hamsters (2mm); he has polar bear parts and walrus bits, wall-mounted and floating in jars. But most Icelandic of all is the folkloric section – in a nation where much of the population admits to believing in 'hidden people', it's good to see elves' on the shelves.

The museum is open noon to 6pm daily from 20 May to 10 September; entrance costs ISK600.

990 THE SECRET ROOM, NAPLES, ITALY

This collection of salacious treasures from volcano-hit Pompeii has proven a troublesome trove. The ancient Romans had a more liberal sexual outlook than the archaeologists digging them up; their frescos were racy, their statues prurient. So what were respectable 18th-century men to do with all this naughtiness? Hide it away, of course, which is why Naples' archaeological museum houses the Gabinetto Segreto – the Secret Room. Variously open, closed, then bricked up altogether, it was only in 2000 that it became properly accessible, and its secrets – terracotta penises, a stone satyr making love to a goat – finally revealed.

The secret collection is in rooms LXII and LXV on the mezzanine floor of the Museo Archeologico Nazionale, Naples.

MOST RISQUÉ SITES

SIGHTS MOST FEATURED IN THE MOVIES

Front up to the world's most popular backdrops – each stars in their own right.

991 ROYAL PAVILION, BRIGHTON, ENGLAND

The exotic palace-cum-playpad of Prince George, later Prince Regent then King George IV, is one of the most self-indulgently decadent buildings in England. Even the forest of Indian-style domes and minarets outside is only a prelude to the palace's lavish chinoiserie interior, where no colour is deemed too strong: dragons swoop and snarl from gilt-smothered ceilings, gem-encrusted snakes slither down pillars and crystal chandeliers seem ordered by the tonne. It's an irresistible setting for film. *Oh! What a Lovely War, Richard III, The End of the Affair* and *Brighton Rock* have all used it as a backdrop.

Check out the current art exhibitions and plan your visit on its website (www .brighton-hove-rpml.org.uk).

992 ALNWICK CASTLE, ENGLAND

The Duke and Duchess of Northumberland call this not-so-humble place home, but it's only been a family residence for a mere 300 years or so. It started out as a medieval fortress, and it still likes to relive the old days by playing castle roles in films such as *Elizabeth* and Ridley Scott's *Robin Hood,* as well as TV series including *Blackadder.* But its greatest role is as Hogwarts (exteriors and interiors) in the Harry Potter films. What kid wouldn't want to down a glass of butterbeer here? Adults may prefer to visit for the Renaissance art and porcelain collections.

Alnwick Castle is just off the A1 in Northumberland. The nearest railway station is Alnmouth (15 minutes away).

993 CHARLES BRIDGE, PRAGUE, CZECH REPUBLIC

Take a stroll across the Charles Bridge and you'll see why directors can't resist it. The atmospheric mists, the blackened statues, the Castle District rising steeply above you – it's a heaven-sent location for Gothic movies such as *Van Helsing.* The bridge was also used as a set for *Mission: Impossible* and *xXx.* It was famously used in the film clip for INXS' 'Never Tear Us Apart', which showed off Prague's charms to the West when it was barely known there. More recently, Kanye West has upheld the Charles Bridge clip tradition.

The bridge can get impossibly crowded with tourists and touts. Hit it at dawn for a chance of solitude and unforgettable views.

994 BROUGHTON CASTLE, ENGLAND

Broughton in Oxfordshire is a quintessentially romantic English castle. There's a king's chamber where both James I and Edward VII once hit the royal hay, a great parlour with an elaborate plastered ceiling, and a garden with hedged fleur-de-lis beds and a heady profusion of roses. It's been the setting for *The Madness of King George, Lady Jane, The Scarlet Pimpernel, The Slipper and the Rose* and (cough cough) *Three Men and a Little Lady.* It also provided the setting for a scene in *Shakespeare in Love* – quite fitting as its star, Joseph Fiennes, is related to the family that still lives at the castle.

The castle only welcomes visitors on certain open days. Check www .broughtoncastle.com for the latest.

Visit the Spanish town of Tabernas to come face to face with Hollywood's Wild West, straight from central casting

995 MINI HOLLYWOOD, TABERNAS, SPAIN

Ever think that the scenery in all those iconic westerns was…Spain? That's right – Mini Hollywood, the nearby Texas Hollywood and the desert surrounding them played the Wild West in Sergio Leone's classic spaghetti westerns, legends of the genre such as *A Fistful of Dollars*, *For A Few Dollars More*, and *The Good, The Bad and the Ugly*. It also served as a location for *Indiana Jones and the Temple of Doom*. These days, Mini Hollywood, built in 1965 by Leone as a film set, is rarely used for filming, and has become a theme park.

The Tabernas desert is in the province of Almería. The region also acted as a backdrop for *Cleopatra* and *Lawrence of Arabia*.

347

996 EMPIRE STATE BUILDING, NEW YORK, USA

This fabulous art deco needle of a building is a magnet for film-makers: it's appeared on screen in more than 100 movies. And it's a versatile performer, too, doing its stately thing in musical comedies, romances, art-house films and action flicks. If you're making a film in which the city is a character, it's a must-have: Woody Allen used it in *Annie Hall* and *Manhattan*, Scorsese used it in *New York, New York*. But its most memorable moments are probably as a meeting spot for Cary Grant and Deborah Kerr in *An Affair to Remember* and in the climactic scene of *King Kong*.

The view from the observation desk is at its romantic best as dusk melts into night. The last elevator up leaves at 1.15am.

997 MILLENNIUM BILTMORE HOTEL, LOS ANGELES, CALIFORNIA, USA

This classic LA hotel is a film veteran. The list of movies shot here is encyclopaedic, and includes *Beverly Hills Cop*, *Bride and Prejudice*, *Spiderman*, *Fight Club*, *Romy and Michele's High School Reunion*, *Pretty in Pink*, *A Star is Born* and *Chinatown*. Hitchcock used the staircase in *Vertigo*. It's also been the setting for commercials, photo shoots and film clips (including Britney Spears' 'Overprotected'). What makes it so photogenic? Fantastically elaborate Spanish Revival architecture with chandeliers, twisted pillars, fountains and statues, not to mention the Crystal Ballroom with its classical frieze. No wonder it's been a popular venue for the Academy Awards.

Have a Black Dahlia cocktail in the Gallery Bar – it's named after a murdered starlet who was last seen leaving the lobby.

998 EIFFEL TOWER, PARIS, FRANCE

Designed by Gustave Eiffel and built in 1889 for the Universal Exhibition and to celebrate the centenary of the French Revolution, Paris' most famous landmark was roundly derided when it first burst upon the skyline (critics sneeringly dubbed it 'the Metal Asparagus'), and it only survived because it served as a decent platform for radio transmissions. But over the years it has thrust its way into hearts and imaginations, including those of directors as diverse as François Truffaut, who used it in *The 400 Blows* and *Breathless*, and Vincente Minnelli in *Gigi*. And who will ever forget Grace Jones jumping off it in the Bond movie *A View to a Kill*?

Take your latest *amour* up to the top-floor champagne bar (open 5pm to 10.30pm) so you can drink bubbly like Greta Garbo in *Ninotchka*.

999 MULBERRY STREET BAR, NEW YORK, USA

It used to be called Mare Chiaro in the days when Frank Sinatra drank here (and until recently, when it changed hands). Sinatra's still on the jukebox, and the bar still looks more or less the same – old-school Little Italy, perfect for bumpings-off. It's this vibe that's made it a fave with directors of such movies as *Godfather III*, *Donnie Brasco* and *9½ Weeks*, and with the producers of *The Sopranos*. The walls are crammed with memorabilia. Slouch

RICHARD I'ANSON / LONELY PLANET IMAGES

The jutting silhouette of the Empire State Building is the perfect landmark in New York's movie-star skyline

into a fedora and mooch along for an Old Fashioned at the elaborate mirrored bar.

You'll find the bar on Mulberry Street (who'd have guessed it, huh?) between Broome and Grand Streets.

1000 10 ADELAIDE STREET EAST, TORONTO, CANADA

A gracious Edwardian number built in 1909, this was once a financial building and is now home to the Ontario Heritage Centre, which has had it carefully restored. It still has the gravitas of its original incarnation, with heavy oak panelling and trimming and a marble gallery that was once a banking hall. You might recognise it from the background of shots in *Serendipity*, *Focus* and *Cinderella Man*. The rooms can be hired for functions or events. Check out the oak-heavy Oval Boardroom if you're up for a really stylish meeting.

Call the Heritage Centre on 416 314 3585 to talk about holding a gathering in its rooms.

SIGHTS MOST FEATURED IN THE MOVIES

SIGHTS
SUBINDEX

1000 ULTIMATE SIGHTS
September 2011

Published by

Lonely Planet Publications Pty Ltd
ABN 36 005 607 983
90 Maribyrnong St, Footscray,
Victoria, 3011, Australia
www.lonelyplanet.com

10 9 8 7 6 5 4 3 2 1

Printed in Singapore.

Lonely Planet's preferred image source is
Lonely Planet Images (LPI)
www.lonelyplanetimages.com

ISBN 978 1 74220 293 8

Lonely Planet Offices

Australia Locked Bag 1, Footscray, Victoria, 3011
Phone 03 8379 8000 Fax 03 8379 8111
Email talk2us@lonelyplanet.com.au

USA 150 Linden St, Oakland, CA 94607
Phone 510 250 6400 Toll free 800 275 8555 Fax
510 893 8572
Email info@lonelyplanet.com

UK 2nd Floor, 186 City Rd, London,
EC1V 2NT
Phone 020 7106 2100 Fax 020 7106 2101
Email go@lonelyplanet.co.uk

Acknowledgements

Publisher Piers Pickard
Associate Publisher Ben Handicott
Commissioning Editor Bridget Blair
Designers Mik Ruff, Samantha Curcio
Image researchers Sabrina Dalbesio,
Aude Vauconsant
Layout Frank Deim, Paul Iacono
Coordinating Editor Nigel Chin
Editors Carolyn Bain, Paul Harding, Kate James,
Helen Koehne, Simon Sellars, Jeanette Wall, Kate
Whitfield
Pre-Press Production Ryan Evans
Print Production Yvonne Kirk

Written by

Andrew Bain
Carolyn Bain
Sarah Baxter
Bridget Blair
Paul Bloomfield
Belinda Dixon
Ben Handicott
Abigail Hole

Nana Luckham
Rose Mulready
Andy Murdock
Tim Richards
Kalya Ryan
Nigel Wallis
Rachel Williams

Images

Front cover images (from left to right)
1: **Mark Newman / Lonely Planet Images**, Grand
Canyon, Arizona, USA
2: **Martin Moos / Lonely Planet Images**, Plitvice
Lakes, Croatia
3: **Ariadne Van Zandbergen / Lonely Planet
Images**, Pyramid of Khafre at Giza, Egypt
4: **Tim Hughes / Lonely Planet Images,** Stari Most
(Old Bridge), Mostar, Bosnia & Hercegovina